Urban Education in the United States

Previous Publications

Education and Social Change (2002)

DePaul University: Centennial Essay and Images (1998)
(with Charles Suchar)

Seeds of Crisis: Public Schools in Milwaukee Since 1920 (1993)
(with Frank Cassell)

Education and Women's Work (1991)

URBAN EDUCATION IN THE UNITED STATES

A HISTORICAL READER

Edited by

John L. Rury

palgrave
macmillan

URBAN EDUCATION IN THE UNITED STATES
© John L. Rury, 2005.

First published in 2005 by
PALGRAVE MACMILLAN™
175 Fifth Avenue, New York, N.Y. 10010 and
Houndmills, Basingstoke, Hampshire, England RG21 6XS
Companies and representatives throughout the world.

PALGRAVE MACMILLAN is the global academic imprint of the Palgrave Macmillan division of St. Martin's Press, LLC and of Palgrave Macmillan Ltd. Macmillan® is a registered trademark in the United States, United Kingdom and other countries. Palgrave is a registered trademark in the European Union and other countries.

ISBN 1–4039–6777–6
ISBN 1–4039–6778–4 (pbk.)

Library of Congress Cataloging-in-Publication Data

Urban education in the United States : a historical reader / John L. Rury, editor
   p. cm.
Includes bibliographical references and index.
ISBN 1–4039–6777–6
ISBN 1–4039–6778–4 (pbk.)
   1. Education, Urban—United States—History. I. Rury, John L., 1951–

LC5131.U684 2005
370'.9173'2—dc22   2004059984

A catalogue record for this book is available from the British Library.

Design by Newgen Imaging Systems (P) Ltd., Chennai, India.

First edition: May 2005

10 9 8 7 6 5 4 3 2 1

Printed in the United States of America.

To Carl F. Kaestle

TABLE OF CONTENTS

Acknowledgments   ix

Works Republished in this Book   xi

Contributors and Their Current Affiliations   xiii

1. Introduction: The Changing Social Contours of
   Urban Education   1
   John L. Rury

      Part One   The Origins of Urban School Systems   13

2. Common Schools before the "Common School Revival":
   New York Schooling in the 1790s   17
   Carl F. Kaestle

3. The Origins of Public Education in Baltimore, 1825–1829   37
   Tina H. Sheller

4. Popular Education in Nineteenth Century St. Louis   57
   Selwyn K. Troen

      Part Two   Bureaucracy and Curricular
                    Differentiation, 1870–1910   69

5. Bureaucracy and the Common School: The Example of
   Portland, Oregon, 1851–1913   75
   David Tyack

6. Urban Reform and the Schools: Kindergartens in
   Massachusetts, 1870–1915   97
   Marvin Lazerson

7. Progressivism and Curriculum Differentiation: Special Classes
   in the Atlanta Public Schools, 1898–1923   119
   Barry M. Franklin

Part Three   Policies and Politics in
Urban Schools, 1900–1940   137

8. Taxation and Social Conflict: Teacher Unionism and
   Public School Finance in Chicago, 1898–1934   143
   Marjorie Murphy

9. Missing the Mark: Intelligence Testing in
   Los Angeles Public Schools, 1922–32   159
   Judith R. Raftery

10. The Politics of Educational Retrenchment in Detroit,
    1929–1935   179
    Jeffrey Mirel

Part Four   The Postwar Era: 1945–1980   213

11. Race and the Politics of Chicago's Public Schools:
    Benjamin Willis and the Tragedy of Urban Education   219
    John L. Rury

12. Bureaucratic Order and Special Children: Urban Schools,
    1950s–1960s   241
    Joseph L. Tropea

13. "The Community is Beginning to Rumble": The Origins of
    Chicano Educational Protest in Houston, 1965–1970   257
    Guadalupe San Miguel, Jr.

Part Five   Urban School Reform in
the Late Twentieth Century   275

14. After the Fall: Continuity and Change in Detroit, 1981–1995   283
    Jeffrey Mirel

15. The Milwaukee Voucher Experiment   309
    John F. Witte

16. High Stakes in Chicago   333
    Brian Jacob

Epilogue: The Uncertain Future of Urban Education   341

Index   349

Acknowledgments

The idea for this book came about several years ago as I began to plan a course on the history of urban education. Looking around, I was struck by the scarcity of recently published material on the topic. This was odd, because in the past it had been the object of keen interest among historians. Indeed, for a time urban education had become something of a preoccupation in the field of educational history, but more recently attention seems to have shifted to other issues. This pattern of inquiry and publication resulted in a rather peculiar situation: a very rich body of work in the past, some of it more than thirty years old, and a comparative dearth of more recent writing. Thus was born the idea for this reader, a book pulling together some of the best of this scholarship, lightly edited and with connecting notes and current bibliography, to provide students with a broad survey of urban educational experience in American history. Constraints of cost and the availability of certain materials have limited the scope of the volume somewhat, but I hope it nonetheless will offer a stimulating point of entry for students interested in learning more about the history of city schools, and provide an aid for exploring the subject further.

This is a collection of works by other authors, and it is these scholars to whom we all owe the largest debt of gratitude for allowing their work to appear in this book. As suggested above, most of the articles republished in this volume have received editorial attention. In most cases this has consisted of simply removing some of the historiographic references from an earlier time, discussions probably of little interest to most readers today. In certain instances an author has suggested editorial changes that might be helpful. In some of the articles I have tried to reduce technical discussions to a minimum, and I have curtailed statistical data and methodological description where possible. This has helped to make the length and cost of the book more reasonable. Since all of these articles have been published elsewhere, readers interested in learning more about such matters can simply look them up in an academic library. The original references for each of these selections have been included in the book, but attentive readers may notice changes in the notation where portions of the text have been edited. Again, anyone interested in examining the full text of a given article can consult the original version as first published.

Like every project of this type, this one has necessitated contributions from many quarters. Amanda Johnson, my editor at Palgrave Macmillan, was encouraging from the very beginning, and has been a continuing source of support and guidance since then. Feedback from anonymous reviewers of the initial proposal proved helpful, as were suggestion from the editorial board at Palgrave. Of course, the biggest contributions came from the authors who agreed to allow their work to be republished, and the publishers who extended permissions to use this material. Discerning readers will doubtless note the large number of essays first published in the *History of Education Quarterly*, a testimony to this particular journal's centrality to the field. Its current editor, Richard Altenbaugh, is owed a special debt of gratitude for his cooperation in securing publication rights for these articles. Similar facilitation was offered by John Lane at Johns Hopkins University Press, Michael Degnan of the American Educational Research Association, Carol Peterson at *Education Next*, and Kay J. Carr, Editor of the *Journal of the Illinois State Historical Society*. At the University of Kansas, Sylvia Mendez kept the project on track by performing all sorts of critically important tasks, not the least of which was continually asking about the work to be done, and additional assistance was provided by Angela Liddeke. Copy editors and the production staff at Newgen Imaging Systems did a marvelous job with the manuscript. My spouse, Aida Alaka, has been a steadfast source of support and encouragement as I have endeavored to complete the book on schedule, as have my colleagues in the Department of Teaching & Leadership at KU. Specific acknowledgments of the authors and initial publishers of these works are listed below.

Finally, I would like to dedicate the book to Carl F. Kaestle, who in addition to being author of the first chapter, also has been a mentor and friend for nearly three decades. He helped to introduce me to the history of urban education, and has provided a model of scholarship and sustained critical engagement with education and history throughout the course of his career. His work has set a standard for everyone working in this field, and his insight, personal warmth, and good humor have long been sources of guidance and comfort for those with the good fortune to know him. Thank you Carl.

John L. Rury
July 2004

WORKS REPUBLISHED IN THIS BOOK

"Urban Reform and the Schools: Kindergartens in Massachusetts," by Marvin Lazerson, *History of Education Quarterly* Summer 1971 11:2: 115–142. Reprinted by permission of the *History of Education Quarterly*.

"Common Schools before the 'Common School Revival': New York Schooling in the 1790s," by Carl F. Kaestle, *History of Education Quarterly* Winter 1972 12:4: 465–500. Reprinted by permission of the *History of Education Quarterly*.

"Popular Education in Nineteenth Century St. Louis," by Selwyn K. Troen, *History of Education Quarterly* Spring 1973 13:1: 23–40. Reprinted by permission of the *History of Education Quarterly*.

"The Origins of Public Education in Baltimore, 1825–1829," by Tina H. Sheller, *History of Education Quarterly* Spring 1982 22:1: 23–42. Reprinted by permission of the *History of Education Quarterly*.

"The Politics of Educational Retrenchment in Detroit, 1929–1935," by Jeffrey Mirel, *History of Education Quarterly* Fall 1984 24:3: 323–358. Reprinted by permission of the *History of Education Quarterly*.

"Bureaucratic Order and Special Children: Urban Schools, 1950s–1960s," by Joseph L. Tropea, *History of Education Quarterly* Fall 1987 27:3: 339–361. Reprinted by permission of the *History of Education Quarterly*.

"Missing the Mark: Intelligence Testing in the Los Angeles Public Schools, 1922–32," by Judith Raftery, *History of Education Quarterly* Spring 1988 28:1: 73–93. Reprinted by permission of the *History of Education Quarterly*.

"Progressivism and Curriculum Differentiation: Special Classes in the Atlanta Public Schools, 1898–1923" by Barry Franklin, *History of Education Quarterly* Winter 1989 29:4: 571–593. Reprinted by permission of the *History of Education Quarterly*.

"After the Fall: Continuity and Change in Detroit, 1981–1995," by Jeffrey Mirel, *History of Education Quarterly* Fall 1998 38:3: 237–267. Reprinted by permission of the *History of Education Quarterly*.

"Race, Space and the Politics of Chicago's Public Schools: Benjamin Willis and the Tragedy of Urban Education," by John L. Rury, *History of Education Quarterly* Summer 1999 39:2: 117–142. Reprinted by permission of the *History of Education Quarterly*.

"Bureaucracy and the Common School: the Example of Portland, Oregon, 1851–1913," by David B. Tyack, *American Quarterly* 1967 19:3: 475–498. Reprinted by permission of the Johns Hopkins University Press.

"Taxation and Social Conflict: Teacher Unionism and Public School Finance in Chicago, 1898–1934," by Marjorie Murphy, *Journal of the Illinois State Historical Society* 1981 74:4: 242–260. Reprinted by permission of the Illinois State Historical Society.

"The Community is Beginning to Rumble: The Origins of Chicano Educational Protest in Houston, 1965–1970," by Guadalupe San Miguel, *Houston Review* 1991 13:3: 127–147. Reprinted by permission of the *Houston Review*.

"The Milwaukee Voucher Experiment," by John F. Witte, *Educational Evaluation and Policy Analysis* Winter 1998 20:4: 229–251. Reprinted by permission of the American Educational Research Association.

"High Stakes in Chicago," by Brian Jacob, *Education Next*, Winter 2003, 3:1: 66–72. Reprinted by permission of *Education Next*.

Contributors and Their Current Affiliations

Barry Franklin is Professor of Education at Utah State University.

Carl F. Kaestle is University Professor of Education, History and Public Policy at Brown University.

Brian Jacob is Assistant Professor of Public Policy, Kennedy School, Harvard University.

Marvin Lazerson is Professor of Education at the University of Pennsylvania.

Jeffrey Mirel is Professor of Education and History at the University of Michigan.

Marjorie Murphy is Professor of History at Swathmore College.

Judith Raftery is Professor of History at California State University, Chico.

John L. Rury is Professor of Education at the University of Kansas.

Tina Sheller teaches American History at Townson University.

Guadalupe San Miguel is Professor of History at the University of Houston.

(Selwyn) Han Troen is the Lopin Professor of Modern History at Ben-Gurion University.

Joseph Tropea is Professor of Sociology at George Washington University.

David Tyack is Professor Emeritus of Education and History, Stanford University.

John Witte is Professor of Political Science at the University of Wisconsin.

Introduction: The Changing Social Contours of Urban Education

John L. Rury

There is a widespread belief today that city schools are an unrelenting dilemma. Just the mention of urban education can conjure images of disorder, negligence, and low academic achievement. Problems of the city schools find their way into the news: drug abuse, gang violence, teenage pregnancy, and dismal test scores. Middle-class urbanites often send their children to private institutions or to magnet schools to keep them away from the problem-plagued public systems. Big city schools are seen as serving the students left with no alternatives.[1]

Things were not always so bad. Less than fifty years ago urban school systems were judged much less harshly, and in some cases they were considered quite good. In 1958 *Life* Magazine featured a story depicting the Chicago schools as representative of the United States; nearly thirty years later U.S. Secretary of Education William Bennett declared Chicago's schools the worst in the nation.[2] Of course, urban school systems have always had problems seemingly endemic to the diverse constituencies they serve, and they have long been marked by great extremes in inequality. But because of their size, these districts historically had greater resources than schools in smaller communities. Aspects of modern schooling taken for granted today started in urban settings: age-grading, uniform textbooks, specialized classes and summer school, among many others. Historically, big city schools offered a wider range of courses, and sometimes specialized in programs such as college prep or vocational training. Back then, teachers were paid better in the city and as a result these schools generally got the most experienced educators. Because they often were seen as superior, big city schools attracted gifted students, many of them from modest backgrounds. Even if some of the worst schools were in the city, so were the very best.[3]

These conditions changed, however, for reasons that were rooted in a sweeping historical process, one that also transformed many other aspects of urban life. The problems that grew from this change, moreover, have proven impervious to innumerable reform campaigns, and the work of tens of thousands of dedicated educators. Because of this, it is crucial to understand the social and economic forces that have shaped the development of urban education in the United States. It also is advisable to examine the changing structure of urban institutions, as they too have evolved over time. The many complicated problems of urban schools today are the products of a continuing process of change. Apprehending just how this happened may be essential to improving urban education in the future.

Such historical understanding is the object of this book. To begin, this introductory essay offers a brief account of national trends in education and urban development over the course of American history, with particular reference to the twentieth century. It is intended to serve as a preface to the more focused studies that comprise the remainder of the volume. The chapters that follow this essay have been drawn from articles published over the past four decades, written by some of the leading historians of urban education in the United States. Most of them appeared during the 1970s and 1980s, something of a "golden age" in the historiography of city schools; others were written more recently. They represent a variety of places and problems, and cover nearly the full course of American history since the eighteenth century. As such, this collection offers a glimpse into the people and processes that have shaped the development of urban schools across the country. Forces that have affected education nationally, after all, have taken a distinctive course in particular settings and at certain points in time. The historical circumstances of these developments will be evident in the chapters that follow.

URBAN SCHOOLS IN HISTORICAL PERSPECTIVE

To fully appreciate the changes that have occurred in city schools, it is important to begin at the earliest stage of American history. Most schools today are public, secular institutions, but the very first urban schools were private or connected to churches. During the colonial era cities were much smaller and all types of institutions were correspondingly diminutive in scale. Governmental obligations were few, and education was widely considered an individual or family concern. The earliest schools in North American cities appear to have been church-sponsored or conducted by individual masters who taught for a fee. New England had the longest tradition of schools established by community or governmental authority, and these too were predominantly religious in purpose. Even in Boston, with its staunch heritage of public support for schools, private institutions of one sort or another proliferated. In most colonial cities these small proprietary schools served all segments of the population, although there certainly were distinctions in wealth and status that marked both students and institutions. When undertaken, public funding usually was intended to assist the education of the poorest students. By the time of the American Revolution, the largest cities had acquired loosely structured systems of private, church-sponsored, and publicly supported schools linked to different classes of the population. The vast majority of these institutions served White males, the sons of the middling classes. Wealthy families often employed private tutors. Special schools existed for Blacks and for women, but they were few in number. In the eighteenth century formal education was largely a patriarchal preserve, and the best schooling was reserved for the boys. All of this would change in the years to follow.[4]

In the decades following the American Revolution, and leading up to the Civil War, cities grew rapidly, propelled by industrialization, improved transportation, and large-scale immigration. As cities became larger and more diverse, dramatic new developments reshaped education. This is the topical focus of Part One of the book, which features articles about New York, Baltimore, and St. Louis. At the start of the period, private masters and charity schooling ran urban schools, but there was considerable pressure to create public institutions to broaden the reach of popular education. There was resistance too, as the case of Baltimore demonstrates, as traditions of popular support for formal schooling varied considerably from one region of the country to another. In most large cities, however, the appeal of tax-supported public education proved very hard to resist, especially as various institutional forms, policies, and educational practices spread from one city to another. At the same time, industrialization and the growth of trade transformed the social profile of most urban areas, making the small-scale private institutions of the past seemingly archaic. Large-scale immigration began in the nineteenth century, and accelerated with the advent of industrial development. The appearance of more poor and unskilled working class city-dwellers gave rise to a new atmosphere of diversity and cultural dissonance. The arrival of newcomers, many of them foreign-born immigrants, contributed to perceptions of growing social disquiet and discord. Schools came to be seen as an important way to reach out to these members of the urban polity and to train their children to be useful citizens.[5]

By and large, it was an era of institution building, and urban schools were in the forefront of campaigns to insure greater social stability through education. Whether maintained by private groups (such as the New York Public School Society) or public agencies (like the public schools in Boston) "free" (no tuition) primary schools were first established to serve the children of the indigent classes, and to teach them correct behavior and proper morality. Eventually these institutions developed into fully articulated public educational systems, complete with high schools and even colleges, intended for all groups. As Selwyn Troen's study of St. Louis demonstrates, however, not all groups made full use of these opportunities. Immigrant families sometimes objected to the assimilationist orientation of American schools, and working-class parents often sent their children to work. Even when there was broad public support for education, it was those in the social and cultural mainstream that came to embrace the schools most enthusiastically.

In other places, such as New York, the transition from charity schooling for the poor to public education for all spanned the nineteenth century, and was fraught with difficulty. There was conflict on cultural and religious grounds, especially the Catholics, who decided to form their own school systems. Taxpayers objected to rising costs, challenging expensive new institutions, such as public high schools, and other reforms. Gradually, however, continued agitation by reformers resulted in change in most places. Larger numbers of families were persuaded to enroll their children in public institutions, even if many did not remain in the schools very long. Following the Civil War, the political question of public support for city schools was largely settled, much like the larger common school movement on the national stage. Reformers continued to advocate for greater public support of the expanding school systems and new professional standards for educators. City schools helped to pave the way for these developments across the country, laying the foundation for today's highly evolved educational institutions.[6]

As suggested earlier, the cities gave rise to many educational innovations in the latter nineteenth century, new institutional forms to address changing needs. This is addressed in Part Two of the book, which deals with reforms in Portland, Atlanta, and the greater Boston area. A new class of administrators came to lead the urban schools, professional superintendents who strove to build systems in keeping with the latest innovations sweeping the country. These men (and very few women) created professional networks whereby information and ideas were constantly exchanged. The challenges they faced were legion, especially the task of addressing the manifold educational requirements of the nation's rapidly evolving urban industrial society.[7] Accordingly, as city school systems grew they became more complex and differentiated, featuring institutions for various levels of education and a growing array of specialized purposes.

By 1900, for instance, most large urban school systems had established kindergartens for the youngest pupils, and grammar and high schools for those seeking higher levels of instruction, along with schools for manual training, commercial education, and any number of other particular purposes. As pointed out in Barry Franklin's study of Atlanta, certain schools or classes also were designated for children deemed "slow," or prone to chronic misbehavior. Inevitably, some institutions became markers of social status. Only a relatively small number of students ever attended secondary schools, for instance, less than 25 percent in most cities, but these institutions came to be seen as important repositories of learning and culture. In setting entrance requirements, usually by examination, the high schools also helped raise academic standards across the districts, as other schools strived to keep pace. Manual training institutions and commercial high schools served a different purpose, preparing youth for the skilled trades or providing business skills. Some big city school districts established normal schools (teachers colleges) to meet the rapidly growing demand for teachers. Curricular innovation, often under the banner of "progressive" reform, created programs of study to link schools to the job market. It was an age of increasing specialization in many spheres of life, and the urban schools helped prepare students for new roles. These institutions offered credentials that conferred status in the ever-changing urban environment.[8]

The latter nineteenth and early twentieth centuries were a time of rapid growth for most American cities, especially in the industrial Northeast but elsewhere too. The pace of immigration picked up after 1890, with as many as a million new arrivals per year, the vast majority headed to the cities. In Chicago, one of the period's great boomtowns, the population doubled every decade, approaching three million by the 1920s. Other places expanded nearly as quickly. In the wake of such growth, simply keeping pace with enrollments was a major challenge facing school districts. Questions of social and cultural diversity became ever more important, as a veritable kaleidoscope of languages and customs eventually dotted the urban landscape. In education, new controversies erupted over matters of curriculum and various mechanisms for the control of schools, often affecting local political arrangements. Teacher organizations recurrently were embroiled in such debates, fighting to increase the scope and efficacy of public education. At the same time, parochial (religious) school systems grew in parallel to the public schools. Educating about a fourth of the population in some cities, these schools represented an important alternative to state sponsored institutions, particularly in the industrial Northeast. All of these developments, coupled with continuing differentiation and organizational change, made for a period of great ferment.[9]

Part Three of the book is concerned with school leadership and political organization during these years, examining cases in Chicago, Los Angeles, and Detroit. In most cities public schools were first organized in a decentralized fashion, with control often focused at the local level (usually the city ward). Eventually, in the wake of frenetic building campaigns to accommodate rising enrollments, this led to an atmosphere rife with conflict and the potential for corruption. Local politicians doled out teaching jobs to friends and associates, other positions went to the highest bidders, and school-supply companies offered kickbacks for lucrative orders. Practices such as these led to drastic changes in the way schooling was organized. Reformers aimed to take the schools "out of politics" by instituting highly centralized bureaucratic administrative systems. The creation of the modern school superintendency in the early twentieth century marked the apogee of this reform impulse, creating an ideal of impartiality, efficiency, and operational control for school leaders everywhere. But reform was uneven, and corruption and political conflict continued to be problems in many cities, as demonstrated in Marjorie Murphy's study of Chicago teachers. Political battles raged in some districts, as dissenting groups challenged the newly dominant management ethos, as was the case in Los Angeles teachers and intelligence testing, discussed in the essay by Judith Raftery. The path of resistance was hard to sustain, however, and the newly professionalized school leaders gradually consolidated their authority. Although it was seriously tested at times, such as during the financial crisis of the Great Depression, as described in Jeffrey Mirel's account of Detroit in the 1930s, the prevailing "progressive" model of school administration thrived in most city school systems well into the second half of the twentieth century.[10]

SOCIAL CHANGE AND URBAN EDUCATION: THE TWENTIETH CENTURY

As suggested earlier, perhaps the most basic factors in the development of urban school systems were demographic and economic. American cities have grown since the early 1900s, but important changes in urban life have revolved around the social and economic profile of the population. Overall, the relative number of Americans living in large cities has changed little since 1920. At that time about one in five lived in places of a quarter million or more, about the same as today. These cities today, however, contain a lower share of the nation's urban population than smaller municipalities. This is because the major thrust of urban development has shifted due to suburbanization, the movement of people out of the large cities to adjacent communities ringing the urban core. These people were replaced in the city by successive waves of new residents, some native-born, others foreign-born, and most of them rather poor. Despite relatively stable population size, in that case, the nation's largest cities have witnessed a dramatic process of social change over the past eight decades. The urban population has remained culturally diverse, but its composition has shifted and cities have not benefited uniformly from the affluence of the expanding national economy.

In the 1920s large American cities began to assume some of the dimensions of their contemporary form, with modern transportation systems, bureaucratic government services, and the very first stages of suburbanization. Large-scale immigration from abroad slowed significantly after World War I, so urban growth was a consequence of natural increase and domestic migration, particularly from the rural South. Black migration, which had started before the war, increased when factories in the North looked to new sources of unskilled labor. Following the decades of the Great Depression and World War II, the 1950s saw a return to the model of city growth first glimpsed in the 1920s: continued industrial development fueling domestic in-migration and population growth, moderated by rapidly accelerating suburbanization.

Suburban development was especially striking in this period, simply because it occurred on an unprecedented scale. Made possible by the popular ownership of automobiles and a boom in home building, suburbanization became a critical theme in metropolitan development. At the same time, the introduction of mechanized farming in the South during the 1940s and 1950s resulted in a massive displacement of African American workers, fueling migration to the North and West. Following 1950, ever-greater numbers of Black Americans left the South to find employment in the nation's major urban centers, especially those needing industrial labor.[11]

Black migration to northern industrial cities continued in the 1960s, and so did suburban development. Large African American ghettos developed in most major American cities, and when suburbanization accelerated in these years, it often was described as white flight. Urban school systems became highly segregated because of changing residential patterns in the cities. This led to glaring disparities within many urban districts, and dramatic protests erupted over the unequal educational resources available to various groups of students. When larger numbers of middle- and upper-class Whites left their old urban neighborhoods for suburban communities, the tax base of city governments and school systems began to weaken. Most of the newcomers to the cities during this period were not wealthy, and could hardly afford to support the rising costs of high quality urban schools. As a result, urban educational systems began to face dire budget shortfalls in the 1960s and 1970s, just about the time that their student populations became predominantly African American or Hispanic. These schools required a growing level of support from such external sources as state and federal grants just to maintain services.

The process of suburbanization thus created two different kinds of problems for city schools. The first was the matter of segregation, or racial and cultural isolation, which resulted from minority groups settling in certain urban neighborhoods while Whites moved out to the suburbs. The other was financial: the declining tax base that suburbanization brought to the cities. Consequently, at the same time that urban schools had larger numbers of disadvantaged children to teach, educators had to look farther afield to acquire the necessary resources. These issues have continued to bedevil urban districts up to the present.[12] Part Four of the book deals with these questions, and others that arose during the postwar period, by considering developments in Chicago, Houston, and greater Washington, DC.

The decade of the 1970s saw a number of developments that further aggravated these problems. First, government-enforced desegregation plans and middle-class fears about crime and deteriorating urban neighborhoods contributed to an accelerated rate of suburban development in many parts of the country. Second, although Black migration from the South slowed, new immigrant groups started to appear in major American cities in large numbers. Like previous newcomers, many members of these groups were poor and unskilled, and they too experienced cultural and linguistic exclusion in their new homeland. The largest groups of new immigrants were those who spoke Spanish, most of whom came from Mexico, Central America, or the Caribbean (Puerto Rico in particular). These groups had been important minorities in American cities during earlier times, of course, but their numbers grew especially quickly in the 1960s and 1970s. By 1980 nearly a fifth of New York's population was Spanish-speaking, and Chicago counted more than 400,000 residents of Hispanic heritage. This posed yet a new challenge to the urban schools, one of educating a diverse population of recent immigrants while dealing with longstanding problems of racial segregation and poverty.[13]

In addition to these changes, the economic base of major cities began to shift as well. In the 1960s manufacturing employment began to decline substantially, a process often described as "deindustrialization," and it accelerated in the 1970s and 1980s. It was concentrated in cities and occurred for a number of reasons, some of them linked to growing industrial competition from abroad. Consequently, employment opportunities in inner city communities decreased significantly. As leading sociologists have noted, the movement of industry out of American cities, whether to locations overseas or simply to the suburbs, has resulted in historically unprecedented social dislocation. The resulting loss of good-paying jobs brought a host of other problems, many with dire implications for education. Since 1970 the number of female-headed households in American cities has grown enormously, as marriages became difficult to sustain in the wake of rising unemployment and poverty. Illegal drug sales, violent crime, and teen pregnancy also have increased sharply in the wake of these developments. And as the popular media has amply documented, these are issues that have a direct bearing upon children and youth.[14]

By the 1990s more than half of all Black children in large American cities were born in poverty, most of them in female-headed families. With the virtual collapse of urban industrial employment, Black communities that traditionally relied upon the factory for successive generations of employment found themselves in a state of crisis. These changes had a palpable impact on urban schooling. While suburbanization changed the economic and demographic profile of the city, problems once restricted to only the poorest areas became far more ubiquitous in urban America. Like their predecessors in poor immigrant areas some 60 years earlier, educators in high poverty schools worked with children contending with deprivation and neglect every day in their home lives. But because of unemployment, crime, racial discrimination, and a host of other factors, the problems today are far worse than those faced by earlier generations of urban children. In many inner city communities of the 1990s, destitution and isolation contributed to an atmosphere of nihilistic self-destruction, where gang membership and illegal activities became important elements of indigenous peer culture. Dropout rates among urban teenagers came to be more than 50 percent in many large American cities, with thousands of adolescents turning to the street in the absence of any real prospects of stable and meaningful employment. Historically, the number of poor, single-headed families and the severity of crime and social dislocation in these communities can be directly linked to the duration and severity of under-employment. In this fashion, the crisis in education can be linked to the economic crisis in inner-city minority communities. This remains a great challenge facing the leaders of urban educational institutions in the years ahead.[15]

Each of these events has contributed to a context of dramatic change in American cities in the postwar period, and together they have had a profound effect on urban public schools. The twin processes of in-migration by Blacks and other disadvantaged groups and out-migration of affluent Whites to suburban areas has transformed the urban landscape. Although downtown areas of the big cities have continued to develop economically, and there has been some movement of middle- and upper-class Whites back into certain urban neighborhoods, the overall pattern of metropolitan development since World War II has isolated minority groups in the city while eroding the fiscal base of city government and local school systems. Because of tensions created with federally mandated plans for integration of city school systems and the growing number of students from poor families, many middle-class White families in the city simply have abandoned the public schools.

As a consequence, in most large urban districts today a substantial majority of students come from minority backgrounds, and are at a disadvantage regarding school success in both cultural and economic terms. With these circumstances, the democratic tenet of the nation's public school tradition that education is to be shared by all members of the society is considerably less viable in today's cities than it was for previous generations of urban children. It is possible to say that there are two systems of public education in many metropolitan areas today: one for the disadvantaged and disenfranchised in the cities, and the other for those who can afford to live in the suburbs or send their children to a "good" school.[16]

Part Five of the book deals with the impact of these events upon urban schools, and some of the reform strategies that school systems have undertaken to respond to them, with reports from Detroit, Milwaukee, and Chicago. The cries for reform have grown increasingly strident in recent decades, with proposals ranging from voucher programs to support the development of private alternatives to the public schools, to sweeping accountability systems based on systematic testing of student learning on a massive scale. Whether any one of these strategies can succeed is an open question, and there continues to be great debate about the real prospects for meaningful change. Meanwhile, the continuing crisis of urban education menaces the lives of millions of children. Until an effective policy response is determined, there is only faint hope for their future.

CONCLUSION

Urban schools in the United States have come a long way from the eighteenth century, when city children, if schooled at all, were educated in private schools run by individual teachers on a proprietary basis. During the nineteenth century public schools were established to help assimilate immigrants and the working class, to teach proper morality and the habits of industry. Later these institutions were organized along the lines of bureaucratic efficiency, even while continually immersed in political controversy. In the latter twentieth century, schools have been buffeted by the tides of urban change, particularly suburbanization—the movement of White, middle-class families beyond the city limits. Those who remained in the inner cities have been disproportionately disadvantaged, both economically and in educational terms. With the appearance of larger numbers of poor and minority students in their classrooms, urban schools have acquired an unenviable reputation for low academic achievement and high failure rates. They also have become associated with a myriad of social problems, ranging from drug addiction to teenage pregnancy. These generally are not issues stemming from the policies of urban school districts or the behavior of educators. Rather, it appears that the troubles of the big cities have become the problems of the schools.

Other factors that affected urban education in the twentieth century, such as curricular reform and organizational change, have been less important than social context. These factors have affected most public schools in the United States, even those that most observers agreed were good schools. People today generally do not think urban schools are acceptable, however. Once the proud sentinels of academic standards, and vehicles of opportunity for generations of students, urban schools eventually came to represent the most severe problems in American education. Despite federal support, material resources in urban schools continue to lag behind those in many suburban school districts. Teachers chose school systems with better working conditions and more highly motivated students. And gross inequities in American education continued to sharpen as the twentieth century came to an end.[17]

Looking at the history of urban education, it is clear that city schools have suffered the consequences of a historic transformation of urban life. As indicated throughout the chapters that follow in this book, it is a process that has certainly shaped the development of schools in many settings, and one that may lie beyond the power of individual urban communities to remedy. Given this, it seems safe to say that ending the current crisis in urban education will require monumental national resolve, and a historic change in policy, to affect basic changes in the metropolitan social structure. While education would no doubt play a vital role in such a transformation, fundamental questions of social and economic inequality must also be addressed. This is the great, unfinished task facing the nation's metropolitan regions, and the on-going challenge to educators concerned with improving the lives of urban children.

NOTES

1. It is important at the outset to define "urban," as it can take a number of different meanings. The term urban in this discussion and the remainder of the book refers to large American cities, most of which today lay at the center of metropolitan areas. For discussion of the term and an introduction to relevant theory and research in connection with education, see John L. Rury and Jeffrey Mirel, "The Political Economy of Urban Education," in Michael Apple, ed. *Review of Research in Education* 22 (Washington, DC: AERA, 1997) pp. 49–110.

2. The story in *Life* was about differences in U.S. and Soviet schools, and even though it focused on deficiencies in the American system, the very fact that Chicago schools were featured was a telling contrast with today's urban schools. Howard Sochurek, "Two school systems" *Life*, March 24, 1958. Regarding Bennett's remarks about Chicago schools, see *Chicago Tribune*, November 7, 1987, 1.

3. This point is perhaps most graphically demonstrated in Jeffrey Mirel's prize-winning study of the Detroit schools. See Jeffrey E. Mirel, *The Rise and Fall of an Urban School System, Detroit, 1907–1980* (Ann Arbor: University of Michigan Press, 1993) especially ch. 2. Also see the essays in John L. Rury and Frank Cassell, *Seeds of Crisis: Public Schooling in Milwaukee Since 1920* (Madison: University of Wisconsin Press, 1993) especially chs. 1, 3, 4, 5, & 6. Also see David L. Angus,

Jeffrey Mirel, and Maris Vinovskis, "Historical Development of Age Stratification in Schooling," *Teachers College Record* Winter 1998 90(2): 211–236.

4. The best study of urban education at this time is Carl F. Kaestle, *Evolution of an Urban School System: New York, 1750–1850* (Cambridge: Harvard University Press, 1973) chs. 1 & 2. Also see Stanley K. Schultz, *The Culture Factory: Boston's Public Schools, 1790–1860* (New York: Oxford University Press, 1973) ch. 1, and Farley Grubb, "Educational Choice in the Era before Free Public Schooling: Evidence from German Immigrant Children in Pennsylvania, 1771–1817," *Journal of Economic History* 1992 52(2): 363–375.

5. Schultz, *The Culture Factory*, chs. 2 & 3; Kaestle, *Evolution of an Urban School System*, chs. 3, 4, & 5.

6. Diane Ravtich, *The Great School Wars, New York City, 1805–1973: A History of The Public Schools as Battlefield of Social Change* (New York: Basic Books, 1974) Part One; Kaestle, *Evolution and an Urban School System*, ch. 6; Selwyn Troen, *The Public and the Schools: Shaping the St. Louis System, 1838–1920* (Columbia, MO: University of Missouri Press, 1975) chs. 1 & 2.

7. On the early development of the urban school superintendent, see David B. Tyack and Elisabeth Hansot, *Managers of Virtue: Public School Leadership in America, 1820–1980* (New York: Basic Books, 1982) Part One.

8. David B. Tyack, *The One Best System: A History of American Urban Education* (Cambridge: Harvard University Press, 1974) Part One; Barbara Beatty, *Preschool Education in America: The Culture of Young Children from the Colonial Era to the Present* (New Haven: Yale University Press, 1995) ch. 6; Troen, *The Public and the Schools*, ch. 5; Marvin Lazerson, *The Origins of Urban Education: Massachusetts, 1870–1930* (Cambridge: Harvard University Press, 1971) ch. 2; Herbert M. Kliebard, *The Struggle for the American Curriculum, 1893–1958* (New York: Routledge, 1995) ch. 2.

9. Perhaps the best discussion of this era can be found in Tyack, *The One Best System*, Part 2. On Catholic schools, see James W. Sanders, *The Education of an Urban Minority: Catholics in Chicago, 1833–1965* (New York: Oxford University Press, 1977) Part One.

10. Tyack, *The One Best System*, Parts 4 & 5; Raymond C. Callahan, *Education and the Cult of Efficiency* (Chicago: University of Chicago Press, 1962) chs. 4 & 5.

11. For an overview of urban development during this time, see Eric H. Monkkonen, *America Becomes Urban: The Development of U.S. Cities & Towns, 1780–1980* (Berkeley: University of California Press, 1988) ch. 3.

12. Harvey Kantor and Barbara Brenzel, "Urban Education and the 'Truly Disadvantaged': The Historical Roots of the Contemporary Crisis, 1945–1990," *Teachers College Record* 1992 94(2): 278–314; also see Harvey Kantor, and Robert Lowe, "Class, Race, and the Emergence of Federal Education Policy: From the New Deal to the Great Society," *Educational Researcher* 1995 24(3): 4–11.

13. Alejandro Portes and Rubén G. Rumbaut, *Immigrant America: A Portrait* (Berkeley: University of California Press, 1990) chs. 1 & 2; Alejandro Portes, Rubén G. Rumbaut, *Legacies: The Story of the Immigrant Second Generation* (Berkeley: University of California Press, 2001) ch. 1.

14. Barry Bluestone and Bennett Harrison, *The Deindustrialization of America: Plant Closings, Community Abandonment, and the Dismantling of Basic Industry* (New York: Basic Books, 1982) passim; William Julius Wilson, *When Work Disappears: The World of the New Urban Poor* (New York: Knopf, 1996) Part One,

also see Wilson's earlier work, *The Truly Disadvantaged: The Inner City, the Underclass, and Public Policy* (Chicago: University of Chicago Press, 1987) passim.

15. William W. Goldsmith and Edward J. Blakely, *Separate Societies: Poverty and Inequality in U.S. Cities* (Philadelphia: Temple University Press, 1992) ch. 4; Kantor and Brenzel, "Urban Education and the 'Truly Disadvantaged,'" 310–312.

16. On these points, see Nathan Glazer, "The Real World of Urban Education" *Public Interest* 1992 106: 57–75; Paula D. McClain, "Thirty Years of Urban Policies: Frankly, My Dears, We Don't Give a Damn!" *Urban Affairs Review* 1995 30(5): 641–644; Lee Sigelman and Jeffrey R. Henig, "Crossing the Great Divide: Race and Preferences for Living in the City versus the Suburbs" *Urban Affairs Review* September 2001 37(1): 3–18.

17. On the low state of public opinion regarding big city school systems, particularly regarding perceptions of bureaucratic control, see Dan A. Lewis and Kathryn Nakagawa, *Race and Educational Reform in the American Metropolis: A Study of School Decentralization* (Albany: State University of New York Press, 1995) ch. 1.

PART ONE

THE ORIGINS OF URBAN
SCHOOL SYSTEMS

There are many issues to consider when thinking about the early development of school systems in American cities during the nineteenth century. For one thing, it was quite different from today's educational arrangements. As noted in the introduction, the first urban schools were established by churches or other religious groups and by independent teachers (or "masters"). In the opening essay of this section of the book, Carl F. Kaestle has examined the circumstances of schooling in New York City at the end of the eighteenth century. New York was much smaller than today, of course, and educational organizations were haphazard compared to today's state-regulated school systems. Formal education was left largely to the prerogative of individual families. Charity schools, usually sponsored by churches, were intended for the children of the poor. Others attended schools maintained by independent teachers, who offered classes for students spanning a variety of ages and backgrounds. Tutors often instructed the offspring of the very wealthy. Few children appear to have attended any type of school for years on end. Instead, most probably enrolled just long enough to learn what their parents felt was essential to know, before leaving the classroom to embark on their first jobs, apprenticeships, or for young women, marriage.

Kaestle explored the changing circumstances of these educational arrangements in the 1790s, a time when the old ways of conducting schools were giving way to new ones. Eventually the city's informal network of independent schoolmasters would yield to an emergent bureaucratic school system supported by public funds. At first, this took the form of a network of "charity" schools run by philanthropists, often featuring "Lancastrian" or monitorial methods, which utilized older students to supervise younger ones. But this quasi-public solution to the growing need for some sort of education for New York's rapidly growing population did not prove satisfactory to everyone, especially the immigrant Catholic population. Amidst controversies over the religious content and funding of education, the city finally established a duly authorized board of education in 1842, to supervise the schools in the public interest. The process of arriving at this endpoint was hardly preordained, yet a similar path to educational development was also undertaken in most other large cities at the time. Newer places sometimes curtailed the charity school phase or skipped it entirely, foreshortening the process by adopting the most recent forms of school organization from the East. Such was the course of system formation in the first half of the nineteenth century; Carl Kaestle's chapter described its very first steps in one of the nation's leading cities.

In the second chapter, Tina Sheller has considered the experience of a different place: Baltimore, Maryland. Like New York and Philadelphia, Baltimore was a large and growing metropolis by nineteenth-century standards, but it was rooted in the educational traditions of the distinctive regional culture of the upper South. This meant that the heritage of popular education that had taken root in Northern states was considerably less palpable there. It is telling, in that case, that Sheller observed the New England background of so many of the city's early educational reformers. She has carefully outlined the sources of popular support for public schools in Baltimore, which had long featured by an informal educational system not unlike the one Kaestle found in New York at the end of the previous century. An important difference between the two cities, however, was the influence of civic leaders in Baltimore, and in the state legislature, who were fundamentally indisposed to the very idea of public schooling. As Sheller noted, Baltimore would eventually follow in the same line of educational development as New York and other large cities. But the first campaign for popular education in this Southern city did not find immediate success. Even if the proponents of urban public education were ultimately triumphant in the urban South, they often had to struggle against the weight of traditions not altogether sympathetic to the cause.

The final chapter in this section is Selwyn Troen's study of the St. Louis schools in the latter years of the nineteenth century. As Troen noted, by the 1880s St. Louis boasted a well-developed educational system, led by the redoubtable William Torrey Harris, one of the great schoolmen of the age (later U.S. Commissioner of Education). St. Louis was a younger city than either New York or Baltimore, and consequently its school system got a later start. But this proved to be something of an advantage, for following an initial period of resistance to public education, school promoters there were able to draw upon the experience of other cities to erect a system comparable in most respects to the larger urban districts to the East. As Troen pointed out, this meant that public primary education was available to virtually all segments of the city's population, and the most successful students could aspire to enrollment in one of the system's new academic high schools.

This did not mean, however, that everyone chose to take full advantage of these opportunities. As Troen also observed, schooling did not hold quite the appeal that it commands today. For most of the city's population, working-class families with limited aspirations, educational attainment was not a high priority. Many were immigrants who may have harbored suspicions about the schools' Protestant and acculturating overtones. Consequently, many children appear to have attended just long enough to learn the basic reading and calculating skills they would need for their blue-collar jobs. For others, attending the higher grades may have helped to build character, but it was not clear that it conveyed many advantages in the labor market. Young women who attended the high schools could become teachers, but this was not a life-long career for most of them (they usually left the schools within a few years). It was a time of transition, when city school systems offered students a growing range of choices, but relatively few were interested in anything more than the most elementary fare. Such was the state of urban public education in the latter years of the nineteenth century, a strange legacy for the reformers who had started these systems in earlier decades. Things would change profoundly, however, in the years to come.

ADDITIONAL READING

The historiography of the early period of urban education is quite rich, but many of the leading studies were published in the 1970s. Among the most important was Carl F. Kaestle's *Evolution of an Urban School System: New York, 1750–1850* (Cambridge, MA: Harvard University Press, 1973), which extended the research reported in his essay herein. Similar treatments of other cities can be found in Stanley K. Schults, *The Culture Factory: Boston's Public Schools, 1790–1860* (New York: Oxford University Press, 1973) and Selwyn Troen, *The Public and the Schools: Shaping the St. Louis System, 1838–1920* (Columbia, MO: University of Missouri Press, 1975). There is a discussion of early schooling in New York in Raymond Mohl, "Education as Social Control in New York City, 1784–1825" *New York History* 1970 51(3): 219–237. Also see a second essay by Mohl, "Humanitarianism in the Preindustrial City: The New York Society for the Prevention of Pauperism, 1817–1823" *Journal of American History* 1970 57(3): 576–599. A discussion of historiographic issues can be found in Jay M. Pawa, "Workingmen and Free Schools in the Nineteenth Century: A Comment on the Labor–Education Thesis" *History of Education Quarterly* 1971 11(3): 287–302. On early Sunday schools, see Paul Boyer, *Urban Masses and Moral Order in America, 1820–1920* (Cambridge: Harvard University Press, 1978) ch. 3; and on Lancastrian schools, see Carl F. Kaestle, ed., *Joseph Lancaster and the Monitorial School Movement: A Documentary History* (New York: Teachers College Press, 1973) Introduction.

For interregional comparisons, see Jane H. and William H. Pease, "Social Structure and the Potential for Urban Change: Boston and Charleston in the 1830s" *Journal of Urban History* 1982 8(2): 171–195, and David W. Galenson, "Educational Opportunity on the Urban Frontier: Nativity, Wealth, and School Attendance in Early Chicago" *Economic Development and Cultural Change* 1995 43(3): 551–563. Treatment of urbanization in one important state can be found in Carl F. Kaestle and Maris A. Vinovskis, *Education and Social Change in Nineteenth-Century Massachusetts* (New York: Cambridge University Press, 1980). Also see discussions of urban schools in Michael B. Katz, *The Irony of Early School Reform* (Cambridge: Harvard University Press, 1968), Carl F. Kaestle, *Pillars of the Republic: Common Schools and American Society* (New York: Hill & Wang, 1982), and Maris A. Vinovskis,

"Schooling and Poor Children in 19th-Century America" *American Behavioral Scientist* January–February 1992 35(3): 313–331. On secondary education, see William J. Reese, *The Origins of the American High School* (New Haven: Yale University Press, 1995), and Maris A. Vinovskis, *The Origins of Public High Schools* (Madison: University of Wisconsin Press, 1985).

There was considerable social and cultural conflict over schooling during this time. In addition to the above books, see Diane Ravitch, *The Great School Wars, New York City, 1805–1973* (New York: Basic Books, 1974). On religious issues, see Vincent Lannie, *Public Money and Parochial Education* (Cleveland: Case Western University Press, 1968); also see Vincent Lannie and Bernard C. Diethorn. "For the Honor and Glory of God: The Philadelphia Bible Riots of 1844" *History of Education Quarterly* 1968 8(1): 44–106. Regarding immigrants, see David W. Galenson, "Neighborhood Effects on the School Attendance of Irish Immigrants' Sons in Boston and Chicago in 1860" *American Journal of Education* May 1997 105(3): 261–293; Farley Grubb, "Educational Choice in the Era Before Free Public Schooling: Evidence from German Immigrant Children in Pennsylvania, 1771–1817" *Journal of Economic History* 1992 52(2): 363–375, and Murray W. Nicolson, "Irish Catholic Education in Victorian Toronto: An Ethnic Response to Urban Conformity" *Histoire Sociale* [Canada] 1984 17(34): 287–306. On early African American education, see David Freedman, "African American Schooling in the South Prior to 1861" *The Journal of Negro History* Winter 1999 84(1): 1–47. Also see John L. Rury, "The New York African Free School, 1827–1836: Conflict Over Community Control of Black Education" *Phylon* 1983 44(3): 187–197; and Rury, "Race and Common School Reform: The Strange Career of the NYSPECC, 1847–1860" *Urban Education* January 1986 20(4): 473–492.

Common Schools before the "Common School Revival": New York Schooling in the 1790s

Carl F. Kaestle

In late colonial America schooling was plentiful but unorganized; schools were increasing in importance but still supplementary to the family, the church, and apprenticeship. Throughout the colonies schools provided training in rudiments for the many, classical training for the few, and some supplementary schooling in technical subjects for a growing number of town dwellers. Common schooling was not "neglected," as historians of the public school system once asserted; rather, the legacy of the colonial period was a mode of schooling quite different in structure and operation from that to which we have been accustomed since the mid-nineteenth century. In coastal towns like New York, parents bought schooling as a commodity in an open market. Schoolmasters competing for students offered subjects ranging from the alphabet to astronomy, for children of all ages, at all times of the day. Schooling arrangements were haphazard and temporary; people in all ranks of society gained their education in a patchwork, rather than a pattern, of teachers and experiences.[1]

By 1850 this legacy had been supplanted. Americans had accepted the notion of unified, articulated, hierarchical school systems amenable to public policy decisions, and in the pace-setting cities, such systems were a reality. Before the Civil War the nation's pre-eminent metropolis, New York, boasted a "perfect system" of schools, a system that displayed many of the character-istics we now associate with urban school bureaucracies: uniform curriculum, standardized promotion of students, downward hierarchical authority, professional supervisors, and central policy making. These early urban school systems were an institutional response to population growth and the prob-lems of crime, vagrancy, and intemperance; they were seen as a means to convert the poor, the raucous, and the culturally offensive—or at least their children—into industrious, cooperative city dwellers. Cultural and religious diversity, in addition to socioeconomic stratification, strained the community's consensus on behavior. Public leaders strove to impart a unifying culture through schooling.[2]

The most important turning point between the informal colonial mode of education and the nineteenth-century concept of a consolidated system was not, in New York City at least, in the 1830s and 1840s, but around the turn of the century. The research described below suggests that the colonial mode of education survived in New York beyond the Revolution into the 1790s. Inexpensive, independent schools provided widespread rudimentary instruction for the city's children. The second point of this chapter follows from the first: the decision to give public aid to the city's free charity schools rather than its independent pay schools was not inevitable but proved to be a crucial preliminary to the creation of the nineteenth-century public school system. A central episode in this development, linking public schooling with charity schooling, was a ruling by the New York City Common Council in 1796, which will be described below. Like so many public policy decisions, it was a blend of tradition, confusion, and political animosity. In order to understand the importance of the Council's decision for later educational developments, we must know the alternatives they faced; and in order to do that, we must look at the economics of schooling in New York in the 1790s: who was educated by whom, where, and at what cost?

Schools were limited in function and were independent of any collective policies. Schooling for social discipline was not a matter of serious public debate; there was a considerable lag between first awareness of urban problems and systematic attempts to solve them through schooling. The demographic, economic, and cultural forces that prompt change in education were gathering, but these had been neither severe enough nor abrupt enough to affect actual schooling practices. Access to common schooling was broad in New York in the 1790s. Between the extremes of the church charity school and the expensive private tutor, a large group of independent schoolmasters and mistresses presided over pay schools that most parents could afford.

Despite rising costs and enduring unemployment, the 1790s were years of improvement for many New Yorkers. The postwar depression had begun to lift in 1787, although a newspaper writer still complained in 1791 that "many of our industrious small tradesmen, cartmen, day labourers, and others dwell upon the border of poverty and live from hand to mouth."[3] Wages for laborers did not rise from 1785 to 1792, it seems, when they averaged about 50 cents a day. By 1795 workmen's rates had increased to about $1 a day, with wages for skilled workers as high as $2. A laundress, said Moreau, earned 50 cents a day in 1794, and a sailor $1.75.[4] These wages may be compared with the usual price for the common pay schools of the day, $2 per quarter. It is difficult to estimate how marginal $2 was to a New York workingman, especially without specific information about rents, but at $2, schooling was within the reach of many workingmen.[5]

Other aspects of New York's economic and cultural life in the 1790s are relevant to education but are even more difficult to assess. Apprenticeship may have begun to decline, but the evidence is not clear.[6] The only indentures that have survived in quantity are for the Almshouse children. Of 135 pauper children bound out from 1792 to 1794 all were placed with masters in the traditional skilled trades except 11 of the youngest, who were sent out of the county to learn farming.[7] Craftsmen were a prominent group in the occupational structure of New York.[8] The economic system of New York still offered much opportunity for the skilled manual worker, and thus for meaningful apprenticeship. Housing and ship construction occupied many carpenters, and iron production employed many blacksmiths. In these businesses craftsmen worked in larger groups, in the shipyards, sail lofts, or air furnaces. However, the small workshop and partnership were still more typical. Small work units meant that more men were likely to work where they lived. Both craft and literary education within the family were thus more possible than in later years.

The living patterns of the city were in transition between the mixed neighborhoods that had reinforced the personal deference traditions of the colonial town and the more impersonal, economically segregated neighborhoods of the nineteenth-century city. Slum areas were already developing in New York by the 1790s. Poor people crowded into the low, marshy areas around the Collect and on the East River. With stagnant water in the cellars and uncollected garbage in the narrow streets, these areas were more prone to disease.[9] Noah Webster pointed out that while the wealthy could escape summer epidemics by leaving the city, "the poor, whose lot it is to labor daily for bread, must remain in their crouded hovels, where their infants pant for fresh air and die." New York was beginning to experience the problems of urban density that would plague the city as the nineteenth century progressed. Moreau noted that the crime rate was much higher than in the state as a whole and said that "in many parts of the city whole sections of streets are given over to street-walkers," especially in the area "called 'Holy Ground' by the irreligious." The city's wards were becoming differentiated economically, and by the 1790s the general pattern of a merchants' downtown and a mechanics' uptown had emerged.[10]

Nevertheless, economic segregation was not thorough in the city. Residential patterns were in transition; although some historians have emphasized the contrast with the more integrated colonial period, the contrast with the increasingly fractionalized nineteenth century is equally important. The wards were quite similar in the percent of electors (or eligible voters) in 1790. The West Ward is low with 12.8 percent, and Harlem, then "a little Dutch village," was notably prosperous with 22.4 percent eligible to vote in state elections. With the exception of these wards, however, the variation in total eligible electors ranged only from 16.0 percent to 21.4 percent, and the differences among categories of voters are not striking.[11] The living standards of the rich and the poor aried greatly, of course, but the variety still existed within each ward. Alleys, rented rooms, and backyard cottages provided many of the poor with housing among the more substantial residents. Narrow, unpaved streets, unpotable water, and refuse were not unique to the poor areas but were problems throughout the city. Speaking of the slums, the historian of the Bowery notes that "other well-to-do and prominent persons lived just around the corner from this ugliness. . . ."[12] The persistence of integrated living patterns in the 1790s is further supported by the mixed enrollment of the common pay schools, which will be analyzed below. Compared with 1850, the city of the 1790s was still small and its residential patterns were still mixed. This integration, one suspects, helped maintain the city's precarious social stability.

This does not mean, necessarily, that the poor and the well-to-do liked each other better or helped each other more because they lived closer and sometimes went to neighborhood schools together. Stephen Allen's reaction to class mixing in schools of the late 1770s suggests quite the reverse:

> In all schools of the day, there was an evident partiality shown by the Master in his treatment of the children of those persons in eligible circumstances. This was the fact here [at Mr. Wingfield's], for it was plain to me that the children of those who were considered rich, were not only treated with more consideration and lenity than others differently situated, but they were seated in more conspicuous places in the school.[13]

The point is not that there was more equality because of the mixing but rather that social stratification was learned and enforced in personal relationships. As economic segregation by neighborhoods increased in the nineteenth century, people in different economic groups learned to live apart as "rich" or "poor." Institutional relationships were interposed in place of personal contact.

In the 1790s this process had barely begun, but the decade saw other ominous demographic developments. After the relatively placid coexistence of Dutch and English cultures in the colonial period, New York in the 1790s experienced a new ethnic conflict that took on political and class dimensions and foreshadowed the great problems of nineteenth-century immigration. Tensions became politicized in the mid-1790s as the Federalist-Republican rivalry grew fierce and French and Irish immigration alarmed the natives. Although the number of non-English immigrants settling in New York City in the 1790s was small compared with the great nineteenth-century waves, the numbers were increasing, and, in addition to New Yorkers' traditional fear of Catholicism, two characteristics made immigration more threatening to conservatives than it had been in colonial times: they began to associate immigrants, first, with radical politics and, second, with poverty and crime.[14] The arrival of French West Indian refugees and United Irishmen made the Federalists worry about maintaining social order and political control; indeed, they thought the two were synonymous. New societies were begun to aid the destitute, and schemes were discussed both for providing work for the idle and for limiting future immigration; but even these responses tended to be partisan, the Republicans promoting assistance, while the Federalists were concerned about limitation. Tammany and the Mechanics' Society lost their nonpartisan character and swung to the Jeffersonian party. In 1794 the

Republicans formed a "Society for the Information and Assistance of Persons Emigrating from Foreign Countries" and announced they would help newcomers find "the most eligible mode of establishing themselves in their several professions." By September 1795, they were receiving "*numerous* and *distressed* applications." Noah Webster, a Federalist, wrote in 1795,

> I consider as a matter of infinite consequence the cautious admission of foreigners to the rights of citizenship. . . . Many of them are warm democrats; and the Emigration Society here is headed by Democrats of our own—in short, the opposers of our government are literally wriggling themselves into all sorts of company to carry their points.

There was tension between political partisans over the reception of Citizen Genet as ambassador and over other demonstrations of support for the French Revolution. In 1798 the quelling of the Irish Rebellion sent a new group of impoverished radicals, or so the Federalists thought, to the port of New York. The editor Hugh Gaine recorded simply in that year, "Too many United Irishmen arrived here within a few Days."[15]

The fears aroused were due in part merely to the Federalists' justified assumption that French and Irish immigrants would increase Republican strength. But there was also uneasiness with cultural values different from the mainstream of Protestant New York, prompting, for example, a more stringent Sabbath law from the Common Council. In 1794 the Presbyterian minister John Rodgers became president of the new Society for Promoting Christian Knowledge and Piety, which aimed to distribute Bibles and tracts among the poor.[16] This kind of response was to become widespread in the nineteenth century. The new urban missionaries began to connect foreign birth with poverty and crime. In 1795 the Commissioners of the Almshouse reported a disproportionate number of Irish among the city's paupers. Enumeration by foreign and native birth became a standard feature of prison and almshouse reports from the 1790s on, always with the same worrisome implications about increasing immigration.[17]

Still, these problems were new, and their scale was not yet oppressive to native New Yorkers. First approaches to postwar immigration and ethnic complexity did not affect schooling. It was the adults, not the children, who were the problem, and New Yorkers turned to tract societies, employment schemes, and proposals that would restrict poor immigrants from entering their city. Immigration, like other social changes, did not prompt a fundamental change in New York's mode of education in the 1790s. One important but generally unrecognized reason for this lack of action was that the city already had extensive provision for common schooling under the same conditions that had prevailed during the late colonial period. When a state law for common education did provide the city officials with an opportunity to systematize schooling, tradition, confusion, and politics combined to prevent any substantial innovation. The remainder of this essay is devoted to examining how the informal mode of schooling worked and why it did not change overnight.

Noah Webster assured the readers of his April 1788 *American Magazine* that there were many good schools in the city "kept by reputable and able men." Nevertheless, he thought, there were not enough first-rate teachers, especially in the lower schools. With his usual zeal, he said he would "almost adore the great man, who shall make it respectable for the first and best men to superintend the Education of youth."[18] If they were not the "first and best men," however, at least some of New York's teachers achieved respect and middle-class income. The *New York Directory for 1796*, the 1796 New York tax lists, and a survey of schools made by the Common Council in the same year provide information that, although not statistically sophisticated, is at least suggestive.[19] While some teachers may have been lost in the tax lists due to changing residence, other listings provide useful information.[20] Over one half of the male teachers were assessed at £20 of personal property or more, and nine owned their houses. Actual income is revealed by the extant reports to the Common Council. The lowest teaching income reported was £46, the highest, £208. The average income of the 18 teachers whose incomes are known is £122. This was not a great income at the time, but considering that many teachers supplemented their income, and some received fuel or lodging in addition to their fees, the occupation seems to have been a relatively attractive one, perhaps comparable in income potential to the skilled crafts, but with the additional advantage of easy entry into the occupation.[21] Easy entry provided an even greater attraction for women than for men because few jobs were open to women, and widowhood provided recruits for New York's dame schools.[22] As in the colonial period, the lack of regulation allowed diverse members of society to join in teaching on a short-term basis. This openness may have invited the incompetent to teach, but it also encouraged teaching by future lawyers and ministers. Success depended solely on satisfied customers. The number, quality, and cost of schools in the city were determined by demand, not by social policies that decided who needed to be educated. The charity schools were exceptions to this generalization, but the pay schools were the characteristic mode of common schooling.

The services of these independent masters of the 1790s were not expensive. Among the extant school reports, 16 gave the quarterly rates of tuition, and the average beginning rate is about 16 shillings, or $2. Masters charged slightly more for advanced subjects, but the rates vary only slightly from one school to another. Masters teaching elementary subjects generally conformed to the 16- to 24-shilling range. The Rev. Peter, whose school enrolled 55 children of the poorer members of his United Brethren Church, charged 8 shillings for readers to 16 shillings for writers and grammarians. He said that these fees were possible because he paid no rent and he desired to educate the poor, and he described the rates as "rather lower than in other schools."[23]

The impression that the city's pay schools were limited to the wealthy, then, is incorrect. The description of these schools as simply "private" is misleading, first, because it has a connotation of exclusiveness that developed at a later time, and second, because "private" education in the 1790s, as in the colonial period, often meant home tutoring, in contrast to "public" classroom instruction. Thus, in a sense, the private pay schools, with the charity schools, were the public schools of New York City in the 1790s. Although nomenclature is not important per se, the term "common pay schools" better conveys the function of the schools described here. They were common in three ways: first, they were the most common, or prevalent, kind of schools; second, most of New York's schoolmasters were engaged in giving children what was called a common education; and third, attendance at these schools was common to the children of families with a broad range of income and occupations. This third fact is the most important, for it is this sense of the word that was central to the ideology of the "common school" reformers of the nineteenth century. The data below suggest that their reform, whether they knew it or not, was an attempt to restore the social mixing that had existed, at least in New York, before the creation of the free schools. The difference, of course, is that as the century progressed, economic and ethnic differences greatly increased, and the independent pay schools were not adequate to meet new educational problems. Nevertheless, it is important to note that this informal mode of schooling was working rather well in the 1790s, a fact hitherto masked by the absence of data about schooling in the period and by the denigration of "private" schools by early writers anxious to promote the fledgling public system.[24]

The common pay schools were not educational Utopias, of course. It is impossible to determine how many truly poor children attended school, but they were undoubtedly underrepresented; at the other end of the scale, although many quite substantial families sent their children to the common schools, others opted for tutors and more expensive boarding schools. Nevertheless, the mix was broad, and the contrast between charity and pay school families, though real, was less distinct than one might expect. An analysis of the children enrolled in the Dutch charity school and in Benjamin Romaine's pay school will illustrate these points. The results are not easily conveyed in statistical form, especially because the same information was not available for every child. Of the 101 children who attended the Dutch charity school between April 1795 and April 1796, the parents of 37 have been identified. There were five pairs of siblings; thus, 32 families are involved.[25]

Nineteen of the 32 families were not listed in the tax lists at the address given in the *Directory* and thus either had no property worth more than £20 or they had moved. More interesting among the charity scholars' parents are the 13 who were successful enough to be taxable. Cartmen were the most numerous among these parents, which is not surprising, for they belonged to an economically diverse occupational group. Of the 11 cartmen whose children attended the charity school, 5 were taxed, and 4 of these owned their own homes. These men could have afforded to pay for education, and indeed many cartmen did, but, whether from frugality or an attachment to the Dutch church, these five men were getting free schooling for their children, thanks to the Dutch consistory, which apparently had a rather loose definition of eligibility. The other tax-paying parents included two city workers—a wood inspector and a measurer—two shoemakers, a tavern keeper, a blacksmith, and a brass founder. The Dutch charity school, then, was not simply a pauper's school. The point, however, should not be over-emphasized. The school did serve primarily workingmen of the upper wards, many of whom probably would have found education difficult to finance.

Romaine's school contained only one free scholar, but, like the Dutch school, it brought together a collection of boys and girls whose parents repre-sented diverse occupations and incomes. Twenty-six parents (of 32 students) were identified. At the lower end of the social scale they included a mariner, an oyster picker, and four others not listed on the tax list. The 20 who were taxed ranged from the substantial businessmen like Oliver Cromwell, William Irving, and Bernardus Swartout, to the baker John Ruckel, who rented quarters in Green Street but had £80 in personal property and sent his son first to Martin Evans' school and then to Romaine's. The most typical of Romaine's clients, however, were successful craftsmen, like master builder Anthony Post, sadler Benjamin Haight, silk dyer George Gunn, and stoneware maker John Crolius.

Fourteen of the twenty taxpayers owned their houses or shops. These were generally in the middle wards, three through six; the Bowery (Ward 7) was represented only by the children of Christian Schultz, a substantial brewer. However, this is not strictly an economic bias: numerous pay schools were scattered throughout the city and charged similar prices. Therefore they tended to attract children from a smaller area than the six charity schools, whose religious affiliations influenced attendance.

James Liddell's school, located in the Bowery on the line between the sixth and seventh wards, attracted more students from the eastern part of the city than Romaine's, which was on the west side, but it also had at least two pupils from quite far downtown. Twelve parents of Liddell's students have been identified. One might expect them to be less prosperous than Romaine's clients, since the eastern area included more laboring people. This impression is borne out, to the extent that fewer of the 12 were found on the tax lists (six), but the same broad range of occupations and wealth is also evident. At Liddell's school the children of wealthy merchant Andrew Mitchell, assessed at £2,500, mingled with the son of middling-class painter-glazier Henry Furman, assessed at £400, as well as many children from poorer homes.

The reports from Romaine, Liddell, and the Dutch school, with those from the 11 other masters who included lists of students in their reports, show that these schools offered children of different family backgrounds a common experience. Adding to the free education given by the charity schools, some pay schoolmasters reduced or omitted fees for poor parents. William Payne informed the Council that, "for this year, and for several before I have taught two poor Scholars gratis."

Although it is impossible to know exactly how many children from different income groups were in school, a rough estimate can be made of the total school enrollment. Total enrollment, compared to the estimated number of children age 5 to 15 in 1795, results in a remarkable enrollment rate: 52 percent.[26] Even if this estimate were high by 10 to 15 percent, it would still be impressive, especially because it compares attendance in a given year with all children age 5 to 15, while actually very few individuals would have gone to school every year during that whole 12-year span. Modern enrollment rates reflect not only compulsory education laws but an assumption that children need continuous education throughout their school age years. In the 1790s, however, a man decided what was appropriate for his children: nothing, or a few semesters for the alphabet, or three to five years for a good common education, or a few more for accounting or navigation, or a full grammar education. Therefore, many children not yet 16 would already have been bound to a trade (although some of these might be among the evening school students counted); others, especially those 5 to 7 years old, might not have gone to school yet but would in the future. Nevertheless, in the 12 months from April 1795 to April 1796, it seems, about half of all of these children attended some kind of school for some time. The estimate of 52 percent, then, if accurate, does not mean that 48 percent of New York's children never went to school. Schooling was such a discontinuous and informal procedure that a 52 percent enrollment rate might occur in a given year even if 80 or 90 percent of the population got some schooling during their childhood.

Materials are not available to correlate common schooling with occupational success. Schooling had a closer relationship to success in some occupations than in others, of course. Above the level of common laborer, cartman, and other unskilled jobs, and below the level of the professions, there were many jobs where a good common education could contribute. For the skilled craftsman a knowledge of arithmetic and some accounting might mean the chance to become a manufacturer employing others and branching out; for the mariner training in reading and navigation might mean the chance to rise to able seaman or mate at double and triple the wages.[27] Clerks and civil servants were a small proportion of the labor force in the 1790s, but innkeepers, grocers, brewers, and other proprietors comprised nearly 15 percent, and schooling could help them too.

Causal statements about the effects of education are very hazardous. Whatever the effects of this mixing of classes and religions, however, the mix was later assumed to be a desirable goal in the educational development of New York City and the nation; but because of the profound changes in economic and ethnic composition of the city brought on by immigration and urbanization, it took the whole of the nineteenth century and beyond to recapture this situation in the schools of American cities. Indeed, New York City's common schools may have been more comprehensive in socio-economic terms in the 1790s than today, if individual schools are considered. No ideologues promoted the schooling arrangements of New York in the 1790s; they just grew that way. Yet the 1796 school returns make it clear that education in the city was inexpensive, with independent masters serving a broad cross-section of the population.

No urgent social needs prompted schoolmasters or philanthropists to organize schools in this decade, but other influences led to organization and, potentially, to a systematization of the schooling of New York's children. During New York's postwar period of population growth there was a great proliferation of associations, some on an ethnic basis, like the Friendly Sons of St. Patrick (1784), and some on occupational lines, like the cartmen (1792) and the printers (1794). There were political groups, like the Democratic Club (1794), and literary societies, like the Calliopean (1788) and the Drone (1792). Many of these associations, to the Federalists' alarm, had a decidedly Republican cast. It was thus typical of the period that in 1794, 15 schoolmasters met to form a society, and several of their number were active Republicans.[28]

By September 29 teachers were on the rolls of the Society of Associated Teachers of New York City. Each member was asked at first simply to communicate "anything which he conceives may have a tendency to promote useful knowledge." In addition to a weekly evening of conviviality and the discussion of shared problems, the Society provided teachers for the first time with a potential mechanism for developing group standards. A committee was established to "make enquiry into the merits and abilities of any person who shall apply to this Society for a Testimonial." The Society also acted as an accrediting group concerning textbooks. A textbook by their vice president, Donald Fraser, carried their approval, as did a geography by Charles Smith, a speller by John Barry of Philadelphia, and a revision of *Dilworth's Assistant* by one of their members, James Gibbons. The Society established a small professional library, including Smith's *History of New York*, a life of Franklin, and a volume on education by Joseph Priestley, a Republican hero of the day.[29] The activities of the Society illustrate its political as well as its fraternal purpose. For example, they met at Gad Ely's schoolroom in 1794 to march out as a group along with other associations to help build the fortifications on Governor's Island, an anti-British gesture, and, like the Cartmen's and Mechanics' Societies, the Associated Teachers extended aid to indigent members.[30]

The Associated Teachers' most important activity was debating. Each week a question of educational theory or practice was argued and voted upon, and the minutes tell us what interested the teachers of the day and how they felt. On the question, "might not schools be well governed without corporal punishment?" the pedagogues decided in the negative. Not surprisingly these schoolmasters also decided, after "copious discussion," that "a private education in a family" was not as advantageous as that acquired in a school.[31] In December 1797, Benjamin Romaine posed the nature-nurture question for debate: "Does the difference of ability, so apparent among mankind arise from a superior intellect or from external causes?" The tie vote was considered important enough to record the aye's and nay's in the minutes, along with a decision to reconsider. Fraser, for example, voted for "original" differences, while Benjamin Romaine argued the environmentalist position. Another prominent member, Jonathan Fisk, declared himself "doubtful." The votes of Romaine and Fisk against inherited differences is indicative of the optimism that informed their oratory as educational leaders.

In his inaugural address as president of the Society in March 1797, Romaine declared,

> The unmeaning names of Titular Distinctions and hereditary privileges are discarded, substituting in their stead the standard of merit, to the most exalted stations in Government . . . when America (to whom seems reserved the perfecting of human establishments) shall arrive at meridian Glory, the virtuous and indefatigable school man shall stand as a bright shining light.[32]

Fisk, invited to give the anniversary oration in 1798, carried the two themes of environmentalism and republicanism to their logical conclusion in a peroration that presages his later success as a lawyer:

> Tho Genius may be the gift of heaven; it is not the precious possession of a chosen few: But like the animating beams of light and heat, is diffused among all classes, and colours, who have the form and feelings of men. If the means of cultivation were equal to all, we should not be able to find that vast disparity in their improvements which many have been ready to imagine. . . . The doctrine of native superiority is nearly exploded, and we are at this day taught the humane, and benevolent creed, that all men are naturally equal, the children of one great family. If all have by nature equal rights, all ought to be informed of those rights, that they may estimate them suitably, enjoy them freely, and preserve them inviolate.[33]

Such views, needless to say, were not self-evident to all New Yorkers; indeed, they were considered dangerously partisan by the reigning Federalists.[34] Association with Republican politics was surely one reason why the Common Council rebuffed the Society's effort to obtain public funds for the city's independent schoolmasters, but there were other reasons more important for the future of public education in the city.[35] The elements of tradition and confusion will emerge from an analysis of the Council's interpretation of the New York State law of 1795 for the encouragement of common schooling.

Governor George Clinton had argued that the colleges and academies assisted by the state Regents served only "the children of the opulent" and that "a great proportion of the community is excluded from their immediate advantages." He urged the establishment of common schools. Led by upstate common school advocates, and spurred on by the availability of funds from state land sales, the legislature passed in April 1795 an "act for the encouragement of schools," which appropriated £20,000 a year for five years, to be apportioned to the counties on the basis of population.[36] Counties were required to match one-half the amount of their share with school taxes in order to receive the state aid. New York County's share from the state was £1,888, so they had to raise £944 for schools as part of the city's property tax in order to qualify.

The law stated that the money should be used to maintain schools where children learned English, arithmetic, mathematics, "and other branches of knowledge as are most useful and necessary to complete a good English education." In a rural district where there had been a single schoolmaster the local school commissioners would have no problem parceling out the money. But in New York City, where there were nearly a hundred teachers offering a common education, the distribution posed a problem for the Common Council. Recognizing that the city was a special case, the law had stipulated that there the Common Council could act in lieu of school commissioners and that the money could be used to support the charity schools as well as "all other schools" where the common subjects were taught.

This did not solve the problem of who should receive the money, however. A committee on schools appointed by the Council in June 1795 did nothing until the following spring, when the Society of Associated Teachers began lobbying for a decision favorable to its interests. In March 1796, the Society appointed a committee "to solicit a conference with the Commissioners who may be appointed to put the Law of this State in force," but this committee was unsuccessful because no such commissioners were appointed. In May the teachers assigned a new group "to await upon the Recorder to obtain information respecting the public law for the support of *schools*." In that month the Council committee recommended that a survey be taken of existing schooling arrangements. Accordingly they directed the clerk to publish in the newspapers a request that all schoolmasters "employed in teaching the English language" submit a report on the number of students taught, the subjects studied, their length of attendance, and tuition charged. The results of this survey have been summarized above.[37]

The Teachers' Society, encouraged by the fact that they were asked to submit reports on their schools, awaited the Council's decision with great interest. By September, however, the law was 17 months old and the Council had not acted. Since the state aid was not only optional, but conditional upon local taxation, the teachers feared that New York City would forego the opportunity. In a petition on September 12, 1796, they urged the Council to take action before the upcoming session of the legislature. They told the Council that they understood the reports requested of them had been "a part of the duty which a late Act of the State enjoins." The act had required county commissioners to collect individual school reports similar to those the Council had requested the previous spring, as the basis for distribution within the counties, and the New York City teachers, not unreasonably, had assumed that the Council had already determined to apportion the money to them. "Under this view, we did not hesitate to comply with a demand which being unprecedented was not otherwise to be accounted for," they argued. "We consider ourselves as a Party contemplated in the Act," they wrote, ". . . an Act which could not have been intended for an unequal Distribution of its Benefits."[38]

Here, then, was a critical point in the development and systematization of New York's common schools. The state legislature had left decisions on the distribution of aid in the hands of the Council. The teachers, recently organized and capable for the first time of collective action, argued that the money designated for common school education should be theirs. That they were already providing common education for large numbers of the city's children was indisputable; that they charged tuition was no automatic barrier, for upstate common schools did so as well and continued to until 1867. The schools of men like Romaine, Fraser, and Campbell were public, common, and eligible under the New York City clause of the 1795 law to share in the school money. The charity schools, on the other hand, though free, enrolled only a small portion of the city's school children, and were restricted to children of their respective denominations, or, in the case of African Free School, to blacks. They represented the received English tradition of church charity education, generally admitting poor students for a three-year period and then apprenticing them to a trade.[39]

The Common Council, however, did not analyze the situation the way the Teachers' Society did. The councillors' definition of a public school was not clear, but they decided that the common pay schools did not qualify. On September 23, 1796, "the Committee on Schools made a verbal report; question was raised if it would be proper to distribute any part of the Monies granted by the Legislature and raised by Tax in this City among the Schoolmasters or Teachers in the City. Unanimous negative."[40] Because the report was verbal, nothing more of the debate survives, but their vote was unequivocal. They obviously could not conceive of the Council distributing £2,832 to a constantly shifting multitude of common school teachers over whom they had no control. It would have been quite legal, but, quite apart from the question of teachers' politics, it would have been too intricate for a governing body that had never had anything to do with education.

The Council apparently made a distinction between a single teacher hired on salary by the inhabitants of a defined area and a group of nonsalaried teachers competing in a free market. The former they looked upon as engaged in public education and eligible for assistance in the same manner as in upstate counties, but they had few such schools. The inhabitants of Bloomingdale village, in the outer reaches of the Bowery ward, provide the contrast that illustrates the point. They had engaged a teacher in 1797 on the promise of £120 a year, but they found they could only raise £80 by subscription. In November they petitioned the Common Council for assistance, explaining that "the Situation of this place being Such, the Greatest part of those who support the School in Summer, Remove to town in Winter, a Number of Children remaining, several of whose parents are not able to pay for Tuition." They prayed aid from the money provided by the legislature. The Council awarded the trustees of this school £20, half of the deficit.[41]

The petition of the Teachers' Society, however, was another matter entirely. Never having collected or distributed any money for common education, the Council was suddenly forced by the state's action into developing a definition and a plan for governmentally sponsored common schooling. Since the need for such schooling had not been widely felt in the city, and the pressure for a program came only after the state had provided the money, the Council was able to procrastinate. They had not yet received the state's share for 1796, and they voted, eight to three, to distribute the amount collected from city taxes, £944, to the city's six charity schools.[42]

The Council had resolved at the time of their September decision to apply to the legislature "for legal provision to establish public schools in the city." Accordingly, in October, after receiving the state share, they drafted a memorial in which they informed the legislature that they had complied with the provisions of the law and received their money, but "from the manner in which the private Schools in the said City are conducted it is impracticable to distribute the said monies according to the Direction of the Act." Having made its decision, the Council began using the terms "private" and "public" in a manner roughly equivalent to our modern usage. The Council asked the legislature to determine what portion they should distribute to charity schools in the future and to authorize them "to apply the Residue to the erecting and supporting of one or more public Schools in the said city." The Council by this time seems to have been thinking of public schools in terms of buildings, and the funds from the Act of 1795 had been limited to salaries.[43] The distinction between salary and construction was not simply a budgeting decision. It sealed the Council's rejection of the independent masters' claim to public funds and committed the Council to a concept of "public school" that involved first erecting a public building similar to other official edifices like City Hall and the Almshouse. Until now, "public school" had generally meant places open to the public where children learned together; henceforth it was to mean places of education erected and maintained with governmental assistance and administered either by governmental representatives or a surrogate board acceptable to them.

The legislature complied with the Council's request and passed a supplemental law in 1797 that allowed the city to use funds for school construction and to allocate 1/6 of the annual school moneys to charity schools, leaving 5/6 for the promised public schools, which were by this time significantly restyled "free schools."[44] Considering the absence of real functional demands, it is not surprising that they continued to postpone their commitment. The city's problems—disorder, ethnic diversity, and poverty—were ominous, but not urgent enough to precipitate a new relationship between government and education. Each year the Council apportioned 1/6 of the funds to the charity schools and set aside 5/6.

In 1800 the school law expired. The funds available from state land sales and the interest on surplus capital had not proved sufficient for the state-wide school program, and in 1799 the state had to institute a direct property tax, for the first time in its brief history, to meet its commitment. This the Federalist Senate was not willing to continue.[45] The termination allowed New York City an excuse to divert the remaining funds earmarked for public schools to the charity school subsidies. The school committee had declared in the spring of 1800, despite the accumulation of nearly $30,000, that establishing free schools "upon as liberal and extensive a Plan as the Funds will admit" was not advisable. The Council decided to invest the money in United States or other bonds for later use. After the rejection of the

1795 law, however, the Council requested, and the legislature passed, another new bill allowing them to divide the capital itself among the 11 charity schools then operating in the city.[46]

These charity schools were now styled "free schools," and the city's earlier plans for erecting "free schools" were dropped. The accumulated funds were paid over to the trustees of the various schools, who were required to invest them and use the interest to operate their schools.[47] In New York City, then, the funds from the school law were used only to sustain existing charity schools rather than create new common schools, and the Council continued the aid after 1800 by using the unexpended 5/6 of the capital. The law had been intended to encourage common schools on the New England model, but New York City already had an adequate, though different, arrangement for common schooling. In the end the Council was completely traditional. They refused to allocate the money to the independent masters, which would have required new standards for judging schools and disbursing funds; but they also delayed and finally abandoned their commitment to build new public schools directed and supported entirely by the city. The old arrangements worked; there was no crisis. They allocated the money where tradition suggested, to church charity schools.

The ambiguous use of terms by both the Council and the Associated Teachers during these five years illustrated the prevailing confusion about the role of the government in education. The schoolmasters had reality on their side, but not precedent. They were in fact in charge of the common education of most children in the city, but the allocation of tax funds to them would have required a complicated involvement of the government in schooling that the Council was not prepared to undertake. By delay and by amendment of the law the Council chose a course that affected fewer children but for which there was long-standing precedent: aid to charity schools. Through occasional grants and privileges, government had customarily extended this kind of aid as far back as pre-Reformation England. Far from seeing a conflict between church and state, the Council reinforced this tradition of aiding churches to educate the poor. There was no establishment and no favoritism; all denominations shared alike. However, the decision also reinforced an association of state intervention in education with charity to the poor. While the Regents assisted colleges and academies that were too expensive for all but the wealthy (at least as far as New York City was concerned), the city aided common education only for those too poor to pay. Both policies tended to increase segregation of education on class lines in the city as the nineteenth century progressed and made it difficult for the free schools aided by the city to become a truly common school system. What was settled in the years 1795 to 1800 was that a common school system in New York City would evolve from the free charity schools and not from the common pay schools.

Thus, the familiar complaint heard later in the nineteenth century, that the public schools were looked upon as charity schools, was not simply a result of the refusal of wealthy people to patronize them, but was also a result of decisions such as that of the New York Common Council in 1796, to devote common school funds only to charity schools, according to received tradition. Meanwhile, the role of the independent school, which thrived during the 1790s, providing inexpensive schooling for perhaps more than half of the city's children, was transformed during the nineteenth century. Hundreds of thousands of resourceless and exploited immigrants swelled the poor neighborhoods of the city, and reformers attempted to reach them through a massive extension of the charity school system. Independent schools gradually became more expensive, more exclusive, and less central in the city's educational life.

NOTES

1. See also Bernard Bailyn, *Education in the Forming of American Society* (Chapel Hill, 1960), and Lawrence A. Cremin, *American Education: The Colonial Experience, 1607–1783* (New York, 1970).

2. Kaestle, *The Evolution of an Urban School System*, chaps. 3–6; see also, Michael B. Katz, *The Irony of Early School Reform: Educational Innovation in Mid-Nineteenth Century Massachusetts* (Cambridge, Mass., 1968); Stanley K. Schultz, "The Education of Urban Americans: Boston, 1789–1860" (Ph.D. diss., University of Chicago, 1969); Raymond A. Mohl, "Education as Social Control in New York City, 1784–1785," *New York History* 61 (Spring 1970): 219–37.

3. *New York Daily Advertiser*, January 13, 1791, cited in Sidney I. Pomerantz, *New York, an American City, 1783–1803*, 2nd ed. (New York, 1965), p. 216; on the economics of the 1780s, see E. Wilder Spaulding, *New York in the Critical Period, 1783–1789* (New York, 1932), pp. 28–29.

4. Pomerantz, *New York*, p. 216; Kenneth Roberts and Anna M. Roberts, eds., *Moreau de St. Mery's American Journey, 1793–1798* (New York, 1947), pp. 157–60. These sources imply that the wage increase represented increases in real income.

5. On commodity prices, see Moreau, *Journey*, pp. 157–60; on rents, see James G. Wilson, *The Memorial History of the City of New York* (New York, 1893), 2:21, and Pomerantz, *New York*, pp. 169, 227–28. The best proof that workingmen could afford school tuition is that so many of them in fact appear in the pay school lists analyzed below.

6. See Paul H. Douglass, *American Apprenticeship and Industrial Education* (New York, 1921); Samuel McKee, Jr., *Labor in Colonial New York* (New York, 1935); Richard B. Morris, *Government and Labor in Early America* (New York, 1946). Douglass wrote that apprenticeship was unchanged after the Revolution and began to decline with industrialization after the War of 1812, while McKee (p. 62f.) saw signs of decline before the Revolution, and Morris (p. 200) says the system began to decline at the close of the Revolution. There are no figures available to document any of these contentions, but impressionistic evidence, such as is presented here, indicates that while apprenticeship may have begun to "decline," it had not, by any means, "declined."

7. New York City Almshouse Commissioners, Apprentice Indentures, 1792–1794, New York Historical Society (hereafter cited as NYHS). By 1850, in contrast, there was less demand for craft apprentices in the city and a trend toward exporting the children. In 1850–1851, 58 of 108 poor children were sent away to become

farmers, and 21 more were bound to craftsmen outside New York City. New York City Apprentice Indentures, Boys, 1850–1853, NYHS.

8. The assumption that city directories underrepresent common laborers and especially mariners is probably correct, although the directories of the late 1790s seem to be more inclusive than the first efforts of the 1780s or the later nineteenth-century directories. Low's *Directory for 1796* contains approximately 10,100 entries, of which approximately 1,900 are female household heads or redundant firm names, leaving 8,200 male adult entries. The estimated population for 1795 is 46,397 (see note 27 later), of which about 25 percent, or 11,579, were white males over 16. This would yield an inclusion percentage of 70.8 percent. However, the male adult figure (based on the percentage in the 1800 Census, 25.3 percent) is for whites, whereas the *Directory* included some black household heads. This would make the inclusion figure too high, perhaps by 5 percent. On the other hand, and more importantly, many men between 16 and 21, or even older, were apprentices or still lived with their families and thus would not appear in the *Directory* as heads of households. This would more than compensate for the omission of blacks in the population estimate. Thus (granting that the total population figure is hypothetical), Low's *Directory* seems to have included over 70 percent of the city's male adults. Furthermore, we must not assume that those omitted were all common laborers or mariners; indeed, in this case we can disprove it. Fortunately, a competing directory for the same year survives, Longworth's *New York Directory for 1796*, which includes well over 1,000 names of male adults not found in Low's *Directory*. The occupations of the first ten nonduplicated names are as follows: tobacconist, cartman, mason, rope-maker, carpenter, laborer, goldbeater, mason, cartman, mariner.

9. See Alvin F. Harlow, *Old Bowery Days* (New York, 1931), p. 90; Elinor Barnes, "The First Federal City, New York in 1789," *New York History* 21 (April 1940): 160; Alfred Young, "The Mechanics and the Jeffersonians, New York, 1787–1801," *Labor History* 5 (Fall 1964): 260–61.

10. Noah Webster to William Currie, December 20, 1797, in *Letters of Noah Webster*, ed. Harry N. Warfel (New York, 1953), pp. 168–69; Moreau, *Journey*, pp. 156, 166; Alfred Young, *The Democratic Republicans of New York* (Chapel Hill, 1967), pp. 471–74.

11. The higher concentration of renters in some wards and owners in others was increasing and is emphasized in Young, *Democratic Republicans*, e.g., p. 474. The remark of Young and Lynd, however, that "the suffrage bottle may be viewed as half full or half empty," applies to residential segregation as well; it is a matter of emphasis (Staughton Lynd and Alfred Young, "After Carl Becker; The Mechanics and New York City Politics, 1774–1806," *Labor History* 5 [Fall 1964]: 223). The description of Harlem is from John Bernard, *Retrospections of America* (New York, 1887), p. 50.

12. Harlow, *Bowery*, p. 91; see also Kenneth D. Miller, *The People Are the City: 150 Years of Social and Religious Concern in New York City* (New York, 1962), p. 25. For a similar assessment of Boston in this period, see Schultz, "Education of Urban Americans," p. 47, and Oscar Handlin, *Boston's Immigrants, 1790–1880*, rev. ed. (Boston, 1959), p. 15.

13. Stephen Allen, Letters, typescript, NYHS, p. 22.

14. Richard J. Purcell, "Immigration to the Canal Era," in *History of the State of New York*, ed. Hugh M. Flick, 10 vols. (New York, 1934–1937), 7:7, 12 f.; Wilson, *History*, 3:71; Young, "Mechanics and Jeffersonians," p. 264 and passim.

15. Pomerantz, *New York*, pp. 334, 337–38; I. N. Phelps Stokes, *Iconography of Manhattan Island*, 6 vols. (New York, 1895–1928), May 22, 1794 [dates refer to his "Chronology"]; *New York Argus*, September 3, 1795; Webster to Theodore Sedgwick, January 2, 1795, in Warfel, *Letters*, p. 124; the Gaine quotation is found in Pomerantz, *New York*, p. 203.

16. Wilson, *History*, 3:84; *New York Argus*, June 11, 1795.

17. Almshouse Report, in *Minutes of the Common Council of the City of New York, 1784–1831*, ed. Arthur E. Peterson, 21 vols. (New York, 1917, 1930), 2:125.

18. *American Magazine* 1 (1788): 215, 226.

19. [Low's] *New York Directory . . . 1796* (New York, 1796). The *Directory* lists 97 teachers for 1796; four others have been added from other sources. When the Columbia professors and the dancing and music teachers are eliminated, the number is reduced to 91 teachers engaged in precollegiate academic schooling. The figure is probably low because some wives who were not listed separately probably taught, and some ministers, like the Reverend Christopher Peter of the United Brethren Church, were also schoolmasters. See Christopher Peter to Common Council, May 18, 1796, New York Municipal Archives (here after cited as NYMA). The Rev. Staughton advertised for grammar scholars in 1795, and his wife opened a full school for girls. See *The New York Argus*, August 14, 1795. Instructors such as these tend not to appear in directories as teachers.

20. The group for whom no tax listing was found is ambiguous. Some were rated at less than £20 and thus paid no taxes; for example, teacher Jeremiah Connor was listed, probably by error, then rated at £0. Others, however, had simply moved between the time the *Directory* was prepared and the property assessments were made; for example, teacher Samuel Rudd was not listed in the tax rolls at the address given for him in the *Directory*, but at a different address in the tax lists, rated at £25. It was not possible to check the entire tax list for all names. Sources: *1796 Directory*; New York City Tax Lists, 1796, NYHS; Teachers' Reports to the Common Council, New York City Clerk, Filed Papers, Box 6459, NYMA.

21. Income reported, April 1, 1795–April 1, 1796, in 18 of the teacher reports, ibid. There is no systematic study of wages and occupations to provide context for this figure. In lieu of such information, the occupation and tax assessments of teacher Benjamin Romaine's neighbors will provide a sketchy comparison. The first 25 names on Partition Street, Fourth Ward, whose occupations are known, were chosen (these are not annual incomes but tax evaluations, real and personal combined): 5 house-carpenters (£20, £305, £390, £550, and £1,000); 5 cartmen (£20, £20, £20, £20, and £390); 2 lawyers (£250 and £450); 2 blacksmiths (£20 and £1250); others, one each: painter glazier (£80), weighmaster (£400), customs weigher (£50), minister (£800), block and pump maker (£20), surgeon-dentist (£50), coachmaker (£20), dry good seller (£500), and deputy sheriff (£50).

22. Of the 31 women, none was assessed at even £20 except the wealthy widow Henshaw who owned and operated a "young ladies academy." Thirteen were listed as widows, eight as "Mrs." (some of whom, like Mrs. Henshaw, were widows), one as "Miss," and nine whose marital status was not given.

23. Teachers' Reports, NYMA.

24. See Albert Fishlow, "The American Common School Revival: Fact or Fancy?" in *Industrialization in Two Systems*, ed. H. Rosovsky (New York, 1966), pp. 41, 46.

25. The 64 children whose parents were not found in the *Directory* may have included a higher proportion of poorer families because the *Directory* probably omitted more poor men than others. Student names were matched with parents

in several ways. The most secure are those matched through baptisms. Except with very common names, these identifications are fairly certain. Second, children with the same family name, especially if listed next to each other, were generally assumed to be siblings, so some baptismal identifications led to further matching of brothers or sisters with parents. Third, in the case of the Dutch charity school, the parents' names and addresses were recorded on the register and are reprinted in Dunshee, *Dutch Church*. These three means of identification provided the parents' names for about half of the final sample. The others were identified from wills, or, with less certainty, by the general combination of probability factors, that is, whether the name was less than common, whether there was only one such adult listed in the *Directory*, whether that adult lived close to school, and whether the family structure of that household head (as recorded in the federal Census of 1790) allowed the possibility of a child of the right sex and age. These factors were combined in judgments that yielded probable, if not positive, identifications. Many possible matches were discarded. The materials used, in addition to the Teachers' Reports, Low's *1796 Directory* and the 1790 Census, *Heads of Families . . .* (Washington, 1908), included: First Presbyterian Church (12 West 12th Street), Baptisms, MS, Vol. I (1728–1790), Vol. II (1791–1802); Trinity Church, Baptisms, transcript, New York Genealogical and Biographical Society, Vol. I (1749–1813); Methodist Episcopal Church Records, Vol. 233, Baptisms, NYPL; Tobias A. Wright, ed., *Records of the Reformed Dutch Church . . . Baptisms, 1731–1800* (New York, New York Genealogical and Biographical Society, 1902; reprinted, Gregg Press, Upper Saddle River, New Jersey, 1968); Rev. James H. McGean, "The Earliest Baptismal Register of St. Peter's Church, New York City," *Historical Records and Studies* 1 (Part I, 1899, Part II, 1900): 97–107, 387–99; and New York City Wills, New York Surrogate's Court, Room 402.

26. The estimated population in 1795, on the basis of a simple arithmetic increase between the 1790 and 1800 federal census returns (which tends to overestimate the 1795 population, and therefore to underestimate percentage of school attenders) is 46,397. The percentage of children 0 to 15 (i.e., under 16) was estimated to be 41 percent on the basis of the following known figures: the ratio of such children to total population was 40.1 percent for whites in 1786, 39.9 percent for whites in 1790, 42.1 percent for whites in 1800; 42.9 percent for blacks in 1747, 35.7 percent for blacks in 1771. Using this 41 percent figure, children 0–15 are estimated at 17,023 in 1795. The ratio of children 5 to 15 is estimated to be 59 percent of the 0–15 figure on the basis of the slightly strained analogy that 61 percent of children 0–14 were 5–14 in 1850 and 57 percent in 1855, the closest relevant figures available. The estimated school age population for 1795, then, is 59 percent of 17,023, or 10,043. The estimated enrollment, 5,249 children, is 52.2 percent of the estimated school age population.

27. See Pomerantz, *New York*, p. 430; for seaman's wages, see Stanley Lebergott, *Manpower in Economic Growth; The American Record Since 1800* (New York, 1964), p. 531.

28. Society of Associated Teachers of New York City, MS, NewYork State Library, Albany, published in full in the *37th Annual Report of the State Superintendent for the School Year . . . 1889–90* (Albany, Department of Public Instruction, 1891), to which page references cited here refer. On the Republican complexion of the Associated Teachers, see Young, *Democratic Republicans*, p. 406.

29. Associated Teachers, Minutes, pp. 253, 256, 267, 287.

30. Stokes, *Iconography*, May 10, 1794; Associated Teachers, Minutes, p. 290.

31. Ibid., pp. 282, 288.

32. Ibid., pp. 300, 274.

33. Jonathan Fisk, "On Education," Anniversary Oration to the Society of Associated Teachers of the City of New York, May 19, 1798, MS, NYHS, pp. 21, 30–31.

34. *New York Argus*, May 21, 1796.

35. Ibid.; on Campbell, see ibid., June 2, 1795; Associated Teachers, Minutes, p. 279.

36. George Clinton, speech to the legislature, 1795, in *State of New York, Messages from the Governors* . . . , ed. Charles Z. Lincoln (Albany, 1909), 2:350; Samuel S. Randall, *History of the Common School System of the State of New York* . . . (New York, 1871), pp. 7–10; *New York Laws*, 1795, chap. 75.

37. *Minutes of the Common Council*, 2:154; Associated Teachers, Minutes, pp. 273–79; *Minutes of the Common Council*, 2:237.

38. Petition of the Teachers of the City of New York to the Commissioners of Schools in and for the City and County of New York, September 12, 1796, Box 6415, NYMA; *Minutes of the Common Council*, 2:154.

39. On the charity schools see Henry W. Dunshee, *History of the School of the Reformed Protestant Dutch Church in New York* . . . . (New York, 2d ed., 1883); William W. Kemp, *The Support of Schools in Colonial New York by the Society for the Propagation of the Gospel in Foreign Parts* (New York, 1913); David and Tamar de Sola Pool, *An Old Truth in the New World; Portrait of Shearith Israel, 165–1954* (New York, 1955); Charles C. Andrews, *The History of the New York African Free School* (New York, 1830).

40. *Minutes of the Common Council*, 2:281.

41. Trustees of the Bloomingdale School to the Common Council, November 30, 1797, Box 6415, NYMA; *Minutes of the Common Council*, 2:410.

42. *Minutes of the Common Council*, 2:281; Report of the Committee on the Distribution of Monies to the Charity Schools, October 24, 1796, Box 6459, NYMA.

43. Ibid.; Memorial of the Mayor, Aldermen and Commonalty of the City of New York to the Legislature of the State of New York, October 24, 1796, draft, Box 6459, NYMA.

44. Elsie G. Hobson, *Educational Legislation and Administration in the State of New York, 177–1850* (Chicago, 1918), p. 83.

45. Ibid., p. 29; Randall, *Common School System*, pp. 9–11; see also Robert F. Seybolt, *The Act of 1795 for the Encouragement of Schools and the Practice in Westchester County*, New York State Local History Service Leaflets (Albany, 1919).

46. *Minutes of the Common Council*, 2:309; 2:628; 3:12.

47. The extant required reports on these grants are found in Box 2990, NYMA.

3

The Origins of Public Education in Baltimore, 1825–1829

Tina H. Sheller

The third and fourth decades of the nineteenth century witnessed nationwide agitation for public schools. While our understanding of this movement is far from complete, it is apparent that the receptivity of American communities to this institution varied considerably. Theoretically, large cities experiencing the shift to capitalist modes of production and the accompanying social disorder should have been most receptive to the common school idea. Indeed, in some (Eastern) cities undergoing these dramatic socioeconomic changes, the proposal to introduce a system of uniform, publicly controlled and operated schools which would instruct children from all classes in the community was adopted with considerable public approval and a minimum of opposition.[1] In St. Louis, Selwyn Troen has documented the existence of widespread opposition along class and ethnic lines to the institution of public schools.[2] Public education also received a hostile reception from community leaders in Baltimore, which was, in 1820, the third largest city in the United States.

Obviously, contemporary responses to similar types of problems generated by the rapidly changing conditions of early nineteenth century urban life were not identical—public education was not embraced uniformly and simultaneously in the second quarter of the century as a solution to alleviate middle and upper class anxieties over social change and disorder. The timing and nature of educational reform reflected the particular cultural and political context, as well as the socioeconomic setting in which it occurred. As Michael Katz has observed, community debates over the nature of educational institutions "reflected fundamental value conflicts and alternative visions of social development."[3] The experience of Baltimore, in this regard, is instructive.

In the third decade of the nineteenth century, Baltimore was the largest and northernmost city in the South. A relatively young city, Baltimore had grown rapidly and dramatically from a town of 200 inhabitants in 1752 to a major urban center of over 62,000 inhabitants in 1820. Its growth and prosperity derived from an agriculturally based trade economy. Baltimore merchants exported wheat, flour, tobacco, iron, and lumber, and imported finished European products, and sugar, cocoa, rice, and coffee from the lucrative West Indies market. The agricultural underpinnings of Baltimore's economy were critical to the city's early social and political development. Trade imperatives dictated close ties between agricultural and mercantile interests. Economic relationships gradually bonded through the solder of marriage and friendship, giving rise to the formation of a landed gentry-merchant elite. This conservative elite dominated the social and political development of Baltimore through the first three decades of the nineteenth century, and exerted a substantial influence in the city throughout the antebellum period.[4]

Baltimore's political subservience to the state government added to the power of rural interests in shaping the city's growth. Dominated by the slave-owning landed gentry, the government at Annapolis possessed considerable control over the city's affairs until 1818. At that time, Baltimore was granted effective fiscal and political autonomy. However, the state's ultimate power over the city, and the intense rivalry of rural–urban economic interests within Maryland were critical factors in Baltimore's progress throughout the nineteenth century. Political as well as social ties to the old landed gentry of the southern Chesapeake contributed heavily to the values and forms of life in the port town.

In the 1820s, Baltimore was an important commercial center with a developing manufacturing capability. Similar to other major American cities of this period, it was suffering the major social disruptions—crime, riots, vagrancy—associated with rapid urbanization, fluctuating economic fortune, and changes in the mode of production.[5] Baltimoreans, like other urban residents, attributed many of the problems of social disorder not to these processes, which they themselves did not comprehend, but to deficiencies within the individual. These deficiencies could be addressed in many ways. Educational reform was one of several different efforts which Baltimoreans pursued to deal with the troublesome failings of a growing number of inhabitants in their community.[6]

Early nineteenth century attempts at educational reform in Baltimore were largely unsuccessful. Between 1799 and 1824, charity schools were established by Episcopalians, Methodists, Catholics, and Quakers, as well as by the Irish Hibernian Society. Constantly plagued by financial problems and unable to attract extensive support, these schools instructed only a relatively few children and generally remained a limited educational force in the city.[7]

The Sunday School movement, begun in 1816, also proved inadequate. Unable to attract students to their schools, Sunday School leaders believed that their major problem was one of persuasion—how could they induce poor families to send their children to school? One solution, according to some, was to offer the promise of further gratuitous education for meritorious Sunday School students. Once the poor understood that the opportunity for more advanced education would allow their children to rise above their humble positions in life, the schools would be filled with children eager to learn. Although the Sunday Schools failed to develop free schools to reward their students, in 1821 several Sunday School leaders expressed the hope that Baltimore would establish a system of publicly supported and operated schools similar to those which they had examined with "unreserved admiration in Boston." They conceded, though, "that so important and radical change in the plan of education" could not be accomplished until public opinion was prepared to accept it.[8]

Four years after these hopes were voiced, several Sunday School leaders joined with other educational reformers in an effort to establish public schools in Baltimore. Their campaign began with a series of ward meetings in January 1825. At these meetings, the Baltimore citizenry heard school proponents extol the virtues of public education as demonstrated by the experiences of other cities. Public schooling, advocates informed their audiences, was much cheaper than a system of private schools. The cost per child was but a fraction of the price of private schooling, thus resulting in considerable savings to the entire community. Furthermore, they argued, these schools offered quality instruction for their pupils. School supporters took special pains to emphasize the qualifications of urban public school teachers. Citing a letter from the Boston School Committee, they explained that the schoolmasters of that city were all university graduates and a highly respected group in the community. Chosen by the School Committee, and paid by the city, these schoolmasters could remain impartial toward all students, even the children of the most influential members of the district.[9]

This vision of equal treatment of all pupils was an important part of the public school appeal, and school supporters expounded upon it at length. In Boston, they found "the most perfect republicanism, for here rich and poor literally meet together." In the public schools of that city, the son of a poor immigrant triumphed over the son of a respected and wealthy descendant of an original settler after numerous and difficult examinations. Honorary rewards were "distributed equally to children of day laborers and of the most accomplished statesman." Immune to the biases of class and religious affiliation, the public schools could draw out and reward the natural talents of its students. In this impartial institution, all could compete and achieve on terms not hindered by the artificialities of class and caste.[10]

Public school advocates anticipated the charge that children of respectable families might be morally tainted by associating with children of the lower classes. Again, referring to Boston, they assured Baltimoreans that the public schools "advance the moral standing of the poorer class of society and never have been found injurious to others." As proof of the harmlessness of this type of association, school supporters explained that "men of the largest wealth and still more . . . those of the most enlightened and religious character" sent their children to public schools.

School proponents concluded their remarks with a call to establish a state-supported, "economical, well-organized" system of schools, such as could compare to the best that private schools offered. They then sounded a solemn warning: ". . . one consideration alone is sufficient to justify it . . . and that is that ignorance is a great cause of crime, and therefore, it is the part of wisdom as well as humanity to provide means of education adequate to its removal."

Following this series of meetings, ward representatives met in a city-wide convention of public school supporters. This convention sent a carefully drafted public school bill and a petition to the state legislature, which had ultimate control over education in the city. In their petition, school advocates once again stressed that the experiences of other cities, especially Boston, had demonstrated clearly—the "astonishing" effects public schooling had on the moral character of the students, the low cost of the schools, and the high quality of the schoolmasters, in comparison with the "great expense incurred in educating only a part of those children at private schools in a less satisfactory manner." Describing their intentions to include all classes of children in the public schools, the petitioners explained: ". . . it has been justly noticed that one of the most beautiful and republican features of this system is its bringing our youth of the higher as well as the lower classes to know and respect one another's rights at a tender age . . . and to teach them . . . that rich and poor must submit alike to the wholesome discipline of the laws and can only be respected in proportion as they fear God and love one another. Surely nothing can be more evident than that it is the right, the duty, and the interest of the public to take into its own hands and to regulate with especial care the education of youth."[11]

Repeatedly, though in different ways, public school advocates stressed two themes which were central to their plans—class mixture and government support and operation. In response to the growing physical and socioeconomic distances between classes in Baltimore, the schools would attempt to reestablish contact on the basis of a common education—that is, a common commitment to certain values, attitudes, and skills.[12] This commitment would be nurtured through the rewards bestowed by an impartial educational hierarchy, thus demonstrating the relationship between particular kinds of behavior—that is, moral, industrious behavior—and the promise of achievement and success in a republican setting. For city and state authorities, class mixture in the schools offered an effective system of moral training, while on a more popular level, the arrangement assured the people equality and upward mobility in a democratic society. Far from contradicting themselves, school supporters believed their system would realize both of these possibilities. Experience had shown, however, that voluntary support of educational endeavors had repeatedly failed to provide the necessary financing. If the public schools were to succeed and provide quality education for all classes, as Boston had demonstrated, some type of taxation would be required. Certainly, their importance to the "advancement of the moral improvement and permanent prosperity to the city of Baltimore" warranted mandatory public support.[13]

To realize their aims, public school proponents submitted a carefully detailed piece of legislation to the Maryland General Assembly. "An Act for

the Establishment and Support of Public Schools," unlike much of the legislation of the period, was a complete and effectively drawn bill which provided
for the establishment, administration, and financial support of the schools, as
well as providing the means for its enforcement.[14] In good republican fashion, the proposed bill provided for a system of schools to be administered by
a combination of directly and indirectly elected officials. Under threat of a
large fine, civic authorities were instructed to call for and conduct biannual
city-wide elections. Each ward was to elect nine of its "most discreet, sensible, and virtuous citizens" to administer its schools. These nine school commissioners, as they were labeled, would then elect one of their number to
serve on the city-wide Union Committee of Public Schools. The Union
Committee would consist of one representative from each of the city's twelve
wards, and "such other person as the said Committee shall think proper
to elect as their President, if they should elect a President not a member of
their body."

Designed as a corporation, the Union Committee was to regulate school
operations and formulate school policy. In order to carry out the former
function, the Union Committee was empowered to decide the financial
needs of the schools, and then assess and collect local income taxes to
meet them (the rate of taxation not to exceed $1 per $100 of income).
Administratively, the Union Committee was responsible for designating the
number of schools and teachers for each ward, the courses of study, the books
to be used, the tuition fees, if any, and the salaries and qualifications of teachers. The Committee was also authorized to appoint the teachers for all of the
schools. In all of these matters, the law instructed the Union Committee to
"take care to preserve as much uniformity as the wholesome administration
of the schools may admit." Furthermore, the Union Committee was periodically to inspect the schools and examine the students, providing for the
distribution of prizes "among the most meritorious scholars of each school."
When they deemed it expedient, the Committee could authorize the establishment of a Classical School of Merit for advanced instruction in science
and literature, open only to those boys with distinguished achievements in
the public schools.

The "Act" specified that only orphans and children of taxable inhabitants—
defined as all registered voters, or any person over twenty-one years of age
who had resided in the city for at least twelve months, and who was a house-
holder, head of a family, or unmarried person having an occupation for his or
her support—could enroll in the schools. After publication of the "Act" in
the *Baltimore American* and considerable public outcry against the apparent
discrimination against children of the poor, supporters of the proposed legislation clarified this provision, explaining that those who were not assessed,
but who paid a dollar, could send their children to public schools. These people could, thus, "demand as a right, what they would be unwilling to receive
as a charity."[15]

On the whole the "Act" was an extremely bold proposition for the
Baltimore community in 1825. Educationally, it was a dramatic departure

from the city's tradition of private and charity schooling. In place of diversity in the quality and content of formal education, the school bill proposed to standardize the schooling experiences of all children in the city. Administratively, the "Act" proposed to establish a political body independent of the municipal government, and to endow it with the power to assess and collect taxes. Even the taxation provisions were radical. Under the contemporary Maryland system, government only assessed taxes on property and not on income.

How should the boldness and design of the school bill be explained? An examination of the leadership of the movement is key to an understanding of the legislation and public debate surrounding the issue of public schooling. Through this type of examination, it is possible to reconstruct the peculiar blend of historical impulses—social, cultural, economic, and political—which at a particular moment in time both gave birth to a strong movement for reform, and, as will be considered later when the opposition leadership is studied, doomed it to failure.

The leadership of the public school system represented a coalition of men with diverse backgrounds.[16] Including a mixture of age, cultural, religious, and middle-class occupational groups, the leadership did not reflect a single interest group, nor did it consist of a tightly knit, self-conscious elite. Instead, the men who formed the public school leadership brought a variety of concerns to the movement. Some of these concerns can be directly established, while others can be inferred.

Part of the impulse to school reform derived from a long-standing interest in providing effective moral education for the lower classes. As noted earlier, several individuals involved with the Sunday School movement were early supporters of the public school idea in Baltimore. Two individuals associated with this early support, George Hume Steuart and Hugh Davey Evans, played leadership roles in the school campaign. Both were young, Episcopalian attorneys with Federalist sympathies. Steuart, one of the most important leaders in the school movement, had become active in the Maryland Federalist party early in his career, serving as a member of the state central committee in 1815, as well as belonging to the Washington Benevolent Society of Maryland, a Federalist party organization. In 1821, he chaired the Sunday School committee that recommended the establishment of free schools, and eventually public schools, and in that same year, organized a procession of Sunday School students designed to impress the citizenry with the importance of "publick instruction."[17]

Steuart and Evans found important allies in three New England-born Unitarians, Edward Hinkley, Charles H. Appleton, and Henry Payson, whose religious and cultural heritage led them to exert an influential role in the school campaign. Devoted to a religion that placed a strong faith in the moral tendencies of mature human reason, Unitarians viewed universal education as the key to social order. This was epitomized by Jared Sparks, Baltimore's first Unitarian minister, who argued in 1821 that "To bring into salutary action these two great instruments of human happiness, morals and religion, nothing is of so much importance as to multiply the facilities of education and quicken the spirit of enlightened inquiry."[18] Hinkley, Appleton, and Payson were all active in this effort to "multiply the facilities of education" in Baltimore. Hinkley was a founder of the Baltimore Athenaeum (1824) and the Apprentice's Library (1821); Appleton was also a founder of the Athenaeum; and Payson worked for the establishment of the Maryland Institute for the Promotion of the Mechanic Arts (1826).

Of these three New Englanders, Edward Hinkley was the most active figure in the school movement. Born in Barnstable, Massachusetts in 1790, Hinkley was a member of an old Bay State family which traced its lineage to the last governor of the Plymouth Colony, Thomas Hinckley. Hinkley attended Harvard during its early nineteenth-century period of liberal theological upheaval. After graduation, he left Massachusetts to study law in Delaware, finally settling in Baltimore in 1815. In Baltimore, he joined a close-knit New England community, which maintained a social cohesiveness at the same time its members played integral roles in the city's commercial and political life. Over the next several years, Hinkley, in collaboration with other New Englanders, attempted to transplant literally New England institutions into what was perceived to be fertile Baltimore soil. In 1819, Hinkley invited his former Harvard classmate, Jared Sparks, to assume the pulpit of the newly founded Unitarian church. Writing to Sparks two years earlier, he had assured the young minister of the ultimate success of his efforts in Baltimore: "In regard to opposition or persecution, nothing is to be apprehended. The variety of people, opinions, and doctrines here does not admit of any formidable alliance. . . . Williams [a native of Boston] says he would rather be opposed to the whole city of Baltimore than to a few individuals in Boston. This sentiment is not without foundation. There is among the common people in this city a sort of indifference about things new and strange which renders their introduction easy, their establishment undisturbed and secure."[19]

A few years later, Hinkley, together with six other Unitarians and several other Baltimoreans founded the Baltimore Athenaeum, a literary and cultural center patterned on those in Boston and Philadelphia. Hinkley and the Athenaeum's other directors hoped their new institution would act as a spur to other educational endeavors. At the laying of the cornerstone of the Athenaeum, in August 1824, Hinkley made a fervent appeal for the establishment of schools, academies, colleges, and universities in Baltimore. "Let us make it [Baltimore] an emporium not only of merchandise," he urged, "but also of the arts and sciences. Let us encourage intellectual commerce. . . . The inhabitants of other cities in reputation at least, have already acquired intellectual preponderance. Shall we submit to tell strangers who may visit us and even our own children that they must go to other cities for mental repast." Determined to provide "mental repast" for his own new-born son, Hinkley, five months later, joined with Payson, Appleton, and prominent Baltimoreans to transplant yet another New England institution to Baltimore—the public school system.[20]

Working with the Unitarians and Sunday School leaders in this effort, and adding prestige to the movement, were a number of prominent well-established Baltimoreans known for their commitment to liberal causes. Alexander McKim, chairman of the school convention and long-time civic leader, had been president of the Republican Society and vice-president of the Maryland Society for the Abolition of Slavery in the 1790s.[21] Other public school advocates, Isaac Tyson, son of Quaker abolitionist Elisha Tyson, and William G. D. Worthington had also at some point in their careers favored the abolition of slavery. In addition, W. G. D. Worthington was one of the leading spokesmen in 1825 in the state legislature of the so-called "Jew Bill," which granted full political equality to Maryland's Jewish population.[22]

The public school campaign was also strengthened by the participation of activists in other educational projects of the 1820s. The third decade of the nineteenth century in Baltimore witnessed a heightened interest in the spread and advancement of knowledge both as a force of moral improvement and commercial progress in the community. Besides the Baltimore Athenaeum, this decade saw the establishment of the Apprentice's Library (1821), the Maryland Institute for the Promotion of the Mechanic Arts (1826), and the Maryland Academy of Science and Literature (1825). These institutions served different groups, and in some ways very different needs, yet they all shared the underlying belief that knowledge, especially, "useful knowledge," could both improve the individual as well as contribute to the material advancement of society. The revolutionary impact of recent inventions such as the steam engine spurred Baltimoreans to focus their attention on the educational resources in the city in order to encourage the cultivation of inventive minds. As one supporter of the Maryland Institute wrote: "We cannot recollect the numerous inventions and vast improvements which have been made in the Mechanic Arts in the last half-century . . . without being aware of the influence of inventive minds, and the importance of adding to their numbers, and augmenting to them the facilities of knowledge by every means in our power."[23] The growing interest in encouraging the advancement of applied knowledge may well have been part of the appeal of public schooling. Almost half of the thirty-six school leaders were involved with the founding of at least one of these institutions.[24]

Personal needs no doubt proved an important motivating force among public school leaders. At least ten members of the group had either been married or fathered children between 1819 and 1825. Their interest in public education, like that of Edward Hinkley, may well have been grounded in their own child-rearing considerations, as well as in concerns for the educational needs of the lower classes. Anxious about their ability to meet the educational needs of their offspring in a world of rapid and unpredictable change, aware of the good reputation of the Boston schools, and attracted to the values embodied in these schools, middle- and upper-class parents sought the introduction of this form of schooling in Baltimore for the benefit of their own children, and for the welfare of the community as a whole.[25]

The participation of still others may have been motivated largely by political considerations. The egalitarian rhetoric of the public school campaign meshed well with the democratic impulse ignited by the 1824 presidential campaign of Andrew Jackson. Politicians out of office could use the school issue to stimulate this impulse, and in so doing, further their own office-seeking ambitions. The political climate in Baltimore was ripe for this type of exploitation. The mayoral election of 1824 had brought into office an individual with strong connections to the state's landed gentry. Preparing for the next election in just two years, the urban-based opposition, headed by Samuel Smith, the powerful United States senator, sought to align itself with a middle-class mechanics' group to support a man-of-the-people for mayor, namely Jacob Small, the well-known builder. In their campaign, they would launch an attack on the incumbent as a representative of oppressive, aristocratic interests. Preparing for this election, Smith faction members as well as others with political ambitions may have viewed the public school movement as a golden opportunity to establish themselves as champions of "the people." At least two school leaders, James H. McCulloh and Hugh McElderry, were important Smith allies.[26]

These, then, are the key elements which explain the development of the public school movement in Baltimore in the 1820s. At this time, educational reform was a compelling issue for many in Baltimore. The concern for reform could be found among several overlapping groups—among those interested in securing effective moral instruction for an increasingly disruptive society; among well-to-do parents anxious about their ability to properly educate their offspring to succeed in a rapidly changing environment; and among those desirous of raising the general educational level in line with the growing technological needs and aspirations of the city. The desire for educational improvements found a promising mode of expression in the public school idea, developed, praised, and promoted in New England, and introduced into Baltimore through newspaper reports, and the influx of New Englanders into the city in the second and third decades of the nineteenth century. New England Unitarians and other educational reformers campaigned for public education with the aid of liberal-minded members of the city's elite, and with the aid of a political climate receptive to the egalitarian rhetoric of the school movement. Their efforts, however, met considerable resistance in the southern port city.

Immediately following the publication of the school bill in the *Baltimore American*, vehement opposition appeared in the form of published statements and counter-petitions. One small but astute segment of the opposition focused on the educational implications involved. Citing the sectarian diversity in Baltimore, one correspondent to the *Federal Gazette* argued that unlike a relatively homogeneous city such as Boston, a general system of education would never suit the city, but would generate conflict. "The Union Committee," he stated, "have the choice of teachers; one is to be chosen—is there no danger that the several societies will each interest themselves to procure a master of their own sect? Or is it intended to risque the measure and take the chance of bringing the population to one way of thinking by the instrumentality of the Public Schools?" A Presbyterian, he contended, would not send his children to a Catholic master, nor would an Episcopalian send his children to a Unitarian. Consequently, many parents, forced to send their children to private schools, would have to bear the financial burden for both public and private schools. "No measure," he concluded, "ought to be thrown before the public for them to act on which in the remotest degree threatens on this score controversy and conflict."[27]

Another correspondent advised those interested in public schools to collect donations from among themselves to establish their school system. "Thus, they will be enabled to give to their children such an education as they wish, without interfering with the rights of others, or coercing those who are not disposed to abandon the modes they have heretofore pursued in bringing up their children." Along the same lines, "Z" argued that it was poor policy to take the education of children from competent parents and make it a matter of public operation.[28]

As controversial as the very concept of a school system supported and operated by the public was, most protests ignored this issue and focused instead on the more obvious issues of administration and taxation. Numerous public letters condemned the income tax as "repugnant to the feelings of free men," "odious," and "oppressive." The machinery for administering the schools was viewed as "an alarming grant of power," "inquisitorial," "unwieldy and expensive," and "an infringement upon individual liberty."[29] According to one opponent, public schooling was merely "a timeserving, popularity seeking scheme," for the rich clearly could afford to send their children to existing pay schools, while under-utilized free schools and Sunday Schools demonstrated that the poor did not even care to send their children to school.[30]

In a more private context, Samuel Hoffman, an established Baltimore merchant, echoed these same objections in a rather anxious letter to his friend Virgil Maxcy, a state legislator. "You may have observed," he wrote, "a feverish excitement in our city for sometime past, exhibiting itself in a project for ward schooling, which has at length come to a crisis as you will perceive by a Bill to be laid before the Legislature for enactment. Some of the features of this bill are so very objectionable, offensive, and I may add outrageous, that it would appear next to impossible that they should be passed by your body." One of the most outrageous features, according to Hoffman, was the scheme of taxation, "inadmissable in a government like ours unless in the very last resort and in the most extreme case." Public schooling was hardly an "extreme case." "I am informed by the managers of the Oliver, McKim, St. Peter's, and the Methodist Charity Schools that they are all in want of scholars; if this be so, where is the necessity of those ward schools at all, and certainly the occasion for them is not so urgent as to resort to the way proposed to raise money for their support. . . ."[31]

In response to attacks on the need for public schools and the mode of financing them, proponents sought publicly to clarify their intentions.

A correspondent to the *Baltimore American* argued that those who pointed to half-empty free schools were not aware of the difference "between these charity schools and the public schools in the eastern states." Another school supporter wrote: "We do not want charity schools—we do not want free schools—we want schools for freemen; such schools as the honest and independent mechanics and merchants of this city will send their children to."[32]

Those opposed to public education took concrete measures to defeat the proposed school bill. Several of the city's wealthiest and most influential citizens published and signed their names to resolutions condemning the "Act." This group also petitioned the City Council to use its influence to prevent passage of the bill in the state legislature. The Council complied with their request, directing the city's delegates to vote against it. The Council's opposition to the "Act," according to a joint committee report, stemmed from the unsuitability of the Boston system of schooling to "our habits, our manners, and our system of education," and, from the fact that the schools would be "burthensome and oppressive" to already overtaxed real estate owners; the "odious" and "revolting" income tax was totally out of the question.[33]

A closer look at those wealthy and influential Baltimoreans who publicly denounced the school bill further reveals the nature and meaning of the public school debate. In comparison with school proponents, these men shared similar occupations, though on the whole, they were older, more conservative, and almost exclusively native-born.[34] The identifiable opposition, though smaller in number than the identifiable school advocates, included important members of the landed elite—such as John Eager Howard, Philip Evan Thomas, and George Winchester—as well as several prominent merchants—namely, John Hoffman, John McKim, Jr., and Robert Purviance—all sons of founding merchants of Baltimore. In the young city, these men represented old Baltimore and old Maryland families.

In contrast to the proponents, none of the opponents, with the exception of William Steuart, was involved in the educational reform efforts of the 1820s. They *were* active, however, in community efforts to develop *external controls* over the growing numbers of disruptive elements in the population. They worked with the House of Industry, for instance, an unsuccessful attempt to establish an institution to encourage industrious habits among the poor; the Society for the Prevention of Pauperism, a short-lived group organized in 1820 for the purpose of supervising the habits of the poor, through the control of liquor dealers, houses of prostitution, and charitable institutions; and the Maryland Colonization Society, an organization devoted to encourage free black migration to Africa.[35] These activities, like the crusty old patriarch, John Eager Howard, who was involved in all of them, suggest the orientation of a status-bound, paternalistic society characteristic of the previous century. In this static view of society, the poor were seen as a permanent social group needing occasional aid and supervision; the free black, on the other hand, was seen as undesirable, and indeed was a threat to the slave-owning order.

This social perspective differed from that of public school advocates who adhered to a relatively more fluid conception of society. In their view, poor children could rise above their humble origins through both their willingness to accept prescribed patterns of conduct and their ability to achieve mental discipline. School leaders accepted social mobility if it were accompanied by rational and moral behavior. Traditional Baltimoreans, on the other hand, held fast to a fixed social structure stratified by inherited status.[36]

Cultural conservatives, the opponents included some of the most commercially aggressive and daring men in the city. With the devastating depression in foreign trade gripping the city in the 1820s, many looked to domestic markets for new opportunities. Reaching those markets, however, required improved and effective means of transportation. Internal improvements were of prime importance for the very future of the sagging Baltimore economy. In the early 1820s, Philip Evan Thomas investigated the possibility of introducing a newly developed means of transportation, the railroad, to Baltimore. In 1825, this possibility may have appeared quite strong, for in just two years from that date, he and twenty-five others, including William Steuart and John McKim, Jr., were granted the right to incorporate the Baltimore and Ohio Railroad, the first of its kind in the country. Around the same time, George Winchester and Robert Purviance became directors of the newly formed Baltimore and Susquehanna Railroad.[37] The involvement of these men in railroads and other internal improvements suggests that at the time of the public school agitation, these opponents, six of whom were merchants, may have viewed the expense of the schools as an unnecessary drain on the city's dwindling monetary resources—resources which they hoped could be tapped to rejuvenate commerce and prosperity in Baltimore.[38]

The background of known opponents, together with the arguments used against the public school, imply the cultural, economic, and political bases of the opposition. Clashing views of the role and nature of the community, the potential of the individual, and the future of society, in combination with the imperatives of a depressed economy, and the political challenge of an independent educational authority, provoked a strong, and ultimately triumphant attack on the proposed school law. Arguments such as Samuel Hoffman's, which questioned the need for public schools when free schools and Sunday Schools were half empty, point to either an unwillingness to accept, or an inability to understand, one of the fundamental thrusts behind the public school movement—class mixture. Furthermore, assertions of parental prerogative in childhood education suggest the conservatives' preference for the private, and religiously and ethnically segmented nature of city life. The Boston school system was ill-suited to the status-bound individualism and sectarian divisiveness of Baltimore society. During a period of commercial depression, its introduction into the city was especially unlikely.

The 1825 school bill failed to achieve passage in the Maryland General Assembly. Reporting on that failure, school leader George Hume Steuart advised his allies: "as I am confident that the refusal of the City Council to recommend our bill was the moving cause of its being rejected, so I trust that the people at the next election will take care to give their suffrage to those supporting public schools."[39] The next round in the contest over public education would be fought in the upcoming elections for local office.

Prior to the municipal elections of October 1825, several ward meetings were held to urge the election of those candidates supporting public schooling. At a meeting of the Twelfth Ward, which had led the earlier drive for public schools, the citizens adopted several resolutions calling for passage of a law in the General Assembly to establish public schools, for the collection of income taxes to support the schools, and for the support of candidates who favored the school system. Other wards were more cautious in their support. The citizens of the Eleventh Ward, noting that there was considerable disagreement in the city over the means of funding the schools, came out in favor of a law to authorize the Mayor and City Council to establish public schools. The municipal authorities, according to the ward resolution, could best understand "the sense of the People," in regard to this issue.[40]

The October election failed to alter in a significant way the membership of the Council since it only involved the First Branch, and not the more staunch opponents within the Second Branch.[41] However, election debates, like the earlier school bill defeat, demonstrated to public school leaders that their efforts would be futile without the support of the Mayor and City Council. Their next proposal to the state legislature in December 1825 bore little resemblance to the previous elaborate plan for public schools. No longer patterned on the Boston model, the bill simply authorized the Mayor and City Council to establish public schools and empowered them to collect taxes for this purpose. Despite the open opposition of the Second Branch of the Council, the bill passed through the General Assembly in February 1826, with the stipulation that the Mayor and City Council approve the legislation and establish schools within five years, or else control over schooling would automatically be placed in the hands of the state.[42]

With their work cut out for them, school supporters sought to influence the more critical municipal elections of October 1826, where members of both houses of the City Council were running for re-election. Various ward meetings again adopted resolutions favoring the election of those candidates in support of public schools. At the same time, letters to the city newspapers alerted voters to those councilmen who had opposed public education, urging them to vote against these candidates or, in the absence of a choice, to erase the names of known opponents from the ballot. The campaign rhetoric continued to play on status tensions in the community as supporters harangued against "rich men, who wish to keep the common people in ignorance."[43]

The results of the 1826 election were both rewarding and disappointing for public school proponents. In the First Branch, they achieved considerable success. Seven of ten publicly announced opponents of the schools were not re-elected, and were replaced by at least two strong school supporters. At the same time, four staunch advocates won re-election. In the Second Branch, they made only minimal, non-decisive gains. Out of the nine known opponents, only three lost re-election bids. Two of the three losers, however, were replaced by school supporters.

The failure to alter the composition of the Second Branch was a significant setback for the school movement. While in January 1827, both branches unanimously passed an ordinance adopting the 1826 school law, the system failed to materialize during the following two years. Repeatedly, the Second Branch thwarted First Branch proposals to convene a joint committee to consider the formation of schools. Finally, in April 1829, the Council passed an ordinance establishing "one or more schools on the Monitorial Plan. . . ." It refused, however, to assess any specific tax for the schools. The system was to be financed by the minimal amount due to the city as its share of the state school fund, and by bequests and donations.[44]

In response to obvious Council opposition, the six newly appointed school commissioners took the matter into their own hands. Aware of the fact that if the city failed to establish schools, the state would assume eventual control, they opened three schools in the fall of 1829. Attempting to force the Council into action, they rented one room in the basement of a Presbyterian Church in the western part of the city and two rooms in the eastern section, and hired three teachers for six months, pending the financial support of the city.[45] This tactic succeeded, and in February 1830, the Council authorized a tax of $12\frac{1}{2}$ cents on each $100 of assessable property for support of the schools.[46] The battle in the municipal government as well as in the public at large, however, was far from over. For the first ten years of their existence, the public schools suffered the hostility or indifference of powerful elements within the Council and community.[47]

CONCLUSION

Searching for new modes of educating lower class children, and anxious about the future of their own offspring, many Baltimoreans responded enthusiastically to the promises of public schooling in 1825. Introduced into the city by way of recently settled New Englanders and by the glowing reports of public school success in Boston and New York published in the local press, the public school idea offered a promising alternative to the inadequate educational facilities in Baltimore. Public school promoters portrayed their institution as a proven vehicle for developing social cohesion and republican virtues at the same time it advanced the careers of meritorious students. The public school offered a defined and well-regulated system to a society plagued by increasing uncertainties, and it sung the virtues of achievement, equality of competition, industry, uniformity, and morality—all values which an evolving Protestant, libertarian, capitalist society would find attractive. In addition, it promised to raise the level of knowledge in a community vitally aware of the impact of technology on community prosperity, and interested in nurturing "inventive minds" and "ingenious mechanics" amidst the "fund of latent talent" in the city.[48]

The public school movement received considerable support in Baltimore. Its cause was advanced by a coalition of New Englanders, local educational reformers, liberal native elites, and political hopefuls, and it was championed by the local press. However, not all shared in the belief that public schooling would be beneficial for the city. A heated exchange over the issue took place in the city's newspapers, with opponents attacking the homogenizing effects of the schools, the administrative apparatus, and the income taxes proposed for their support. Several members of the city's conservative elite publicly condemned the 1825 school bill, and exerted political pressure to defeat it. Their opposition stemmed not only from the challenge to their authority which the establishment of an independent schooling administration represented, but also from cultural and, to a lesser extent, economic considerations. Public schooling held little appeal to those whose values derived from an eighteenth-century, hierarchical, status-based culture. During a period of economic decline especially, there would be little willingness to fund a promising, but costly educational experiment which deviated from the social order they upheld. The school bill thus failed to gain passage in the state legislature. Political pressure over the next few years, however, forced some important concessions from municipal leaders, and they provided for a nominal public school system. Yet in their legislative response—in establishing schools on the monitorial plan, and in reluctantly conceding a minimum of funding—and in their neglect of the schools over the next ten years, members of the city's dominating elite demonstrated that they were unwilling at this time to support schools for the middling and upper classes, and would continue to render aid only for the education of the poor. Ultimately, though, in granting legal authorization for a system of municipally operated schools, the Baltimore leadership of the 1820s provided the basis for the eventual development of the public school idea in their city.

NOTES

1. Michael B. Katz, "The Origins of Public Education: A Reassessment," *History of Education Quarterly* 16 (Winter 1976): 391–93; Stanley K. Schultz, *The Culture Factory: Boston Public Schools, 1789–1860* (New York, 1973), p. 41; Carl F. Kaestle, *The Evolution of an Urban School System: New York City, 1750–1850* (Cambridge, 1973), pp. 85–88.
2. Selwyn Troen, *The Public and the Schools: Shaping the St. Louis System. 1838–1920* (Columbia, Missouri, 1975).
3. Katz, "The Origins of Public Education," 385.
4. Carville Earle and Ronald Hoffman, "Staple Crops and Urban Development in the Eighteenth Century South," *Perspectives in American History* 10 (1976): 48–50; Gary Lawson Browne, *Baltimore in the Nation, 1789–1861* (Chapel Hill, North Carolina, 1980), pp. 12, 95. An important component of this elite was a dynamic group of Scots-Irish merchants. See LeRoy J. Votto, "Social Dynamism in Boom-Town: The Scots-Irish in Baltimore, 1760–1790" (M.A. thesis, University of Virginia, 1969).

5. Browne, *Baltimore in the Nation*, pp. 51–114; Dennis R. Clark, "Baltimore 1729–1829; The Genesis of a Community" (Ph.D. dissertation, The Catholic University of America, 1976), pp. 191–239.

6. For other reform efforts, see note 21, later.

7. Clark, "Baltimore 1729–1829," pp. 243–53.

8. *First and Second Annual Reports of the Board of Delegates from the Male Sunday School Societies of Baltimore* (1820); "Report of a Meeting of the Union Board of Delegates," *Baltimore American and Commercial Advertiser*, 24 July 1821.

9. A report on the meeting was printed in the *Federal Gazette and Baltimore Daily Advertiser*, 11 January 1825.

10. "AH" here would, of course, exclude free black children. Their status, really non-status, in the community was well understood by the citizenry. In all of the discussions surrounding the public schools which I found there is no mention of education for free black children. White girls were to be included in the system, but not beyond the grammar school level.

11. Printed in the *Federal Gazette*, 27 January 1825.

12. For the growing class polarization during the 1820s in Baltimore, see Browne, *Baltimore in the Nation*, pp. 96–98; Whitman H. Ridgway, *Community Leadership in Maryland, 1790–1840* (Chapel Hill, North Carolina, 1979), pp. 89–95.

13. *Federal Gazette*, 13 January 1825.

14. The "Act" was printed in the *Baltimore American and Commercial Advertiser*, 7 February 1825. Two printed copies of the bill (one an amended version) can be found in the John Pendleton Kennedy Papers, Peabody Institute Library, Baltimore.

15. *Federal Gazette*, 16 February 1825.

16. Of 162 known school supporters, I derived the leadership of 36 men from those who served in at least one of the following capacities: officer or speaker at ward meetings; member or officer of the city-wide school convention; member of the committee which petitioned the City Council; member of the committee which petitioned the state legislature. Because of their influence in the community, newspaper editors favorable to public schooling were also included among the leadership.

    This information was gleaned from the daily press, especially the *Federal Gazette* and *Baltimore American*, between January and March 1825; also from the Journal of the First Branch of the City Council, 4 February 1825, Baltimore City Archives.

17. *Baltimore American*, 24 July 1821; David Hackett Fischer, *The Revolution of American Conservatism: The Federalist Party in an Era of Jeffersonian Democracy* (New York, 1965), pp. 82, 120–21, 368; "Recollections of the Life of Hugh Davey Evans," Subject File, Maryland Diocesan Archives, Maryland Historical Society; "Correspondence from the Male Sunday School Societies to the Baltimore City Council," 9 November 1821, Document #603, Baltimore City Archives.

18. Jared Sparks, "Appropriation of Public Lands for Schools," *North American Review* 33 (October 1821): 337. For the Unitarian commitment to promoting education, see Daniel Walker Howe, "At Morning Blest and Golden Browed; Unitarians, Transcendentalists, and Reformers, 1835–1865," in Conrad Wright, ed., *A Stream of Light: A Sesquicentennial History of American Unitarianism* (Boston, 1975). "Among the secular activities reflecting Unitarian religious commitment were many relating to the promotion of literacy and learning. . . . the

Unitarians of the middle third of the nineteenth century were remarkable even among Yankees for their devotion to education" (p. 34). William Ellery Channing and Samuel May, two prominent Unitarian ministers, were active in the Boston public school reforms of 1818. Stanley Schultz, *The Culture Factory*, p. 39.

19. Dielmanand Hayward File, Maryland Historical Society; Edward Hinkley to Jared Sparks, 19 April 1817, in Herbert B. Adams, ed., *The Life and Writings of Jared Sparks*, Vol. 1 (New York, 1893; reprint ed., Books for Libraries Press, 1970), p. 128.

20. *Baltimore American*, 11 August 1824. The Edward Otis Hinkley Papers, Maryland Historical Society, contain Hinkley's sons's autobiography, which notes that he attended Public School #1, his father "having been instrumental in establishing the system of public education. . . ."

21. L. Marx Renzulli, *Maryland: The Federalist Years* (Rutherford, NJ, 1973), p. 62; *Resolutions Held at a Meeting of the Maryland Society for the Abolition of Slavery, February 1792* (Baltimore, 1792).

22. Leroy Graham, "Elisha Tyson, Baltimore, and the Negro" (M.A. thesis, Morgan State University, 1975), pp. 43, 84; W. G. D. Worthington Diary, 1825, Box 270, Joseph Toner Collection, Library of Congress; Isaac Fein, *The Making of an American Jewish Community* (Philadelphia, 1971), pp. 32–36.

23. *Baltimore Gazette and Evening Advertiser*, 3 November 1825.

24. Significantly, the group included one of the state's leading spokesmen for the advancement of "useful knowledge," John Stuart Skinner, editor of the *American Farmer*, and an outspoken advocate of scientific agriculture and animal husbandry.

25. Two of the several themes of the public debate surrounding the schools concerned the rising cost and unsatisfactory quality of education in Baltimore. One correspondent to the *Baltimore American* (7 February 1825) complained that "at the present enormous charges for education, there exists a virtual prohibition of learning to all but the children of the rich." Another correspondent (15 February 1825) in a seeming reference to the New Englanders, reported that parents who investigated "the manner in which this concern [education] was managed by the town" found that notwithstanding the high cost of the schools, "the children were very badly educated and their parents sometimes egregiously imposed upon, that the teachers were not altogether so moral in their deportment or so well qualified in learning or so disinterested in their views as to be fit for the great duties they had undertaken."

26. Browne, *Baltimore in the Nation*, pp. 103, 106; conversation with Gary L. Browne. Ridgeway, *Community Leadership in Maryland*, p. 81.

27. *Federal Gazette*, 12 February 1825.

28. Ibid., 21 February 1825; *Baltimore Gazette and Evening Advertiser*, 18 September 1825. For similar arguments, see also *Baltimore American*, 11 February 1825; and *Federal Gazette*, 18 February 1825.

29. *Baltimore American*, 9, 10, 12 February 1825.

30. *Federal Gazette*, 11, 17 February 1825.

31. Samuel Hoffman to Virgil Maxcy, 9 February 1825, "Correspondence," Box 63, Virgil Maxcy Papers, Galloway-Maxcy-Markoe Papers, Library of Congress.

32. *Baltimore American*, 9, 14 February 1825.

33. For the published resolutions, see *Federal Gazette*, 16 February 1825. For the City Council report, see *Baltimore American*, 9 February 1825, and *Federal Gazette*, 15 February 1825.

34. While the opposition did not include any merchant-manufacturers, at least two opponents were active supporters of manufacturing interests. Opponents John McKim, Jr., and John Eager Howard were officers in the American Society for the Promotion of Domestic Manufacturers and National Industry, organized in 1817. Scharf, *History of Baltimore City and County* (Philadelphia, 1881; reprinted Baltimore, 1971), p. 393.

35. For the House of Industry, see Scharf, *History of Baltimore City and County*, pp. 826–27; "Report of the Trustees of the House of Industry," December 26, 1822, Documents 514, 515, Baltimore City Archives. For the Society for the Prevention of Pauperism, see Blanche D. Coll, "The Baltimore Society for the Prevention of Pauperism, 1820–1822," *American Historical Review*, 61 (October 1955): 77–87. For the Maryland Colonization Society, see *Fifth Annual Report of the American Society for Colonizing the Free People of Color* (Washington, D.C., 1822), p. 111.

    The fate of the House of Industry further points up the type of conflict surrounding the public schools. In December 1826, the trustees of the House of Industry suggested that the City Council sell the House of Industry property, donate the proceeds to the Almshouse, which accomplished what the H. of I. had originally intended to do, and then obtain "an efficient vagrant act, by which vagrants, the youthful portion of them at least, may be removed from our streets and placed under the care and control of the Trustees of the Almshouse." The following month, a committee from the First Branch argued that since the City Council had recently been authorized to establish public schools, the proceeds ought to go to these schools, "the best corrective of pauperism." The Second Branch defeated this proposal, favoring instead the suggestion of the H. of I. trustees. "Report of the Trustees of the House of Industry," 28 December 1826, Document 1288; "Report of the Committee on the House of Industry." 16 January 1827, Document 771; "Report of a Committee on the House of Industry," 29 January 1827, Document 772, Baltimore City Archives, Journal of the Second Branch of the City Council, 8 February, 30 January 1827, Baltimore City Archives.

36. In their views of education and social organization, traditional Baltimoreans were representative of the Southern mindset. See William R. Taylor, "Toward a Definition of Orthodoxy: The Patrician South and the Common School," *Harvard Educational Review* 36 (Fall 1966): 412–26.

    The views of public school proponents, on the other hand, resembled those William Cutler has described in his analysis of the trustees of the New York Public School Society: "Theirs was not a distaste for social mobility by anyone, regardless of his background. For years they helped to send a few of the Society's brightest graduates to Columbia College, the University of New York, and the Rutger's Female Institute. But the Trustees firmly believed that social mobility, as well as citizenship, had to entail habits of moral order including a respect for industry, authority, and self-discipline." "Status, Values, and the Education of the Poor: The Trustees of the New York Public School Society, 1805–1853," *American Quarterly* 24 (March 1972): 81.

37. Scharf, *History of Baltimore City and County*, pp. 317, 343.

38. School supporters shared opponents' concerns over the city's economic growth. Henry Payson, Solomon Etting, John P. Kennedy, John S. Skinner, and Isaac Tyson were very active in promoting internal improvements. The point here is that pressing commercial concerns, *in conjunction with an eighteenth-century*

view of community, tended to further inhibit one's willingness to accept a new and costly scheme of education.

Eventually the city did contribute heavily to the railroads. In 1831, it allocated $50,000 to the B & O, and $12,000 to the B & S. The allocation to the fledgling public schools in that year was $3,915. "Register's Summary," January, 1831, in *Ordinances of the Major and City Council of Baltimore*, 1831. This school budget contrasts strikingly with that of Boston, which spent $76,154 in 1825 and $120,244 in 1835. Schultz, *The Culture Factory*, p. 80.

39. *Baltimore American*, 23 February 1825.
40. *Baltimore Gazette*, 9, 27 September 1825; *Baltimore American*, 28 September 1825; *Baltimore Patriot and Mercantile Advertiser*, 30 September 1825.

    The citizens of the Twelfth Ward held a referendum on the school issue. The results were: 607 For 14 Against; *Baltimore Gazette*, 4 October 1825.
41. Traditionally, the Second Branch had been the upper house of the Council. Originally, its members were elected by the First Branch, although this changed in 1808 when popular elections were instituted. The property qualifications for the Second Branch ($500) were higher than those for the First Branch ($300). The Second Branch included only one representative per ward, while the First Branch included two per ward.
42. *Baltimore American*, 23 February 1825, 2 January 1826. For the opposition of the Second Branch, see "City Council Resolution," 27 January 1826, Document 1031, Baltimore City Archives; *Laws of Maryland*, 1824–25, Chapter 130.
43. *Baltimore Gazette*, 31 August, 4, 23, 25 September 1826; *Baltimore Patriot*, 19, 23, 29 September 1826.
44. *Ordinances of the Mayor and City Council of Baltimore*, #3, 17 January 1827; W42, 6 April 1829. For example of Second Branch opposition, see Journal of the First Branch, 26 January 1829, 27 March 1829.
45. For the struggles of the opening year, see *First Annual Report of the Commissioners of Public Schools*, December 1829.
46. *Ordinances*, #9, 25 February 1830.
47. See annual reports of the school commissioners, 1829–39.
48. *Baltimore Gazette*, 3 November 1825.

4

Popular Education in Nineteenth Century St. Louis

Selwyn K. Troen

It is both encouraging and gratifying to the members of this Board to witness the unexampled success of our school system, and the great popularity of the schools. This is still the more gratifying, when we feel a consciousness that this popularity is deserved; and that the more our schools are tried and the closer their operations are examined, the greater will be their popularity, and the confidence reposed in them.[1]

So Isaiah Forbes concluded his annual report as president of the St. Louis Board of Public Schools in 1855. Mid-nineteenth-century school directors, superintendents, and heads of departments universally echoed this confidence in the success of the schools and their continued growth. Moreover, they attempted to substantiate their claims with an impressive array of statistics that both summarized yearly operations and placed them in historical perspective. Beginning with Forbes' report, successive Boards published through the end of the century, in English and German, an average of five to seven thousand copies for local and national distribution to broadcast the triumphs of the public schools.

These *Annual Reports* dramatically delineate the expanding popularity of the public schools both in absolute and relative terms. Between 1840, or shortly after the first schools were established, and 1880, when they had evolved into a complex and diversified system ranging from kindergartens to evening, high and normal schools, the student body had grown from 266 pupils to 55,870. When correlated with the city's total population, these numbers show that between 1840 and 1850, its first full decade of operation, the system reached about one in fifty of the city's population. By 1880, one out of every six or seven persons came into contact with the schools, with the greatest proportion of this rise occurring in the post–Civil War period.[2] By this date, the schools had become one of the city's most important social institutions, touching the lives of more people on a daily and continuing basis than perhaps any other.

Nevertheless, while public education expanded, some of the system's basic features remained constant. Despite its increased complexity and size, it performed much the same kind of work in 1880 as it had in previous decades. In the 1850s, the period when good records become available, as well as during the next two decades, the average student was between nine and ten years of age.[3] Furthermore, little change took place in the length of schooling since the burden of the system's work was devoted to instructing seven through twelve-year-olds who were in the first three grades. Thus, the Board continued to be primarily involved in teaching the fundamentals of reading, writing, arithmetic, some geography and group singing.[4] These comprised the natural limits of public education for the majority of parents permitted their children to drop out despite the availability of free higher schooling. This study is concerned with defining who continued, who left, and what factors influenced their decisions.

Of prime importance in exploring these questions are the cumulative tables in the *Annual Reports* that deal with such matters as enrollments, age and sex of pupils, occupations of parents, and the number in each grade. However, since it was uncertain how representative school records were of the patterns operating in society at large, and since the variables present in the tables are limited, a collective biography of more than fifteen thousand children, drawn from the manuscript census of 1880, was established. The biography yields a cross section of the community's economic, social and racial groups and is based on an analysis of about 45,000 persons or one eighth of the nation's fourth largest city, in twenty-six selected election precincts.[5] Since the data revealed that race was a critical factor in educational and vocational opportunities and in the character of the family, only an analysis of the population of white children is presented here. Moreover, blacks were denied public schooling until 1866 and engaged in a limited boycott until 1876. The story of the black child, therefore, necessitates separate treatment and has been presented elsewhere.[6]

In addition to emphasizing the importance of elementary education, the *Annual Reports*, by themselves, suggest that the major difference between those who left school and those that remained was the level of the fathers' occupations. Although St. Louis educators prided themselves on an open and democratic system, clearly children in higher economic groups used the schools to better advantage. About 50 per cent of the system's students were children of unskilled or skilled workers with an approximately equal division of the two categories between 1860 and 1880.[7] Despite their large representation in the system as a whole, they exhibited a disproportionately low distribution in the higher reaches of the system. For example, in 1880, they comprised about 21 per cent of the high school and 18 per cent of normal school students.

The relationship between class and education becomes even more striking when the category of unskilled labor is isolated and examined. In 1880, for example, they comprised 27 per cent of day students, that is, pupils in the district, high and normal schools, but supplied only 3 per cent to the high and

7 per cent to the normal school. Breaking this category down into its constituent parts, it becomes clearer how few advanced beyond elementary instruction. There were 8,262 children of "laborers," the major component in the unskilled classification, in the district schools, but there were only 23 in the high and 2 in the normal school. Similarly only one child of a "laundress" was found in the high school and none was preparing for teaching but 1,711 were in the district schools. Yet another component, "draymen and teamsters," made the same kind of showing, sending 1,984 to district schools, four to the high and two to the normal school. On the other hand, "professionals," with a number approximate to that of "laundresses" and to "draymen and teamsters" sent 113 to the high school, 9 to the normal school, and 1,866 to the district schools. This pattern of unequal distribution by class, established with the first high school class in 1857, remained one of the constants in the social structure of the schools.[8]

Gender is another area of maldistribution. While there is no way in which differentiation can be made by grades, it is possible to delineate differences between levels. In the day schools as a whole, there was approximately equal distribution of males and females, with males predominating by one per cent in 1860 but with one to two per cent more females during the 1870s. In the high school there were somewhat more males than females in the early years, but after 1865 an increasing proportion of girls enrolled. Between 1855 and 1860 it was 46 per cent female, but between 1875 and 1880 it was 59 per cent.[9] The normal school, however, was from its beginnings in 1857 almost completely a female institution. This data suggests that commencing in the post war period, girls were receiving more schooling in the teen years. Such a conclusion may be unwarranted since it does not take into account the opportunities available for males at non-public institutions found in the city and elsewhere. Indeed, for a refinement and elaboration of all the dynamics described above—ages of attendance, the significance of class and sex for educational advancement—as well as additional factors influencing attendance, it is necessary to turn to the manuscript census.

An important advantage to the census data is that it relates school to other experiences, allowing for a profile of the stages in the development of children. After five years at home, schooling began at six for 56 per cent; the peak years of education were from eight through eleven when about 90 per cent enrolled; then, beginning at twelve, ever-larger numbers of youngsters left school. The exodus became so massive that less than half of the fourteen-year-olds and less than a fifth of those sixteen continued to take advantage of St. Louis' diverse schools. Based on the patterns of education and employment, children can be divided into four age groups: one through five; six through twelve; thirteen through sixteen; and seventeen through twenty. Only the second group was involved with schooling *en masse*, confirming the data drawn from the *Annual Reports*. Thereafter, most children either became unknowns, probably returning home, or graduated into the world of work.[10]

The kind of job a child was able to obtain when he dropped out was related to the age at which he left school. Throughout this period there is an expansion of the work force in all the categories and movement into jobs of greater status and complexity with the advance of years. For example, whereas 20 per cent of the twelve-year-old boys had left school, only 58 per cent of these had jobs, and most of them, 88 per cent, were employed in semi-skilled or unskilled occupations. By sixteen, 15 per cent remained in school. Of their peers who left, 86 per cent were employed: 47 per cent were semi-skilled and unskilled workers; 15 per cent were now in skilled categories; 21 per cent held white collar jobs as various kinds of clerks; and 3 per cent were even in the higher occupations. At eighteen and twenty, at least 50 per cent of all males were skilled workers or better.

While a few girls also began to work at age twelve, a greater proportion of twelve to sixteen-year-olds stayed in school. At ages twelve, fourteen, and sixteen there are 5, 6, and 9 per cent more girls in school than boys. By eighteen and twenty, there is a return to parity as education becomes increasingly less significant for both sexes. When females left school, however, it was for experiences fundamentally different from those of males. Fewer girls worked. At age twelve, 6 per cent less were employed; at fourteen, 20 per cent; at sixteen, 27 per cent; at eighteen and twenty, 25 per cent. Moreover, those employed generally worked as maids, seamstresses, laundresses, or kept house for their own families. Only about one out of ten girls, by the late teens, had left the home, whether her own or someone else's, for the factory, shop, and office.[11] After several years in school, large numbers simply returned home. At sixteen, 30 per cent were unemployed and in the family. Between seventeen and twenty, the average rose to 36 per cent. By contrast, only about 9 per cent of the boys were similarly disengaged from both work and school.

One wonders why more girls, faced with the prospect of returning home and not contributing to the family income, did not take greater advantage of the city's schools. The fact that they did not, even though they received, on average, more schooling than males probably means that education was not considered of particular value for girls and reflects indulgence and minimal parental economic expectations as they awaited their real vocation. While for boys school was a prelude to a lifetime of work, for most girls it served as a hiatus between the freedoms of early childhood and the responsibilities of marriage. Thus, despite this distinction, the most significant trend for children of both sexes was their abandonment of education in their early teens.

The relationship of a child to his household is another factor which affected the length and quality of his school experience. Children who lived with both or even one of their parents were at a decided advantage. Those living in institutions, in households headed by a relative other than a parent, or as boarders, went to work earlier. In their case, too, the beginning of adolescence marks a convenient demarcation point. While children in families in the six to twelve group had a somewhat greater opportunity for going to school, as their chances increased to almost two to one through the teen years.

Not only does the educational gap between children within and without the family grow wider through the teen years, but those children who reside outside the family attend school under less favorable circumstances. For example, in the thirteen to sixteen group, less than 1 per cent of family children who went to school also held jobs as compared with 28 per cent of those who were not in the family. In the seventeen through twenty group, the proportions become 4 per cent as opposed to 29 per cent. Clearly the family provided a protective umbrella for the child in its midst, giving him an opportunity for prolonged schooling, and for an education without the distractions of work.

In addition, children who lived at home were not required to work as soon or in the same numbers as those who were on their own. In the seventeen to twenty group, 11 per cent of the males and 55 per cent of the females living with their families were unemployed as opposed to only 3 per cent of those who were outside the family. The family, then, also provided some young men and especially the young ladies with a base of support where they might await the creation of their own households. It therefore may have made possible for some females such avocations as reform and charity work.[12]

For children living at home, the school and job experience was further influenced by the father's occupation. Its influence was minimal for youngsters between six and twelve. At this stage with an average of 82 per cent in school, there was a large measure of equality of experience. For example, children of unskilled and skilled workers had attendance rates of 83 and 80 per cent, while children of professionals and petty officials and businessmen had rates of 88 and 87 per cent. Moreover, if a child were not in school he was at home. Age, not economics, was important.

The earnings and status of the father were of greater importance in the thirteen through sixteen-year-old, for as participation in education diminished, significant variations based on class occur. Distinctions between subgroups widened as the average attendance dropped from 81 per cent for six to twelve-year-olds to 43 per cent for thirteen to sixteen-year-olds. We find at one extreme, children of professionals with 80 per cent in attendance, and at the other children of unskilled workers with 32 per cent. While from six through twelve there was a difference of 5 per cent between children in these categories, for the four-year span after twelve the gap had widened about ten-fold to 48 per cent. It made little difference whether the father of a child eight or twelve was a physician or a boatman; for most children it made all the difference a few years later.

Based on a hierarchy of parental occupations (the data), delineate a critical factor for the nineteenth century drop-out. The community of drop-outs was initially and largely drawn from the male children of skilled, semiskilled, and unskilled workers. These sons had attendance rates ranging from 32 per cent to 36 per cent with a median of 33 per cent. Sons of fathers with higher occupational levels had a median of 65 per cent with a range of 56 per cent for petty officials and businessmen to 80 per cent for professionals. The clear point of division was whether one's father wore a white or a blue collar.

While unemployment rates were nearly identical with sons of blue and white collar workers at about 11 per cent, significantly more working-class children were employed. Although sons of blue collar workers had more than doubled the employment rate, 57 per cent to 25 per cent, and entered the labor force at an earlier age, they held inferior jobs, with the majority in unskilled areas, and diminishing numbers in more highly skilled positions. Although some sons of white collar workers also took unskilled jobs when they left school, many more of them worked as clerks or held other white collar jobs. For example, sons of unskilled workers had eight times as much chance to be themselves unskilled as to hold a white collar job, while children of high officials and businessmen had a five-to-one chance to escape unskilled positions and find white collar jobs. In sum, sons of households with higher occupational levels could not only stay in school longer, but could also begin at a better job than children from working-class homes.

The disparity between children of different classes was most marked among the seventeen through twenty group. The higher the father's position, the greater the son's chance for schooling, the better his job, and the smaller the chance of unemployment. As an illustration of the critical importance of father's occupation, sons of blue collar workers had one-third the chance to become clerks and twice the likelihood of holding unskilled jobs as those sons who came from white collar families. The same inequalities affected the experiences of the daughters. Females from blue collar families were more likely to leave school and enter domestic service, while daughters of white collar workers remained in school longer, or stayed at home. Class distinctions impinged on the experiences of children of both sexes.

As was anticipated, the social structure of education as revealed in the census data complements the information in the *Annual Reports*. It is now clear that schooling was nearly universal during mid-century, with about 90 per cent of all children between eight and eleven in school and the great majority in public schools. The efforts expended by public and non-public institutions to reach the mass of the city's children and to create generations of literate individuals were successful.

As both the census and school records also indicate, several factors were responsible for a significant divergence in experience and opportunity for children beyond age twelve. Gender played a minor role as girls become a small majority in the public schools, although this may not have been true of the non-public academies. Also, presence in a family headed by a parent was significant, probably because it provided the kind of security necessary to delay entry into the labor market. The importance of economic security is underscored by the critical impact of the fathers' occupations. While some working-class children went beyond the district school, prolonged education was more likely to occur in white collar families. Thus, while the system was open and free, children of different classes did not make equal use of it. Equipped with a basic education, particularly working-class children embarked in large numbers during the early teens into an increasingly industrialized and complex society. The stratification of the public system necessarily mirrored society at large. Class became the most important parameter and, in effect, controlled the length of childhood and the nature of the options available to the young.

That many children from the lower classes failed to attain more schooling is not surprising. Large numbers had to work to assist their families. There is no data available on children's earnings or on family income, but numerous writers have commented on the phenomenon of nineteenth-century urban families required the income of their offspring. Before the widespread adoption of cash registers, telephones, and child labor laws, there was ample opportunity for unskilled work as cash boys, messengers, and light manual laborers.[13]

While drawing attention to the importance of economics, the census data suggested that other factors also contributed to extended schooling. Working-class children may have entered the work force earlier through press of circumstances, but many children of businessmen and especially white collar workers also left. They departed in smaller numbers and perhaps a year or two later, but the fact is that most ended their education in the early teens instead of taking advantage of the public high school and similar institutions. Of all the groups, it is the sons of professionals, who had themselves experienced extensive training, that have the highest and most persistent attendance records. Not only income but attitude probably kept the lawyer's son in school and sent the businessman's or clerk's son out to work.[14] The extraordinary percentages of professionals' children in school may reflect the value their households placed on learning.

On the other hand, if children outside the working class were not required to augment the family income, their employment suggests that the experience of working in factories, offices, and stores was deemed by their parents as being more worthwhile than the classical or modern curriculum of the high school. Professionalization, or the concept of attaining the skills required for modern industrial society through formal education, was only just forming in late-nineteenth-century America.[15] It is possible that employment for these sons was viewed as a quasi-apprenticeship system. Thus, while elementary instruction was widely appreciated by both parents and schoolmen alike, clearly the value of more education was far less understood. Perhaps it is because of this perception that the *Annual Reports* express no dismay over the fact that there were ten times as many children enrolled in the first three grades of the district school as in the three years of high school.[16]

Indeed, the patterns of school attendance and employment which emerge from the St. Louis census and school records in 1880, when placed together with data from other studies, suggest a broad continuum of practice and attitudes. While research beginning with the census of 1840 is underway to test this hypothesis, there is some evidence from other sources that offer support. As late as 1908 the Dillingham Commission on Immigration reported that the St. Louis public schools contained about 65 per cent of their students in the fourth grade and below.[17] Attendance levels began to advance only with the popularization of the high school and of vocational and commercial courses around the turn of the century.[18] It is possible, therefore, that from the middle of the nineteenth century, when St. Louis developed extensive public and parochial systems, through the first decade of the twentieth century, the patterns of school attendance remained the same—a few years of schooling in the pre-teen period.[19] Thus, 1880 may be a mid-point for a condition that spanned several generations. Certainly educational practices in the first ten years of this century were more similar to those current in mid-nineteenth century than to our own.

The continuity of educational practice may be further inferred from Joseph Kelt's recent analysis of children in rural New England from 1800 to 1840. Among his conclusions are that children attended school between eight and twelve, after which sons passed into apprenticeship or employment. Sons of ministers and other wealthy parents, who correspond to professionals' children in this study, tended to stay in school longer than children of mill owners and manufacturers, demonstrating the importance of parental values.[20] The continuum of behavior in these aspects of growing up between rural New England in the first part of the nineteenth century and St. Louis in the latter part, suggests that for the history of childhood and education there are limits to the significance of a rural–urban dichotomy and to a chronology that would divide the nineteenth century. Rather, traditions firmly rooted in American culture persisted throughout the period.

Certainly St. Louis educators accepted as natural and perhaps even desirable the practice of initiating children into the work force after a few years of formal learning. Superintendent William Torrey Harris (1868–1880) was the most systematic and well-known spokesman for this view.[21] Perceiving that society had entered a period of extensive and continuing transformations, he rejected vocational training on the grounds that specialization could result in exposing workers to the dangers of obsolescence. He preferred that the schools equip children to be adaptive and flexible in a dynamic society. On this basis, Harris could be viewed as a proponent of liberal education. More to the point, however, he held a very traditional notion concerning the individual's responsibility for his own destiny. Arguing, for example, that the fundamental purpose of the public school curriculum was "providing the pupil with the mental discipline, and an equipment of tools and intelligence, so that he may help himself," he expected that the individual would continue his education outside the school. "With the proper discipline," Harris observed, "the pupil becomes an industrious investigator; let him loose in the library and he will become learned." The result would be that the "public school and the library render possible a perpetual education in the community." Harris reiterated this belief on numerous occasions, explaining that the nation's educational system was based on "the American idea of self-help."[22]

Thus, while Harris and his contemporaries were convinced of the possibility of individual and social betterment through education, it is not difficult to understand their expectation that a relatively short period of formal schooling was sufficient to insure it. Inequalities of attendance in the higher reaches of the system aroused little concern in a society which did not especially demand formal and specialized instruction. Since the schools were representative during the important few years of nearly universal education, the fact that the higher grades were undemocratic in character and rather poorly attended troubled neither professional educators nor the public. Significantly, St. Louisans in the 1860s and 1870s complained that the system offered too much rather than too little education, charging that the high school's curriculum was aristocratic, not that its student body was unrepresentative.[23] In a society where schooling consumed such a small portion of childhood, and where its relation to work was still imprecise, inequities did not command serious attention.

The lack of concern for educational equality is related to a fundamental difference in attitudes over the role of schooling between the nineteenth century and the present. Pointing to the relationship of educational attainment and job-level, the sociologists Lipset and Bendix have written concerning mid-twentieth century that "education was the principal avenue for upward mobility in most industrialized countries." Furthermore, they suggest that an open society is supported by the openness of the educational system through which even the poor can advance.[24] In this society, the deprivation or obstruction of individual or group access to schooling of quality has important and measurable economic and social consequences. Similarly, failure to exploit opportunities can be disastrous. With the widespread recognition that so much is at stake, the assessment of the educational system and of its relationship to society becomes an issue of paramount importance. In addition, as the child and society come to expect so much from the child, the schools come to demand a great deal from the child, exacting a seemingly ever-increasing commitment of time and energy.

While much was also expected of education in the nineteenth century, the popular investment in schooling was far less. There were two related factors accounting for this. First, educators had confidence in the ability of a good teacher to teach and in the capacity of children to learn. Among the many examples of this belief two may be offered here. Harris introduced the kindergarten to the public system with the conviction that even one year of exposure to educational "games" would benefit the young child for the rest of his life, endowing him with the capacity to engage successfully in a wide variety of employments from the needle trades to the foundry, to the preparation of foods in the home.[25] In addition, St. Louis educators justified evening schools on the basis that they would render adult newcomers to the city and those natives who had missed the district school, literate, capable of self-improvement, and qualified participants in a democratic society. All this was to be accomplished by teaching an abbreviated elementary school curriculum for two hours on sixty-four nights during the year.[26] In the context of this confidence, it was reasonable to hope for a great deal from the three, four, and perhaps five years spent in the system.

Moreover, the mass of society, from unskilled workers to businessmen, shared this belief. They gave it expression by insisting that their children go to school and then by withdrawing them by the early teens in the expectation that they were now adequately equipped to begin their careers. Except for males headed for the professions, for females destined to be teachers, and for

those few whose families valued higher learning, the encounter with education was relatively brief. Its brevity testifies to how little direct impact school
made on one's career. Among the most telling evidence for the lack of a
measurable connection between school and vocation is the fact that girls
stayed in school, on the average, longer than boys. Parents were generally
reluctant to delay the entry of sons into the world of work.

Thus, in mid-nineteenth century, young children attended as popular and
democratic an educational system as the nation ever possessed. Divorced
from the stigma of a charity venture,[27] the public schools were not yet
marked by hierarchies of quality and specialization as their importance was
not recognized. The result was a remarkable homogenization of experience
that was enhanced as the graded curriculum was standardized. The ideal of a
common school where children from all segments of society would have a
common experience was approximated. It was this achievement that led
St. Louis schoolmen to broadcast with such confidence the progress of their
schools.

NOTES

1. Isaiah Forbes, "President's Report," *Second Annual Report of the Superintendent
   of the St. Louis Public Schools for the Year Ending July 1, 1855* (St. Louis, 1855), p. 6.
2. *Annual Report, 1880*, pp. cxxviii–cxxix, and the *Tenth Census of the United States*,
   XIX, Pt. II, p. 567.
3. In 1860 the proportion under ten was 66 per cent; in 1865, 54 per cent; in 1870,
   49 per cent; in 1875, 53 per cent; and in 1880, 56 per cent. *Annual Report, 1860*,
   p. 55, and *Annual Report, 1880*, p. 31.
4. The curriculum is broadly outlined in *Annual Report, 1879*, p. cvi.
5. The data was taken from the Second Enumeration of the manuscript census for
   1880, and was processed in an SPSS file that is stored at the Computer Center of the
   University of Missouri/Columbia. Information was gathered on 15,312 children,
   with child defined as any person at any age who resided in the household of his
   mother and/or father, and any person twenty-one and younger who lived outside
   the family unit.
6. Selwyn K. Troen, "Measuring the Black Response to Public Education in Post
   Civil War St. Louis," a paper delivered at a symposium on "Urban Education and
   Black Americans in the Nineteenth Century," Division F, AERA Annual Meeting,
   April 5, 1972.
7. The table was constructed by aggregating the data on specific occupations which
   were recorded by the *Annual Reports*. For a discussion of the system of classification and tables illustrating the raw data, see Selwyn K. Troen, "Schools for the
   City: The Growth of Public Education in St. Louis 1838–1880," Ph.D. diss.,
   University of Chicago, 1970, Appendix D.
8. *Annual Report, 1855*, pp. 116–121. For a discussion of a parallel structure in
   Massachusetts, see Michael B. Katz, *The Irony of Early School Reform: Educational
   Innovation in Mid-Nineteenth Century Massachusetts* (Cambridge, Mass., 1968),
   pp. 39–40, and Appendix C.
9. *Annual Report, 1881*, p. 100.

10. Unknowns represent those for whom the census enumerators marked "at home" or left a blank. It is assumed that these omissions represent those who were neither employed nor at school and they are, therefore, calculated with those whom we know to be "at home." The assumption is based on three considerations. First, since the enumerator is accounting for nearly all children between nine and twelve, with an average unknown of about 8 per cent, it appears unlikely that he was less accurate or less avid in determining occupations or school attendance at other ages. Secondly, the curve reflected by unknowns is so well ordered as to suggest important meanings rather than chance. Thirdly, the pattern of employment and school attendance conforms to expectations. We know from school reports that children began dropping out in large numbers at about twelve when they gradually began to be absorbed into the work force.

11. Of 734 girls seventeen through twenty-one who were listed as unskilled laborers, 66 per cent (488) were servants and maids, 20 per cent (144) were keeping house, 9 per cent (63) were seamstresses, and 5 per cent (39) were in various other occupations, including 15 prostitutes.

12. For a portrait of comfortable females who make reform their vocation, see Christopher Lasch, *The New Radicalism in America, 1889–1963: The Intellectual as a Social Type* (New York, 1965), chapters 1, 2, and 4.

13. A classic progressive accounting of poverty is Robert Hunter, *Poverty: Social Conscience in the Progressive Era*, ed. by Peter d'A. Jones (New York, 1965). An example of contemporary scholarship is Stephan Thernstrom, *Poverty and Progress: Social Mobility in a Nineteenth-Century City* (Cambridge, Mass., 1964).

14. Although the census does not include information on income, it is possible to establish occupational hierarchies that reflect both status and wealth. The occupational matrix for the prosopography is an adaptation of the one developed by Stephan Thernstrom and Peter Knights in their studies of occupational mobility in Boston, and has been modified to include children's and women's vocations. A copy can be sent on request. For an abbreviated version of the matrix see Peter R. Knights, *The Plain People of Boston 1830–1860* (New York, 1971), Appendix E.

15. On professionalization see Robert H. Wiebe, *The Search for Order, 1877–1920* (New York, 1967), pp. 111–132. Also, the teen years were not yet defined as a distinct period in the life-cycle and special attention in the form of institutional care had not yet developed. Hence, the shift from the fourth or fifth year of school into the factory or office was considered natural. On attitudes towards teens, see John Demos and Virginia Demos, "Adolescence in Historical Perspective," *Journal of Marriage and the Family* (November, 1969), 632–638.

16. *Annual Report, 1880*, pp. cxviii–cxix. There were 22,954 in grades one through three but only 2,233 in grades seven through nine.

17. Report of the Immigration Commission, *The Children of Immigrants in Schools* (Washington, 1911), pp. V, 213–219.

18. For a discussion of the expansion and the popular appreciation of the high school around the turn of the century, see Edward A. Krug, *The Shaping of the American High School* (New York, 1964), pp. 169–189.

19. There are no precise figures available for parochial schools on a regular basis. Catholic parish schools comprised the largest group and they were not yet organized into a system. Based on Catholic directories and newspaper descriptions of students and curricula in the *Western Watchman*, which was sponsored by the

St. Louis archdiocese, at least 80 per cent of the students were receiving elementary instruction and the ages of the students ranged from seven to sixteen. *Sadler's Catholic Directory, Almanac, and Order for the Year of our Lord, 1880* (New York, 1880), pp. 155–158; "The Catholic Schools," *Western Watchman*, August 20, 1870; "Examination of St. Patrick's Parochial Schools," *Western Watchman*, May 20, 1871; "The 'Globe' on the Public Schools," *Western Watchman*, May 3, 1873.

20. Joseph F. Kelt, "Growing Up in Rural New England, 1800–1840," in *Anonymous Americans: Explorations in Nineteenth Century Social History*, ed. Tamara K. Hareven (Englewood Cliffs, N.J., 1971), pp. 1–16.

21. A major source for Harris' ideas are the *Annual Reports* from 1867 through 1880. Other sources include Merle Curti, *The Social Ideas of American Educators* (Paterson, N.J., 1959), pp. 310–347; John S. Roberts, *William T. Harris: His Educational and Related Philosophical Views* (Washington, 1924), and Kurt Leidecker, *Yankee Teacher* (New York, 1946).

22. *Annual Report, 1867*, p. 71; *Annual Report, 1871*, p. 165, and *Annual Report, 1872*, p. 150. Harris never tired of this refrain. In 1900 as United States Commissioner of Education, he wrote: "In the United States the citizen must learn to help himself in this matter of gaining information, and for this reason he must use his school time to acquire the art of digging knowledge out of books." William T. Harris, "Elementary Education," in *Education in the United States*, ed. by Nicholas Murray Butler (Albany, N.Y., 1900), p. 11.

23. Indicative of popular feelings are the letters to the editor in the month preceding the April elections for school directors. For example, see *St. Louis Globe-Democrat*, March 14, 15, 18, and 29, 1878. For the Catholic viewpoint, see "Our Common Schools," *Western Watchman*, September 22, 1883.

24. Seymour Martin Lipset and Reinhard Bendix, *Social Mobility in Industrial Society* (Berkeley, Calif., 1964), pp. 91–101.

25. *Annual Report, 1879*, pp. 131–133.

26. *Annual Report, 1856*, pp. 46–47, and *Annual Report, 1879*, pp. 142–144.

27. Paul Monroe, *Founding of the American Public School System* (New York, 1940), I, pp. 295 ff. For the problem of the charity stigma in a neighboring state, see John Pulliam, "Changing Attitudes toward the Public Schools in Illinois, 1825–1860," *History of Education Quarterly*, VII (Summer 1967), 191–208.

PART TWO

BUREAUCRACY AND CURRICULAR DIFFERENTIATION, 1870–1910

The decades between the end of the Civil War and the advent of World War I witnessed dramatic changes in American cities, and in urban education. It was a time of frenetic growth, large-scale immigration, and rapid institutional evolution. These themes are evident in the second part of the book, which considers the dynamics of urban school organization, curricular development, and related issues in the late nineteenth and early twentieth centuries. It opens with a classic article first published nearly forty years ago by David Tyack, examining the development of the school bureaucracy in Portland, Oregon. As Tyack noted, school reformers in that city, like many others, were faced with the challenge of organizing a coherent system of education that could efficiently and impartially serve the growing number of children in their burgeoning metropolis. The challenge they faced was similar to that of other school leaders of the nineteenth century, dating from Horace Mann and his campaigns to improve the common schools of antebellum Massachusetts. It was a matter of establishing a coherent set of standards for everything from the behavior of students and teachers to a common curriculum. In undertaking this task, these men saw themselves as crusaders, combating the parochialism and corruption of the old district schools, where teachers' qualifications often mattered less than who they knew on the local school committee.

As Tyack observed, Portland's reformers modeled their policies on those promulgated in other cities, and they drew inspiration from the example of business and industry. Order and uniformity were watchwords of the day, not only to instill lessons of discipline and responsibility in the students, but also to make educators accountable to goals and standards established for the system as a whole. Tyack documented the extreme measures that some of the most zealous schoolmen undertook in the name of higher standards, in pursuit of both behavioral and academic perfectability. He also identified the opponents of reform, many of them businessmen concerned about the rising cost of public education. In the end, however, the development of educational bureaucracy in Portland and other cities proved difficult to resist, even for its most vociferous critics. The logic of impartial rules to govern the rapidly growing school systems of the largest cities seems to have been unavoidable in practical terms, as urban school systems grew ever larger and more complex. The result was a system that eventually would seem to run almost on its own momentum, and this would become a problem in the distant future.

The next chapter deals with a rather different impulse in urban education during this period of reform. While some school leaders were busy devising better methods of instilling discipline in urban classrooms, others were intent on making schools more humane and compassionate. Among the most important curricular innovations of this sort was the kindergarten, a special type of class for the very youngest of students, inspired by the humanistic German educational theorist Friederick Froebel. Although the champions of the kindergarten envisioned it as a universal educational innovation, some thought it especially appropriate for the poor children of the cities. In his study of this development, Marvin Lazerson has traced the evolution of the kindergarten as a reform initiative in certain Massachusetts cities in the years around the turn of the century. Industrial cities in the northeast attracted thousands of impoverished immigrants each year. Alarmed at the harsh conditions under which the children of many urban families lived, especially those of immigrant workers, school reformers saw the kindergarten as a way of introducing these students to the larger world of nature and social relations, while helping to animate a spirit of curiosity and trust. Kindergartens thus were thought to be a way to combat a troubling new feature of city life: the urban "slum." Lazerson documented the successes and shortcomings of these efforts, describing their ultimate demise in the face of budgetary constraints and concerns about the socialization of poor immigrant children. As city schools in Massachusetts were required to accommodate more of these students, the purposes of the kindergarten changed, to a focus on basic language skills and school-readiness. In the end, innovative measures as comprehensive as the kindergarten were difficult to sustain for institutions faced with the task of accommodating ever larger numbers of poor and untutored children. Even if it eventually became a standard feature of American elementary education, the kindergarten was something of a failed experiment in urban educational reform at the turn of the century. It showed the limits of educational change in a time of massive growth in city schools, and perhaps the naivete of its most outspoken advocates.

This section's final chapter concerns yet another critical question in early urban education, one that continues to pose challenges to educators today. In his study of the Atlanta schools, Barry Franklin examined the process by which schools dealt with the problem of students classified as "slow," disorderly, or otherwise disruptive to normal classroom procedures. While some historians suggested that educational leaders had looked to business institutions for answers to their problems, Franklin argued that it was pressure from teachers that led to the development of "special" classes for students deemed too demanding or unruly or inept to instruct with "normal" students. He documents the process by which the very first classes for these students were developed in Atlanta, noting once again the importance of models from other cities in shaping district policies. By and large, the decision to create separate classes and school for "special children" represented an early example of a critical impulse evident in many urban school systems at the time. Historians have referred to this as "differentiation," or the idea that children with dissimilar aptitudes and behavioral dispositions ought to be segregated from one another, to receive instruction especially designed to meet their presumed needs and interests. Eventually, differentiated curricula would be tailored for women, African Americans, and a number of other groups deemed appropriate for specialized education of one sort or another. As Franklin found in Atlanta, however, the early development of such measures was not greeted with universal acclaim. In fact the business community questioned their necessity when the cost of making accommodations for slow and disorderly children finally came to light. Even so, the development of these classes represented a significant curricular innovation, one that eventually would affect all types of schools but was first undertaken in the cities. Atlanta may not have been a leader in these practices, but its experience mirrored that of many other urban districts at the time. Differentiation became a watchword of urban school reform during this crucial period. Again, this was a standpoint that would exist for decades before eventually being challenged in a later era.

ADDITIONAL READING

There are a few broad studies of this era in the history of urban education, and again the best known date back several decades or more. David Tyack's *The One Best System: A History of American Urban Education* (Cambridge, Massachusetts: Harvard University Press, 1974) picks up the story where his article on Portland leaves off, providing perspective from a number of additional cities. Yet another classic study of this period focuses on the development of urban school administration, Raymond G. Callahan, *Education and the Cult of Efficiency* (Chicago: University of Chicago Press, 1962). On early school leaders, also see David Tyack and Elisabeth Hansot, *Managers of Virtue: Public School Leadership in America, 1820–1980* (New York: Basic Books, 1982). A more chronologically limited view is provided in William A. Bullough, *Cities and Schools in the Gilded Age: The Evolution of an Urban Institution* (New York: Kennikat Press, 1974); also see Bullough's article, " 'It is Better to Be a Country Boy': The Lure of the Country in Urban Education in the Gilded Age" *Historian* 1973 35(2): 183–195. On the development of bureaucracy, see Michael B. Katz, "The Emergence of Bureaucracy in Urban Education: The Boston Case, 1850–1884" *History of Education Quarterly* 1968 8(2 and 3): 155–188, 319–357, or his more recent treatment of these issues in Katz, *Reconstructing American Education* (Cambridge, Massachusetts: Harvard University Press, 1987). For widely differing takes on the development of certain urban districts at this time, see Marvin Lazerson, *Origins of the Urban School: Public Education in Massachusetts, 1870–1915* (Cambridge: Harvard University Press, 1971), Paul E. Peterson, *The Politics of School Reform, 1870–1940* (Chicago: University of Chicago Press, 1985), William J. Reese, *Power and the Promise of School Reform* (Boston: Routledge & Kegan Paul, 1986), and David E. Labaree, *The Making of an American High School* (New Haven: Yale University Press, 1988). For treatment of children labeled disorderly or "slow," see Barry M. Franklin, *From "Backwardness" to "At-Risk"* (Albany: State University of New York Press, 1994).

On the humanitarian impulse that began to emerge in education and urban reform during this time, especially as it concerned elementary schools and younger children, see Maureen A. Flanagan, *Seeing With Their Hearts: Chicago Women and the Vision of the Good City, 1877–1933* (Princeton: Princeton University Press, 2002), William J. Reese, "After Bread, Education: Nutrition and Urban School Children, 1890–1920" *Teachers College Record* 1980 81(4): 496–525, Michael B. Katz, "The 'new departure' in Quincy 1873–1881. The Nature of Nineteenth Century Educational Reform" *New England Quarterly* 1967 40(1): 3–30, Janice K. Schemenauer, "New Ideas in Education: Toledo and the Urban School, 1870–1930" *Northwest Ohio Quarterly* 1997 69(2): 71–95, and Janet A. Miller, "Urban Education and the New City: Cincinnati's Elementary Schools, 1870 to 1914" *Ohio History* 1979 88(2): 152–172.

On regional tendencies in urban education, see John L. Rury, "Urbanization and Education: Regional Patterns of Educational Development in American Cities, 1900–1910" *Michigan Academician* 1988 20(3): 261–279, and Keach Johnson, "The State of Elementary and Secondary Education in Iowa in 1900" *Annals of Iowa* 1987 49(1–2): 26–57. Regarding smaller cities in the Midwest, see William J. Reese, ed. *Hoosier Schools: Past and Present* (Bloomington: Indiana University Press, 1998), Ch. 2. On the South, see David N. Plank and Rick Ginsberg, eds., *Southern Cities, Southern Schools: Public Education in the Urban South* (New York: Greenwood, 1990), and Plank's article, "Educational Reform and Organizational Change: Atlanta in the Progressive Era" *Journal of Urban History* 1988 15(1): 22–41. For studies of Baltimore during this period, where many of these dynamics also were evident, see Andrea R. Andrews, "The Baltimore School Building Program, 1870 to 1900: A Study of Urban Reform" *Maryland Historical Magazine* 1975 70(3): 260–274, Bayly Ellen Marks, "Liberal Education in the Gilded Age: Baltimore and the Creation of the Manual Training School" *Maryland Historical Magazine* 1979 74(3): 238–252. On African American education in the urban South at this time, see Carl V. Harris, "Stability and Change in Discrimination Against Black Public Schools: Birmingham, Alabama, 1871–1931" *Journal of Southern History* 1985 51(3): 375–416, Dale A. Somers, "Black and White in New Orleans: A Study in Urban Race Relations,

1865–1900" *Journal of Southern History* 1974 40(1): 19–42, Walter T. Howard and Virginia M. Howard, "Family, Religion, and Education: A Profile of African-American Life in Tampa, Florida, 1900–1930" *Journal of Negro History* 1994 79(1): 1–17. Studies of immigrant education are listed in the next section of the book.

5

BUREAUCRACY AND THE COMMON SCHOOL: THE EXAMPLE OF PORTLAND, OREGON, 1851–1913

David Tyack

"The most fundamental principle observed in the present conduct of the Portland school system is the maintenance unchanged of a rigidly prescribed, mechanical system, poorly adapted to the needs either of the children or of the community."[1] So concluded a team of educational experts led by Ellwood P. Cubberley of Stanford in a 1913 study of the Portland Public Schools. "Because of lack of opportunity to exercise initiative," they observed, teachers and administrators were "carrying out a system in whose creation they had little or no part. The result is a uniformity that is almost appalling." Administrators were mere inspectors, certifying or compelling compliance with rules. The curriculum was "vivisected with mechanical accuracy into fifty-four dead pieces." Children trotted on one stage of the treadmill until they could advance to the next by passing an examination. "School board and superintendent, as well as principals, teachers, and pupils, are victims of the system for which no one is primarily responsible."[2] The origin of the bureaucracy was a mystery; pride, ritual and fear maintained it. Cubberley and his colleagues were describing—with some caricature—a social pathology which had afflicted urban schools for decades. In 1880 Charles Francis Adams Jr. blasted school superintendents as "drill sergeants" and described their schools as "a combination of the cotton mill and the railroad with the model State-prison."[3] In a series of articles in the *Forum* in 1892, Dr. Joseph M. Rice attacked regimentation in city schools of the East and Midwest. That same year President Charles W. Eliot of Harvard denounced mass education which "almost inevitably adopts military or mechanical methods, . . . [which] tend to produce a lock-step and a uniform speed. . . ." Inflexible routine degraded the "teacher's function. . . . There are many persons who say that teachers in the graded schools ought not to serve more than ten years at the outside, for the reason that they become dull, formal, and uninteresting; but, if this be true, it is certainly the fault of the system rather than of the teachers."[4]

During the mid-nineteenth century most American urban school systems became bureaucracies, though schoolmen did not use that term. They developed elaborate rules to govern the behavior of members of the organization, and a great premium was placed on conformity to the rules; they created hierarchies of appointive offices, each with careful allocations of power and specified duties; and objective qualifications governed admission to the various roles (whether "superintendent" or "third grader").[5] The schools, like other organizations, were trying to cope rationally with large numbers of heterogeneous pupils. Indeed, schoolmen commonly thought bureaucratization essential to progress. In 1890 the Committee on City School Systems of the National Education Association quoted Herbert Spencer on the value of "a differentiation of structure and a specialization of function," and concluded that urban schools needed not only "combination and unification for general purposes" but also specialized administrative structures "with well-defined functions and powers."[6] In the actual organization of the schools, however, schoolmen of the nineteenth century tended to favor simple military or industrial bureaucratic models in which uniformity of output and regularity of operation took precedence over functional differentiation. Thus in practice they often created a curriculum which was identical for all children, preferred teaching methods which promised standardized results, and based the hierarchy more on a distribution of power than on specialized expertise.

The educational statesmen of Horace Mann's generation had tried to create system where they saw chaos. Urban school bureaucracies institutionalized this quest for standardization. Reformers believed that in order to unify the people they must first unify the common schools. They were dismayed by the heterogeneity of typical public schools: teachers untrained, mostly young and inexperienced, lacking a sense of professionalism; curriculum haphazard, textbooks miscellaneous; classes composed of students of wildly varying age and ability, irregular in attendance and unruly in behavior; buildings rough and messy, serving as general community centers for church services, lantern slide lectures, social occasions and political assemblies.[7] The rural school was especially subject to the caprice of the community, the tyranny of the tribe which Edward Eggleston describes so clearly in *The Hoosier Schoolmaster.* In the small district school, authority inhered in the person, not the office, of the schoolmaster; the roles of teachers were overlapping, familiar, personal rather than esoteric, strictly defined and official (the same teacher in a rural school might be brother, suitor, hunting companion, fellow farm worker, boarder and cousin to the different boys and girls in the class). Normally the only supervisors were laymen, school board members or ministers who dropped in from time to time on the local school. The school played a relatively small and often unpredictable part in the total socialization of the young.[8]

Reform, then, meant standardization. Schoolmen sought to grade classes, to prescribe a uniform curriculum and textbooks, to train teachers in approved methods, to give them a sense of vocational identity and spirit, and to appoint officials to supervise the schools. Such bureaucratization was easiest in cities (where the population was concentrated and the tax base adequate). Urban residents were familiar with bureaucracies arising in manufacturing, commerce, transport, the military and government. Posing the rhetorical question "Why the expense and machinery of a superintendent?" one school administrator replied:

> In industrial establishments, as well as in enterprises requiring unskilled manual labor, employers insist upon abundant supervision. A great railroad company places one man to boss three or four. Every factory, large or small, has its foremen and its bosses. Experience has taught that such an arrangement pays financially. The conclusions are quite as reasonable in the conduct of schools; where even a small aggregation of schools is, there an able superintendent can be profitably engaged.[9]

Increasing ease of transportation and communication, together with the migration of teachers and administrators, spread the new patterns of organization. Richard Wade has observed that the new cities arising by the banks of the Ohio and the Mississippi—St. Louis, Cincinnati and the rest—emulated the educational systems of "the great cities across the mountains" even though they were "freed from. . . . old restraints and traditions." Louisville sent a new principal to study eastern schools to eliminate the need for "expensive errors and fruitless experiments."[10] Similarly, Portland, Oregon—a fir forest in 1840—had organized by the 1870s a school system based on eastern models. By copying the most recent organizational reforms such cities could skip earlier, piecemeal stages of bureaucratization.

In 1874 leading American city and state school superintendents and college presidents signed *A Statement of the Theory of Education in the United States* written to explain American educational practices to Europeans. In this outline they justified bureaucratization in matter-of-fact rather than crusading language. "The commercial tone prevalent in the city," they said, "tends to develop, in its schools, quick, alert habits and readiness to combine with others in their tasks. Military precision is required in the maneuvering of classes. Great stress is laid upon (1) punctuality, (2) regularity, (3) attention, and (4) silence, as habits necessary through life for successful combination with one's fellow-men in an industrial and commercial civilization." They seemed to accept employers' specifications as to the ideal character of workers. They saw the school as "a phase of education lying between the earliest period of family-nurture . . . and the necessary initiation into the specialties of a vocation. . . ." Because "the peculiarities of civil society and the political organization draw the child out of the influence of family-nurture earlier than is common in other countries," the American school had "to lay more stress upon discipline and to make far more prominent the moral phase of education. It is obliged to train the pupil into prompt obedience to his teachers and the practice of self-control in its various forms, in order that he may be prepared for a life wherein there is little police-restraint on the part of the constituted authorities." Therefore urban schools must socialize children to take part in an increasingly bureaucratic society: the new size and complexity of "corporate combinations . . . make such a demand upon the community for directive intelligence that it may be said that the modern industrial community cannot exist without free popular education carried out in a system of schools ascending from the primary grade to the university."[11]

Across the nation urban school bureaucracies won acclaim. The best teachers and administrators flocked to these systems in search of higher pay and prestige.[12] But the reformers' very success became an affliction, as is often the case when reforms become institutionalized. Orderly grooves became ruts. In 1903 Charles B. Gilbert, the superintendent of schools in Rochester, New York, warned that large institutions tend "to subordinate the individual. . . . This is particularly true in great school systems. . . . The demands of the organization itself are so great, it requires so much executive power to keep the machine running, that the machine itself attracts undue attention and we are in danger of forgetting that the business of the school is to teach children." He knew, he said, superb teachers who were "driven from the school system because they did not readily untie red tape." Worst of all was a "shifting of conscience" from teaching to pleasing petti-fogging superiors. "I know of cities in which supervisors go about from schoolroom to schoolroom, notebook and pencil in hand, sitting for a while in each room like malignant sphinxes, eying the terrified teacher, who in her terror does everything wrong, and then marking her in that little doomsday book." A school is not a factory, he said, "with a boss, sub-bosses, and hands." Like Charles W. Eliot, Gilbert looked back with nostalgia on "the small unpainted schoolhouse in the remote country district" as a place where the individual child, the individual teacher counted, where flexibility flour-ished. When the urban school bureaucracy turns children into robots and "grinds out the power of initiative from the teacher," said Gilbert, "then it is time to smash the machine; and there are countless machines all over this land that need to be smashed."[13]

Just such a machine was the Portland school system when Cubberley and his colleagues arrived in 1913. There they found all the dysfunctions which Robert Merton describes in his essay on "Bureaucratic Structure and Personality."[14] What had originally been a thoughtful response to problems of disorganization in mass education became archaic ritual. "Passive, routine, clerical"—these adjectives described "the attitude of principals and grammar school teachers toward their work," said the investigators. "And the attitude of the pupils is inevitably the same." With the exception of one lesson, they "heard not a single question asked by a pupil, not a single remark or com-ment made, to indicate that the pupil had any really vital interest in the sub-ject matter of the exercise. . . ." Like experienced enlisted men, teachers "feared to advocate anything out of the routine, for that would mean more work, and more work—with its intended accomplishment—in one part of the system, would threaten other parts of the system with a like affliction!" The system was bound by rules which had so long outlived their usefulness that no one could recall their origin or state their rationale.[15]

"There is no study," Charles Bidwell has observed, "of the prevalence or incidence either of bureaucratic structures or processes in school systems. . . ."[16] This oversight is not coincidental. As Marvin Bressler has pointed out in his essay on "The Conventional Wisdom of Education and Sociology," scholars in education have tended to stress individual volition, broad social needs and a "credo of unlimited hope."[17] Reformist and optimistic in temper, many educationists have written from an individualistic psychological perspective. They have often represented teaching styles and philosophies of education as if they were options independent of organizational patterns. The behavioral effects of institutional structure have more often been taken for granted than examined, while tacitly it was assumed that a teacher could choose to be "progressive" or "traditional." But the experience of Portland up to the time of the Cubberley survey suggests that the rigid bureaucratic system had an internal momentum and influence which largely shaped the conduct of teachers, administrators and students. The persistence of this system in the face of major social and intellectual changes cannot be explained simply by conventional categories of individual intent, rational adaptation or psychological or social needs.[18] Although the founders of the bureaucracy knew the reasons for their actions, before long the structure of the organization began to produce in its members what Veblen called "trained incapacity" and what Dewey deplored as "occupational psychosis."[19] People acted the roles which the institution demanded with little thought about the purpose of education.

So it was with the Portland bureaucracy. While this essay deals, perforce, with the individuals who built the system, the bureaucracy itself is the central subject rather than the actors. The essay will also explore the relevance of bureaucracy to "progressive education," in the conviction that this reform movement was a "revolt against formalism" quite as much in educational organization as in educational thought.[20]

When the Rev. Thomas L. Eliot, a public-spirited Unitarian minister in Portland, became superintendent of schools in Multnomah County in 1872, he was convinced that Portland needed the kind of educational system his father had helped to build in St. Louis. "Economy of power and efficiency in our schools," he wrote in his annual report in 1873, "depends in great degree upon a proper division of responsibilities. As in the army, so here; and I have suggested to the Directors [of the Portland schools] some steps looking towards a more thorough supervision by the Principals of their subordinates."[21] The next year he welcomed the appointment of a city superintendent (Eliot worked only part-time as county superintendent and his territory was far too large to supervise adequately):

This measure was . . . dictated by that common sense which sees the need of a head to every organization consisting of diverse and complex parts. Our 25 schools, like so many separate units, or "feudal baronies," were governed by as many systems and precedents as there were teachers. The grades were, indeed, supposed to be defined, but were in a decidedly nebulous state. It was

not, nor could it be, expected of the Directors to spend their whole time in
the details of school methods, discipline and examinations. It remained . . .
to follow . . . the example of other cities throughout the country where
Superintendents or visiting principals are appointed.[22]

The early days of public education in Portland had a certain rustic charm: the
first teacher, bearing the unfortunate name of John Outhouse, unloaded
ships and built roads when he was not teaching school; a successor "graded"
her ninety pupils by ranking them on steps in the old loft which served as her
classroom; one dapper teacher went for his certificate to the home of a minister who was serving as county superintendent, found him at the washtub,
and smartly answered his questions while the minister was drying himself and
rolling down his sleeves; a canny class of children persuaded their teacher not
to use the rod by threatening her with a roomful of mice.[23]

But for Eliot and his predecessor as county superintendent, the Rev. George
Atkinson, such haphazard schooling had grave flaws: how could such teaching
render the next generation "homogeneous in habits of thinking, feeling,
and acting"?[24] Atkinson was a pioneer Yankee Congregationalist minister
who taught for a while in the Oregon City schools. He patterned the system
of grading and examinations in Oregon City on the Boston plan, and when
he moved to Portland, he sought to standardize its schools as well.[25]
Eliot agreed; graded classes and strict examinations brought healthy uniformity, hard work and moral indoctrination. "As a field of clover, well rooted,
admits no weeds," he wrote, "so the mind of a child, thoroughly employed
and interested, has little room for the culture of low imagination and vice . . . an
ill-regulated school system will bear fruit in the lack of self-control, punctuality, order, perseverance, justice, truth and industry, in its citizens." Eliot
believed that well-run schools could counter "the pitiful fallacies which
plunge nations into years of social misery and political disorder. . . . The
barest knowledge of political economy, widely diffused, would prevent
the notion of sumptuary laws, communism and interference with trade and
circulating media, which even now delude the minds of large portions of the
people."[26] Immigration, immorality, class conflict, corruption—these threats
demanded efficient schools.

These two ministers, architects of the Portland school system, borrowed
freely from eastern educational ideology and structure. The product of the
schools was to be the homogeneous good citizen—sober, moral, industrious,
one who would preserve rather than question the social and economic
system; the means of production was to be a prescribed curriculum and a
semi-military bureaucracy. Atkinson and Eliot were educational strategists:
they saw the schools as only part of a total process of socialization and civilization, and they worked as well to establish libraries, churches, colleges and
a host of other stabilizing institutions and associations.[27] But many of the
schoolmen who followed them were not strategists but drillmasters who
mistook bureaucratic means for social ends.

When Samuel King, first city school superintendent, took office in 1874, Portland had about ten thousand residents, 1,168 of whom were enrolled in the public schools. A consummate bureaucrat, King believed that children's behavior must be precisely controlled, reliable, predictable. Regular attendance and punctuality—surely necessary prologues to schooling—became an obsession with King. His war on irregular attendance, also waged vigorously by his successor Thomas Crawford, made Portland students in a few years the most punctual in comparable cities across the nation (by 1881 only .04% were reported tardy).[28] Superintendents continued well into the twentieth century to report attendance and tardiness statistics down to the second and third decimal point. In 1876 the school board adopted a policy of suspending any student absent (except for sickness) or tardy four times in four consecutive weeks. King and his successors also publicly reported the tardiness of teachers, and fined principals for not opening schools at 8:30 A.M. sharp. "A school with an enrollment of fifty, daily attendance fifty and none tardy," King wrote lyrically in 1876, "is a grand sight to behold in the morning and afternoon."[29] So great was the stigma of tardiness, and so keen the competition among schools for a good record, that children sometimes hid all day to avoid coming into class late and teachers sometimes sent children home to avoid marking them tardy. Sometimes Crawford complained of teachers who had "overdrawn the evils of tardiness"; but he set the style by patrolling the streets to spot absent or late children. And Crawford proudly listed in a roll of honor the names of children who had perfect attendance from one to six years.[30]

Getting the children and teachers to school on time was only the beginning. King and his principals worked out a "system of instruction and a division of school labor" which included a uniform curriculum, primary, intermediate and grammar departments divided into six grades (further subdivided into A and B sections), and a plan of written examinations to ensure that the children had been "thoroughly drilled in the work assigned."[31] As a Yankee who believed that "a perfect system of school management is indispensable to the welfare of our Public Schools," King paid examinations the supreme compliment: "System, order, dispatch and promptness have characterized the examinations and exerted a healthful influence over the pupils by stimulating them to be thoroughly prepared to meet their appointments and engagements. Next to a New England climate, these examinations necessitate industry, foster promptness, and encourage pupils to do the right thing *at the right time*."[32]

The results of the first round of examinations might have dismayed a heart less stout than King's. In seven classrooms out of a total of twenty-one, none of the children passed. Only in six classrooms were more than half of the children promoted. But King maintained that the operation was a great success, though most of the patients died. Not surprisingly, in the next examinations teachers and pupils improved somewhat: this time between 13 and 75 per cent of the children were promoted (in some of the classes, though, fewer than three-fourths of the students got up nerve to take the test).[33] King published the results of the examinations in the newspaper, with the child's score and school next to his name. Parents could draw their own conclusions about the diligence of the child and the competence of the teacher, and they did. Incensed and anxious, the teachers joined irate parents to force King's resignation in 1877.[34]

The new superintendent, Crawford, promptly abolished the practice of publicizing the test results. He wrote in his report in 1878 that "incalculable injury has been done, both to the teachers and to the pupils of our free schools, resulting from a spirit of rivalry on the part of the teachers." Some teachers had gone to great lengths to protect their reputations, urging children to withdraw from school shortly before the examination and even advising the superintendent to suspend slow students for trivial offenses so that they wouldn't drag down the percentage of promotions. The system of publicity had led, he said, to cramming, "bitter animosities," and "unpleasant wran- glings, over arbitrary standards in marking papers." Yet Crawford was no Paul Goodman; he was a good bureaucrat who wanted harmony in the ranks. He retained the examination system, elaborating it in Mandarin detail while softening its rigors, but he kept the examination results the property of the bureaucracy.[35]

Despite occasional rhetoric about independence of mind, King and Crawford made it clear in their reports that the school system was to incul- cate certified thoughts and proper deportment. "Habits of obedience, atten- tion, promptness in recitation, neatness of copybooks, and a carefully prepared program of the daily work, are some of the characteristics and attractions of most of the schools," said King in 1875. He believed that "children should be taught to obey the commands of their teachers at once, and a slight tap of the pencil [should] be intelligible to any class."[36] As children passed from class to class, they displayed "a military air and discipline that is truly com- mendable and pleasant." Even compositions should display martial virtues as pupils "draw up their words in orderly array and march through many sentences preserving order in the ranks and an unbroken line."[37] Eliot believed that in their handwriting students "should strictly conform to given positions and rules, however awkward and constrained they may seem at first; for in penmanship, as in everything else of man's development, true liberty is obedience to law."[38] And the law, there was no doubt, was the curriculum prescribed by the bureaucracy.

The uniform curriculum of the common school—an unbroken "chain" King called it—[39] included the three R's, grammar and a smattering of natu- ral and social science. From test questions it is possible to discover what chil- dren learned to remember long enough to repeat on the examinations.[40] The curriculum was neatly parceled into semester segments, the teachers were closely supervised and had to drill students on the material covered in the tests, and a premium was placed on uniformity of output. King's report for 1877 listed the questions asked at the end of the eighth grade and the examinations in the various high school subjects. With few exceptions the questions required definitions, facts, memorization of textbook explanations. These are some examples: (the last three are aimed at eighth graders, the others at high school students):

A man pays 6 dollars yearly for tobacco, from the age of 16 till he is 60, when he dies, leaving to his heirs $500; what might he have left them if he had dispensed with this useless habit and loaned the money at the end of the year at 6 per cent, compound interest?

Define Imaginary Quantity, Surd and Pure Quadratic Equation.

What system did Kepler adopt? Give his three laws. Tell how he discovered each.

Define Diction. What is necessary to give one a command of words? What kind of New Words should be avoided? If any, specify the objections to the use of each of the following words: Exit, talkist, alibi, conversationalist, boyist, skedaddle, donate.

How do the two kind of engines differ? How is the power of steam engines estimated?

What was the Kansas-Nebraska Bill?

What causes earthquakes? Describe the Desert of Sahara. Give the area of the Atlantic ocean.

Write and punctuate the Lord's Prayer.

Give the principal parts of the verbs *lay, lie, go, cut, shoe*. Give the second person singular of *elect* in all its moods and tenses.

Give the five provisions of the Compromise of 1850.

Spell: Burlesque, Ichneumon, Heliotrope, Analytically, Diaphragm, Panegyric.[41]

The fact that about 93 per cent of the high school students answered questions like these correctly that year testifies to the marvelous capacity of the human race to suffer trivia patiently. Year after year, until the bombshell of the Cubberley report in 1913, the curriculum changed but little; it was mostly taken for granted.

An essential phase of the bureaucratization of the schools was the establishment of definite qualifications, salaries and duties for teachers. In 1881 Crawford complained about untrained and inexperienced teachers and decried the pressure on the school board to hire incompetent teachers with influential friends. He urged that professional competence be the only criterion for employment. He also suggested a normal "training class" for high school students intending to teach. In 1881 the school board adopted a uniform pay schedule for teachers based on years of experience and level of instruction.[42] Two years later the board set standards of eligibility and performance for each position and published twenty-two rules regulating teachers' examinations and certificates. Although technically there was no segregation into positions by sex, in effect a class system soon developed in which men became predominantly the supervisors and women the supervised; only in the high school was it respectable for men to teach. This feminization of elementary school teaching had gone so far by 1905 that all teachers of the grades were women. Twenty-three out of twenty-seven elementary school principals that year were men—almost, but not quite, a caste system, for some upward mobility was possible for women. This sex differential, coupled with the low pay, low prestige and inadequate education of the elementary school teachers, helped to reinforce the autocratic structure of the bureaucracy.[43]

Although certification is regarded today as a form of professional licensure, in its early stages in cities like Portland certification was a branch of civil service reform: a means of ensuring that public servants possessed at least minimal competence for their tasks and a way of preventing an educational spoils system. These objective standards of competence and rewards were common characteristics of bureaucracies in all fields, though in public agencies during the gilded age corruption and special favors were notorious problems. In Portland, however, civil service reform came early, and with the exception of alleged improper influence of the "book trust" of the American Book Company, in the 1890s, Portland was relatively free from scandal.[44]

In 1883 the school board issued a booklet of *Rules and Regulations* which codified the practices standardized during the previous decade. There was bureaucracy, in black and white: the classification of schools; the uniform curriculum; the hierarchy of offices and delineation of duties; the time schedules; the elaborate plan of examinations and promotions. As chief policeman the superintendent was required to "see that the grade work is strictly followed, that the rules and regulations are observed and enforced, and [to] report any and all delinquencies to the Board." Principals were the intermediate inspectors and disciplinarians, instructed by the board, among other duties, "to prohibit the playing of marbles on or about the school premises." Nothing was left to chance in the duties of the teachers: they were told to open the windows at recess; to suspend a thermometer from the ceilings and to keep their rooms between 67 and 71 degrees; to assemble for at least two hours at their monthly institute (they were fined two dollars for failing to attend and one dollar for being tardy); "to subscribe for, take and read, at least one periodical devoted to educational work"; and to "*cheerfully* cooperate with the City Superintendent in executing the prescribed work of the grades." Uneven in education and skill, teachers were to be governed by rules, not professional norms. Once a month the teachers read to the students the "Duties of Pupils" commanding obedience, punctuality, industry and respect for school property. Thirty-seven rules dealt with absence, tardiness, excuses and suspensions; eight outlined examinations and promotions.[45] Obscurity was not one of the faults of the Portland Public Schools; complacency was.

The bureaucratization of the schools had not gone unchallenged in Portland or elsewhere. In 1880 the crusty and conservative editor of the *Oregonian*, Harvey Scott, launched an attack on the "cumbrous, complex and costly system" of the public schools. "In nearly every city there has been growing up during the last ten years an elaborate public school machinery," he wrote, "largely managed and directed by those whom it supports. Nominally it is controlled by the taxpayers of the districts, but in reality by associations of persons who live as professionals upon the public school system."[46] What was needed, he said, was a return to "the simple yet effective system of the old common schools." Scott was sure that citizens were "decidedly in favor of reducing the 'establishment,'—as the system has been called since it grew to its present proportions." Methods of instruction have grown "to a complexity which puzzles the learner and which works the teacher harder out of school hours in making up trivial reports, calculated on percentages of proficiency, behavior, etc., than in the . . . schoolroom."[47] (Perhaps teachers not inclined to "cheerfully cooperate with the City Superintendent" had been talking out of turn.)

Scott sent reporters out to gather the opinions of the businessmen of Portland about the "new-fangled, finical stuff" going on in the schools; the complex machinery, the new subjects introduced into the grades and the high school (which Scott thought quite unnecessary for the common child). Most of the businessmen interviewed thought common schools necessary, but many questioned the need for expensive "flummery." "A child who has a good English education, if he has any snap about him," said one, "will succeed better than the average graduate of the high school who knows a little of every thing." Another said flatly: "The prominent and useful men of this city are not men of high education." Some glorified the simple, cheap, old-time district school: just the three R's, under the eye and thumb of the community. And one believed that the Portland schools were "being controlled by a school ring and not by taxpayers or directors."[48] Just inculcate the right values cheaply, said the self-made men.

Even George Atkinson had misgivings about the dominant role the school was beginning to play in the life of the child. During pioneer days children had learned the discipline of manual labor at home, he wrote in 1879, but as the school took over more and more of the student's life there was a danger that it might "graduate whole regiments of sickly sentimentalists: young gentlemen unused and unfit to work, and young ladies decked in the latest fashion. . . ." Parents should be forced to certify that their children were doing some manual labor for at least six months of the year, thereby correcting "a good part of the evils which are likely to grow out of improved public instruction."[49]

Atkinson's comment that "evils . . . are likely to grow out of improved public instruction" suggests the complexity of the issues raised in the revolt of 1880 against the school bureaucracy. Many motives impelled Scott and his fellow critics. Scott thought the schools were producing "shyster lawyers, quack doctors, razor-strop and patent-soap peddlers, book canvassers, and bookkeepers"—not willing workers. Many opposed higher taxes, especially for secondary education. Some believed that education beyond the common school should be the province of private schools (and they were encouraged in this belief by many private schoolmen who luxuriated in laissez-faire rhetoric). Some wanted the simple days of the old district school when parents saw the school as a community center in which families were more citizens than subjects. Others resented the fact that the schools were taking over functions previously performed by family, church and economic units. And above all, the schools seemed to be out of touch, insulated, irresponsible and irresponsive to the public, remote and haughty.[50]

Scott had said that no one could expect self-criticism from the professional establishment; the letters to the press of administrators like Crawford and the state superintendent of public instruction displayed a shocked and self-righteous attitude.[51] The depth of feeling against the bureaucrats was illustrated in a letter from "C" which appeared in the *Oregonian* on February 26, 1880: "We, the defenders of the common school system, are between the upper and nether millstones, the impracticables and the destructives. . . . It can only be perpetuated by relieving it of the complex character it has assumed by reason of the inflated, pedantic and self-aggrandizing character of the faculty, who from one entrenched foothold of aggression against popular rights have advanced to another, until we see the result in the superficial, overloaded and overtaxing system now prevailing."

Such attacks hurt and bewildered Crawford. He had earnestly gone about his business of liquidating tardiness and ignorance, organizing the schools according to the best eastern models, cultivating his own bureaucratic garden.[52] The impersonal rules, the uniform curriculum, the school hierarchy— did these not serve as a buffer between the teacher and the community, affording protection against the tyranny of parents, the spoils system of urban politicians, the insecurity of ambiguity? Crawford did admit that school patrons "have an undoubted right to sit in judgment on the general and even particular conduct of teachers who are public servants. What a teacher does out of the school room as well as in it comes within the purview of the public."[53] Then as now, the superintendency was an anxious profession and the school a vulnerable institution. Bureaucracy became the schoolman's moat and castle, and bureaucrats tended to regard an attack on their particular system as an attack on the principle of public education. That label which would be heard again and again in the years to come—"enemies of the public school"—they tried to pin on their opponents.

In 1880 the main task of defending the schools fell to the Rev. George Atkinson, then general missionary for the American Home Mission Society. Atkinson knew how to smother brush fires by committee. Thus at a heated meeting of taxpayers on March 1, 1880, Atkinson as private citizen diplomatically proposed an impartial investigation of the charges which had been leveled against the system and a report on the condition of the schools.[54] He summarized the complaints: that the machinery of the schools was too costly and cumbersome; that the studies were too difficult and numerous; and that the high school was not properly a part of the common school system (certain college preparatory subjects had been singled out for attack). Atkinson was chosen chairman of the investigating committee. This was rather like asking the Pope to study irregularities in the Vatican, for Atkinson was the most eloquent advocate of the bureaucracy (though not technically a member of the "school ring").

As author of the report Atkinson said that the "machinery" of education, far from being too cumbersome and costly, "seems hardly to keep pace with the growth of the city." He maintained that "large classes permit the best division of labor" and that the systems of grading and examinations "encourage every class in habits of promptness, order and diligence." Over a third of the grammar school graduates of the past five years were continuing their education, over one-half were working at home or in trades, and only 1 per cent were "of questionable character." But Atkinson reiterated that parents should "train their children, in manual labor" and teachers should give "lessons about the real work of life." The best proof of the quality of the schools was "that few idlers or hoodlums have ever been connected with the public schools of Portland." The high school he saw as an "extension of the grades and classes," well justified as a means of spreading "the purest morals and the best possible culture among great masses of people, who make and execute their own laws."[55]

In this report Atkinson reminded the people of Portland of the rationale for uniform and efficient public education: "The self-government of the people is still on trial, and every hour great currents sweep from other lands against its foundations and test the pillars of its strength. How shall the incoming tens and hundreds of thousands be moulded into our body politic and made homogeneous with ourselves except by the public school—training every child in our own tongue and habits of thought, and principles of government and aims of life?"[56] The perils of diversity dictated uniformity in the schools. Thomas Eliot concurred:

> The justification of our public school system really lies where people seldom look for it, viz.: In the necessity of a republic's preserving a homogeneous people; the necessity of having one institution which effectively mingles and assimilates *all* classes and castes. It is the "imperium in imperio," the democracy *within* the democracy of our national existence. The nation can afford to trust education of every kind to the parental instinct; but, it cannot afford to trust to chance the unifying processes; the sentiment which welds the people; and the common school as bringing all classes together at an impressionable age is the forge it sets up and maintains as its most powerful instrumentality against aristocracy and mobocracy (communism) and every other "ocracy."[57]

Still grumbling about the establishment, Portland accepted Atkinson's report and its rationale.[58] Not until Cubberley and his team of experts descended in 1913 would there be another full-scale investigation of the bureaucracy.

When Crawford resigned from the superintendency in 1888 the basic character of the school system was well established. For the next three years a talented woman, Ella Sabin, was superintendent. During her brief tenure she attempted to recast the curriculum and teaching methods in accord with "the enlivening influence of the 'new education' " (the movement which later became "progressive education"), but the patterns of behavior already established in the bureaucracy persisted and were reinforced by the regimentation required by her successors; she left her mark chiefly by a residue of progressive rhetoric, here and there, in the teachers' guide.[59] Irving Pratt, who took her place in 1891, became best remembered for declaring that "19 of his teachers [were] excellent. . . . All the rest were a poor lot."[60]

Frank Rigler spent his seventeen years as superintendent (1896–1913) largely in perfecting the machine he had inherited. In his first report he assured the taxpayers that *he* was no devotee of the "new education": "The friends of our schools who are apprehensive that the schools have become too modern are needlessly alarmed. I am not aware that our schools have any (approved) features that were not to be found a generation ago. . . ." Like a good general, he supported his troops: "every teacher now in our schools is making an effort, each according to her ability, to do the kind and extent of work that has been done by the best teachers for many years."[61] The *Oregon Journal* reported the claim of one of Cubberley's colleagues that there had been no changes for the better during Rigler's long regime, an accusation which infuriated the superintendent.[62] In Rigler's final report, written just before his resignation, he listed the improvements made during his tenure— manual training schools, a program for deaf and defective children, medical examinations of pupils and so on—but his sense of priorities was evident in the first three items on his list of achievements:

1st.   The construction of the buildings has changed from wood to steel and concrete.
2nd.   A system of ventilation and heating has been introduced which expresses the latest views of competent ventilating engineers.
3rd.   The toilet facilities of the schools have been made equal to those of the best dwellings and hotels.[63]

Indeed, a committee of leading educators admitted in 1890 that community pressures on imaginative administrators were such that "It is not surprising that so many really capable superintendents settle down to the running of the school machine as it is. . . . the strongest and wisest of educators may be pardoned if he degenerates into a not ignoble specimen of arrested development."[64]

Rigler, however, never was tempted to be anything but a guardian of tradition. His maxim "was to play the game straight according to the prescribed rules."[65] Criticized he was, for conservatism and autocracy; never for being too liberal. Stern, efficient, logical, a master of detail, he ran the bureaucracy like an army.[66] At teachers' meetings he went through the textbooks page by page, telling his staff what questions to ask and what answers to accept. It was common knowledge in Portland that Rigler "could sit in his office and know on what page in each book work was being done at the time in every school in the city." He revived Crawford's plan of internships in teaching for high school graduates and personally indoctrinated the young girls in his rigid course of study.[67] (The bureaucracy in Bel Kaufman's *Up The Down Stair Case* seems permissive by comparison.) The basic curriculum remained what it had been in the 1870s: the three R's, grammar, history, civics, geography, drawing and various subjects in natural science.[68] But Rigler took great pride in splitting the former thirty-six divisions of the curriculum into fifty-four "cycles" (each spelled out by pages in the textbooks) and in turn subdivided them into fast and slow sections.[69]

In Rigler's monotonous reports one looks in vain for reflections on the philosophical or sociological rationale of his administration.[70] A fellow superintendent, Aaron Gove of Denver, was not so reticent; in an NEA address he bluntly expressed the premises which underlay the Portland bureaucracy as well as his own. Gove opposed " 'soft pedagogy' and 'mellow education' " and believed that the grammar school years were "the time for drill, memory training, severe application to tasks with an accounting for their accomplishment."[71] Similarly he had no taste for democratic school administration. The limits of the superintendent's authority should be clearly stated, he said, "in the formal rules and regulations of the board of education." Within these bounds the superintendent's authority was unlimited, though he would be well advised to exercise it politely: "The autocracy of the office of the superintendent of a public-school system is necessary for the accomplishment of his purposes, but that despotism can be wielded with a gloved hand." Teachers can no more constitute a democracy than can policemen. Teachers may from time to time give *advice*, but "dictation must come from the other end." The teacher has only "independence like that of a man in a shoe factory who is told tomorrow morning to make a pair of No. 6 boots"—that is, he "can work rapidly or slowly," but he must make the boots. Gove saw in the "War Department of the nation" the best analogy for proper school organization. The general—the superintendent—must control all his troops, but must leave first-hand inspection up to his inspector-general's department. "The executive department of a school system of thirty thousand pupils would be ideal with one superintendent and four school inspectors who shall spend their entire time, as does the inspecting officer of the army, in reviewing and examining in detail every part of the enterprise and reporting promptly and often, in a very careful way, what he finds. . . ."[72]

So far had bureaucracy gone down the down staircase that the nature of education had been subordinated to the demands of the organization. To the survey team in 1913 schooling seemed a vast percolation of words for the student, teachers robots, administrators themselves captives of the rules and the system. This was the trained incapacity, the blindness to alternatives, which bureaucracy often (though not necessarily) produced.[73] Cubberley and his colleagues were determined to jar Portland out of its rut.

To Cubberley's group Portland symbolized much that was wrong with "traditional education." They deplored the abstract, uniform curriculum and gagged on grammar tests that asked students to define attribute complements and independent elements. They attacked the military model of teaching by routine and drill. They satirized the autocratic and rule-constipated structure of the schools. They believed that the new science of education, new conceptions of learning, new tasks for the school and new views of the teacher's role had rendered obsolete most of the bureaucratic system which Portland had labored for fifty years to build.[74]

Cubberley was convinced that education should be functionally differentiated according to the needs of students and society. Furthermore, he was committed to professional expertise for both teachers and administrators. These are elements of what has come to be called educational progressivism. The old-fashioned military model of bureaucracy in which hierarchy depended more on power than on function made sense only so long as the goals of education were stated in very generalized terms, such as producing homogeneous good citizens. By 1913 many school administrators believed that educational progress depended on Spencer's "differentiation of structure and . . . specialization of function," and their model of such functional specialization was contemporary industrial organization.[75] In Cubberley's view,

> Our schools are, in a sense, factories in which the raw materials [children] are to be shaped and fashioned into products to meet the various demands of life. The specifications for manufacturing come from the demands of the twentieth century civilization, and it is the business of the school to build its pupils to the specifications laid down. This demands good tools, specialized machinery, continuous measurement of production to see if it is according to specifications, the elimination of waste in manufacture, and a large variety in output.[76]

Cubberley believed in "large variety in output," for one of the key faults of traditional education was its lack of specialization. Portland's schools were "much in the condition of a manufacturing establishment which is running on a low grade of efficiency," said Cubberley, for it was based on an antiquated bureaucratic model. "The waste of material is great and the output is costly—in part because the workmen in the establishment are not supplied with enough of the right kind of tools; in part because the supervision of the establishment is inadequate and emphasizes wrong points in manufacture; but largely because the establishment is not equipped with enough large pieces of specialized machinery, located in special shops or units of the manufacturing plant, to enable it to meet modern manufacturing conditions."[77] Cubberley believed that urban schools should "give up the exceedingly democratic idea that all are equal, and that our society is devoid of classes,"[78] and should adapt to existing social classes. For leaders "should apply to the management of their educational business principles of efficiency similar to those which control in other forms of manufacturing."[79] He believed that the school system should train students for specialized roles in the economy while still striving to produce *morally* homogeneous citizens.

The school should have a highly trained staff headed by a captain of education similar in stature to a captain of industry. A bureaucracy it should be, but a specialized one controlled by professionals, not drill sergeants. The caliber of a school, said Cubberley, "depends much more on the quality of the leadership at the top and the freedom given the leader or leaders to work things out in their own way, than upon any scheme of organization which can be devised." The Portland School Board was still trying to oversee minute administrative details and relied on rules rather than men, not realizing that "What a school system is, it is largely because of the insight, personality, and force of the Superintendent of Schools." Likewise, this leader should be given responsibility to select administrators and teachers who could exercise professional discretion within their specialized spheres. Cubberley believed that a staff which had grown from 294 in 1900 to 928 in 1913 needed effective supervision; but he also was convinced that no one man could decide what was best for the 43,000 children in the district. To professionally trained teachers fell "the responsibility, under wise guidance and leadership, of adapting the educational process, both in content and method, to individual needs." In short, the bureaucracy was to be looser structurally, the superintendent and his administrative staff adapting the schools as a whole to the needs of society, and the teachers adapting lessons to the needs of the child.[80] A new tension was thus introduced which had hardly existed in Rigler's despotic system: the uneasy and sometimes conflicting demands of consistent and orderly administration on the one hand and professional autonomy and freedom to experiment on the other.[81]

Cubberley had really stated a dilemma rather than solved a problem, a dilemma faced by urban schoolmen everywhere. As Cubberley knew, bureaucracy in some form was here to stay in large American school systems, however it might be modified by new conceptions of education, and inherent in bureaucracy was the impulse toward regularity. In a small rural school, or in a Freud-inspired private school, an individual teacher might single-handedly put the tenets of progressive education into practice. Progressives might protest against the regimentation common in urban school systems at the turn of the century, but the effects of rigid bureaucratization could not easily be erased by reading *Democracy and Education*, by introducing new subjects into the curriculum, by workshops on new methods, by developing new ways to classify pupils, by new theories of administration, by new patterns of professional training. It was difficult indeed to capture the spirit of progressive education in a crowded slum school, to transform a class of forty polyglot children into the sort of family at cooperative work which Dewey described as the ideal school.[82] As a result, many "progressives" like Cubberley sought essentially to substitute a new version of bureaucracy for the old. But at the turn of the century perceptive schoolmen recognized that the quest for standardized schooling—that once had been a reform—had become a kind of despotism. It would require all their ingenuity to control their creation and to subordinate the schools to education.[83]

NOTES

1. Ellwood P. Cubberley, *The Portland Survey* (Yonkers-on-Hudson, N.Y., 1916), p. 125.
2. Cubberley, *Portland*, pp. 40, 128, 125, 41–42, 46; Cubberley's colleagues were education professors and school administrators, including Edward C. Elliott, Frank E. Spaulding, J. H. Francis, Lewis Terman.

3. "Scientific Common School Education," *Harper's New Monthly Magazine*, LXI (Oct. 1880), 935–40.

4. Rice's articles were republished as *The Public School System of the United States* (New York, 1893); Charles W. Eliot, "Undesirable and Desirable Uniformity in Schools," National Education Association [hereafter cited as NEA], *Journal of Proceedings and Addresses . . . 1892* (New York, 1893), pp. 82, 86; on the condition and ideology of the schools of the period see Oscar Handlin, *John Dewey's Challenge to Education* (New York, 1959).

5. On school systems as bureaucracies see Charles E. Bidwell, "The School as a Formal Organization," in *Handbook of Organizations*, ed. James G. March (Chicago, 1965), p. 974; on bureaucratic structure generally see *Reader in Bureaucracy*, eds. Robert K. Merton et al. (Glencoe, IL, 1952).

6. "School Superintendence in Cities," NEA, *Journal of Proceedings and Addresses . . . 1890* (Topeka, KS, 1890), pp. 309, 312–13.

7. On early district schools see Clifton Johnson's *Old-Time Schools and School-Books* (New York, 1904); the quest for standardization is a theme of practically all histories of the common school reform and reports of state superintendents—as an Oregon sample, see Oregon Superintendent of Public Instruction, *First Biennial Report* (Salem, OR, 1874), pp. 24–27.

8. David Tyack, "The Tribe and the Common School: the District School in Ashland, Oregon, in the 1860's," *Call Number*, XXVII (Spring 1966), 13–23; Marshall Barber, *The Schoolhouse at Prairie View* (Lawrence, KS, 1953); Milton E. Shatraw, "School Days," *American West*, III (Spring 1966), 68–71.

9. Aaron Gove, "Duties of City Superintendents," NEA, *Journal of Proceedings and Addresses . . . 1884* (Boston, 1885), p. 27; for a similar point of view see Superintendent of Public Schools, San Francisco, *Twenty-Second Annual Report* (San Francisco, 1875), p. 140; T. L. Reller, *The Development of the City Superintendency of Schools in the United States* (Philadelphia, 1935).

10. Richard C. Wade, *The Urban Frontier* (Chicago, 1964), pp. 314, 317; see *Third Annual Report of the General Superintendent of the St. Louis Public Schools* (St. Louis, 1857), pp. 324–29, 354–69.

11. Duane Doty and William T. Harris, *A Statement of the Theory of Education in the United States of America as Approved by Many Leading Educators* (Washington, D.C., 1874), pp. 14, 13, 12; see Oscar Handlin's discussion of the urban demand for chronological precision in *The Historian and the City*, eds. Oscar Handlin and John Burchard (Cambridge, 1963), pp. 13–14.

12. NEA, *Report of the Committee on Salaries, Tenure, and Pensions of Public School Teachers in the United States* (Winona, MN, 1905), p. 195.

13. "The Freedom of the Teacher," NEA, *Journal of Proceedings and Addresses . . . 1903* (Winona, MN., 1903), pp. 165–67; Eliot, "Uniformity," pp. 87–88.

14. *Social Theory and Social Structure* (rev. ed.; Glencoe, IL, 1957), pp. 197–200.

15. Cubberley, *Portland*, pp. 155, 158, 36–39.

16. "School as Formal Organization," p. 992; there is no lack of historical data for such analysis—indeed, much of what educational historians have been describing all along is in fact the creation of bureaucratic structure.

17. *Sociology and Contemporary Education*, ed. Charles N. Page (New York, 1964), pp. 83, 76–114.

18. In a study that provides a useful comparison with Portland, Michael B. Katz discusses the "implausible ideology" of Massachusetts educators that "had helped set the stage for the rigid, sterile bureaucracies that soon would operate most

urban schools": *The Irony of Urban School Reform, Ideology and Style in Mid-Nineteenth Century Massachusetts* (Washington, D.C.: United States Office of Education, Cooperative Research Program, Project S-085, 1966), pp. 152–213.

19. See Merlon's discussion of these concepts, *Social Theory*, pp. 198–99.

20. See Lawrence Cremin, *The Transformation of the School* (New York, 1961).

21. *Oregonian*, Jan. 4, 1873.

22. *Oregonian*, Mar. 14, 1874.

23. Thomas H. Crawford, "Historical Sketch of the Public Schools of Portland, Oregon, 1847–1888" (typescript, Oregon Collection, University of Oregon Library), pp. 9, 13–14; Alfred Powers and Howard M. Corning, "History of Education in Portland" (mimeographed W.P.A. Adult Education Project, 1937), p. 48.

24. George Atkinson, "Early History of the Public School System of Oregon, with a General Outline of its Legal Aspects," in State Superintendent of Public Instruction, *Biennial Report*, 1876, p. 15.

25. State Superintendent of Public Instruction, *Biennial Report*, 1878, pp. 59–60; *Biography of Rev. G. H. Atkinson, D. D.*, comp. Nancy Atkinson (Portland, 1893), pp. 25–26.

26. *Oregonian*, Mar. 22, 1876.

27. David Tyack, "The Kingdom of God and the Common School: Protestant Ministers and the Educational Awakening in the West," *Harvard Educational Review*, XXXVI (Fall 1966), 447–69.

28. City Superintendent of the Public Schools, City of Portland, Oregon, *Eighth Annual Report for the Year Ending June 28, 1881* (Portland, OR, 1881), p. 28. The Portland superintendents' reports were printed yearly beginning in 1874; hereafter they will be listed by year only (e.g., *Report for 1874*).

29. *Report for 1876*, pp. 8–9; Powers and Corning, "History," p. 51.

30. *Report for 1881*, p. 29; *Report for 1882*, pp. 27–28. In 1899 A. E. Winship, editor of the *Journal of Education*, decided that the best analogy for the school superintendent was the train conductor whose "watch is the only standard" on the pedagogical train: "What The Superintendent Is Not," NEA, *Journal of Proceedings and Addresses . . . 1899*, p. 309.

31. *Report for 1874*, p. 4.

32. *Report for 1877*, p. 16.

33. *Report for 1874*, pp. 8–9.

34. Powers and Corning, "History," pp. 45, 327; Otis W. Caldwell and Stuart A. Courtis describe the founding of the standardized examination in Boston in *Then & Now in Education, 1845: 1923* (Yonkers-on-Hudson, N. Y., 1925).

35. *Report for 1873*, pp. 16–18; *Report for 1882*, pp. 37–39; on Max Weber's concept of "official secrets" see *Reader in Bureaucracy*, p. 26.

36. *Report for 1875*, p. 9; *Report for 1876*, p. 37.

37. *Report for 1875*, p. 12.

38. *Oregonian*, Mar. 22, 1876; Eliot was concerned that "*individuality may be sacrificed, or that as a result* [of bureaucratization] *machine work may take the place of the production of thinking power*"—but he believed that large numbers dictated system and that the work of King was "in the right line of development."

39. *Report for 1874*, p. 9.

40. Horace Mann found the standardized examination a useful weapon in his war against the Boston schoolmasters—see Caldwell and Courtis, *Then & Now*, chap. i and pp. 235–72.

41. *Report for 1877*, pp. 51–62.

42. *Report for 1881*, pp. 32–41.

43. *Report for 1883*, pp. 23–26; *Report for 1884*, pp. 41–44; NEA, *Report of the Committee on Salaries, Tenure, and Pensions . . .* , p. 195; it seems likely that feminization of teaching depended as much on bureaucratization as upon the economies it brought.

44. Lucien Kinney, *Certification in Education* (Englewood Cliffs, N. J., 1964), pp. 77–79; the discussions in the department of superintendence of the NEA at the turn of the century dealt extensively with the problems of the spoils system in education, as did the series of articles on public education in *Atlantic Monthly* in 1896; on the issue of the "book trust" see the *Oregonian*, Sept. 23 and 24 and Oct. 28, 1894.

45. *Rules and Regulations and Course of Study of the Public Schools of District No. 1, Portland, Oregon* (Portland, 1883), italics added.

46. *Oregonian*, Feb. 9, 1880; in *Class, Bureaucracy and Schools* (New York, 1971) Michael Katz examines attacks on bureaucratic education elsewhere.

47. *Oregonian*, Feb. 23, 1880.

48. *Oregonian*, Feb. 21, 1880; examination of Portland School Board minutes for the period suggests that actually the Directors took a very detailed, not to say picayune, interest in managing the schools—e.g., resolution of Sept. 28, 1883, concerning the monthly reports of the principals on efficiency of teachers, or the discussion on Sept. 17, 1884 about rules for use of the school library.

49. *Oregonian*, July 31, 1879.

50. *Oregonian*, Feb. 19, 1880; Bidwell, "School as Formal Organization," pp. 1009–10, points out that one reason for opposition to consolidation—and bureaucratization—of rural schools in recent years has been the symbolic importance of the community school as an integrative force for the primary groups of the neighborhood.

51. *Oregonian*, Feb. 18, 1880; Mar. 1, 1880; it must be admitted that some of Scott's charges were ill-tempered and unfair.

52. Wallace Sayre, in "Additional Observations on the Study of Administration," *Teachers College Record*, LX (Nov. 1958), 73–76, analyzes some of the "serviceable myths" developed by educational bureaucrats in their quest for autonomy and outlines some issues that need to be studied to clarify the *external* relations of schools to their environment; I am indebted to his suggestions.

53. *Report for 1880*, p. 28; *Oregonian*, Feb. 28, 1880.

54. Scott declared—*Oregonian*, Mar. 3, 1880—that Atkinson's investigation was "quite unnecessary," for he had no desire to be confused by Atkinson's facts.

55. *Report for 1880*, pp. 31–34.

56. *Report for 1880*, pp. 34–35.

57. *Oregonian*, Feb. 25, 1880.

58. The defeated Scott was still spluttering in the *Oregonian*, Jan. 8, 1899, that the typical educator was "a mere drillmaster," one who was unfit "to make public policies as to education."

59. *Report for 1889*, pp. 25, 71 ff; Miss Sabin was educated at the University of Wisconsin; she was the only superintendent from 1874–1913 to have more than essentially a high-school education.

60. Powers and Corning, "History," p. 140; Miss Sabin in her *Report for 1891* disagreed, saying that the top four-fifths of Portland's teachers were as "enlightened and devoted" as any in the nation.

61. *Report for 1896*, pp. 29–30.

62. *Oregon Journal*, Apr. 24, 1913; Rigler had anticipated the charge of being "unprogressive" in an article he wrote in the *Oregonian*, June 5, 1912.

63. *Report for 1913*, p. 85.

64. "School Superintendence in Cities," p. 312.

65. E. H. Whitney, "Partial History of the Portland School System, 1896–1913, with Biographical Sketch of Frank Rigler" (Seminar Paper, University of Oregon, 1922).

66. Rigler's associate Daniel Grout gave a perceptive sketch of Rigler in the *Oregonian*, July 18, 1914.

67. Lee A. Dillon, "The Portland Public Schools from 1873 to 1913" (Master's thesis, University of Oregon, 1928), pp. 26–27.

68. *Report for 1898*, pp. 67–70, 87–117; *Report for 1903*, pp. 87–88.

69. *Report for 1898*, pp. 82–83; *Report for 1901*, p. 76.

70. Cubberley, *Portland*, pp. 393–96.

71. NEA, *Journal of Proceedings and Addresses . . . 1901* (Chicago, 1901), pp. 188–89.

72. "Limitations of the Superintendents' Authority and of the Teachers' Independence," NEA, *Proceedings and Addresses, 1904* (Winona, MN, 1904), pp. 152–56.

73. Michel Crozier, *The Bureaucratic Phenomenon* (Chicago, 1964), p. 187, defines bureaucracy as "an organization that cannot correct its behavior by learning from its errors"; at a meeting of school patrons on Dec. 27, 1912, a citizen (not a school board member), W. B. Ayer, was the person who proposed that the investigation of the schools be made (*Report for 1913*, pp. 32–33); for a bitter indictment of the Rigler machine see *The Telegram*, Mar. 21, 1914.

74. Cubberley, *Portland*, pp. 140–41, chap. xi.

75. Raymond Callahan, *Education and the Cult of Efficiency* (Chicago, 1962).

76. Cubberley, *Public School Administration* (Boston, 1916), p. 338.

77. Cubberley, *Portland*, p. 417.

78. Cubberley, *Changing Conceptions of Education* (Boston, 1909), pp. 56–57.

79. Cubberley, *Portland*, p. 418.

80. Cubberley, *Portland*, pp. 15, 27, 53, 181; some insisted that laymen still had an important role to play, like William G. Bruce, editor of the *American School Board Journal*. "Quo Vadis, School Board?" NEA, *Journal of Proceedings and Addresses . . . 1899* (Chicago, 1899), p. 1130: "the new fad . . . likens a school to a factory plant. Like the factory superintendent, the school superintendent is to employ all hands, fix all salaries and boss the job from beginning to end."

81. In 1917 P. W. Horn did a follow-up study to see if the Cubberley recommendations were followed: *Report of Supplementary Survey of Portland Public Schools* (Portland, 1917).

82. John Dewey, *School and Society* (Chicago, 1956), pp. 7–11; Dewey was somewhat ambiguous in posing an organizational model for the school, for he realized that large-scale organizations were a permanent feature of modern industrial society, and he wished workers to realize the functional significance of their contribution to these enterprises.

83. Since I have painted a rather grim portrait of the Portland Public Schools prior to 1913, I should like to record my conviction, based on close acquaintance with the system, that the Portland district is today one of the most innovative and effective school systems in the United States.

6

Urban Reform and the Schools: Kindergartens in Massachusetts, 1870–1915

Marvin Lazerson

Origins and Ideology

In the decades after the Civil War, no individual did more to popularize the kindergarten in America than Elizabeth Palmer Peabody. Her advocacy was an "apostolate," kindergartening a religion, a "Gospel for children." All children, Peabody and her associates believed, were self-centered. In their earliest years they discover their bodies, senses, and power to act. Without an agency external to the family in which socialization among peers and to society's mores occurs, childhood would thus ultimately become self-destructive. It was here that the kindergarten became necessary, allowing the child "to take his place in the company of his equals, to learn his place in their companionship, and still later to learn wider social relations and their involved duties." "A kindergarten, then," Peabody wrote, "is children in society—a commonwealth or republic of children—whose laws are all part and parcel of the Higher Law alone."[1]

Since the kindergarten's primary goal was socialization, children could not be allowed to run free. In the garden of children, the trained kindergartner helped the child develop by carefully removing obstacles to natural growth and by providing nourishment. As the gardener must know plants, the kindergarten teacher had to understand children, bringing together the natural instincts of motherhood with special training in child development. "The mother," one speaker at a National Education Association meeting declared, "as handmaid of the Lord, will recognize in the consecrated kindergartner a fellow-worker in the garden of the Lord." The kindergarten thus stood as an extension of ideal Motherhood, an institution which would effect the transition between the individualistic education of the home and the social necessities of the broader society.[2]

Although socialization was frequently discussed, what the term actually encompassed varied. On the one side stood the emancipation of the child from traditional and insensitive restrictions, the enhancement of spontaneity and creativity. On the other, emphasis was given to uniformity and control. Early kindergartners often pointed to the former as their new institution's primary contribution, calling for love and understanding of the child, creative expression, youthful teachers, and the elimination of corporal punishment and parrot like memorization. They advocated movement and activity for children who desired and needed both, introduced new play objects into the environment, and were willing to accept noise as a healthy corollary to happy play. "Of the two evils," Elizabeth Peabody wrote, "extreme indulgence is not so deadly a mistake as extreme severity."[3]

But while kindergartners urged emancipation, they also argued that their ultimate goal was order. The kindergarten was, after all, a "guarded company of children," and children could not be left "to a chaos of chance impressions." Individualism, with its potentiality for disorder and conflict, was another form of self-centeredness, vitiating the primary goals of kindergarten learning. "All government worthy of the name begins in self-government," Peabody declared, "a free subordination of the individual in order to form the social whole." The need for such socialization could hardly be underestimated. "The child is doubtless an embryo angel; but no less certainly a possible devil. . . ." Obedience, Mary Mann similarly concluded, was essential for order, and order "I regard as 'heaven's first law.' "[4]

To produce this socialization, which channeled spontaneity into order, the kindergartners evolved a complex and highly structured methodology of play activities. Building on Froebel's assertion that play represented the highest and purest form of activity for young children, they created an ordered environment within which the child learned by doing. The child's own activity—spontaneous, natural, and satisfying his most basic needs for movement and self-mastery—became the mechanism for positive social growth. All play activities, however, were not equally valid. Music, song games, and marching which called for great activity but kept children within a highly structured program and prevented "disagreeable romping" were fundamental. Formalized games helped the child internalize rules. As one kindergartner put it, "The ordinary child remembers to be good; the kindergarten child forgets to be naughty." Froebel's "gifts"—soft cloth balls, blocks, cubes, rings, triangles, spheres, and cylinders—introduced the child to geometrical forms and suggested the harmony and symmetry of life. Less important but still necessary in a well-run kindergarten were such utensils as paper, scissors, clay, pencils, and paint to elicit creative activity and help develop manual dexterity. Small gardens offered the child an object lesson in organized natural growth. Above all, early kindergartners warned, avoid the overuse of books, let the child learn the use of objects before the words of adults.[5]

These views of childhood education received impressive support in the closing decades of the nineteenth century from a new emphasis upon early habit formation and from the emerging child-study movement. Although earlier Lockean ideas had laid the basis for an emphasis on childhood learning, not until the end of the nineteenth century did American educators generally acknowledge the importance of the early years in shaping adult behavior. To the kindergartners, this was an article of faith. The young child, they argued, was both malleable and perceptive. "The first seven years of the child's life," wrote Angeline Brooks, "Froebel saw to be the most important for purposes of education; for, as he said, during that time tendencies are given and the germs of character are set." Having found that the child's social and moral character could be shaped at an early age, the kindergartners also asserted that the influences would be lifelong. In 1886, the *Journal of Education* simply concluded that "In the first 7 or 8 years of a child's life it will probably be settled whether he is to be swayed by superstition or intelligence, whether he is to live terrorized by fear or buoyed up by hope and courage." Under these circumstances, the kindergarten appeared vital.[6]

Further support for the kindergarten appeared as a by-product of the child-study movement, particularly the ideas formulated by G. Stanley Hall. President of Clark University, indefatigable organizer, prolific author, editor, and public speaker, Hall played in the years prior to World War I a seminal role in the fields of child and adolescent psychology. To the kindergartners, he was the "father of the child study movement," the individual who made of childhood "a gospel." Hall provided a scientific rationale for Froebel's views that education was evolutionary and developmental, that human growth was a process of stages, and he urged the public to allow children to express their needs and peculiarities. His injunction that teachers and parents "get out of Nature's way and allow her free scope, and avoid excessive checks and inhibitions" was readily echoed by the kindergartners. His calls for teachers to know their children confirmed what early childhood educators already knew. The extraordinary breadth and proliferation of his studies and those inspired by him made child study a national topic of discussion. It was thus not surprising that in 1880 when Hall sought to study children entering the first grade in Boston's public schools, he should be financed by Boston's leading supporter of kindergartens, Mrs. Quincy Adams Shaw, or that four of Mrs. Shaw's kindergarten teachers should act as investigators.[7]

"The Contents of Children's Minds," the 1880 study, propelled Hall to the forefront of the child-study movement, and it revealed some of the reasons Hall's early theories found such ready support from the kindergartners. Determined to take an "inventory of the contents of the minds of children of average intelligence on entering the primary schools" of Boston, Hall formulated questions which "should lie within the range of what children are commonly supposed or at least desired or expected, by teachers and by those who write primary text-books and prescribe courses of instruction, to know." The findings were shocking. City children existed in almost total ignorance of the commonplaces of life: 80% of the children were ignorant of beehives, 54% of sheep, 87% of a pine tree, 40% of a pond, 92% of a triangle. Such alarming results, however, contained some positive affirmations of the kindergarten. Children who had been to the charity kindergartens where "superior intelligence of home surroundings can hardly be assumed," did substantially better than the other children. Most primary teachers found children from the kindergartens better fitted for school work, though often more restless and talkative. Perhaps most revealing was the relationship between Hall's standards of intelligence and the activities of the kindergarten. The test items were heavily weighted toward rural imagery, and consciously so. "As our methods of teaching grow natural," Hall believed, "we realize that city life is unnatural, and that those who grow up without knowing the country are defrauded of that without which childhood can never be complete or normal. On the whole, the material of the city is no doubt inferior in pedagogic value to country experience. A few days in the country at this age has raised the level of many a city child's intelligence more than a term or two of schooltraining could do without it."[8] These views paralleled basic assumptions of the early childhood educators. Kindergartners conceived of the city as an artificial environment antipathetical to natural growth, and sought in the "children's garden" a surrogate for urban life. Nature walks, small gardens, and freedom to play which were assumed to be the life style of the rural child were essential ingredients of the kindergarten, while the strenuous play activities of the countryside found their parallel in the marching and games. The wood carving, sewing, drawing, sand and mud manipulation which Hall thought fundamental to growing up intelligently were recreated in a variety of forms in the children's classes. Most kindergartners, then, could find Hall's assumptions and his study of the "contents of children's minds" gratifying. Not merely had kindergarten children outdistanced the others, but the general solution advocated by the child psychologist pointed directly to the expansion of their institution.[9]

KINDERGARTENS AND SOCIAL REFORM

While the ideology of the early kindergarten movement stressed its universality, its applicability to all children, the first kindergartens catered to the affluent. The earliest practitioners were cultured women whose daily associations were with individuals of wealth. Even when Boston established a publicly supported kindergarten in the early 1870s, "circumstances made it necessary," former Superintendent of Schools John Philbrick later wrote, ". . . to locate it among the better class of population. . . ."[10]

But despite this initial identification with the affluent and cultured, the kindergarten received its most important support in late nineteenth-century Massachusetts as an institution of the urban slum. In the 1880s and 1890s the social problems of the city came under more intensive investigation and received more publicity than ever before. Heightened concern for the slum helped spawn a new view of poverty which looked at the results of economic hardship rather than simply condemning them as a cause of social ills. Americans began to define poverty in terms of insufficiency and insecurity, and no longer as desirable or necessary. The belief that poverty was debilitating paralleled assertions that its evils—disease, want, disrupted families— could be eradicated by the social measures of an aroused public, by a reorganizing of the environment in which the poor lived. Simultaneously, the child and his home, not simply as symbols of the child-study movement, but as special objects of social amelioration, received new attention. Children's aid organizations sprouted and flourished. Volunteer charity workers reported that "labor among the children" was the most important feature of their work. "Here [in the homes of the children], by means of books, games and pictures, the visitors can bring brightness and activity instead of dreariness and idleness. The comfortable and interesting home will be the best safeguard against outside temptations."[11]

Not all educators adopted this new view of urban poverty; few were as articulate. But the kindergartners and those who supported them found the attitudes and the goals of the social welfare movement congenial. The kindergarten's antiurban bias accentuated the horrors of the slum and provided a vantage point from which to view poverty. Kindergarten advocates argued that healthy family life could not occur in the slums, that children of the poor were "uncared for." The urban street and home seemed environments of terror. Mary Mann, usually a sympathetic observer, was reported to have characterized slum children as "little savages from three to five, the pests of the street, their mouths full of profane and obscene language." In the immigrant ghetto—by the late nineteenth century in Massachusetts, poverty and immigrants were deemed synonymous—an institution adaptable to children, willing to recognize their need for activity and play, while introducing order to their lives appeared vital if society was to avoid adults bred in anarchy. The kindergarten, the editor of *Century Magazine* declared, was "our earliest opportunity to catch the little Russian, the little Italian, the little German, Pole, Syrian, and the rest and begin to make good American citizens of them."[12]

Between 1880 and 1900, similar expressions revolving around the preschooling of the urban poor came from almost every educational leader in Massachusetts. In Lawrence the superintendent of schools in 1881 recommended public support for kindergartens in the less fortunate areas of the city. Lynn's superintendent pleaded for just one kindergarten especially adapted to "little ones from homes of the poor and the uncared for." The school committee in New Bedford, arguing for kindergartens, believed that "the great majority of children who do not attend school between five and seven are unfortunately those of foreign parentage, and, as a rule, often of the most ignorant kind. They are the very children who should be in school at the earliest permissible age, as they, as a rule, are the first to leave school to go to work." In 1897, the new superintendent of schools in Haverhill summarized the prevailing ideology:

> In my opinion the Kindergarten should be established not for the benefit of those children who come from homes of culture and refinement; but on the contrary, it should receive those children that have had little, if any, good home-training. If it were established in such a portion of our city, and were properly conducted, it would furnish a happy transition from those homes and the unwholesome influences of street life to the healthful schoolroom surroundings.[13]

These views were not isolated phenomena. They reflected a growing sense of urgency about the relationship of education and schools to slum life, manifest to some extent in almost all the educational innovations of the late nineteenth century. Schooling and social welfare were becoming synonymous as individuals desperately sought to correct the dysfunctional institutions of the urban environment. In their efforts, educational change was seen both as a way of improving the schools and of ameliorating broader urban social problems. Not surprisingly, then, school reform received much of its impetus from social settlement workers and philanthropists engaged in reshaping the urban environment. To these individuals, the kindergarten was a unique institution, distinctive in its approach to child development and a means of entering the home and neighborhood. To the social reformers, the kindergarten was more akin to the settlement house than to the school, and they joined with the early formulators of the kindergarten ideology to keep kindergarten education distinct from the narrow pedagogy and academic goals of the regular school classroom.[14]

In the late nineteenth century, the settlement was seen as an agency for melting families into a neighborhood. The kindergartens would participate in that work primarily by harmonizing and socializing individual families. Proposing a club for little children along kindergarten lines, one settlement worker wrote, "They would be easy to manage, and would give us an entree into the homes of the mothers." Settlements and kindergartens gave the highest priority to taking the child off the streets by providing him with attractions unattainable on them. Both viewed the poor, particularly the immigrant poor, with a mixture of sympathy and contempt. Kindergarten teachers, the Pittsfield, Massachusetts *Sun* wrote in 1898, would explain their methods and objects, teach the games and songs to mothers, thus allowing mothers to play with their children at home. And, "if the mothers happen to be poor, ignorant, uncultivated women, as so many are who have children in the public or free kindergartens, the kindergartner does real missionary work in the talks she can give on hygiene—proper food and clothing and neatness in every way. . . ." Mothers' meetings, kindergartner Nora Smith argued, for those "hard-worked, unlettered women" whose children attended the charity kindergarten classes, should be social gatherings in spotless rooms containing flowers, light refreshments, and cloth-covered tables. "It will be," she wrote, "a cosmopolitan audience thus gathered together in any of our free kindergartens, and somewhat uncongenial in its elements, comprising, as it does, Italians, Germans, French, Irish, Scandinavians, Hebrews, Africans, a few native-born Americans possible, and perhaps even some wanderers from Syria or Armenia." Indeed, even the settlement house itself might be considered a "kindergarten for adults." "The settlement may not have intentionally preached the doctrines of Froebel, but it has practiced them in every phase of its work. In the playground, the children's club, the vacation school, nay, in the very settlement itself, one may read the philosophy of the kindergarten writ large."[15]

A striking manifestation of the kindergarten as urban reform was the philanthropic kindergarten activities of Mrs. Quincy Adams Shaw. Daughter of famed Harvard scientist Louis Agassiz, stepdaughter of Radcliffe College's first president, Elizabeth Gary Agassiz, and wife of a copper mining heir who claimed three of Massachusetts' most distinguished names, Mrs. Shaw epitomized the socially concerned philanthropist. In the last year of her life, she wrote her children that she had "had too much—you will all have too much—and it will require great effort with God's help to determine 'to give' rather than 'to hold'. . . ." Considered the richest woman in Boston and the city's "greatest woman philanthropist," Mrs. Shaw was a major sponsor of settlement houses, a strong supporter of women's rights, and founder and president of the Boston Equal Suffrage Association. Many of the educational innovations of the period—sloyd (a Swedish method of woodworking), industrial education, and vocational placement bureaus—received their initial support from her proselytizing and financial activities. Of all her concerns, however, none so involved her interest and money as the kindergarten and day nurseries, believing that "the bringing up of children is the vital question of life—the great problem of the race."[16]

Mrs. Shaw was probably converted to kindergarten work by Elizabeth Peabody during the 1860s. In 1870, when Peabody's school appeared ready to close for lack of funds, Mrs. Shaw provided additional financing, and shortly thereafter helped open a charity kindergarten in Boston's North End, followed by two similar ones in suburban Jamaica Plain and Brookline. Within a decade, she was supporting 31 such ventures in and around Boston, spending more than $200,000 on them between 1882 and 1889. Even after her kindergartens were incorporated into the Boston public school system in 1888, she continued her philanthropy, providing funds for training courses for kindergarten teachers, Christmas parties, and an assortment of related activities.[17]

The most famous of Mrs. Shaw's charity kindergartens were undoubtedly those in Boston's densely populated, immigrant North End. In this district, housing twenty-five nationalities in 1900, most recently arrived from Eastern Europe, wrote Francis Parker, a former supervisor of primary schools in Boston, "hundreds of parents turn their children out into the streets in the morning to care for themselves, while they, by selling fruit, grinding organs, begging, or even worse, strive to eke out a miserable existence." To meet the needs of these children, two charity kindergartens had been established in the early 1870s, "to collect," its sponsors wrote, "some of the neglected children who swarm in the streets, while yet too young for the primary schools, and give them facilities for intellectual and moral training at an age most tender and sensitive to every surrounding influence."[18]

It is unclear how long these schools remained in existence, but by 1880, Mrs. Shaw had helped establish at least three separate kindergarten classes, receiving permission from the Boston School Committee to hold two of them in rooms of a local public school. That is, from their inception, the philanthropic kindergartens were provided with some facilities by the public schools. All furnishings, heat, teachers, and assistants were paid for by Mrs. Shaw, the classes catering to children between twenty-two months and five years of age. Physical needs were met first: each child was greeted by daily face washing, his clothes cleaned, and milk and bread provided. The kindergarten room, one observer of a North End class wrote, "is warm and cheery; bright pictures hang on the walls; on one blackboard is a crayon sketch of swans floating on still waters; on another are notes and words of simple songs; on the shelves at one side of the room is a company of dolls, while various childish treasures are scattered here and there within easy reach of tiny hands." The activities of these classes in the heart of the immigrant ghetto had a certain bizarre quality to them. Children marched and sang about a "little birdie"; they learned that wooden balls come from "the great, tall trees," and talked about pussy willows, the sun, and walks in green fields. Committed to memory were such verses as:

> I'm an oriole, I'm an oriole,
>> My nest hangs on high Where the breezes are singing
>> Their sweet lullaby. They rock in their cradle,
>> My birdies and me, And we are as happy,
>> As happy can be.[19]

But the North End kindergartens were more than play spots dedicated to introducing rural imagery into the life of the ghetto child. Both Mrs. Shaw and her supervising teacher, Laliah Pingree, were devoted to reaching the neighboring homes. Mothers were invited into the classes; parents' gatherings were held in the evenings to explain kindergarten methods and to suggest improvement in child care. The kindergartners placed great faith in the belief that the habits children learned while under their care would pervade the slum home. Forced to overcome apathy among parents toward the new classes, kindergarten teachers systematically and consistently visited the homes of enrolled and prospective pupils, teaching only half a day for this purpose. Kindergartners were enthusiastic about such tales as Lucy Wheelock's "A Lily's Mission" in which two "ragged, dirty children" bring a flower home to their dingy tenement apartment. The mother has failed to keep the house clean; the father is out drinking. Overjoyed at seeing the flower, the mother places it on a window sill only to discover that dirt prevents any sunlight from shining through the window to the flower. With the window clean, sunlight reveals the filth of the apartment which is then quickly cleaned; mother washes and dresses, and father, overcome by his new environment upon his return home, vows to give up the bottle. Such tales revealed only the most spectacular of powers attributed to the kindergarten as an instrument of reform. "The interest manifested in the children and families," Laliah Pingree wrote of Mrs. Shaw's kindergartens, "does much to encourage the parents to do something for the children themselves, and to make them more responsible for them. The impression made upon the mothers by the patience and gentleness of the teacher is a deep one. . . ." Pointing to the need to instruct slum parents, Pingree told of the kindergarten child who after being struck by her mother declared, "God did not give you those to strike me with; he made them to do nice and good things; my [kindergarten] teacher said so." To the philanthropists and settlement workers, the kindergarten thus emerged as a crucial wedge to bring order to the child's growth and to his life at home, on the street, and in the classroom. Through the child, the adult poor would be instructed in the mores of the dominant society. As the kindergarten moved from the organizations of charity to the public schools, it would retain that ideology of reform, but not for long.[20]

INSTITUTIONALIZATION AND COMMUNITY

Tied to and invigorated by the settlement houses and philanthropists, the kindergarten soon found its way into the public school systems of urban Massachusetts. By 1914, seven of the ten largest cities and twelve of the twenty largest had public kindergartens. In almost every case, they developed out of a philanthropic base, and particularly in the first years of the transition from charity to public education continued their allegiance to the ideals of social philanthropy and their commitment to the kindergarten as distinctive from the regular school classroom.[21] Almost invariably, the first kindergartens under public auspices focused on the peculiar needs of the slum child, and upon the role kindergartens could play in elevating the home and neighborhood, while preparing the child for the elementary grades. Ultimately, however, the incorporation of early childhood training into urban school systems represented a withdrawal from the broad goals of community reform. An emerging consensus developed among educators and philanthropists that all education, whatever its social justification, should be centered in the schools, that social change occurred best through classroom practices. In Massachusetts, this would lead in the decades after 1900 to a gradual narrowing, rather than broadening, of social commitments, a turning away from urban reform. For reasons of economy and theory, public kindergartens began to eliminate mothers' meetings and home visits, while their supporters on the eve of World War I spoke less about reforming and elevating the family and about social amelioration than they did about smoothing the child's progress in grade school and separating him from his social background. The processes of transfer from philanthropic to public, and the need for an institutional rationale acceptable to the professional educator worked a subtle but nonetheless radical transformation in the philosophy of the kindergarten. The transition from philanthropic to public occurred first in Boston, and it was there that the initial continuity between schooling and social reform was most clearly apparent. Although the city had briefly experimented with a public supported kindergarten in the 1870s, preschooling before 1887 remained almost exclusively a philanthropic-social settlement activity, dominated by Mrs. Shaw. During the mid-1880s, however, rising costs forced Mrs. Shaw to cut back her commitments, and she and her associates began pressuring the Boston School Committee to finance its own kindergartens. Receiving strong support from Superintendent of Schools Edwin P. Seaver,

Mrs. Shaw agreed to turn over her program to the city, thereby enlarging charity into a broader public responsibility. The rationale for accepting this responsibility emerged in two areas, one involving the relationship of pre-schooling to social reform, the other focusing on early childhood education as a prerequisite for future school success. The former reflected a direct trans-fer of philanthropic ideals to public education. In an immigrant, working class city like Boston, few families could be considered positive agents of socialization, and any improvement in family life depended upon bringing children into more adequate institutions. Calling for the adoption and expan-sion of kindergarten classes as a regular feature of the Boston public schools, Superintendent Seaver declared, the kindergarten "affords a much-needed protection from the injurious influence of the street." "For those unfortunate children—and there are many, who suffer from parental carelessness, indif-ference, ignorance, or poverty, the kindergarten measurably supplies what the home does not—kindly nurture in the virtues and graces of a more refined and elevated democratic life." Simultaneously, the kindergarten also seemed an effective way of getting children ready for further schooling. This view was best summarized by an experienced teacher who had taught primary school for thirty years—beginners for about twenty years. She had received ten or twelve children each year from kindergarten for about ten years. Their train-ing "in habits of neatness, cleanliness, order, self-reliance, and prompt obedi-ence," she wrote, was "a great saving of time to the primary teacher." They had also "formed habits of observing closely, and using their hands properly." "All their faculties" were "so cultivated that no time" was "lost in preparing them for Primary School work." Those children who belonged to cultivated families, she continued, might not need kindergarten training, "but it is almost a necessity for the majority of children under our charge."[22]

Inherent then in the Boston School Committee's adoption of the kinder-garten, a step taken in 1888, were these two interrelated themes: community reform as epitomized by the social settlements, and school achievement defined by adequate preparation for primary grades. Both themes depended upon a consensus among philanthropists, reformers, and educators that urban social life had failed, that the children of the city needed a special insti-tution if they were to learn proper habits of behavior. While community reform and school achievement initially seemed complementary, however, public education would be hard-pressed to achieve either among the poor, and educators would soon be choosing schools rather than community as their central concern.

The dominant role philanthropy and philanthropic ideals played in estab-lishing kindergartens in Boston also appeared in other Massachusetts cities. In Cambridge, kindergartens were initiated by Mrs. Shaw in the late 1870s. A decade later, she and other philanthropists convinced the Cambridge School Committee to incorporate their charity classes into the public schools. As occurred in Boston, philanthropy continued to play a role in the classes even after their adoption by the public system. Mothers' clubs, evening receptions for fathers, and home visits by teachers all designed to improve family life remained integral to Cambridge's kindergarten program through to the end of the century. This blurring of public and philanthropic similarly occurred in Fall River, where as late as 1912, Mrs. Spencer Borden was supplying furniture, materials, and all other equipment to the public school system's five classes. Even in the wealthy Boston suburb of Brookline, considered by an observer in the 1890s to possess "one of the most unique school systems in the country," charity overtones persisted. Discussing educational activities in the town, Superintendent of Schools Samuel Button noted that the Brookline Education Society and Child Study Association brought "cultured women" together with "those less favored" to explain the care of children. Dutton, one of the most articulate and active exponents of innovation among the state's professional educators and a propagandist for widespread kindergarten education, remained committed, like other educators, to the particular applicability of such classes to "all neglected children and those whose breeding and environment are likely to result in criminal habits."[23]

If Massachusetts' major cities thus drew upon philanthropic initiative to establish kindergartens as part of their public school systems before World War I, the elan and vitality which marked the movement's early years, especially the commitment to community reform, suffered a noticeable decline in the decade and a half after 1900. Despite continuing assertions that kindergartens were essential for children of the ghetto, despite affirmations of their importance to all children, despite a resolution by the Massachusetts Teachers' Association in 1895 and proposed legislation in 1909 that all cities and towns with populations over 10,000 have public kindergartens, and despite the activities of individual superintendents of schools, public classes showed only moderate growth.[24] While the number of children enrolled in public kindergartens increased from about 3,000 to 14,000 between 1890 and 1900, annual enrollment climbed to only 18,000 by 1914, with Boston and Worcester, the state's largest cities, accounting for half the latter figure.[25] Whereas Massachusetts in 1898 accounted for 8.8% of all kindergarten-registered children in the United States, its proportion gradually dropped to 5.4% by 1912. Even where public kindergartens were established, they sometimes catered to as few as 6% of the eligible population (ages 4–6), although Boston's 22%, Cambridge's 31%, Springfield's 61%, Holyoke's 23%, and Worcester's 28% were outstanding among the larger cities.[26]

The most obvious question arising from these statistics is why the lessening of commitment. Many educators continued to affirm the kindergarten's importance in implementing proper habits of behavior, in educating urban parents, and as an introduction to early school life, yet the movement's enthusiasm waned and its implementation slowed. In part, this reflected heightened concern with costs. Many cities and towns, already heavily taxed to support elementary and high schools, and particularly burdened by overcrowded classrooms, found kindergartens an unjustifiable luxury. Between 1889 and 1909, while enrollment in the Boston kindergartens climbed, the city paid about $20 a year for each pupil. By 1914, however, expenditures

had increased to $27 a pupil. Cambridge found itself in a similar situation
when instruction per kindergarten pupil increased from $14.78 (1890), to
$19.33 (1898), to $27.15 (1908), and finally to $39.77 (1915) as compared
to expenditures per primary school pupil of $12.92, $13.94, $16.11, and
$24.46 for the same years. Expenses in Fall River went from $12.37 in
1904–1905 to $21.65 per pupil in 1913–1914, while Lowell, which cut its
kindergarten enrollment between 1904 and 1914, found that its expenditures per pupil continued to increase. Although these rises reflected a general
trend in school costs, kindergartens remained more expensive than the lower
primary grades. As distinctive institutions, they demanded special treatment,
and to varying degrees they got it. In a study of 20 American cities in 1911,
the Boston Finance Commission found that five of the seven Massachusetts
cities analyzed averaged fewer pupils per teacher in kindergarten than in the
elementary schools, and in some cases the difference was dramatic.[27]

Lessening commitment to the kindergarten, however, represented more
than a reaction to high and rising costs. Cities were invariably involved in
choosing educational innovations or expanding their educational services;
kindergartens could have received more priority than they did. "More fundamental [than costs]," David Snedden, State Commissioner of Education,
wrote in 1915, was ". . . whether the aims and the field of the kindergarten
have been defined to the satisfaction of educators." "It is widely assumed that
the chief value of the kindergarten is to compensate for deficiencies of home
environment." Such an assumption, the Commissioner claimed, implied that
educators knew what the ideal environment for healthy growth was and that
the "compensatory functions" of the kindergarten provided such an environment. If this were so, why did the "cities having conditions of environment
least favorable to the normal growth of children [viz., the immigrant-
industrial cities] have usually the fewest kindergartens." In effect, Snedden
argued, kindergarten advocates asserted they offered an ideal environment to
overcome home and neighborhood conditions, without proving their case to
the public. But there was more to the criticism, for implicit in the argument
was a sense that the essential failure of kindergartners had been their attempt
to establish their institution distinct from the primary grades, the unwillingness of kindergarten advocates to see their programs as simply the beginning
of the regular school process. "Children of English-speaking parents living in
good environments," Snedden wrote, "could most afford to delay their
school work until the age of six, either by remaining at home or engaging in
the play activities of the kindergarten." Children of the slums, however, especially the non-English speaking, needed early exposure to a more rigorous
school atmosphere, one which combined certain kindergarten methods with
systematic primary school training.[28]

This issue, the conflict between essentially structured and formalized
learning versus "play" learning, effectively undercut appeals for kindergartens as distinctive public institutions. Within the kindergarten movement
itself, the distinctions that had developed between the needs of all children
and those peculiar to children of the poor, the differences between early

childhood schooling for children from healthy homes and those from the urban slums, were reflected in controversy over kindergarten methods. As Snedden implied, once educators differentiated among categories of children, methods and goals had to be modified. Those who remained committed to the universal child and Froebel's methods therefore came under constant criticism by kindergarten reformers who demanded programs adapted to such categories as the child's nationality, class, age, approximation to normality, physical handicaps, environmental background, and material and social development. Conflict within the kindergarten movement itself over the extent to which young children should be differentiated undercut expansion of preschooling programs.[29]

Concern over costs and confusion among kindergartners as to the true nature of their institution soon led Massachusetts educators to focus on the relationship between primary and kindergarten education, evolving a compromise situation which effectively curtailed the latter's distinctiveness, and helped terminate the philanthropic commitments to social amelioration. The establishment of subprimary classes, or in less defined form, the absorption of the kindergarten by the lower primary grades had particular appeal to those concerned with the slum child. "When . . . children live in crowded quarters," Commissioner Snedden wrote, "and especially if the language of the home be foreign, or else poor English, a twofold gain results from admission at five to a so-called subprimary class. The school will provide for a few hours each day a better environment than the street, and a moderate amount of systematic training will give to the pupil such command of English and training in school behavior in general as to enable him, after entering the first grade, to keep pace approximately with more favored classmates."[30]

The processes which made the kindergarten simply an adjunct of first grade occurred throughout the state, but the most pertinent example can be found in the immigrant-industrial city of New Bedford. There, rapid population growth—from 40,000 to 96,000 between 1890 and 1910—and large numbers of foreign born, reflecting the enormous expansion of the city's cotton textile industry, placed great pressures upon the city's school system. In the lower grades, where a majority of the children by 1913 came from homes of non-English speaking parents, conditions were exceedingly bad. It was to these children of New Bedford's immigrant mill population that the first kindergartens in the city were directed.[31]

In 1894, under the auspices of the City Mission, an aid station for the poor, two charity classes were set up in the mill and immigrant north and south ends of the city. Within two years, pressure developed for public sponsorship of the classes, now accepted as necessary "for children whose home advantages were not of the best." After a minor skirmish between the city council which refused to allocate funds and the School Board, three kindergarten classes were established, under conditions, however, which manifested a significant deviation from earlier philanthropic conceptions. The new classes were not to be distinctive institutions, but "should conform somewhat to the plan or organization which rules in all other grades of the schools if

they are to become a permanent part of the school system." As was true of
primary school teachers, kindergarten instructors were required to conduct
two sessions daily, each containing 50 different pupils, though as a conces-
sion to the particular necessities of the kindergarten, two teachers were
assigned to every 100 pupils. Teachers' home visits, small classes, and an educational and social ethic distinct from that of the primary schools received
little recognition. New Bedford thus initiated its public kindergarten program with virtually no concern for the social reform measures which had
previously dominated much of the movement.[32]

Even with these modifications, New Bedford's educators were unhappy.
None of the three kindergartens was meeting its quota of 100 pupils per day,
making the program more expensive per pupil than originally intended.
"I am a firm believer in kindergartens," Superintendent William Hatch wrote
at the end of the first year's experiment, "and I have so expressed myself
before; but I also firmly believe economical questions must have proper
consideration in school administration. The cost of kindergarten under the
one-session plan [with afternoons devoted to home visits and mothers' clubs]
is too great to warrant their maintenance on that plan. If there is not sufficient appreciation of this class of schools on the part of the parents of the city
to support the double plan, as much as I should dislike to see kindergartens
abandoned here I should feel it my duty to advise their discontinuance."
Five years later, in 1902, attendance continued considerably below expectations. With two teachers in each school, Hatch claimed, kindergarten instructors averaged only 14 pupils contrasted to a primary school teacher's 40 to 50.
Reflecting growing community concern over school costs, the superintendent contended that the kindergartens created more problems than they
solved. While he believed "it would be an excellent thing if most of the
children of our schools could have the advantage of the kindergarten," New
Bedford's schools were already overcrowded with increasing costs already
"causing more dissatisfaction."[33]

The controversy finally came to a head between 1904 and 1909, when
a compromise effectively eliminated kindergartens. In the former year,
Superintendent Hatch enlarged his criticism from economic to theoretical
grounds, claiming that children should not be in school before the age of six,
and suggesting that earlier attendance had no discernible effect on school
performance. With the city in the midst of an economic depression the following year, the School Board narrowly voted in June 1905 to continue the
kindergartens, though it recognized that they were expensive and insuffi-
ciently patronized. Nine months later, however, the Board reversed itself and
moved to abolish the classes, an action which aroused a storm of protest
among prominent individuals in the city. At a special public hearing, a citizen's group headed by the founders of the charity kindergartens of the 1890s
declared: "In an industrial city like ours we believe it essential to begin
the ducation of hand and mind of the child at the earliest possible time. We
therefore petition your Honorable Board to continue the kindergartens we
have already and to establish others where they are needed." Kindergarten

supporters claimed that New Bedford's industrial community urgently needed the classes. The Reverend Paul R. Frothingham, who had started the city's second charity kindergarten in the immigrant north end, declared: "There are some cities where the kindergarten is not so necessary as in New Bedford, cities where all the people are well-to-do, where there are small families, and the parents are able to provide for their children. But in a great industrial center, with large families and crowded conditions, a kindergarten, I believe, plays a very important and necessary part." Indeed, the issue was so important that Frothingham called for the elimination of Latin and Greek from the high school rather than drop kindergartens.[34]

Under intense pressure—the School Board received petitions from boards of directors of the Orphans' Home, Mothers' Club, Woman's Club, and City Mission, all representing prominent New Bedford citizens, as well as petitions from several of the mill corporations— the School Committee engaged in a tactical retreat. In June 1906, two and a half months after the stormy open hearing, the board voted eight to seven to retain the public kindergartens and within six months had added a fourth class in the south end. The 1906 decision, however, did not settle the controversy. Confronting a situation in which more than 50 percent of the children entering first grade did not understand English or could do so only with difficulty, the School Board moved to establish half-time subprimary classes for five and six year olds. These classes would continue the game activities of the kindergarten but would also introduce the children to the routine of school life. No child under the age of seven would be allowed to enter school after the first two weeks of classes unless he was qualified to do so, thus forcing all newly arrived non-English speaking children into the subprimary classes. In effect, New Bedford had found that isolating the immigrant child was an effective way of educating him, but that this could best be done by introducing him to the "routine of school life," rather than by establishing distinctive, socially involved kindergartens.[35]

New Bedford was not an exceptional case. It and seven other of Massachusetts' twenty largest cities had either eliminated or never established public school kindergartens before 1914. More important, a number of other cities which had maintained such classes were by the second decade of the twentieth century eliminating the kindergarten as a distinctive institution, moving away from its earlier conception as a unique environment for children with socially amelioristic goals. The subprimary movement prominent in New Bedford had received strong support from the state's commissioner of education. The emancipatory goals of creative play and expression within a structured environment and the humanization of early childhood education had become confused with the need to bring order and discipline to the slum child. Preparation of the child for the primary grades was becoming the kindergarten's raison d'etre, combining English language instruction with an emphasis on traditional learning and curriculum. What Francis Parker had called "the most important far reaching educational reform of the nineteenth century" was ceasing to be conceived of as an environment in itself and as a supplement to the child's environment, and instead, was assuming a position as a preelementary class whose major function was to remove the child from his home environment and lead him into the schools as quickly as possible.[36]

This tendency was not totally novel. Rather it represented a subtle change in emphasis which, in turn, resulted in the radical transformation of the kindergarten as an urban institution. Antagonism to the slum child's background had always existed within the kindergarten movement, and indeed, provided a major impetus to its growth. A "social quarantine" movement had even become prominent at the turn of the century, calling for a "strict quarantine for the innocents [i.e., "children of the street and of wretched homes"], where "the kindergarten influence and gentle training . . . may overcome the moral starvation from which they suffer, and develop in them human potentialities for goodness."[37] But such views had always coexisted with and even been dominated by philanthropic and settlement goals that had seen the child as a means to larger social reform. The mothers' meetings, social gatherings, child care talks, home visits, and a host of other activities had effectively enlarged conceptions of child schooling. Now, in the first two decades of the twentieth century, Massachusetts' cities began to eliminate or deemphasize these as regular features of the kindergarten. Cambridge instituted a one-year experiment in double teaching sessions for each kindergarten teacher in 1911 necessitating "the dropping of much of the visiting to the homes of the children as well as the mothers' meetings." Worcester believed that kindergarten teachers had to be trained for the primary grades as well as for their particular kindergarten roles. Boston's Finance Commission undoubtedly offered the most extreme proposal: all-day kindergartens in foreign districts with all four year olds attending as the only means of preparing the children for their first grade work.[38] These public pronouncements, however, only partially reflect the changing conceptions of the kindergarten. As revealing was the absence of discussion about the social responsibilities of early childhood educators. Whereas superintendents of schools had once affirmed the key roles kindergartens would play in slum districts, between 1910 and 1914 such discussion practically ceased.[39] Where children of the poor were mentioned, it was now almost invariably in the context of non-English speaking immigrants who needed aid in being propelled through the school and into the work force, rather than in terms of helping reform the larger society of which they were a part. As they became institutionalized in the urban public school, kindergartners moved from the delicate balance they had earlier proposed between freedom and order, emancipation and discipline, to a clear and overriding commitment to control. Slum children, removed from the guiding restraints of healthy, orderly family life, growing up in the anarchic environment of the street needed, above all else, discipline, needed to be prepared for the strict environment of the primary grades. By the time of America's entry into World War I, Massachusetts' educators had resolved the tension that had existed in the kindergarten movement between focusing on the child or using the child for the larger setting. They had turned from the child in the slum home to the slum child in school, a far easier and cheaper means of education, and in the process they were ceasing to believe that positive benefits could be derived from a focus on the former.

NOTES

1. Elizabeth Peabody, *Lectures in the Training Schools for Kindergartners* (Boston: D. C. Heath & Co., 1893), pp. 4, 22, 66–67, 88; The American Institute of Instruction, *Proceedings and Addresses* (Boston, 1871), p. 7; *New England Journal of Education* I (January 2, 1875), 1; Mary Mann, "The Home," *Kindergarten Magazine* I (September 1888), 133–36 and (October 1888), 165–68; Elizabeth Peabody and Mary Mann, *Moral Culture of Infancy and Kindergarten Guide* (Boston: T.O.H.P. Burnham, 1863), pp. 12–14.

   On Elizabeth Peabody, see Ruth M. Baylor, *Elizabeth Palmer Peabody: Kindergarten Pioneer* (Philadelphia: University of Pennsylvania Press, 1965). An early and still useful history of the kindergarten is Nina C. Vandewalker, *The Kindergarten in American Education* (New York: Macmillan Co., 1908). For more extensive documentation of the materials in this article, see Marvin Lazerson, "The Burden of Urban Education: Public Schools in Massachusetts, 1870–1915" (Ph.D. diss., Harvard University, 1969), ch. 2.

2. Peabody and Mann, *Moral Culture*, pp. 10–15; Peabody, *Lectures*, pp. 4–5; Angeline Brooks, "The Theory of Froebel's Kindergarten System," in *The Kindergarten and the Schools*, Anne Page et al. (Springfield: Milton Bradley Co., 1886), p. 47; Mrs. Elizabeth P. Bond, "The Kindergarten in the Mother's Work," National Education Association, *Journal of Proceedings and Addresses* (1885), p. 359.

3. Peabody, *Lectures*, pp. 15–18, 64; Peabody and Mann, *Moral Culture*, pp. 23–24; Peabody, *What is a Kindergarten?* (Cambridge, Mass.: privately published, 1874).

4. Peabody, *Lectures*, pp. 2, 4–5, 14–15, 44–46, 67, 78, 179; Peabody, "Kindergarten Schools," *Massachusetts Teacher* XXIII, 3d ser. (July 1870), 238; Peabody and Mann, *Moral Culture*, p. 182.

5. Lucy Wheelock, "The Purpose of the Kindergarten," *Journal of Education* (July 2, 1891), p. 36; Angeline Brooks, "Philosophy of the Kindergarten," in *The Kindergarten*, Kate Douglas Wiggin, ed. (New York: Harper and Brothers, 1893), pp. 119–21, 131; Alice W. Rollins in ibid., p. 2; Peabody and Mann, *Moral Culture*, pp. 34–51; Nora A. Smith, *The Children of the Future* (Boston: Houghton, Mifflin & Co., 1898), pp. 67–100.

6. Brooks, "Philosophy of the Kindergarten," pp. 103–08; *Journal of Education* XXIV (November 18, 1886), 324.

7. G. Stanley Hall, *Aspects of Child Life and Education* (New York: D. Appleton & Co., 1921), pp. vi, 11; Charles Strickland and Charles Burgess, eds., *Health, Growth, and Heredity: G. Stanley Hall on Education* (New York: Teachers College Press, 1965), pp. vii–viii, 1–3; Merle Curti, *The Social Ideas of American Educators* (Paterson: Littlefield, Adams & Co., 1963), pp. 396–428 remains the best study of Hall.

8. Hall, *Aspects of Child Life*, pp. 10–26.

9. Ibid., pp. 300–21; Strickland and Burgess, *Hall*, pp. 16–18, 53–58. For examples of the antiurban bias of kindergarten supporters, see Peabody, *Lectures*, pp. 1–23; Ellise B. Payne, "The Problem of the City Kindergarten," NEA, *Proceedings* (1896),

pp. 510–14; Edwin P. Seaver in Massachusetts Board of Education, *Report of the Committee Appointed to Investigate the Existing System of Manual and Industrial Education* (Boston: Massachusetts Board of Education, 1893), p. 29. Hall was later to break with the kindergartners over their overformalization of play. See Winifred Bain, *Leadership in Childhood Education: A History of Wheelock College* (Boston: Wheelock College, 1964), pp. 15–16.

10. John Philbrick, "The New Departure in Boston," *New England Journal of Education* XI (February 19, 1880), 116; A.G.W., *The Kindergarten, What is It?* (Boston: privately printed, 1872–74?), copy in Harvard College Library.

11. Robert Bremner, *From the Depths: The Discovery of Poverty in America* (New York: New York University Press, 1956), chs. 1, 3, 5, 8, 9; Nathan I. Hugins, "Private Charities in Boston, 1870–1900" (Ph.D. diss., Harvard University, 1962), chs. 3, 5: Associated Charities of Boston, *Annual Report* (1880), pp. 23–24; ibid. (1886), pp. 33–34.

12. Mary Mann in *Cambridge Chronicle*, May 11, 1878, p. 2; Richard W. Gilder, "The Kindergarten: An Uplifting Social Influence in the Home and District," NEA, *Proceedings* (1903), p. 390.

13. Lawrence, *Annual Report of the School Committee* (1881), p. 40; Lynn, *School Report* (1892), p. 51; New Bedford, *Annual Report of the School Committee* (1902), p. 26; Haverhill, *Annual Report of the School Committee* (1897), p. 29. See also Lowell, *Annual Report of the School Committee* (1880), pp. 22–23; ibid. (1881), pp. 10–12; Cambridge, *Annual Report of the School Committee* (1895), p. 48. (Hereafter reports of school committees and superintendents of schools will be cited as *School Reports*.)

14. Laura Fisher, "The Kindergarten," U.S. Bureau of Education, *Annual Report of the Commissioner* (Washington, D.C.: U.S. Government Printing Office, 1904), p. 692; *Kindergarten News* III (January 1893), 5; Massachusetts Board of Education, *Annual Report of the Board and Secretary, 1897–98* (Boston: Massachusetts Board of Education, 1898), p. 197 (hereafter cited as *Annual Report*); Robert A. Woods, *The City Wilderness* (Boston: Houghton, Mifflin & Co., 1898), p. 237; Joseph Lee, "Kindergarten Principles in Social Work," NEA, *Proceedings* (1903), pp. 378–82.

15. Diary of Nora Smith, January 6, 1893, Denison House Papers, folder 3, Schlesinger Library, Radcliffe College; *Pittsfield Sun* in *Kindergarten Review* IV (October 1898), 118–21; Smith, *Children of the Future*, pp. 52–55; Vandewalker, *Kindergarten*, pp. 108–11. See also Allen F. Davis, *Spearheads for Reform: The Social Settlements and the Progressive Movement, 1890–1914* (New York: Oxford University Press, 1965), pp. 43–45, and Arthur Mann, *Yankee Reformers in the Urban Age* (Boston: Harper Torchbook, 1966), pp. 115–23.

16. Pauline Shaw to "My Dear Children," November 30, 1916, Women's Rights Collection, Schlesinger Library, Radcliffe College; *The Journal of Education* XIV (September 29, 1881), 205; *Boston Evening Transcript*, February 10, 1917 (copy in Schlesinger Library). For biographical information on Mrs. Shaw, see *Pauline Agassiz Shaw: Tributes Paid Her Memory* (Boston: privately printed, 1917).

17. *Pauline Agassiz Shaw: Tributes*, pp. 32–36; *Journal of Education* XXVII (April 26, 1888), 264; *Kindergarten Magazine* II (December 1889), 248.

18. Francis W. Parker, "The Kindergartens of Boston," *Kindergarten Magazine* I (March 1889), 334–35; "Kindergartens: The Need of Their Establishment."

"Establishment and Support" [1874–1875?] (printed copy of letter in Harvard College Library).

19. Alice M. Guernsey, "Schools and Homes," *Journal of Education* XVIII (July 12, 1883), 53; Parker, "The Kindergartens of Boston," p. 335. On the use of public school classrooms for Mrs. Shaw's kindergartens, see Boston School Committee, *Minutes of the School Committee* (1882) (Boston: City of Boston, 1883), pp. 218–19.

20. Lucy Wheelock, "A Lily's Mission," *Voice from the Old Bowrey and Five Points Mission Monthly*, October 1, 1889, Lucy Wheelock Papers, Wheelock College; Laliah Pingree in Boston, *Documents of the School Committee* (1885) (Boston: City of Boston, 1886), no. 4, pp. 51–52 (hereafter cited as *School Documents*). Similar to the Wheelock story is Annie I. Willis, "A Midsummer Story: The Charity Kindergarten," *Journal of Education* XXXVI (July 14, 1892), 55–57.

21. For a general summary of kindergarten developments in Massachusetts and New England, see Lucy Wheelock, ed., "The Kindergarten in New England," presented to the Association for Childhood Education, June 26–30, 1935, Wheelock Papers, Wheelock College. Of the ten largest Massachusetts cities, Boston, Worcester, Fall River, Lowell, Cambridge, Springfield, and Somerville had public kindergartens, while New Bedford, Lynn, and Lawrence did not. Of the next ten cities, Holyoke, Haverhill, Salem, Newton, and Fitchburg had classes. Brockton, Maiden, Taunton, Everett, and Quincy did not.

22. Boston, *School Documents* (1885), no. 4, pp. 50–54; ibid. (1886), no. 3, pp. 46–49; ibid. (1887), no. 3, pp. 28–32; ibid. (1887), no. 21; ibid. (1888), no. 18, pp. 10–13.

23. Cambridge, *School Report* (1889), pp. 28–30; ibid. (1900), p. 41; ibid. (1901), p. 50; Fall River, *School Report* (1912), p. 25; Amalie Hoffer, "Brookline Schools—Well-Equipped, Well-Developed, Well-Poised," *Kindergarten Magazine* IX (December 1896), 282, 285, 288; Samuel T. Dutton, *Social Phases of Education in the School and the Home* (New York: Macmillan Co., 1899), pp. 213–15, 245–46.

24. Massachusetts Board of Education, *Annual Report* (1884–1885), pp. 90–91; ibid. (1894–1895), pp. 189, 191–92; Massachusetts, *Documents of the House of Representatives* (1909) (Boston: Massachusetts General Court, 1910), no. 577, no. 1462, no. 1538.

25. Massachusetts Board of Education, *Annual Report* (1890–1891), pp. 56–57; ibid. (1899–1900), p. 129; ibid. (1913–1914), p. 198. While Boston and Worcester contained over half (9,451 of 18,118) the public school kindergarten children in Massachusetts in 1912, their proportion of total day public school students was only about 25 percent. The United States Bureau of Education estimated that 1,500 children, seven to eight percent of the total enrollment, were registered in nonpublic school kindergartens—tuition charging, charity, and parochial—in 1912. While the figure is probably too low, compared to the 17–18 percent of all Massachusetts school children enrolled in nonpublic day school classes, it does suggest that when children went to kindergarten, they were more likely to do so under public auspices than at a later period in their school life. United States Bureau of Education, "Kindergarten in the United States," *Bulletin* (Washington, D.C.: U.S. Government Printing Office, 1914), no. 6, pp. 28–29, 66–67; Massachusetts Board of Education, *Annual Report* (1911–1912), pp. 57, 61, xlix.

26. U.S. Bureau of Education, "Statistics of Public and Private Kindergartens," *Report of the Commissioner*, 1903, LI; U.S. Bureau of Education, "Kindergartens in the United States," pp. 28–29, passim.

27. Massachusetts Board of Education, *Annual Report* (1899–1900), pp. 126–27; ibid. (1904–1905), pp. 177–78; ibid. (1913–1914), p. 198; Cambridge, *School Report* (1890), p. 17; ibid. (1898), p. 19; ibid. (1908), p. 28; ibid. (1915), p. 49; Boston Finance Commission, *Report on the Boston School System* (Boston: City of Boston, 1911), p. 167.

    Only Springfield's kindergartens contained more kindergarten pupils per teacher than elementary pupils, while Lynn, the seventh city, had no official kindergarten classes. Whereas Boston averaged 43 elementary school pupils per teacher, it had only 26 for the kindergarten. Comparable figures in Lowell were 37 to 19, Cambridge 38 to 25, Worcester 34 to 22, and Fall River 33 to 22. Lawrence dropped its experimental kindergarten in 1898 due to financial pressures. (Lawrence, *School Report* [1898], pp. 15–16.) Kindergarten advocates recognized their difficulties and attempted to persuade the public that the educational benefits were either worth the costs or compromised their methods to cut costs. See Eastern Kindergarten Association, *Does the Kindergarten Pay?* (Boston, 1909) and Vandewalker, *The Kindergarten*, pp. 184–85.

28. Massachusetts Board of Education, *Annual Report* (1914–1915), pp. 48–49.

29. International Kindergarten Union, *The Kindergarten* (Boston: Houghton, Mifflin & Co., 1913), pp. 242, 295–301. This is an excellent summary of conflicting tendencies in the kindergarten movement just before *World War I*.

30. Massachusetts Board of Education, *Annual Report* (1914–1915), pp. 49–50.

31. In 1913, 57 percent and 53 percent of the children in the public first and second grades were from non-English speaking homes. Between 1890 and 1910, the proportion of foreign born in New Bedford went from 34.6 percent to 44.1 percent of the total population, except for Lawrence, the highest in the state. (New Bedford, *School Report* [1913], p. 42).

32. Wheelock, "The Kindergarten in New England," pp. 14–15; New Bedford, "Minutes of the School Committee," July 1, 1895, February 3, 1896, May 4, 1896, May 3, 1897, August 16, 1897 (ms. in the Office of the School Committee, New Bedford); New Bedford, *School Report* (1896), pp. 91–94; ibid. (1897), pp. 97–99.

33. Ibid., pp. 100–01; ibid. (1902), pp. 26, 138–39.

34. Ibid. (1904), p. 142; New Bedford, "Minutes," June 15, 1905, June 30, 1905, February 5, 1906, March 5, 1906, March 19, 1906; *New Bedford Morning Mercury*, March 20, 1906, p. 8.

35. New Bedford, "Minutes," April 2, 1906, June 4, 1906, November 5, 1906, February 3, 1908; New Bedford, *School Report* (1906), pp. 113–15; ibid. (1908), pp. 74–75; ibid. (1909), pp. 71–72.

36. Massachusetts Board of Education, *Annual Report* (1914–1915), pp. 49–50; Francis Parker quoted in *Kindergarten Magazine* (April 1889), p. 381; Boston, *School Documents* (1914), no. 11, pp. 39–41.

37. *Kindergarten Magazine* XI (November 1898), 146–50. The front cover of this periodical in 1899–1900 carried as one of its goals, support for the social quarantine movement in kindergarten and elementary education.

38. Cambridge, *School Report* (1911), pp. 20–21, 29; Worcester, *School Report* (1911), p. 71; Boston Finance Commission, *Report* (1916), pp. 70–71. A number of cities still continued to think in terms of broader social issues, although it

is hard to gauge their actual involvement. See Springfield, *School Report* (1912), p. 60; Fall River, *School Report* (1916), p. 39; Worcester, *School Report* (1913), pp. 84–85.

39. In Lowell, for example, between 1910 and 1916 the superintendent of schools never mentioned kindergartens except to report that one had been added or dropped from the system. A little more than a decade earlier, Lowell's pride in its kindergartens was unbounded. (Lowell, *School Report* [1899], p. 56.)

7

Progressivism and Curriculum Differentiation: Special Classes in the Atlanta Public Schools, 1898–1923

Barry M. Franklin

Addressing the Atlanta Board of Education at its January 1898 meeting, Superintendent William F. Slaton called for the adoption of a regulation to "prevent children of dull minds and weak intellects from remaining 3 or 4 years in the same grade." Their presence, Slaton stated, was leading "to the annoyance of the teacher and detriment of the grade."[1] This call to deal with low achieving students was not the only recommendation to alter existing school policies and programs that the city's Board of Education heard that year or the next. In his annual reports for both 1898 and 1899, Slaton called on the Board of Education to introduce vocational education into Atlanta's course of study to meet the needs of high school students who, as he put it, "are bread-winners early in life and subsequently heads of families."[2] And during May 1899, the Board of Education received proposals urging it to introduce physical education into the curriculum and to establish kindergarten classes in several of the city's schools.[3] Here were the first stirrings of Progressive educational reform, which would lead in Atlanta, as in other urban school systems, to a differentiated program, including vocational education and guidance, kindergartens, junior high schools, and special classes for handicapped children.[4]

During the first two decades of the twentieth century, Atlanta school administrators and certain members of the Board of Education periodically grappled with the problem that Slaton had raised concerning low achieving children in the city's public schools. Unable to settle on an acceptable plan to address this problem in regular classrooms, the school administration would, in 1915, establish its first special classes for mentally defective children, children who were at least three years "behind in mental development."[5] By 1920, Atlanta would have seven special classes in its forty white grammar schools and, for a short time, two special classes in its fifteen black grammar schools.[6]

Progressive Era educational reformers, according to recent scholars, turned to curriculum differentiation as a bureaucratic strategy to respond to an array of external demands and pressures facing turn-of-the-century urban, centralized school systems.[7] Concerned about a school population that was becoming more diverse in class, ethnicity, and ability, reformers sought to design a more functional school program. Adapting such scientific management procedures as time study and job analysis to the task of selecting and organizing the curriculum, they created a school program composed of numerous specialized courses of study.[8] And by vocationalizing the curriculum, these reformers sought to produce a work force essential to industrial expansion and class divisions basic to a capitalist society.[9] Atlanta's attempt to establish its first special classes offers an instructive case for examining recent interpretations of curriculum differentiation.[10] This study of the establishment and operation of special classes in Atlanta demonstrates how important the school system's internal authorities were in driving this reform.[11]

The first concrete proposal for addressing the needs of Atlanta's retarded students was made in September 1908. Two teachers, a Miss Mitchell and a Miss Dunlap, suggested to the Board of Education that students "whose conduct and lessons for the day are satisfactory" be allowed to leave school at 1 P.M. while "slow and backward pupils and those with unprepared lessons" be held to 2 P.M., thereby giving them additional time to complete their work. Neither Superintendent William M. Slaton, who had succeeded his father, William F. Slaton, the year before, nor Assistant Superintendent Leonidas Landrum was willing to accept the recommendation. Slaton claimed that the proposal "would result in injury to all."[12]

The board, however, was more sympathetic to the idea. It asked the Committee on Schools and Teachers to study the matter and to make a report. Two months later, in November, the board accepted this committee's recommendation to dismiss the first grade at 1 P.M. daily. First grade teachers would then be freed from their classroom responsibilities and instead would work with "backward children" in the other grades until the regular dismissal time of 2:30 P.M. (2:00 P.M. in May and June).[13]

Judging by his rhetoric, Slaton was not opposed to all measures for dealing with low achieving students. In 1911, he urged the board to provide some assistance to "backward children."[14] And a year later, Slaton spoke to the board about the need to establish special classes for delinquent children. "It is not just," he said, "that fifty or sixty children in a class should be retarded by two or three refractory members whose parents through weakness or ignorance, have not taught and trained them at home to obey school authority."[15]

Although the board that year did open up a class for deaf children at Ashby Street School and appointed a teacher to work with tubercular children confined to the city's Battle Hill Sanitorium, it was not willing to establish special classes for low achieving children.[16] Two years later, in December 1914, the board, which had recently elected as its president Robert Guinn, a proponent of curriculum differentiation, authorized that several vacation schools be established the following summer. Such schools, the board hoped, would allow students who had failed during the regular year to make up their work and to allow able children to advance more rapidly.[17] The vacation schools, however, did not seem to address the difficulties of all children with achievement problems. In a report to the board after the conclusion of its first session in June 1915, the administrators of the vacation schools, Laura Smith and Ora Stamps, noted the problem created by "children whose mentality is deficient and whose presence in the school room hinders the instruction of normal children." They called on the board to establish special classes for these children. Landrum, who had replaced Slaton as superintendent that month, supported the proposal, and the board approved.[18]

Within several weeks, the city's first special class for mentally deficient white children was opened at Fair Street School.[19] At the end of its first month of operation, the principal, Gussie Brenner, reported to the board on the progress of the program. She noted that the class was instilling "backward children" with self-respect, helping those whose retardation was improvable to return to their regular grade, and preparing the "worst cases" to be self-sufficient. Evidently impressed with her report, the board authorized the establishment of two more special classes for white children by the end of the year, one at Boulevard School and the other at Lee Street School.[20]

For the most part, the explanations that other historians have advanced to account for the appearance of a differentiated curriculum do not help us very much in understanding why Atlanta established its special classes for mentally deficient children. It is not clear, for instance, that Atlanta introduced its special classes in response to the passage of a state compulsory attendance law. Atlanta's first special class was established in 1915, a full year before the state passed its first compulsory attendance law. And that law, which required children between eight and fourteen to attend school for four months a year through fourth grade, exempted, among others, children with mental defects, the very children for whom the special classes were ostensibly designed.[21] Even as late as 1920, when Atlanta had nine special classes in operation, Georgia had not passed legislation either requiring the education of the mentally retarded or providing financial support to those school districts that voluntarily established programs for these children.[22] Georgia's compulsory law may have served over time to bring more low achieving children into the schools, thus requiring the establishment of more of these special classes; nonetheless, this law does not seem to have been the impetus behind these classes.

Events surrounding Atlanta's special classes do not support the view that early twentieth-century school reformers turned to this innovation as a response to the needs and values of businessmen. It is true that the only segment of Atlanta's population that seemed to be interested in the special classes was drawn from the city's business and professional elite. But this elite did not offer a unified response to the issue of special classes. Since a number of business leaders were against special classes, it is not possible to link the business interest directly to their establishment.

The business community was divided into so-called progressive and conservative factions, and within these factions, it was further divided over the issue of special classes. The conservatives were primarily bankers, corporate leaders, and professionals who looked to Clark Howell, editor of the *Atlanta Constitution*, for leadership. The progressive group included, for the most part, lawyers, real estate agents, and insurance salesmen under the leadership of Hoke Smith, publisher of the *Atlanta Journal* and at various times during this period governor of Georgia and United States Senator. Although struggles were often couched in the rhetoric of reaction versus reform, hence the labels of conservative and progressive, what these factions actually fought about much of the time was control of the city's political apparatus and ultimately control over the Georgia Democratic party.[23]

Atlanta's school managers had ties to, or were part of, this business elite. But their association with either the conservative or progressive faction did not determine their position on special classes. For example, the Slatons and Leonidas Landrum tended to align with the city's conservatives, but they joined with some progressives in supporting special classes.[24] And other so-called progressives joined conservatives in opposing this reform. In June 1918, W. H. Terrell, an attorney and Board of Education member who often spoke for the city's conservatives, testified before a special committee of the Atlanta City Council, which was then investigating the schools, that "certain innovations" which the progressive school board president, Robert Guinn, advocated, increased costs while actually decreasing the efficiency of the schools' operation.[25] Speaking before the same committee, another attorney, Harvey Hatcher, who was usually a supporter of Guinn and who was chairman of the City Council's Finance Committee, attacked the special classes on the grounds of their cost. Thus, Hatcher's links to the progressive wing did not preclude him from joining conservatives in opposing special classes. The Finance Committee had actually threatened to abolish these classes early in 1918 when Laura Smith, who, as Primary Supervisor, was in charge of special education, requested a budget increase of one hundred dollars to purchase materials to introduce handwork into the special classes. It was only after Guinn intervened that the committee withdrew its threat.[26]

Whatever there was in the way of a struggle over special classes, and it was minimal, occurred within the city's business and professional elite. The issue never became one that pitted dominant against subordinate classes. The dominant classes were too divided to take a single stand, and the subordinate groups voiced no opinion about special classes. The city's black population, organized labor, and even teachers were virtually silent on the issue.[27]

What then provided the impetus for the establishment of special classes in Atlanta? First, special classes seemed to offer school administrators a way to maintain the common school ideal of accessibility in a changing society. Atlanta school bureaucrats, as did their counterparts in other cities, frequently spoke of the need for a widely accessible system of public schooling. In his 1911 annual report, Superintendent William M. Slaton echoed the sentiments of mid-nineteenth-century common school reformers in calling for the education of all of the city's youth on the grounds that "ignorance and the lack of moral training is the greatest curse of mankind."[28] Two years later, Board President Guinn called for a high school education for all of Atlanta's children in order to insure that they reach "the highest efficiency of which they are able."[29]

Achieving this accessibility was, however, always problematic in Atlanta. From the beginning of the city's school system in 1872, there were never enough classrooms for all the children who wished to attend. Double sessions and class sizes in excess of sixty children were a common feature of the city's schools.[30] Exacerbating this persistent overcrowding was the enrollment growth during the early years of the twentieth century. Between 1898 and 1915, statements of school administrators suggested that the city's schools were feeling the impact of an increasing number of troublesome children, as Atlanta's white, grammar school enrollment grew from 13,254 to 21,190 students, an increase of 67 percent.[31] The growing number of low achieving students forced into overcrowded classrooms made the work of the city's teachers more difficult.

It was evidently burdensome keeping these children in school. At its October 1914 meeting, the Board of Education received a letter from J. E. Ellis, a teacher at Grant Park School, concerning one of her students, who had, as she put it, an "epileptic fit." According to the letter, Grant Park's principal, Mrs. W. P. Davis, would not allow the child to return to school "because the presence of the child was liable to cause distraction in the exercise of the school." At the same meeting, the board also considered a letter from Belle Simpson, the teacher of the deaf class at Ashby Street School, requesting the removal of one Herbert Manning. "He disturbs the class by doing many unusual and unexpected things and continuously distracts the attention of the class and the work of the teacher." Voting to remove both children from the schools, board members stated that incidences such as these indicated that teachers faced a problem of accommodating certain "deficient and disabled children." At the suggestion of Guinn and two other members, a committee was appointed to study the problem, and the following month it proposed the introduction of vacation schools.[32] Establishing first vacation schools and then special classes offered a means whereby the city's schools could remain accessible as the student population became larger and more diverse. Although it was ultimately necessary to segregate low achieving children in special classes, the schools were still able to remain open to them. In creating these special classes, however, Atlanta's school managers were not just reacting to a need to make classrooms more manageable. They were initiating a reform that they believed would allow the schools, despite changing conditions, to remain true to their historic goal of being open to all children.[33]

In addition, Atlanta's school officials called for special classes to enhance their status as professionals and to advance their political agendas.[34] Atlanta's school managers were not the only educators to support special classes during this period. Superintendents in urban school systems throughout the nation made similar appeals. In his 1906 report to the St. Paul, Minnesota, Board of Education, Superintendent S. L. Heeter noted that certain children, "misfits," as he called them, "do not fit into any class." They needed, he went on to say, a separate class staffed by a teacher of "sympathy, tact, skill and courage with such optimism and personality, as would lead and inspire irregular boys and girls."[35] And three years later, Superintendent Stratton Brooks of Boston called for the establishment of special classes to minimize the harm that he believed was posed by the presence of "epileptics" and "others of physical peculiarity" in the regular classroom.[36]

These appeals to expand the school program by introducing special classes and other forms of curriculum differentiation were one phase of a larger effort during the first two decades of this century by an emerging corps of school administrators to legitimate the existence of their profession. By extolling the virtues of such bureaucratic solutions as special classes, these administrators were in effect creating an ideology extolling technical expertise that could justify their standing as a distinct professional specialty within the schools.[37] New programs, such as special classes and vocational education, provided the symbolic trappings of incipient professionalism.[38] Promoting special classes, however, served more than an ideological function. Once school systems introduced special classes, they then had to go out and hire teachers who had expertise in teaching low achieving children. And having such teachers in their employ required these school systems to hire specialized administrative personnel as supervisors. These appeals for special classes not only legitimated school administration as a profession, they actually built the profession.[39]

William M. Slaton used the issue of special classes to solidify his professional standing by linking himself with leading professionals in other cities. On at least two occasions, Slaton held up to the school board examples of cities that had established special classes as a means of spurring on reform. In January 1912, in calling on the board for the establishment of special classes for delinquent children, he noted that these classes were to be found in the "leading cities of the United States." And two months later upon returning from a meeting of the N.E.A.'s Department of Superintendence in St. Louis, he informed the board that this city, unlike Atlanta, provided special classes for deaf, mentally defective, and delinquent children.[40] Implicit in Slaton's remarks on both occasions was the message that if Atlanta wanted to become a progressive city, it, too, would have to establish special classes. Slaton's urgings were not unlike those of other similarly placed professionals in other spheres who were advancing reform. Just as these individuals looked to their counterparts in other cities for innovations, say to reformers in New York for the idea of the municipal research bureau or to those in Galveston for the idea of the commission form of government, so did Slaton look to school managers in St. Louis for the idea of the special class.[41] Thus, the drive for professionalization and the drive for special classes were mutually reinforcing. On the one hand, his support for special classes helped Slaton strengthen his professional standing. On the other hand, his enhanced public image as a progressive superintendent could advance his political agenda, which included special classes.

Robert Guinn was also able to use the issue of special classes to promote his political goals. Guinn came to the Board of Education as a political rival, in the Georgia Democratic party, of the Slaton family, particularly Governor John Slaton, Superintendent William M. Slaton's brother. Not unexpectedly, then, Guinn saw the superintendent as the main obstacle to the introduction of the progressive school reforms that he so favored. Almost immediately upon joining the board in 1914, Guinn set out to embarrass the superintendent by calling for an outside survey of the city's schools. Going further, he arranged with M. L. Brittain, State Superintendent of Public Instruction, to have the State Supervisor of Rural Schools, Celeste Parrish, who was a former student of John Dewey at the University of Chicago and a proponent of curriculum differentiation, conduct the study. Slaton in fact objected to the study on the grounds that "the board could not guard itself against wild statements and prejudices which might enter into a survey prepared by Commissioner Guinn."[42]

In her study, which took two weeks and included visits to approximately one-quarter of the city's white grammar schools and to Girls' High School, Parrish found little to approve of in Atlanta. She was particularly critical of the curriculum because it lacked the kind of connection between the school program and the demands of adult life that she believed typified the best of Progressivism: "In all the cities which have reached a high grade of educational efficiency, there is a distinct attempt to relate the work of the schools to the experience of the children, and to the social and industrial life of the city. The Atlanta course of study has been static for so many years that the city has outgrown it."[43] What was needed, according to Parrish's way of thinking, was a differentiated curriculum. She recommended the introduction of manual training and home economics in the grammar and secondary schools and the establishment of a kindergarten program. For low achieving and troublesome children, she suggested that Atlanta follow the example of other cities and establish vocational schools and special classes."[44]

Not satisfied with simply exposing the weaknesses of Atlanta's schools under Slaton's leadership, Guinn urged the board not to renew the superintendent's contract when it expired in June 1915. The city, Guinn argued, needed a superintendent with "progressive ideas" and "executive ability," qualities that he believed Slaton did not possess. Slaton, however, challenged Guinn's charge. Citing his support of numerous innovations in the city's schools, he noted his commitment to reform: "On my recommendation and advocacy, the department of medical inspection was added to the schools. Was that progressive? On my recommendation the Normal Training School was established to manufacture our own teachers out of our own house material. Was that progressive?"[45]

Guinn, however, prevailed and was able to muster a nine-to-three majority vote of the Board of Education to remove Slaton. Guinn's choice to replace Slaton was State Superintendent Brittain, who like Parrish had attended the University of Chicago and held similarly reformist views. Unable to convince Brittain to leave his elective office to come to Atlanta, Guinn arranged to have Landrum appointed as superintendent and then got Landrum to appoint another former University of Chicago student, Joseph Wardlaw, dean of the faculty of the State Normal School in Athens, as assistant superintendent. In 1917, after Landrum completed one term, the board replaced him with Wardlaw and then went on to create a new position for Landrum, that of business manager.[46] Under Landrum and Wardlaw, Guinn was able to establish the city's first special classes. Creating special classes went a long way toward augmenting the administrative capacities of Atlanta's public schools. These classes provided a mechanism by which administrators tried to keep the city's schools accessible in the face of a changing school population. And in promoting these classes and other forms of curriculum differentiation, Atlanta's school bureaucrats tried to advance their career and political goals.

Although the reform agenda rested on a desire to make the schools more accessible, it remains to be seen how effectively school officials achieved this goal. And it remains to be seen what, if any, relationship existed between curriculum differentiation and the growth of industrial capitalism. To answer these questions, we need to look beyond the political debate surrounding the creation of these classes and consider how these classes actually operated.

There was no distinct curriculum in Atlanta for the grammar school special classes apart from the regular elementary course of study. A 1928 newspaper account of the city's "ungraded classes," a designation adopted in 1924 to replace the term "special classes," noted that children were given "daily lessons in all elementary book work subjects."[47] The task of special class teachers, according to the article, was to involve students in activities that they would enjoy and at which they would succeed. Evidently, teachers in these classes varied the work in accordance with the child's particular ability while seeing to it that assignments were "concrete and practical."

The article then went on to describe two students enrolled in these classes. One, a boy, was unable to do the work of his fourth grade class and exhibited "atrocious" behavior. In the ungraded class, he was not only given work in reading, arithmetic, and geography, he was also involved in a number of practical activities, such as repairing toys for the Junior Red Cross and weaving a rug for his mother's Christmas present. "Since his placement," according to the article, "he has not been absent, nor would he think of leaving his happy schoolroom where his interest is stimulated along 'doing lines.' " A second student, a girl, did not complete grammar school until she was fourteen. Assigned to the ungraded class at Thomson Junior High School, she completed three years of "fine work" and was sent to Commercial High School to study home economics. "This girl, who could not master the regular course of study," the account concluded, "has been salvaged for society by special education."[48] As we might expect from a program supposedly driven by the goals of social efficiency, the mission of the special class was to keep these children in school in hopes of enhancing whatever social contributions they might ultimately make.

The curriculum for the city's junior high special or, as they later came to be called, ungraded classes reveals what those contributions were to be.

Atlanta opened its first junior high school special class in 1924 but did not specify the curriculum until a group of teachers developed a guidebook of suggested units in 1938.[49] Children in these classes spent two periods a day working on units that integrated social studies, English, and spelling to solve everyday problems concerning shelter, conservation, transportation, and vocations, to name a few topics. They then spent a period each in mathematics, practical science, handicraft, shop, home economics, and physical education or music.[50] In the vocations unit, which was designed to instill students with the "desire to be gainfully employed," children were encouraged to explore the possibility of entering such occupations as poultry raising, furniture repair, masonry, telegraph delivery, package wrapping, and industrial labor in meat packing plants, cotton mills, and clothing factories. The handicraft period was to involve the students in making projects that were of a "vocational nature." It was hoped that these activities would teach these children to construct "attractive, salable articles," including end tables, fruit and flower baskets, whisk brooms, chairs, luncheon mats, and sweaters.[51] The ultimate purpose of these special classes, then, appears to have been to keep low achieving students in school long enough to propel them into the unskilled or, at best, semiskilled occupations of the city's industrial work force. To determine how consistent this goal was with the needs of an emerging capitalist economy requires that we look at which students enrolled in the special classes and what happened to them while there.

Between 1921 and 1923, twenty-two of the approximately one hundred and twenty-five children in the city's special classes were enrolled in Lee Street School in Atlanta's West End neighborhood.[52] Ostensibly designed for children with retarded mental development, the policy of the Board of Education dictated that each student referred to the special class was to be given a Binet Test.[53] Yet, of the eighteen children for whom cumulative school records could be located, only one had a recorded I.Q. score.[54] That student, whom I will call John Bell, had an I.Q. of 64, a score that would, according to the practices of the day, lead to a placement in a special class such as the one at Lee Street.[55]

Born in 1911, Bell entered grammar school at age six. He failed to be promoted from the first grade, having earned an A in conduct, a C in language and composition, a D in arithmetic, and Es (failure) in reading and literature, spelling, and penmanship.[56] He repeated the first grade two more times without success. After his second attempt in 1920, he was promoted on Superintendent William F. Dykes's recommendation despite the fact that he earned Ds in language and composition, reading and literature, and penmanship. He then went on to repeat the second grade two times and was promoted to third grade at age ten. He evidently had extreme difficulty in this grade and, before completing it, was placed in Lee Street's special class.

There were two children who began their school careers in the special class and whose records indicate clear reasons for that placement. One, Victoria Poor, who entered the special class at age fourteen, was almost immediately recommended for placement in Ashby Street's deaf class. The other,

William Fews, entered the special class at Lee Street in 1916 at age nine, transferred to the Boulevard School special class the following year, and then left school for a period of three years. In 1921, he returned to Lee Street's special class at age fourteen, at which point his records indicate that he should be placed in a residential institution for the "feebleminded." There was a third student who began school in Lee Street's special class, but there is no indication of why he was placed there.

The remaining fourteen children were sent to the special class after having encountered problems in the regular grades. It is hard to pin down exactly what these problems were. Most of these children had repeated at least one, but often several, grades before being sent to the special class. There were, however, five children who successfully passed the first and second grades and sometime during the subsequent year were transferred to the special class. Interestingly enough, most of these children had received good grades in both conduct and effort.

Although it is difficult to draw conclusions from cumulative records that list the grades that children received without indicating anything about what actually happened in the classroom, these grades do tell us something. Some of these students did consistently earn grades that would seem to fit individuals who were three years behind in their mental development. Jane Richards, for example, always seemed to do poorly in her academic subjects. Although she was promoted to the second grade, she only earned Ds in her first grade courses in reading, spelling, history, and physiology/hygiene and Cs in arithmetic and penmanship. She then went on to repeat the second grade twice, failing on both occasions to be promoted. In her first attempt, she earned Es in composition, spelling, and arithmetic, while in her second, she earned Es in reading and composition. After her second failure, she was placed in the special class where she remained for the next four years. Her record was, in fact, quite similar to that of John Bell who, as was noted earlier, had an I.Q. of 64.

Most of the Lee Street special class children, however, received both good and poor grades, which would indicate a pattern of strengths and weaknesses that is uncharacteristic of the mentally defective. Julius Holt, for example, failed the second and fourth grades. Nonetheless, he had received an A in arithmetic in his first attempt at the second grade and a B in the same subject when he repeated the grade. Later, however, his arithmetic grades did decline. In the third grade, he earned a C in that subject and in the fourth, a D. In the year that he failed the fourth grade, which led him to be placed subsequently in the special class, Julius received Cs in reading and literature, spelling, history, and physiology/hygiene and Ds in composition, arithmetic, and geography. Similarly, John Wynne failed fourth grade, which led to his placement in the special class, but received Bs in penmanship, geography, and history, and Cs in conduct, effort, and literature. His only unsatisfactory grades were Ds in reading, spelling, and arithmetic.

The sketchy and incomplete information contained in the cumulative records of these students makes it impossible to say with certainty why these children were in the special class. The information that is available from Lee Street does suggest that these children were a heterogeneous group. Some, no doubt, were, or at least exhibited characteristics of, children with mental defects. Most, however, had a pattern of grades more characteristic of children whose low achievement was the result of such environmental deprivation as frequent absences, lack of interest, poor study habits, and inadequate parental supervision. These were children who were difficult to teach, and some may have been troublesome to manage.

As we might expect, it was not easy to keep the Lee Street special class students in school. Fourteen of the eighteen children for whom records could be located never completed the Lee Street program. Six of them left the special class after a year or two to go to work or because their parents left the city. It is not clear what happened to the other eight since there are no entries on their cumulative records after their assignment to the special class. It appears that these children dropped out of the special class somewhere along the way.

Four children did complete the Lee Street class and went on to attend the special class at Thomson Junior High School. Mat Hart and Eleanor Gross completed a year at Thomson and left. The other two students, John Bell and Herbert Anderson, completed three years at Thomson. Bell, who supposedly had a 64 I.Q., achieved a mixed record. His best grades were in his vocational subjects where he earned As in metal shop, printing, and electrical shop, a B in wood shop, and a C in drawing. His worst grades were in mathematics where he received two Cs and a D, English where he received a C and two Ds, and business practice where he earned a D. In art, science, and history, however, he earned Bs. Anderson was the only Lee Street special class student to attend high school. In 1930, at age nineteen, he entered the city's Technological High School, which offered a special industrial program for older students. There is no indication on his cumulative record as to what courses he took or whether he was ultimately graduated.

From the Lee Street data, it appears that Atlanta's special class was not particularly effective in enhancing the accessibility of the schools. It provided a place in the schools for low achieving children, but it could not hold them there. And at first glance, it appears that the class was not an effective instrument for producing the work force that the city's economy required. For the most part, white Atlantans, at least males, did not occupy unskilled and semi-skilled jobs. Only 20 percent of the white male population, according to the 1920 census, held jobs that would be so classified. Even when women are included, only 36 percent of the white population held unskilled and semi-skilled jobs. On the other hand, 78 percent of black males held these low level jobs.[57] What role was there for an educational enterprise that channeled white children to jobs that blacks appeared more likely to hold?

In fact, as events turned out, these special classes were useful vehicles for spurring onward processes of class formation corresponding to changes in the city's economy. The years after 1910 witnessed an occupational realignment in Atlanta. As the result of a combination of factors, including an economic downturn throughout the South that drove rural blacks and whites to the city, rising unemployment, and population growth, whites in Atlanta were gradually displacing blacks from jobs which they had once dominated.[58] In 1910, blacks held 75 percent of the over eleven thousand unskilled and semiskilled jobs that existed in Atlanta, while whites held 25 percent of these jobs. By 1920, the actual number of unskilled and semiskilled jobs had virtually doubled to over twenty-three thousand, while the share held by blacks was reduced to 65 percent. Whites, however, increased the proportion of these jobs which they held to 35 percent. Ten years later in 1930, the number of unskilled and semiskilled jobs increased by about five thousand with a slight shift in the black–white distribution. The proportion held by blacks was now 64 percent in comparison to the white proportion of 36 percent.[59]

Of the eighteen special class students for whom school records can be located, the majority had parents who were factory workers, carpenters, plumbers, or railroad engineers, while only a minority had parents who were businessmen or clerks. Using father's occupation as a measure of social class, it appears that about 58 percent of the Lee Street special class children came from working-class homes and about 41 percent from middle-class homes.[60] This was different from the composition of Lee Street's regular classes, where 43 percent of the children came from working-class homes and 56 percent came from middle-class homes.[61] From the Lee Street data, it would appear that Atlanta's special classes served as a vehicle for transforming low achieving white children of working-class backgrounds into an underclass that was ready to assume the unskilled and semiskilled jobs created by changes in the city's occupational structure. In recognition of the small number of special class students whose records are obtainable, this must of course be a speculative finding. Nonetheless, such a finding does explain how the initiatives of school managers taken in the interest of expanding state administrative capacities could ultimately serve the goal of business classes to perpetuate capitalist social relationships.[62]

Progressive Era school reform was one phase of a larger movement to provide an emerging American state with the capacities it needed at all levels to address the problems of twentieth-century urban, industrial society. One such problem was that of fulfilling the public school's historic mission to be widely accessible, while confronting a school population that was growing in size and diversity. These changes were bringing into early twentieth-century urban schools a larger number of low achieving, difficult to teach children. By establishing special classes, Atlanta school bureaucrats thought they could accommodate these children, albeit in segregated settings. Special classes also offered another benefit to Atlanta's school bureaucrats. They were able to use their support for these classes to promote their own professional identities and political agendas.

Special classes, however, neither held children in school nor offered them anything of much worth during the time that they were there. From the beginning, special classes were a flawed reform. Instead of maintaining the common school ideal of accessibility under changed conditions, these classes served to obscure how much early twentieth-century school reformers had departed from that ideal.[63]

NOTES

1. Atlanta Board of Education, *Minutes*, 6 Jan. 1898, 2: 522.

2. Atlanta Board of Education, *Twenty-seventh Annual Report*, 31 Dec. 1898, 52–53, and *Twenty-eighth Annual Report*, 31 Dec. 1899, 28.

3. Atlanta Board of Education, *Minutes*, 4, 23 May 1899, 3: 72, 80.

4. For illustrations of curriculum differentiation in Atlanta, see *Atlanta Constitution*, 13 Nov., 18 Dec. 1927, 1, 8, 22 Jan., 19 Feb., 11 Mar. 1928.

5. Atlanta Board of Education, *Minutes*, 29 June 1915, 6: 317; ibid., 30 July 1915, 6: 330; ibid., 22 June 1916, 7: 43.

6. Atlanta Board of Education, *School Directory*, 1920–1930. The two special classes for black children in existence in 1920, one at Carrie Steele School and the other at Pittsburg Night School, were closed the following year and replaced by two classes at Storrs School. The next year, however, those classes were also closed. There were no other special classes for black children until 1929. For a discussion of special education for blacks in Georgia, see Jane Vivian Mack Strong, "A Study of Educational Facilities Available to Atypical Negro and White Children in Georgia" (M.Ed. thesis, Atlanta University, 1949).

7. David L. Angus, Jeffrey E. Mirel, and Maris A. Vinovskis, "Historical Development of Age Stratification in Schooling," *Teachers College Record* 90 (Winter 1988): 211–36; David Tyack, *The One Best System: A History of American Urban Education* (Cambridge, 1974), 182–88.

8. Raymond E. Callahan, *Education and the Cult of Efficiency: A Study of the Social Forces That Have Shaped the Administration of the Public Schools* (Chicago, 1962), ch. 5; Edward A. Krug, *The Shaping of the American-High School, 1880–1920* (Madison, 1969), 304–27.

9. David John Hogan, *Class and Reform: School and Society in Chicago, 1880–1930* (Philadelphia, 1985), xx–xxv, 138–39, 228–35; Martin Carnoy and Henry M. Levin, *Schooling and Work in the Democratic State* (Stanford, 1985), 80–97.

10. Ira Katznelson and Margaret Weir, *Schooling for All: Class, Race, and the Decline of the Democratic Ideal* (New York, 1985), ch. 6; Wayne J. Urban, "Educational Reform in a New South City: Atlanta, 1890–1925," in *Education and the Rise of the New South*, ed. Ronald Goodenow and Arthur O. White (Boston, 1981), 114–30; Julia Wrigley, *Class Politics and Public Schools: Chicago, 1900–1950* (New Brunswick, 1982), Ch. 3.

11. The definition of the state used in this essay derives from Theda Skocpol, "Bringing the State Back In: Strategies of Analysis in Current Research," in *Bringing the State Back In*, ed. Peter B. Evans, Dietrich Rueschemeyer, and Theda Skocpol (Cambridge, 1985), 3–37; and Martin Carnoy, *The State and Political Theory* (Princeton, 1984). For a discussion of the role of the state as an actor in policy formation, see Skocpol, "Bringing the State Back In." I am indebted to Joseph Tropea for the suggestion that I look at special classes from this vantage point. For his attempt to use a state-centered interpretation for examining the development of special classes, see Joseph L. Tropea, "Bureaucratic Order and Special Children: Urban Schools, 1890s–1940s," *History of Education Quarterly* 27 (Spring 1987): 29–53; and idem, "Bureaucratic Order and Special Children: Urban Schools, 1950s–1960s," ibid. (Fall 1987): 339–61.

12. Atlanta Board of Education, *Minutes*, 24 Sep. 1908, 4: 273.

13. Ibid., 21 Nov. 1908, 4: 285; *Atlanta Constitution*, 26 Nov. 1908.

14. Atlanta Board of Education, *Minutes*, 26 Jan. 1911, 5: 123.

15. Ibid., 4 Jan. 1912, 5: 286.

16. Ibid., 27 June 1912, 5: 356; ibid., 25 July 1912, 5: 361; *Atlanta Constitution*, 28 June, 27 Sep. 1912.

17. Atlanta Board of Education, *Minutes*, 15 Dec. 1914, 6: 246–47; ibid., 8 June 1915, 6: 295.

18. Ibid., 29 June 1915, 6: 317.

19. Ibid., 30 July 1915, 6: 330.

20. Ibid.; *Atlanta Constitution*, 31 July 1915; Atlanta Board of Education, *School Directory*, 1915–1919, 19, 39.

21. United States Department of the Interior, *Report of the Commissioner of Education for the Year Ended June 30, 1916* (Washington, D.C., 1916), 24.

22. Robert Kunzig, *Public School Education of Atypical Children*, United States Department of Interior, Office of Education Bulletin no. 10 (Washington, D.C., 1931), 14, 25.

23. David N. Plank, "Educational Reform and Organizational Change: Atlanta in the Progressive Era" (Unpublished manuscript, 1987), 6–7; David N. Plank and Paul E. Peterson, "Does Urban Reform Imply Class Conflict? The Case of Atlanta's Schools," in *The Social History of American Education*, ed. B. Edward McClellan and William J. Reese (Urbana, Ill., 1988), 217–18; Paul E. Peterson, *The Politics of School Reform, 1870–1940* (Chicago, 1985), 86.

24. Urban, "Educational Reform," 118–19; idem, "Progressive Education in the Urban South: The Reform of the Atlanta Schools, 1914–1918," in *The Age of Urban Reform: New Perspectives on the Progressive Era*, ed. Michael H. Ebner and Eugene M. Tobin (Port Washington, 1977), 137–38.

25. Atlanta City Council, "Evidence and Proceedings before a Special Committee of Five, Appointed under a Resolution of City Council," 12 June 1918, 386–89 (located in Office of City Clerk, Atlanta).

26. Ibid., 263, 316–17.

27. I examined on a daily basis the *Atlanta Independent*, Atlanta's principal black newspaper, between 1916 and 1925 and the *Journal of Labor*, the official newspaper of the Atlanta Federation of Trades, between 1914 and 1921, and found no mention in either paper of low achieving children or special classes. I only found one reference to special classes in the papers of the Atlanta Public School Teachers' Association. At the February 1920 meeting of the Association's Board of Directors, Gussie Brenner, principal of Fair Street School, noted the need for a "centrally located" facility to provide for the city's handicapped children. See Atlanta Public School Teachers' Association, Directors' Meeting, Feb. 1920, folder 3, box 2072, Atlanta Education Association Collection, Southern Labor Archives, Special Collections Department, Georgia State University.

28. Atlanta Board of Education, *Minutes*, 4 Jan. 1912, 5: 288.

29. Ibid., 8 Apr. 1914, 6: 147–48.

30. Melvin W. Ecke, *From Ivy Street to Kennedy Center: Centennial History of the Atlanta Public School System* (Atlanta, 1972), 14, 16–17, passim; *Atlanta Constitution*, 25 Oct. 1914, 3, 4, 7 Feb. 1915.

31. Ecke, *From Ivy Street*, 452–53 (Appendix B).

32. Atlanta Board of Education, *Minutes*, 22 Oct. 1914, 6: 228–29; *Atlanta Constitution*, 23 Oct. 1914.

33. For a discussion of how school reformers saw curriculum differentiation as a means of reconciling the public school's historic democratic goal of accessibility with the demands of a capitalist economy for selectivity in admissions, see David F. Labaree, *The Making of an American High School: The Credentials Market and the Central High School of Philadelphia, 1838–1939* (New Haven, 1988), 7–8, 70–72, 161–62, 173–77.

34. Margaret Weir and Theda Skocpol note that "government officials (or aspiring politicians) are quite likely to take a new initiative, conceivably well ahead of social demands, if existing state capacities can be readily adapted or reworked to do things that will bring advantages to them in their struggles with competitive political forces." See Margaret Weir and Theda Skocpol, "State Structures and the Possibilities for 'Keynesian' Responses to the Great Depression in Sweden, Britain, and the United States," in *Bringing the State Back In*, ed. Evans, Reueschemeyer, and Skocpol, 115.

35. St. Paul Board of School Inspectors, *Forty-seventh and Forty-eighth Annual Reports of the Board of School Inspectors of the City of St. Paul*, 16 June 1906, 67.

36. Boston Public Schools, *Annual Report of the Superintendent*, School Document no. 13, July 1909, 15.

37. Callahan, *Education and the Cult of Efficiency*, ch. 8; David Tyack and Elizabeth Hansot, *Managers of Virtue: Public School Leadership in America, 1820–1980* (New York, 1982), 106–14.

38. For a discussion of the symbolic role of educational policy in legitimizing the educational professions, see Herbert M. Kliebard, "Curriculum Policy as Symbolic Action: Connecting Education with the Workplace" (Paper presented at the annual meeting of the American Educational Research Association, San Francisco, Calif., 27 Mar. 1989).

39. Tyack, *One Best System*, 185–86.

40. Atlanta Board of Education, *Minutes*, 1 Jan. 1912, 5: 286; ibid., 28 Mar. 1912, 5: 309; *Atlanta Constitution*, 1 Jan. 1912.

41. Martin Schiesl, *The Politics of Efficiency: Municipal Administration and Reform in America, 1880–1920* (Berkeley, 1977), chs. 6–7.

42. *Atlanta Constitution*, 27 Feb. 1914; Urban, "Progressive Education in the Urban South," 132–33; Charles Strickland, "Parrish, Celeste Susannah," in *Notable American Women*, ed. Edward T. Jones, Janet Wilson-Jones, and Paul Boyer (Cambridge, 1971), 3: 18–20.

43. Celeste S. Parrish, *Survey of the Atlanta Public Schools* (1914; reprint, Atlanta, 1973), 22.

44. Ibid., 27.

45. *Atlanta Constitution*, 25 Feb. 1915.

46. Ecke, *From Ivy Street*, 107–109; *Atlanta Constitution*, 6, 29 June 1915; *Atlanta Journal*, 29 June 1915; Dorothy Orr, *A History of Education in Georgia* (Chapel Hill, 1950), 387.

47. *Atlanta Constitution*, 25 Mar. 1928.

48. Ibid.

49. Atlanta Public Schools, *Curriculum Suggestions for Ungraded Classes—Junior High Schools* (Atlanta, 1938).

50. Ibid., 32–33.

51. Ibid., 41–44.

52. PTA Association, Lee Street School Enrollment, 1921–22, 1922–23, box 2, Lee Street School Collection, Atlanta Historical Society; George D. Strayer and

N. L. Engelhardt, *Report of the Survey of the Public Schools of Atlanta, Georgia* (New York, 1921–22), 2: 117.

53. Atlanta Board of Education, *Minutes,* 27 July 1916, 7: 59.

54. This information could, of course, have been recorded elsewhere, but the manager of the Atlanta Public Schools Record Center was unaware of the existence of any other records for these students.

55. To protect the identity of the Lee Street special class students, I have given them pseudonyms that indicate their gender. For a discussion of the meaning of the scores on this first version of the Stanford-Binet Test, see Lewis M. Terman, *The Measurement of Intelligence: An Explanation of and a Complete Guide for the Use of the Stanford Revision and Extension of the Binet-Simon Intelligence Scale* (Boston, 1916), ch. 5.

56. In 1914, the Atlanta Board of Education adopted the following grading system: A (excellent), 90–100; B (good), 80–89; C (satisfactory), 70–79; D (fair), 60–69; E (unsatisfactory), below 60. In 1918, the board introduced a new grading system: A (excellent), 90–100; B (good), 80–89; C (fair), 70–79; D (unsatisfactory), below 70. See Ecke, *From Ivy Street,* 101, 129.

57. U.S. Department of Commerce, Bureau of the Census, *Fourteenth Census of the United States, 1920: Population* (Washington, D.C., 1922), 4: 1053–55.

58. James D. Anderson, *The Education of Blacks in the South, 1860–1935* (Chapel Hill, 1988), 229–31.

59. U.S. Department of Commerce, *Fourteenth Census, 1920: Population,* 1053–55; *Thirteenth Census of the United States, 1910: Population* (Washington, D.C., 1913), 4: 536; *Fifteenth Census of the United States, 1930: Occupations by States* (Washington, D.C., 1933), 391–93.

60. The cumulative records of thirteen of the Lee Street special class students listed the occupations of their fathers. I categorized those occupations according to Thernstrom's Socio-Economic Ranking of Occupations as follows: high white collar-owner of a furniture factory (1 child); low white collar—foreman (1), insurance agent (1), postman (1), shipping clerk (1), skilled-railroad engineer (1), carpenter (2), plumber (1), semiskilled/unskilled—packer (1), textile worker (2), waiter (1). I combined semiskilled and unskilled because it was not possible to tell from the information on the cumulative record in which of these categories the occupations fell. See Stephan Thernstrom, *The Other Bostonians: Poverty and Progress in the American Metropolis, 1880–1979* (Cambridge, 1973), 289–302 (Appendix B). Although this data set is exceedingly small, I have decided to report the results. I am doing so because after three years of searching records in Atlanta, I have not been able to identify any other special children.

61. To determine the class background of children from Lee Street's regular classes, I selected every fifth unduplicated name for which school cumulative records could be located from the 1921–22 class roster of 591 children and from the 1922–23 class roster of 568 children. Using Thernstrom's Socio-Economic Ranking of Occupations to categorize these students, I found that 15 (12.1%) of the children's fathers held high white collar occupations; 55 (44.4%), low white collar occupations; 31 (25%), skilled occupations; and 23 (18.5%), semiskilled/unskilled occupations. For the population of Atlanta, I again used Thernstrom's rankings with the occupations of white males reported in the 1920 census. This analysis indicated that 6,349 (16%) of white males held high white collar occupations; 17,728 (44.6%), low white collar occupations; 7,511 (18.9%), skilled occupations; and 8,160 (20.5%), semiskilled/unskilled occupations.

62. For a discussion from a Marxist vantage point of how the initiative of state bureaucrats may be independent of the interests of business classes yet ultimately advance capital accumulation, see Fred Block, "The Ruling Class Does Not Rule: Notes on the Marxist Theory of the State," *Socialist Revolution* 7 (May 1977): 6–28.

63. For a discussion of how Progressive Era school reforms undercut the ideals of the common school movement, see William J. Reese, "Public Schools and the Common Good," *Educational Theory* 38 (Fall 1988): 431–40.

PART THREE

POLICIES AND POLITICS
IN URBAN SCHOOLS, 1900–1940

Rapid urban development ushered in a new political atmosphere, and this helped to shape urban education during the opening decades of the twentieth century. The vast school systems that appeared in American cities entailed a complex array of financial and ideological relationships between various elements of the urban polity. As noted earlier, school leaders often looked to the business community for ideas and advice about how to efficiently manage their rapidly growing educational enterprises. This did not mean, however, that the wealthy and powerful elites who represented the commercial interests in most cities were always favorably disposed toward the schools. When financial pressures became acute during economic slowdowns, or businessmen objected to certain curricular innovations, heated conflicts often burst into the forefront of public discourse over schooling.

There were other interests with a stake in the urban schools, however. One such group was the teachers who worked in them. As school systems grew in size and complexity, the teachers organized, at first in rather loose associations but eventually in the first teacher unions, precursors to today's school-based labor organizations. City teachers bore the brunt of conflicts over money and curricular reform, and they sometimes took it upon themselves to identify the needs of the schools. These women and men agitated for greater resources and curricular reforms, along with traditional bread and butter issues of better pay, pensions, and other benefits. Of course, the residents of the cities, the consumers of education, often voiced strong opinions about financial issues related to public education and curricular questions as well. With urban growth, cities became fragmented along class and ethnic lines, and different social and economic status groups often expressed quite divergent views with regard to public education. During times of public debate over education, all of these voices could rise together in a great cacophony over the fate of the schools. Such conditions periodically made a very complicated political setting for determining the fate of public education in the nation's largest cities.

The chapters in this part of book examine these questions in three different cities. The first is Marjorie Murphy's study of Chicago teachers and their quest for improved financial support for the city's public schools. It is a story of considerable drama, focusing on the bold and tireless efforts of Margaret Haley, the fiery and confrontational leader of the Chicago Teachers Federation, the first organization of its kind in the country. Haley and her allies accused major corporations of avoiding tax payments to the Board of Education, igniting a storm of controversy about issues ranging from the civic responsibility of the business community to the proper role of teachers in determining fiscal policy issues for the schools. Chicago was a famously corrupt town even at the turn of the century, and its commercial elites were especially adept at making under-handed arrangements to dispense with tax obligations and other civic duties. Murphy's essay outlined the decades of conflict that swirled around the schools as a consequence, as some of the city's most powerful men did battle with the teachers, ultimately attacking on their status as workers and an interested party to the future of the schools. The advent of the economic crisis brought on by the Great Depression revealed the inherent weakness of Chicago's system for supporting public education, resulting in thousands of teachers losing their jobs or enduring payless paydays while tax reform shifted a larger share of the support for public schooling to residential taxpayers. As Murphy has pointed out, this put in place the conditions for a new set of tensions in the urban polity, one that eventually served to pit educators against the working-class parents of the children they instructed. This would prove to be an especially important dynamic in decades to come.

The next essay concerns quite a different problem in the politics of education during this era. Standardized testing is a feature of modern schools that many take for granted today, but early in the twentieth century it was a new and somewhat controversial facet of the educational system. Judith Raftery has examined the process by which the earliest intelligence and achievement tests were adopted in the Los Angeles public schools. One of the most critical issues was the district's growing population of Mexican students. In the 1920s these tests represented a new form of technology for measuring the differences between various groups of students, one seemingly well suited to the predilections of system bureaucrats interested in efficiently delivering the appropriate forms of instruction to students of diverse "abilities."

Raftery found, however, that the teachers in Los Angeles schools were not always receptive to the introduction of such measures, and often questioned the utility of these tests and their effects on various groups of children in the schools. This was a different form of politics in education, a subtle but effective resistance on the part of educators to policies and measures promulgated by a growing corps of university experts and central office administrators. Recognizing the flaws in the instruments then being introduced, teachers worked hard to subvert the intentions of the emerging testing regime. In particular, they sought assessments that were sensitive to students' cultural backgrounds. In the course of her research, Raftery uncovered a number of interesting findings about group testing differences in Los Angeles, including those concerning Black children, some of which were seemingly quite contrary to contemporary expectations. She gives voice to the classroom teachers who looked with skepticism on many of the ideas and policies of the educational leaders and reformers of the day. This is a dimension of the politics of schooling in urban education systems that has too often been overlooked in other studies.

The third chapter of this section considers the question of fiscal retrenchment in public education, along with the political conflicts that it seems to invariably entail. In this prize-winning essay, Jeffrey Mirel has examined the political impact of the Great Depression on the Detroit schools. As he noted, this setting provides a unique opportunity to examine the political forces then concerned with the schools. In undertaking a study of these elements, he highlighted certain of the themes suggested in other chapters. Perhaps the most important of his findings concerned the key role of urban commercial groups. During the 1930s, the business community's skepticism about the growing expenditure of public education, especially in the larger cities, came into the forefront of public debates about the future of the schools. These debates not only concerned financial questions of the system's solvency, but also extended to curricular questions. Business elites may have served as important sources of guidance and support for the early captains of the large systems, but they abruptly became education's sharpest critics when confronted with a fiscal crisis. Interestingly, Mirel argued that it was the consumers of educational services, particularly those in working-class neighborhoods, who became the schools' greatest supporters in these conflicts. Altogether, it was a telling time of conflict and debate, and one that would eventually lead to a new political alignment in support of public education. As Mirel has suggested, the conflicts of the depression era helped to set the stage for educational politics of the postwar period.

ADDITIONAL READING

The literature on this period overlaps substantially with the citations provided for the later nineteenth century, as the two periods are often discussed together. David Tyack's *The One Best System* (1974) and Raymond Callahan's *Education and the Cult of Efficiency* (1962), cited in the preceding section, both provide extensive treatments of the issues discussed above (although neither discusses the Great Depression in any depth). The same can be said for William J. Reese, *Power and the Promise of School Reform* (1986), David Labaree, *The Making of an American High School* (1988), and Paul Peterson, *The Politics of Urban School Reform, 1870–1940* (1985), also cited in the previous section. Leadership issues are discussed in David B. Tyack and Elisabeth Hansot, *Managers of Virtue: Public School Leadership in America, 1820–1980* (1982) (also cited earlier). For additional perspectives on the urban politics of era, see Ira Katznelson, and Margaret Weir, *Schooling for All: Class, Race, and the Decline of the Democratic Ideal* (New York: Basic Books, 1985), Paul C. Violas, *The Training of the Urban Working Class: A History of Twentieth-Century American Education* (Chicago: Rand McNally, 1978), Barbara Berman, "Business Efficiency, American Schooling, and the Public School Superintendency: A Reconsideration of the Callahan Thesis" *History of Education Quarterly* 1983 23(3): 297–321, and William J. Reese, "The Control of Urban School Boards During the Progressive Era: A Reconsideration" *Pacific Northwest Quarterly* 1977 68(4): 164–174. On the Great Depression, see David B. Tyack, Robert Lowe, and Elisabeth Hansot, *Public Schools in Hard Times: The Great Depression and Recent Years* (Cambridge: Harvard University Press, 1984).

For studies of particular cities, see Jeffrey Mirel, *The Rise and Fall of an Urban School System: Detroit, 1907–81* (Ann Arbor: University of Michigan Press, 1993), David John Hogan, *Class and Reform: School and Society in Chicago, 1880–1930* (Philadelphia: University of Pennsylvania Press, 1985), Julia Wrigley, *Class Politics and Public Schools: Chicago, 1900–1950* (New Brunswick: Rutgers University Press, 1982), Ronald D. Cohen, *Children of the Mill: School and Society in Gary, Indiana, 1906–1960* (Bloomington: Indiana University Press, 1990), Ronald D. Cohen and Raymond A. Mohl, *The Paradox of Progressive Education: The Gary Plan and Urban Schooling* (Port Washington, NY: Kennikat, 1979), Judith Rosenberg Raftery, *Land of Fair Promise: Politics and Reform in Los Angeles Schools, 1885–1941* (Stanford: Stanford University Press, 1992), Bryce E. Nelson, *Good Schools: The Seattle Public School System, 1901–1930* (Seattle: University of Washington Press, 1988), Diane Ravitch and Ronald K. Goodenow, eds., *Educating an Urban People: The New York City Experience* (New York: Columbia University, Teachers College Press, 1981), Jean Anyon, *Ghetto Schooling: A Political Economy of Urban Educational Reform* (New York, Teachers College Press, 1997), William J. Reese, " 'Partisans of the Proletariat': The Socialist Working Class and the Milwaukee Schools, 1890–1920" *History of Education Quarterly* 1981 21(1): 3–50, and David A. Gamson, "District Progressivism: Rethinking Reform in Urban School Systems, 1900–1928" *Paedagogica Historica* 2003 39(4): 417–434. On a particular reform, consult Kenneth M. Gold, *School's In: The History of Summer Education in American Public Schools* (New York: Peter Lang, 2002), and Gold's article about a Southern city, "What Did You Flunk? Summer Schools and the Race for Promotions in Richmond, Virginia, 1911–31" *Virginia Magazine of History and Biography* 2002 110(3): 339–376.

On urban teachers at this time, the literature is nearly as expansive. See, for instance, Kate Rousmaniere, *City Teachers: Teaching and School Reform in Historical Perspective* (New York: Teachers College Press, 1997), Marjorie Murphy, *Blackboard Unions: The AFT and the NEA, 1900–1980* (Ithaca, NY: Cornell University Press, 1990), and Wayne Urban, *Why Teachers Organized* (Detroit: Wayne State University Press, 1982), along with Ruth Jacknow, *My Daughter, the Teacher* (New Brunswick, NJ: Rutgers University Press, 1993), Doris Hinson Pieroth, *Seattle's Women Teachers of the Interwar Years: Shapers of a Livable City* (Seattle: University of Washington Press, 2004), Victoria-María MacDonald, "The Paradox of Bureaucratization: New Views on Progressive Era Teachers and the Development of a Woman's Profession" *History of Education Quarterly* 1999 39(4): 427–453, Paula O'Connor,

"Grade-school Teachers Become Labor Leaders: Margaret Haley, Florence Rood, and Mary Barker of the AFT" *Labor's Heritage* 1995 7(2): 4–17, Kate Rousmaniere, "Being Margaret Haley, Chicago, 1903" *Paedagogica Historica* 2003 39(1–2): 5–18, Janet A. Nolan, "Irish-American Teachers and the Struggle over American Urban Public Education, 1890–1920: A Preliminary Look" *Records of the American Catholic Historical Society of Philadelphia* 1992 103(3–4): 13–22, Kyle E. Ciani, "Training Young Women in the 'Service' of Motherhood: Early Childhood Education at Detroit's Merrill-Palmer School, 1920–1940" *Michigan Historical Review* 1998 24(1): 103–132, Kate Rousmaniere, "Teachers' Work and the Social Relations of School Space in Early-Twentieth-Century North American Urban Schools" *Historical Studies in Education* 1996 8(1): 42–64, Marta Danylewycz and Alison Prentice, "Teachers, Gender, and Bureaucratizing School Systems in Nineteenth Century Montreal and Toronto" *History of Education Quarterly* 1984 24(1): 75–100, and Cecilia Reynolds and Harry Smaller, "Ontario School Teachers: A Gendered View of the 1930s" *Historical Studies in Education* 1994 6(3): 151–169.

On immigrant education in American cities, see Joel Perlmann, *Ethnic Differences: Schooling and Social Structure among the Irish, Italians, Jews and Blacks in an American City, 1880–1935* (New York: Cambridge University Press, 1989), and James W. Sanders, *The Education of an Urban Minority: Catholics in Chicago, 1833–1965* (New York: Oxford University Press, 1977). More specialized studies include Timothy L. Smith, "Immigrant Social Aspirations and American Education, 1880–1930" *American Quarterly* 1969 21(3): 523–543, Michael R. Olneck and Marvin Lazerson, "The School Achievement of Immigrant Children, 1900–1930" *History of Education Quarterly* 1974 14(4): 453–482, John L. Rury, "Urban Structure and School Participation: Immigrant Women in 1900" *Social Science History* 1984 8(3): 219–242.

On African American urban education in the early twentieth century, see Vincent P. Franklin, *The Education of Black Philadelphia: The Social and Educational History of a Minority Community, 1900–1950* (Philadelphia, University of Pennsylvania Press, 1979), Judy Jolley Mohraz, *The Separate Problem: Case Studies of Black Education in the North, 1900–1930* (Westport, CT: Greenwood, 1979), Michael Homel, *Down from Equality: Black Chicagoans and the Public Schools, 1920–1940* (Urbana: University of Illinois Press, 1984), Lillian S. Williams, "Community Educational Activities and the Liberation of Black Buffalo, 1900–1930" *Journal of Negro Education* 1985 54(2): 174–188, and William B. Thomas, "Schooling as a Political Instrument of Social Control: School Response to Black Migrant Youth in Buffalo, New York, 1917–1940" *Teachers College Record* 1985 86(4): 579–592.

For discussion of the Great Depression, see David Tyack, Robert Lowe and Elisabeth Hansot, *Public Schools in Hard Times: The Great Depression and Recent Years* (Cambridge, MA: Harvard University Press, 1984).

8

Taxation and Social Conflict: Teacher Unionism and Public School Finance in Chicago, 1898–1934

Marjorie Murphy

Increasing school attendance and shifting tax burdens in Chicago spawned a fiscal crisis that grew throughout the late nineteenth century and culminated in the collapse of public schools during the "payless paydays" of the 1930s. The actors pitted against each other in the struggle over tax policy were newly unionized teachers, who flaunted their affiliation with labor and the working class, and a loose coalition of attorneys representing railroad, utility, bank, and real estate interests. The stalemate created on the floor of the Illinois General Assembly and in the courts of law eventually triggered, during the Depression of the 1930s, the mechanism for the collapse of urban public finance.

Underlying the crisis was a sudden shift in working-class life. Workers in America, once with only their labor to sell in a progressively mechanizing, specializing, and expanding economy, began at the turn of the century purchasing homes and sending their children to school in record numbers. As the financial demands of schools grew, there was a tremendous strain on the urban tax structure. In Chicago, the burden of support fell increasingly on the new homeowners. As the sensitive issue of higher taxes emerged, tensions between unionized teachers and other workers grew. The traditional, albeit fragile, trade union support for public education became fragmented along lines of self-interest.

This essay explores four phases of the conflict: (1) the passage of revenue laws that allowed serious tax evasion; (2) the dramatic tax investigation led by the Chicago Teachers' Federation; (3) the shift among working-class Chicagoans toward greater school attendance and home ownership; and (4) the teachers' tax crusade of the 1920s, which, ironically, paved the way for complete urban financial collapse in the Great Depression.

The seeds for the great fiscal crisis of the 1930s were sown in 1898, when the twenty-one members of the Chicago Board of Education debated the priorities of the "educational" and "building" accounts of the school system budget. Confronted by powerfully organized advocates, the politically appointed board made concessions to each group, and the resulting policy proved both contradictory and doomed to failure.

The "educational account" of the School Board budget was represented by the public school teachers, who had organized the Chicago Teachers' Federation (CTF) in 1897. These elementary school teachers, mostly women, were pledged to protect the pension system, secure better pay, and "study parliamentary law."[1] In the first year, the CTF collected the signatures of more than 3,500 teachers on a petition for salary increases, their first in twenty years. Reluctantly, the Board succumbed to the well-publicized campaign and agreed to a new salary schedule.[2]

Almost simultaneously, the other major power group—represented by the Buildings and Grounds Committee of the Board of Education—persuaded the eagerly agreeable full Board that school construction funds (the "building account") should become a separate tax item, independent from the rest of the expenses of the school system. The Buildings and Grounds Committee also advocated legislative remedies that would grant its members the power of eminent domain in acquiring building sites for new schools. By agreeing to support those changes in taxation and administration—embodied in School Law amendments of 1898 and 1899—the Chicago Board of Education gave advocates of building expansion first shot at school revenues and thus invited thirty years of fighting with city teachers.[3]

Formerly, the Buildings and Grounds Committee paid exorbitant prices for school sites, many of which were newly acquired by real estate speculators who then took advantage of the public debates that preceded each purchase. Expecting opposition from real estate agents in the bid for eminent domain, members of the Buildings and Grounds Committee sought the aid of the Chicago Civic Federation.[4]

The Federation consisted of young businessmen and professionals who devoted themselves to centralizing urban decision-making, eliminating the worst excesses of city politics, and generally providing social stability for a new corporate society. Under the guidance of the Civic Federation, the Buildings and Grounds Committee built an alliance with leaders in the real estate business, who were looking for assistance in their plans for a more favorable assessment process.[5]

The Revenue Act of 1898, reflecting the growing recognition of the needs of urban finance, reorganized Cook County as a single tax unit, in place of the rural division of townships that prevailed in the rest of the state. It also recognized the vast growth of the metropolitan area through the annexation of a vast amount of territory, two-thirds its previous size, in 1889. Furthermore, it provided for the County Board's review and possible reduction of existing tax rates for all purposes except "school building." A School Law amendment passed at the same session set maximum Chicago school taxes as no more than 2.5 percent for educational and 2.5 percent for building purposes.[6]

The construction of urban public school buildings made possible by the 1898 Revenue Act remains the greatest public works project of the nineteenth and early twentieth centuries. Contracts awarded by the powerful Buildings and Grounds Committee, with the approval of the Chicago City Council, provided jobs for hundreds of Chicago construction workers. Committee members eschewed the practice of general contracting, instead taking individual bids for each project, and in the myriad of contracts that resulted, the considerable favoritism was obscured by the paper flow alone.

A group of real estate developers, certain municipal reformers, and City Hall interests were meanwhile working for passage of a law that would prevent taxes from becoming "unreasonable." The resulting bill, named for its sponsor State Senator Niels Juul of Chicago, limited property taxes to 5 percent of assessed valuation. Real estate agents claimed that such a limitation would raise property levels in a depressed market. More significant, the Juul Law gave special authority to the Cook County assessors for adjusting tax rates for meeting the 5 percent limitation. (A provision of the 1898 Revenue Act granting similar extra authority to Cook County had been declared unconstitutional in 1900 as "special legislation." The language of the Juul Law was consistently upheld by the courts, however.)[7]

An exemption to the Juul Law's 5 percent limitation was provided for "school building purposes" in cities exceeding 100,000 population. The educational account levy was not exempted. The Juul Law was designed to avoid unreasonable taxation, but it quickly attracted unreasonable amendments.[8]

Illinois' revenue laws were amended at nearly every session of the general assembly after 1898, and the power struggle between Chicago's educational and building accounts continued. The complexity of the revenue laws, especially the Juul Law, served in turn as an alibi for tax evasion. The report of a 1910 tax commission criticized the law as "highly complicated" but failed to offer a solution.[9] Four years later, tax historian Robert Murray Haig commented:

> Even the officials who administer it [the Juul Law] . . . often fail to understand it. This at least seems to be the best explanation for illegal rates extended so frequently in Illinois. Rates above the limits prescribed by law are levied annually in almost every county of the state, and railways and other large taxpayers find it to their advantage to employ attorneys to investigate the rates levied and secure abatements.[10]

Tax evasion produced a shrinking tax base in Cook County. The building account, exempt from the tax limit imposed by the 1898 Revenue Act and the later Juul Law, suffered no setback, while the Chicago Board of Education announced huge deficits in the educational account because of rising instructional and maintenance costs. Fewer teachers were hired, and promised salary increases were postponed. Angered by the Board's action and knowing full well that large corporate interests evaded taxes while construction contracts bolstered political fortunes in City Hall, the Chicago Teachers' Federation led the first serious investigation of the state's taxing machinery.[11]

Teachers chose to investigate in muckraking style rather than by working through the legislative agenda because, as women, they had no political clout other than the right to petition and the right to bring suit in the courts. Legislative lobbying in their behalf was only occasionally successful because they controlled no votes. In 1895, for example, legislators had helped teachers gain state matching funds for their pension system, but only in response to a grass roots campaign. Those gains were precarious gifts, not well-earned rights, as the teachers learned in later years. In 1901, as teachers pursued their tax investigations through the State Board of Equalization and the courts, they were denied matching funds for pensions. Powerful Republican State Representative David Shanahan, a Chicago real estate executive and later Speaker of the House, angrily explained to CTF representative Margaret A. Haley: "When you teachers stayed in your school rooms, we men took care of you, but when you go out of your school rooms as you have done and attack these great, powerful corporations, you must expect that they will hit back."[12]

The story of the teachers' tax crusade was portrayed as dramatically as a Dickens novel, beginning appropriately at Christmas in 1899, when Haley decided to use her holiday for examining the rumor that Chicago corporations were escaping millions of dollars in taxation because of their refusal to report assets, as required by law.

Haley went first to the office of the Cook County Clerk, where, "knowing that the County Clerk of Cook County was a mere politician, a passing show," she asked to see his assistant, Archibald Cameron, "the wizard of tax spreading." A messenger boy led Haley and her teacher companion

> through circuitous passages . . . among book racks, long tables from which men, seated on high stools, peered curiously at us from under green eye shades, on through the gateways, locked on the inside, but opening to the touch of our guide. He finally pointed a cautious finger and said in low tones: "That is Mr. Cameron, the man with the pen over his ear." Then the boy immediately disappeared.[13]

Cameron was lecturing to several city attorneys on the new tax system, while the five-foot two-inch Haley stood on her toes to hear the conversation. She approached him slowly but did not hesitate in her demand to see the assessment schedules. Cameron asked Haley who wanted them. "I told him the six thousand teachers of Chicago," she later wrote. "As I said this I thought of Ethan Allen demanding the surrender of Fort Ticonderoga in the name of the great Jehovah and the Continental Congress."[14]

The real drama was in Haley's discovery that several utilities and railway companies (including the Pullman Company) had not only evaded property taxes but had not been assessed for the intangible property of their franchises. In some cases, companies reported no assets and the assessors made no investigation. The politically adept Haley gathered legal opinions from former Governor John Peter Altgeld and attorney Clarence Darrow. She also persuaded the prominent attorney Isaac T. Greenacre to represent the CTF. At a special meeting of the Chicago teachers, Haley and CTF President Catharine Goggin were given a year's release from classroom teaching in order to conduct a thorough investigation.[15]

Haley chose to examine public utilities and streetcars because she knew that those companies would not move from Cook County. Further, she aimed at the old Populist target of monopoly, which had become particularly controversial because of the excesses of Charles Tyson Yerkes, the streetcar tycoon whose leases had involved bribery in both the Chicago City Council and the Illinois General Assembly. By 1900, Yerkes had left Chicago with $5,000,000 for his sumptuous New York townhouse, while Chicago teachers were being paid less than day laborers and the school board limped through a financial crisis. When Haley disclosed the fact that Chicago companies had escaped millions of dollars in taxation, she gained the sympathy of most Chicagoans.[16]

In October of 1900, Haley and Goggin (in whose name the resulting litigation was carried) began a series *of mandamus* proceedings that forced a reassessment of several railway and utility companies. Using the figures supplied by the Cook County assessor, the women appeared before the State Board of Equalization, which reviewed all assessments. As Haley vividly recalled, however, those smoke-filled sessions often adjourned mysteriously after no business had been conducted. Undaunted, Haley filed writs of *mandamus* compelling the Board "to assess the franchises according to law." Despite threats from corporation attorneys, the CFT (with no support from the Board of Education or other taxing bodies) pursued a suit alleging tax evasion by five of the city's largest corporations—Chicago City Railway Company, Chicago Telephone Company, Chicago Edison Company, South Chicago City Railway Company and People's Gas, Light and Coke Company. A second suit mentioned an additional fifteen traction and railway companies.[17] In 1902, the companies in the first suit appealed the decision to the federal courts, and Judge J. Peter Grosscup reduced the combined tax bill from two million dollars to $600,000. The teachers could still rejoice, however, for they had added substantially to the county's revenue base.[18]

Yet the Chicago Board of Education, with a portion of the teachers' tax rewards (several thousand dollars was enjoined until 1904 because of ongoing appeals), appropriated the new income to what it considered essential services: high school programs, night schools for immigrants, and kindergartens. The Board also paid the fuel bill and funded the Building Repair Department, a controversial part of the educational account that financed sidewalks, drain pipes, furnishings, and paint for new schools constructed from the building account.[19]

When the Board made those appropriations, it charged that the teachers' insistence on salary raises was not only self-seeking but also detrimental to the entire school program. Newspapers delighted in portraying teachers as so selfish that they would deny an education to the kindergartner. Isolated from reformers because of the salary issue, the teachers affiliated with the Chicago Federation of Labor in 1902 and promised to give the Board of Education an unprecedented political battle.[20] According to one tax observer who noted the aggressive style of the CTF, the teachers had "virtually been placed in a position where they had to take the bull by the horns or be gored by it, and they courageously chose the former alternative."[21]

Pursuing the tax money, the CTF finally won the last of the suits on August 23, 1904. Judge Edward F. Dunne, who was to become mayor of Chicago in 1905, expressed his outrage at the way the teachers had been denied their reward for tax vigilance:

> While the defendant, the Board of Education, sat supinely by and while other public officials more specifically charged with the levy and collection of these taxes refused to perform their sworn duty, this complainant [the CTF], acting for and on behalf of these same teachers out of their own limited resources, went out and performed the duties which primarily devolved upon the tax levying bodies of the state and secondarily upon the board of education to see that the tax levying officials of the state collected the taxes honestly belonging to the schools of the city and brought about the payment of dishonestly with-held taxes.[22]

Certainly Haley and the CTF thought that, with a more sympathetic Board of Education appointed by Mayor Dunne in 1905, they would be able to achieve the overall pay raise promised in 1898 and awarded only for the 1900 tax year. Yet the additional tax revenues brought in by the teachers had failed to rescue the Board from its perpetual fiscal crisis. The teachers therefore continued in their attempts to uncover fraud. They achieved reforms in the Building Repair Department in 1907, and in 1909 they appeared in Springfield in support of two bills: an amendment to the Juul Law that would exempt the educational account from the 5 percent tax limit and an amend-ment to the School Law that would transfer school repair expenses from the educational account to the building account. Both measures succeeded.[23] Improvements in teachers' salaries occurred after 1909 because of the appointment of Ella Flagg Young as superintendent. Young, a University of Chicago graduate, was an admirer of Haley's but soon aroused the hostility of teachers' old antagonists.

Real estate interests—who had consistently demanded lower property tax rates—were furious with the teachers over what they called "irresponsibility" in public school finance. At the 1913 session of the general assembly they supported passage of laws that allowed for the reduction of school (but not school building) taxes and exemptions on buildings constructed on school lands. (Many offices in Chicago's Loop occupied such property.) Haley charged that the latest amendment to the Juul Law created more "loop-holes" for tax-dodging. William Rothmann, a 1912 Board appointee and partner in a law firm headed by powerful Republican Roy O. West, won the backing of the Board of Education for the amendment. Haley pledged herself to overturn the "land tax," as she called the revision.[24]

Before the next session of the legislature, however, the Board of Education passed a rule making membership in the CTF or any union tantamount to resignation. The rule was written as a typical yellow-dog contract and was enforced by making teachers sign an oath before receiving their paychecks. Board president Jacob Loeb was the author. The CTF contested the Loeb Rule in a series of bitter court battles that lasted almost two years. Finally, in April, 1917, the Illinois Supreme Court decided in favor of the Board. The CTF was required to disaffiliate with labor, and it continued as a quasi-legal organization until 1924.[25]

Meanwhile, school attendance was rising dramatically among both native-born and foreign-born populations in the city, especially in the higher grades. Attendance among fourteen- and fifteen-year-old foreign-born students rose from 55 percent of their age cohort in 1919 to 94 percent in 1930.[26] A study of the educational aspirations of schoolchildren in 1922 indicated that the increasing school population would continue. From all groups studied, 71.6 percent of eighth graders expressed an interest in high school education. The study concluded that a change in attitude on the part of children and parents was responsible for the shift in school attendance patterns from the early years of the century: "Many principals have mentioned the definite change that has come during the last few years in the attitude of both parents and children toward further education. The social as well as the industrial value of high school is an important factor in increased school attendance."[27]

Home ownership in Chicago was also rising among immigrant groups. Investigations by the Immigration Commission, by settlement house workers, and by sociologists from the University of Chicago confirmed that the immigrants' ambition to own a home was often achieved only by having every family member work. Whereas in 1908 less than 20 percent of second-generation families owned homes, by 1930 approximately 28 percent did; the rate for foreign-born families rose from 15 percent in 1908 to 42 percent by 1930. Over the same period, property values increased. Real estate boomed, and residential property, which had formerly comprised an insignificant portion of the tax base, became the main revenue source.[28]

The relationship between unionized public school teachers and the Chicago working class became increasingly compromised. Although the Chicago Federation of Labor offered unqualified support when the Loeb Rule threatened to destroy the teachers' union, the subsequent shift in working-class life toward more years of school attendance and more widespread home ownership presented a new contradiction between the people as workers and the people as taxpayers. We need not entirely discount the old notion that the working class traditionally supported education; school attendance figures, after all, attested to a growing interest in education. Yet, as corporate giants evaded taxes and moved to shift the tax burden onto the shoulders of new homeowners, a working-class ambivalence toward expansion of education emerged.

The pre-Loeb Rule bond between organized teachers and organized labor was fragile at best. Construction laborers, for example, understandably encouraged the growth of the building account. In 1898 the building trades unions suffered a major defeat when a successful contractors' lockout prevented enforcement of union recognition in public school construction. Consequently, by 1909, when those formerly implacable trade unionists were quietly accepting union as well as non-union contracts, they were in no position to expose the featherbedding that had become common practice in the public construction industry.[29]

Another labor figure whose interests conflicted with the teachers was John C. Harding of the Typographical Workers Union, who served on the Board of Education from 1905 to 1915. Harding, although an outspoken advocate of better salaries for teachers, frequently put the interest of his union well before those of the teachers by jealously guarding the union bug on school textbooks. In a well-publicized "textbook row" with Superintendent Young in 1913, Harding temporarily allied with her fiscal critics because of Young's refusal to approve certain expensive, union-made primers. For the sake of solidarity, the teachers never repudiated Harding publicly, yet that conspiracy of silence blanketed a bitter conflict of interests.[30]

Enemies of the CTF held Young and the predominantly women teachers responsible for the million-dollar deficit in the 1914–1915 budget, calling it an example of "frenzied feminine finance." On closer examination, however, it was not Young but Board President Jacob Loeb who produced the disastrous fiscal crisis in school finance.[31] From 1915 to 1919 the Board indulged in the greatest deficit spending that Chicago taxpayers had ever seen. In 1924 the Board announced a million-dollar plan for alleviating crowding in the high schools by building new junior high school facilities.[32] No one questioned that school costs had risen with increasing school attendance in the upper grades and a corresponding expansion in the teaching force, but little was being done to address the fiscal problem created by those costs. Educational historian David Tyack has shown the administrative pressures on school officials and financial demands on taxpayers nationwide for accommodating the new school population:

> Statistics revealed the magnitude of the transformation and suggested the character of the challenges schoolmen faced as education became increasingly universal through the high school years. The costs of city schools in 1910 were twice as high as in 1900, three times higher than in 1890. From 1890 to 1918 there was, on the average, more than one new high school built for every day of the year. Attendance in high schools increased during the period from 202,963 to 1,645,171, an increase of 711% while the total population increased only 68%.[33]

A major reason for the skyrocketing costs was the salary level of high school teachers and specialists, whose pay was nearly twice that of elementary teachers. Although total salaries did rise, elementary teachers who had supported the CTF gained little. Between 1923 and 1927, the Board of Education constructed seventeen new buildings, principally junior and senior high schools, which were more expensive than the earlier elementary school buildings. The new schools almost immediately demonstrated major structural flaws. Shoddy workmanship and poor architectural plans aroused suspicion that the contracts were politically motivated. (Investigations conducted in the late 1920s into the quality of Chicago schools revealed that only nine of the city's 301 schools passed a standard evaluation.)[34] Perhaps the revelations of school construction fraud (first hinted by Chicago newspapers in 1925), the continually inadequate wages for teachers, and the Board's retirement of the Loeb Rule were what tempted the aging Margaret Haley to take one last stab at reforming Illinois' tax structure in 1926. Her timing proved disastrous.

Haley and the elementary school teachers faced an entirely new environment that was both politically conservative and economically diverse. The automobile was quickly replacing the streetcar, and roads were competing with schools for tax revenues. An act of 1917 greatly eased limitations on the issuing of bonds and anticipation warrants, and members of the Board of Education took full advantage of their increased spending freedom. Haley, convinced that Loop businessmen were evading property taxes, was determined to conduct another investigation. In former campaigns against unfriendly school board presidents and superintendents, she had enjoyed the official and outspoken support of the Chicago Federation of Labor. But by 1926 labor leaders were reluctant to offer wholehearted support to any revision of the city's tax base. Haley, to her chagrin, was to find a Pandora's box of inequities, corruption, and fraud that led to a business tax revolt and ultimately to the insolvency of the school board.[35]

Haley's selective appraisal of likely "tax dodgers" began in summer of 1926. As expected, her investigators found that many major banks and railway companies were evading taxes. The unexpected result was that Haley's much-publicized campaign led some Loop businessmen to conduct their own investigations into tax inequities. Their researchers found that, compared to the city's overall assessment of 25 percent, Loop businesses paid taxes on up to 70 percent of assessed valuation.[36] The regular statewide quadrennial assessment of 1927 raised the overall assessment rate but also revealed the same irregularities uncovered by the Loop study. As a result, angry businessmen refused to pay their taxes. Newspapers reported 103,000 appeal protests. Taxpayers, particularly in the business sector, were in complete revolt.[37]

Still determined to increase corporate rates, Haley in September requested a hearing before the State Tax Commission (which in 1918 had replaced the more political State Board of Equalization). Haley pointed out that the Cook County Board of Review was in violation of the state law requiring full publication of real estate assessments. She was joined in those hearings by members of the powerful Joint Commission on Real Estate Valuation, headed by George O. Fairweather, business manager of the University of Chicago. In May, 1928, the Commission declared that "gross inequalities" and "unjust discrimination" in the 1927 assessments of Cook County rendered them invalid. A full reassessment of all county property was ordered. Illinois Attorney General Oscar E. Carlstrom declared the order void, but Commission members appealed to Governor Louis Emmerson, who immediately called a special session of the general assembly. Revenue laws passed in June authorized the reassessment.[38]

Experts estimated that the project would cost more than $2,000,000. Ironically, Haley's so-called "tax dodging" banks led the campaign for raising the necessary bonds. Harry S. Cutmore, formerly of the Manufacturer's Appraisal Company, was hired as director of the reevaluation.[39]

The point of the reassessment, however, was no longer to find revenue—as had been Haley's original intention—but to find inequities in the system by a "scientific" analysis of published valuations. The need for such systematic study was critical, as Cutmore's colleague Herbert D. Simpson stated:

> 250,000 properties in Chicago were assessed at less than 20%, 90,000 properties were assessed at 50% to 100%; Calumet was assessed at 10%, Rogers Park at $33\frac{1}{2}$%; vacant land was assessed at 20%, commercial property at 36%; small homes were assessed at $33\frac{1}{2}$%, large homes at 28%; the whole assessment was "38% off"; and that portion of taxes collected in Chicago through a process of virtual confiscation amounted to $30,000,000 annually.[40]

As the project was diverted from gaining additional revenue, the teachers' crusade gave way to the call for overall tax reductions. In the process, the burden of property tax was shifted from business to residential property. The reassessers, calling for a scientific assessment of property, refused to allow Loop businessmen the fixed limit on taxation they demanded, but did allow them a full 30 percent depreciation of their taxable business properties. Newspapers focused not on the pressures the larger businesses were creating for a lower assessment but rather on the political corruption involved in the Cook County Board of Review. The *Chicago Tribune*, for example, published photographs on the subject, one showing the home of the Chief of Police Detectives Michael Grady, who paid on an assessed value of $500, while his neighbor with a similar home paid on an assessed value of $2,450.[41] The publicity took the heat off the downtown businesses, some of which were the newspapers themselves, or their neighbors. Taxes, meanwhile, could not be collected as long as the investigation and resulting appeals continued. The final assessment on April 23, 1930, came to $3,336,174,128, which was $223,952,373 less than the 1927 assessment. Much of the total proved impossible to collect because of the Depression, which had been six months underway when the investigation was ended.[42]

As early as December, 1929, the Board of Education conceded that it lacked sufficient funds for meeting its next payroll. In the thirteen months that followed, only five monthly payrolls were met; by May of 1933 the Chicago Board of Education owed the Chicago public school teachers in excess of twenty million dollars. Paying the teachers in script, which was often discounted at rates ranging from 12 percent to 20 percent of face value, the Board entered insolvency.[43] The old business coalition, many of whose participants had still not paid taxes, sought to wring the last ounce of progressivism from the public school teachers, as school principal Elsa Ponselle later recalled:

> There were some stores downtown we will always remember with gratitude. They took those warrants at a hundred percent. Remember the Hub, Lytton's? They were wonderful. Old-timers like us still go there. There are some stores that will not be remembered with any love. They took it with sixty, seventy-five percent discount.[44]

The teachers' union movement, meanwhile, experienced a new upsurge of organization, as the teachers took their protests to the streets.

> We marched down LaSalle Street, we marched down Dearborn, we marched down Michigan Avenue. We marched everywhere. People were appalled. Teachers were supposed to be meek and mild. We were supposed to be the bulwark of the status quo and here we were, joining the revolution. We were on the side of the great unwashed.[45]

An investigation into school affairs made by George Strayer, the distinguished professor from Columbia University, revealed in 1932 that despite the Board's failure to pay teachers, it continued a $15,000,000 construction program and was "inordinately" attentive to its debts. Interest payments alone came to 28 percent of the annual school budget. The Strayer Report, however, did not suggest ways of gaining new revenues. Instead, it focused on curbing expenditures.

In the 1930s teachers abandoned their efforts to broaden the tax base. To solve the problems of their own pay and the continuance of quality education programs they looked at school budgets, not the taxing machinery. In 1939 Margaret Haley died, and in the same year the Illinois legislature revised the state's tax structure—a long overdue remedy for the problems of urban school finance.[46]

Home ownership, school attendance, and taxation became permanent attributes of working-class life during the volatile years of the Progressive period. As more and more workers invested in homes and education, the burden of property tax shifted to their shoulders. The small homeowner inherited a property tax created earlier in a rural, under-populated Illinois. Public school teachers, once organized and strongly identified with the fortunes of this growing constituency, led a campaign for shifting the tax burden to large public utilities and the streetcar and private corporations. Their efforts failed in the spectacular collapse of urban fiscal policy in the 1930s.

NOTES

1. Minutes of the Chicago Teachers' Federation, 1897, Chicago Teachers' Federation Collection. Chicago Historical Society. For the history of the CTF and

the Chicago school system, see Marjorie Murphy, "From Artisan to Semi-Professional: White Collar Unionism among Chicago Public School Teachers, 1870–1930," Diss. University of California—Davis 1981; Cherry Wedgwood Collins, "Schoolmen, Schoolma'ams and School Boards: The Struggle for Power in Urban School Systems in the Progressive Era," Diss. Harvard University 1976; Robert L. Reid, "The Professionalization of Public School Teachers: The Chicago Experience, 1895–1920," Diss. Northwestern University 1968; David Hogan, "Capitalism and Schooling: A History of the Political Economy of Education in Chicago, 1880–1930," Diss. University of Illinois—Urbana 1978.

2. *Forty-fourth Annual Report of the Board of Education . . . 1898* (Chicago: John F. Higgins, 1898), pp. 11–12; Mary J. Herrick, *The Chicago Schools: A Social and Political History* (Beverly Hills, Calif.: Sage Pub., 1971), pp. 96–100.

3. *Forty-fourth Annual Report of the Board of Education . . . 1898*, pp. 33–35, 161–62; *Forty-fifth Annual Report of the Board of Education . . . 1899* (Chicago: John F. Higgins, 1900), pp. 16–17; *Laws of Illinois*, 40 G.A., Spec. Sess. (1897–1898), pp. 54–55; *Laws of Illinois*, 41 G.A. (1899), pp. 349–51.

4. George S. Counts, *School and Society in Chicago* (New York: Harcourt, 1928) pp. 36–40.

5. For the Civic Federation and other urban reform groups, see James E. Herget, "Democracy Revisited: The Law and School Districts in Illinois." *Journal of the Illinois State Historical Society*, 72 (1979), 136–38; Chicago Bureau of Public Efficiency, *Chicago School Finances, 1915–1925* (Chicago: Chicago Bureau of Public Efficiency, 1927); Michael Patrick McCarthy, "Businessmen and Professionals in Municipal Reform: The Chicago Experience, 1887–1920," Diss. Northwestern University 1970, pp. 58–59; Donald David Marks, "Polishing the Gem of the Prairie: The Evolution of Civic Reform Consciousness in Chicago, 1874–1900," Diss. University of Wisconsin, 1974, pp. 89–201; Stephen D. London, "Business and the Chicago Public School System, 1890–1966," Diss. University of Chicago 1968. See also Homer Hoyt, *One Hundred Years of Land Values in Chicago* (Chicago: University of Chicago Press, 1933), pp. 207–08, 351–53.

6. *Laws of Illinois*, 40 G.A., Spec. Sess. (1897–1898), pp. 34–54, 54–55 (revisions of both the revenue and school laws); *Laws of Illinois*, 42 G.A. (1901), pp. 272–74; Hoyt, p. 154.

7. A similar bill, also sponsored by Juul, had earlier passed the Senate but failed in the House: *Senate Journal*, 41 G.A. (1899), pp. 122, 254; *House Journal*, 41 G.A. (1899), pp. 317, 907–08; *Laws of Illinois*, 42 G.A. (1901), pp. 272–74; *Laws of Illinois*, 40 G.A., Spec. Sess. (1897–1898), pp. 34–54 (Sec. 49 was the provision later declared unconstitutional); John Murray Haig, *A History of the General Property Tax in Illinois*, University of Illinois Studies in the Social Sciences, Vol. 3 (Urbana: University of Illinois Press. 1914), p. 190; *Knopf v. The People*, 185 Illinois 20 (1900).

8. See, e.g., *Laws of Illinois*, 44 G.A. (1905), pp. 365–67; *Laws of Illinois*, 46 G.A. (1909), pp. 323–25; *Illinois Revised Statutes*, Ch. 120.

9. J. A. Fairlie, *A Report on the Taxation and Revenue System of Illinois, Prepared for the Special Tax Commission* (Danville: Illinois Printing Co., 1910), p. 16.

10. Haig, p. 193.

11. *Forty-sixth Annual Report of the Board of Education . . . 1900* (Chicago: Hack & Anderson, 1901), pp. 143–46; Counts, pp. 90–92. Later tax reformers charac-terized the CTF approach to tax reform as "narrow" because of the union's search for revenues. See Herbert D. Simpson, *Tax Racket and Tax Reform in*

Chicago (Chicago: Institute for Economic Research, Northwestern University, 1930), pp. 112–24. For more on the tax system in Illinois, see the following reports of the Educational Finance Inquiry Commission, all published by Macmillan in 1924: Nelson B. Henry, *A Study of Public School Costs in Illinois Cities*, Floyd W. Reeves, *The Political Unit of Public School Finance in Illinois*, and Henry C. Morrison, *The Financing of Public Schools in the State of Illinois*.

12. Murphy, ed., "Autobiography of Margaret A. Haley," TS, Ch. 3, p. 153 (original autobiography in the Chicago Teachers' Federation Papers, Chicago Historical Society), hereafter cited as "Haley Autobiography." For the pension law of 1901, which prohibited the use of tax revenues as matching funds, see *Laws of Illinois*, 42 G.A. (1901), pp. 300–01.

13. "Haley Autobiography," pp. 153–85.

14. *Ibid.*, pp. 181–221.

15. *Ibid.*, pp. 200–05; *Proceedings of the Illinois State Board of Equalization . . . 1900* (Springfield: Phillips Bros., 1901), pp. 8–9; tabulated statements in the report indicate that many large companies were not assessed for capital stock and franchise (pp. 43–46).

16. Ray Ginger, *Altgeld's America: The Lincoln Ideal Versus Changing Realities* (Chicago: Funk & Wagnalls Co., 1958), pp. 169–83; *Stormy Years: The Autobiography of Carter H. Harrison, Five Times Mayor of Chicago* (New York: Bobbs-Merrill, 1935), pp. 110–208.

17. "Haley Autobiography," pp. 200–25; *Proceedings of the Illinois State Board of Equalization . . . 1901* (Springfield: Phillips Bros., 1902), pp. 13, 18–20, 22–25 (for *mandamus* proceedings and resulting reassessments), and pp. 14–17, 30–31 (for appeals from the affected companies); *Proceedings of the Illinois State Board of Equalization . . . 1902* (Springfield: Phillips Bros., 1903), pp. 40, 60–62; Herrick, p. 101.

18. *Chicago Tribune*, July 1, 1902, p. 4, col. 7.

19. Counts, p. 93.

20. *Chicago Teachers' Federation Bulletin*, Nov. 14, 1902.

21. Simpson, *Tax Racket and Tax Reform*, p. 123; *Chicago Tribune*, July 10, 1902, p. 4, col. 7.

22. *Chicago Tribune*, Aug. 23, 1904, p. 3, col. 7.

23. Dominic Candeloro, "The Chicago School Board Crisis of 1907," *Journal of the Illinois State Historical Society*, 68 (1975), 397–401; *Laws of Illinois*, 46 G.A. (1909), pp. 323–25.

24. *Laws of Illinois*, 48 G.A. (1913), pp. 517–19, 519–20; Haley, "Stenographic Report of an Address to the Public Ownership League, Chicago," Aug. 28, 1915, Chicago Teachers' Federation Papers; Albert Nelson Marquis, ed., *The Book of Chicagoans: A Biographical Dictionary* (Chicago: A. N. Marquis & Co., 1917), pp. 587, 718.

25. Loeb, an insurance executive, was a member of the Board of Education from 1913 to 1922. For a detailed analysis of the Loeb Rule and its effect on teachers and the community, see Murphy, "From Artisan to Semi-Professional," pp. 209–83; Herrick, pp. 122–29; Freeland Stecker, "The First Ten Years of the American Federation of Teachers," Arthur Elder Collection, Walter Reuther Labor History Archives, Detroit.

26. See Hogan, p. 353.

27. L. F. Merrill, "A Report Concerning the Plans of 596 Children on Leaving Eighth Grade," *Chicago Schools Journal*, 5 (1922–1923), 156.

28. David Hogan, "The Making of the Working Class in Chicago," *History of Education Quarterly*, 18 (1978), 227–70; Michael Katz, "Who Went to School?" ibid., 12 (1972), 432–53. The rise in home ownership is evident in the Chicago census reports from 1900 to 1930.

29. Robert A. Nottenberg, "The Relationship of Organized Labor to Public School Legislation in Illinois, 1880–1948," Diss. University of Chicago 1952, pp. 51–60.

30. For more on labor's debate over textbooks, see the Illinois State Federation of Labor *Proceedings* for 1923, p. 462, and *Weekly News Letter*, Jan. 3, 1920; and Chicago Federation of Labor's *The New Majority*, June 18, 1921. For more on Harding and the CTF, see *Chicago Teachers' Federation Bulletin*, May 5, 1905.

31. See, for example, Joan K. Smith, "Progressive School Administration: Ella Flagg Young and the Chicago Schools, 1905–1915," *Journal of the Illinois State Historical Society*, 73 (1980), 27–44.

32. John A. Vieg, *The Government of Education in Metropolitan Chicago* (Chicago: University of Chicago Press, 1939); Chicago Bureau of Public Efficiency, *Chicago School Finances, 1915–1925*.

33. David Tyack. *The One Best System: A History of American Urban Education* (Cambridge, Mass.: Harvard University Press, 1974), pp. 182–83.

34. Herrick, pp. 188–243; George D. Strayer, comp., *Report of the Survey of the Schools of Chicago, Illinois*, 5 vols. (New York: Bureau of Publications, Teachers College, Columbia University, 1932). For the teachers' view of junior high schools from 1919 to 1925, see *Margaret A. Haley's Bulletin*, and *The New Majority*.

35. Haley wrote a complete manuscript on her investigation; see "The 1926 Assessment" in her autobiographical manuscript, Chicago Teachers' Federation Papers.

36. Simpson, Tax *Racket and Tax Reform*, p. 125.

37. See, for example, the newspaper articles cited in Simpson, *The Tax Situation in Illinois* (Chicago: Institute for Research in Land Economics and Public Utilities, 1929), pp. 58–61.

38. *Tenth Annual Report of the Tax Commission of the State of Illinois . . . 1928* (Springfield: Schnepp & Barnes, 1930), pp. 163–73: *Laws of Illinois*, 55 G.A., 2 Spec. Sess. (1928), pp. 106–07.

39. The $2,000.000 figure was the total for both the first and second assessments. See *Tenth Annual Report of the Tax Commission . . . 1928*, pp. 121–23, 185; Simpson, *Tax Situation in Illinois*, pp. 58–59.

40. Simpson, *Tax Racket and Tax Reform*, p. 136.

41. *Chicago Tribune*, July 30, 1928, p. 3, cols. 1 ff.; *Tenth Annual Report of the Tax Commission . . . 1928*, pp. 173–74; Simpson, *The Tax Situation in Illinois*, pp. 62–73.

42. Simpson, *The Assessment of Real Estate for Taxation in Chicago: A Preliminary Report* (Chicago: Institute for Economic Research, 1929); *Fifteenth Annual Report of the Tax Commission of Illinois . . . 1933* (Springfield: Schnepp & Barnes, 1934), pp. 114–15.

43. Lyman B. Burbank, "Chicago Public Schools and the Depression Years of 1928–1937," *Journal of the Illinois State Historical Society*, 64 (1971), 365–81; Herrick, pp. 177–257; and the testimony of teachers in *Hearings Before a Subcommittee of the Committee on Manufacturers, United States Senate, 72nd*

Congress, 1st Session, May 9, 1932 (Washington, D.C.: Government Printing Office, 1932), pp. 48–51.

44. Studs Terkel, *Hard Times: An Oral History of the Great Depression* (New York: Random House, 1970), pp. 388–89.

45. *Ibid.*, p. 389.

46. *Laws of Illinois*, 61 G.A. (1939), pp. 886–1005.

9

MISSING THE MARK: INTELLIGENCE TESTING IN LOS ANGELES PUBLIC SCHOOLS, 1922–32

Judith R. Raftery

This is a study of how Intelligence Quotient (I.Q.) testing, which was always controversial, became a tool for one of the nation's most advanced and progressive school systems, the Los Angeles public schools. Rather than considering what advocates said about intelligence testing, this essay focuses on the actual testing in schools. It argues that teachers never completely accepted I.Q. tests as the unambiguous instruments their designers had claimed. Instead, teachers immediately detected the cultural biases in the tests, and administrators recognized that they did not provide the revolutionary, educational, or diagnostic tool that had been expected. This essay does not suggest that I.Q. testing played no role in "tracking." What it does demonstrate is that the test generated far more confusion and frustration for teachers and administrators than historians have thought. Educators initially expected that the test would provide a clear-cut pattern for separating students by intelligence. When they discovered that the test was unreliable, many looked for alternatives. Ability grouping in Los Angeles public schools in the 1920s and early 1930s depended less on I.Q. testing than other historians have led us to suppose.

I.Q. testing came under attack almost as soon as it was introduced in the early years of the twentieth century. Some intellectuals criticized the hereditarian bias of the tests; others, less concerned with ideology, held that the tests were not trustworthy evaluators of intelligence.[1] Modern critics have made assumptions and generalizations about how testing affected schooling without looking closely at the entire testing program. They have condemned the reliance on testing as shifting American education away from the democratic liberal tradition, or, less generously, they have depicted it as the ultimate perpetrator of social control and inequality. With less bold strokes, but with vigor, some have accused teachers, administrators, and counselors of purposely using testing to segregate children by race.[2] These criticisms, however, neither explain what made testing possible within the public schools nor contribute to our understanding of how educators interpreted and used the tests. And they shed no light on the complexities and controversies within the educational establishment over this explosive issue.

Furthermore, many historians have taken the writings of eminently quotable leaders such as Lewis Terman, Ellwood Patterson Cubberley, and Kimball Young as indicators of how school testing worked. Yet the claims of theorists are far removed from the actions of rank-and-file classroom teachers. To have a fuller picture of the testing movement, questions should be addressed within narrower perimeters. It is safer to generalize from a case study: the experience of Los Angeles with I.Q. testing over a ten-year period, and the day-to-day practices of classroom teachers and district psychologists who tried to make sense out of one of the most complicated puzzles.[3]

Los Angeles had a population of over half a million people in 1920. It was the fastest growing urban area west of the Rockies and by 1930, the fourth largest city in the nation. The city's leaders epitomized progressivism. They had, by 1903, reorganized municipal government to include innovative procedures such as the initiative, the recall, and the referendum. By 1911 they took pride in seven settlement houses and a successful campaign for women's suffrage.[4]

School leadership also demonstrated this progressive impulse. Angelenos saw themselves on the cutting edge of progressive reform, and to this end, teachers, administrators, and Board of Education members—Los Angeles school people—along with other reformers had established social-services programs within the schools. Penny lunch programs, after-hours playgrounds, day-care centers, and kindergartens aimed at offsetting the poverty in homes and retaining a sense of community as the city changed in size and demographic makeup. Establishing order in an industrializing, urbanizing society became the central task of community leaders throughout the Progressive Era.[5]

Until the First World War no single immigrant group was predominant in the city, and the percentage of foreign born in the population had stood at 19 for several decades. By the 1920s, however, the large number of Mexicans who arrived in the city eclipsed all other arrivals. Discouraged by the chaos of their own revolution and encouraged by United States agricultural interests, Mexicans flocked to the United States, making Los Angeles one of their urban centers. In Los Angeles, with its large agricultural hinterland, Mexicans could enjoy some amenities of urban life while they worked on farms or in agriculture-related industries; and many migrants who labored up and down California's rich valleys made Los Angeles their off-season base. By 1938, school officials counted 48,748 Mexican students in a school population of 186,683.[6] Acutely aware of the Mexican presence, many teachers and administrators sought ways to integrate and accommodate Mexican children within the city schools. In one central response they turned to mental or I.Q. testing, terms used interchangeably at the time, because they hoped it would help them find a suitable curriculum to serve an increasingly diverse population.

Educators in Los Angeles hired the best people available to assist them. Lewis Terman, who taught in the State Normal School in Los Angeles, was the single person in American education most clearly associated with I.Q. testing. A Hoosier, he received his Ph.D. in psychology from Clark University in 1905. Under the leadership of G. Stanley Hall, Clark University was the center for psychological study, and, as a student of the renowned psychologist, Terman acquired his lifelong interest in testing. During his studies, however, Terman contracted tuberculosis and, like many other health-seekers, subsequently came to southern California. After a year in San Bernardino, he accepted a position at the Normal School where his enthusiasm and innovative theories of intelligence measurement influenced the corps of students he trained. His students not only taught in the city's schools but also held positions in the district's Department of Psychology and Educational Research. For instance, the department's statistician, Ellen Alice McAnulty, worked with Terman as his research assistant before she accepted her position. Also closely allied with Terman, Dr. Arthur H. Sutherland directed the educational research for the Department of Psychology and Educational Research. In 1922 Sutherland outlined the workings of the department in a booklet, *Intelligence Tests and School Organization*. Terman, who was a member of the Commission on Revision of Elementary Education, which prepared the booklet, wrote its preface.[7]

Terman began his work on the American version of the classical I.Q. test, the Binet, in Los Angeles and continued the project when he went to Stanford University in 1910. Thus he linked Stanford's name with that of Binet's to give the most widely known test its title.[8] Terman transformed Binet's concept of age-mentality and was one of the first to use the term "intelligence quotient" to express the numerical relationship of an individual's mental age to chronological age. The Stanford-Binet became the model for all other I.Q. tests, including the achievement tests.[9] Terman felt that heredity was the prime determiner of intelligence. He attributed mental retardation to "inferior mental endowment" and discounted irregular school attendance, the use of foreign language in the home, malnutrition, bad teeth, and adenoids as major causes of low I.Q. In his 1919 work, *Intelligence of School Children*, he announced that, contrary to some of the fuzzy theories of progressives, "educational reform may as well abandon, once and for all, all effort to bring all children up to grade."[10]

During this period, as school reform and its concomitant, professionalization, took hold in Los Angeles, progressive administrators and Board of Education members invited outside experts to conduct school surveys to determine how to make their schools more efficient. The experts came from university schools of education or were well-known public school administrators who aimed to centralize and professionalize school districts, making them function as corporate systems.

Hoping the surveys would help create greater order and a differentiated school program to meet the needs of a changing school population, Los Angeles administrators in 1914 invited two experts to conduct a survey.

They could not have chosen two more typical "administrative progressives": Albert Shiels, director of reference and research for New York city schools, and Walter Jessup, dean of the schools of education, State University of Iowa. In 1915, Shiels and Jessup published their results in *Report of the Advisory Committee of the Board of Education*. By 1916 the Los Angeles board had hired Shiels as superintendent, and he immediately began to implement many of the changes he and Jessup had suggested. As one of his first acts, he established the Department of Psychology and Educational Research in 1917, setting up the mechanism for mass testing. The department provided a base of operation for school testing and gave it the autonomy and resources it needed.[11]

The ultimate outcome of the mass testing program depended on a curriculum revision to allow for the variations in mental abilities. To accomplish this task, the board turned to another expert, the University of Chicago's J. Franklin Bobbitt. Bobbitt, known as the father of the progressive curriculum, served as an assistant superintendent from January to April 1922, and again for those same months in 1923. His view of education differed from many of the earlier curriculum reformers. He expressed a more pragmatic, less naive approach, one that was based on a hope for a better society, but one that depended on good management and that left nothing to chance. He used the corporation as a model, always returning to the themes of efficiency and progress. In the *Twenty-sixth Yearbook of the National Society for the Study of Education* he wrote, "The school is not an agency of social reform. Its responsibility is to help the growing individual continuously and consistently hold to the type of living which is the best practical one for him."[12] Not a strict hereditarian, Bobbitt felt that, after making allowance for the heredity factor, the intelligence of any person was primarily determined by experience. He stressed the advantages of ability grouping. The department noted that children progressed five to seven times as rapidly in equal groups as they did in unequal ones.[13]

There is no doubt that Los Angeles welcomed testing programs because they were scientific. Science was playing an ever-greater role in postwar America. Many influential Americans acclaimed science as the new gospel, and an article in the *Nation* expressed the views of the majority in 1928: "A sentence that begins with 'science says' will generally . . . settle any argument in a social gathering or sell any article from toothpaste to refrigerators." Educators especially turned to science for guidance.[14] Perhaps no area of science affected the attitudes and policies of Los Angeles schools more than the work of psychologists, particularly those who concentrated on the measurement of children's intelligence. Their testing program offered the ultimate in effectiveness and efficiency.

The search for efficient, better methods of instruction had led school superintendent James Foshay in 1901 to establish "ungraded" classrooms. The ungraded rooms benefited "those pupils who required more individual training," and they relieved "the busy teacher [in] the crowded classroom."[15] By 1917, when Superintendent Shiels placed the supervision of ungraded classrooms under the Department of Psychology and Educational Research, they had grown to ninety and provided for nearly two thousand children. In an early attempt to streamline education, Shiels had psychologists administer Binet tests, examine health and school records, and take statements from teachers and principals. The new information enabled them to place pupils in more clearly defined categories.[16] The conviction of teachers and psychologists that many students from the ungraded classrooms, who showed intelligence quotients in the low 70s, had actual learning abilities far above their test scores and could, with special help, be brought to an "efficient school level," compelled educators to devise a plan that included separate learning centers for slow English-speaking learners, newly arrived foreign children, and limited English speakers. This plan remained in effect until the mid-1920s.[17]

During the 1920s, Los Angeles school counselors tested nearly the entire school population. Some educators were satisfied with standardized I.Q. tests; others explored different avenues. Those who worked with immigrant children found I.Q. tests an inadequate gauge; many of them turned to achievement tests. Some educators administered tests in such diverse subjects as music, art, handwriting, as well as in the conventional subjects of reading, spelling, and arithmetic.

For instance, school administrators went to great lengths to find suitable tests for non-English-speaking children, particularly Mexicans. In June 1925, Assistant Superintendent Emma Raybold reported on one of the earliest group tests on the Mexican population. This early examination was not to assess intelligence but to determine the most reliable test for future measurements. During the previous fall, school counselors had administered one nonverbal intelligence test and a series of verbal ones to two groups of "unselected" first graders in the San Fernando Valley schools. The groups consisted of Spanish-speaking Mexican children at San Fernando and English-speaking children at Lankershim. The counselor had added the Kohs Block test because the nonverbal performance test required no fluency in English. It did require the children to group together blocks of various colors according to a set pattern.[18]

Correlation coefficients for most of the test scores were quite high. The scores from the nonverbal Kohs tests of Mexican students, however, correlated less well with their scores on verbal tests, such as the Detroit, the Binet, and the Pintner.[19] Unfortunately, Ray bold failed to report the range and standard deviation of any of the test scores. In addition, she did not mention whether she performed statistical tests to determine if the differences between the correlation were quantitatively significant. And finally and most importantly, she failed to give the Kohs test to the Lankershim students, thereby obviating several valuable comparisons.

The test results caused confusion. Testers assumed that the Kohs test would be most suitable for non-English speakers. When Raybold found that Kohs scores of Mexican children correlated least with the verbal tests, she concluded that the Kohs test "was not as reliable with a primary group of

Mexican children who cannot speak English as is a test involving language factors." The Detroit test, however, correlated highly with the other verbal tests. Raybold noted, "Mexican children actually understand the English language more than we realize." In Los Angeles the Detroit test became the standard for testing Mexican children.[20]

By rejecting the Kohs test and selecting the Detroit test, because of its seeming reliability, the board preserved the cultural and economic bias of the testing program. In this case it failed to realize that a nonverbal test should correlate less well with verbal tests than would another verbal test, and that the nonverbal test would provide a different, but no less valid, view of students' mental abilities.

Satisfied with the Detroit test, the psychologists decided to use it with first graders at Belvedere school, an ethnically mixed school located east of the central city. They felt that the Detroit test pointed out individual differences better than either the Binet or the Pintner, and it lent itself more readily to a translation into Spanish. Belvedere counselor Edith Heim proposed that they administer the Spanish translation of the Detroit tests at Belvedere because she hoped that the translated test would determine whether language was the handicap or whether the children suffered from mental deficiencies.[21]

The translated Detroit test probably did not correctly identify the children's abilities. Although it was in Spanish, it undoubtedly had been translated into standard Castilian, an upper-class form lacking many idiomatic expressions common to the barrios, the poor Mexican neighborhoods. Some educators recognized the unreliability of translated tests and wrote their own. Hershel Manuel and his staff in the Department of Education at the University of Texas developed and administered their own Spanish version by 1931.[22] The Texan found that a direct translation ignored cultural biases—those beyond the simple biases of language. Even if the children used Castilian, the same cultural partiality that existed in the English version would continue in the translation. For instance, understanding a story about zoo animals in either English or Spanish requires prior knowledge of a zoo or animals. The same criticism applies more acutely to a nonverbal test. On a picture completion test, some of the pictures are easily completed while others rely on prior experience: one needs to be acquainted with a telephone in order to add a cord, as one must have some familiarity with an American hearth to add a screen, and one must have seen a live elephant or a picture of one to add a trunk. Heim felt that the Spanish translation had only one section where the Mexican children might be at a disadvantage and that section involved marking "five things which we dig out of the ground." Whether that meant fruits and vegetables not familiar to Mexican children is not clear, but since this item was only one out of fifty, or one month out of the mental age, she decided that a wrong answer would not be much of a handicap.[23]

Heim proposed an intermediary class between kindergarten and first grade as a holding place for children lacking proficiency in English, or until they reached a mental age of six. The Cl class, already in operation on a limited basis, would avoid the problem in which "two or three semesters of either drifting or drowning result in indolent, uninterested pupils who become the problem and despair of even the best teachers."[24]

In many ways, the department acted out of a sense of frustration. By trying to develop a test that would record a realistic score for non-English speakers, it demonstrated a sensitivity to the language problem, yet failed to understand that, even though the Mexican schoolchildren in Los Angeles were becoming bilingual and bicultural, they had not acquired sufficient fluency in either language or culture to affect notably a test that was geared to English-speaking, middle-class Americans. Standard I.Q. tests translated into Spanish would not give any more realistic results than those in English. The real problem with the testing program, whether in English or in Spanish, was that the tests had been devised for a middle-class population.

Heim and many others in the profession viewed a lack of English-language proficiency as a manifestation of low mental ability instead of a lack of experience with a new language and culture.[25] Yet she proposed intensive exposure to English in the Cl class to overcome English deficiencies. She stressed homogeneous grouping, where the teacher concentrated on English. Heim's solution exemplifies the contradictory thinking of many Los Angeles educators. On the one hand, she stated that English difficulties reflected low mental ability, and on the other, she wanted to solve the problem by total immersion in special English classes.

In December of 1925 the schools directed another test at Mexican children. This time the test was in an integrated setting at the Palms School. The results appeared in the *Psychology and Educational Research Bulletin*, and the title indicates the community's response to the influx of Mexican children: "The Mexican: An Educational Asset or an Educational Liability?" Palms's principal, Mrs. Leo Gamble, refuting what she called the "feeling of unfairness of dubbing him 'lazy' or of feeling him a liability without first measuring his efforts," chose to administer two different tests, one to measure intelligence and the other to measure achievement.[26]

The school administered tests to two hundred and fifty children in the third through eighth grades, twenty-two of whom were Mexican. Gamble viewed the Mexican community as upwardly mobile; half owned their own homes, and five had automobiles. Most of the children were American born, and not one had immigrated after the age of two. Many of the families spoke some English.

Nevertheless, the I.Q. test results were disappointing and tended to reinforce established biases. The average I.Q. in the school was 100.25, while Mexican children scored an average of 78.75. Not satisfied with the I.Q. results, Palms's counselors administered achievement tests, which told another story. Mexican students consistently scored a higher percentage in achievement when compared to their I.Q. than the rest of the students tested.

What Gamble failed to note, and what a careful examination of the tests might have revealed, was that even though the Palms School's Mexican community seemed upwardly mobile, the tests continued to impose cultural biases against them. The fact that some of the parents spoke English and that English dominated the school yard conversations did not guarantee that the Mexicans knew enough English to perform well on a verbal I.Q. test. Another possible reason for lower test scores of the Mexican children was that they entered school a year or so later than the English-speaking children. In the first grade, Mexican children's average age was 8.5 years, while the average American child was only 6.9 years. The ratio of mental age to chronological age, which defines the Stanford-Binet I.Q., would automatically favor the younger group. Nevertheless, Gamble's use of achievement tests to find a more reliable testing method for the Mexican students' ability showed a continuing sensitivity to and suspicion of the test's adequacy.

Another indication of educators' reluctance to rely solely on I.Q. tests to gauge mental abilities appeared in the *Bulletin* in the fall of 1926.[27] Principal Joseph Kendall of the Lemona Grammar in Van Nuys in rural San Fernando Valley, a newly constructed, completely segregated Mexican school, reasoned that little significance should be attached to the low intelligence scores because the measure used, the National Intelligence Test, presupposed reading ability in English. To make the teachers' work as effective as possible, Kendall had decided to find another method using the National Intelligence Test in spelling, arithmetic, and reading comprehension. The entire school personnel directed their efforts at improving the standard scores.

From the beginning the Lemona educators realized that nonstandard procedures needed to be employed if they were to attain their goals. Actually, the school's scores ranked higher than some expected, considering the fact that so many of the pupils lacked fluency in English. In arithmetic, for example, they ranked almost at the city's norm; in reading comprehension they scored slightly less than a year below the norm, and in spelling they were a little more than a year behind. However, since many of the children were old for their grade, the retardation rate was calculated at two and half years. Their average I.Q. was 75.

The teachers saw their task clearly. Without allotting any extra time for fundamentals, yet not allowing any interference with basic instruction, they went about their mission in the most creative manner. The staff combined standard materials with work that they had designed themselves. They obviously stimulated the children, and the results pleased them. The collective I.Q. scores rose to 81, and Kendall noted that the change "was of course due to the fact that the added knowledge of the English language which the pupils had acquired and the greater reading ability caused them to register to a closer degree their real intelligence."[28] In the teachers' eyes the real gains came in achievement. In only seven months the students' overall gain amounted to fourteen months, or a 100 percent acceleration rate. In arithmetic they gained thirteen months, ten months in reading comprehension, and a remarkable twenty months in spelling.

Kendall imagined what progress could be made if the school were integrated. Although English was spoken in the classroom, on the playground the children spoke Spanish and "continued to think in the Spanish language."[29]

Referring to the success the school achieved, he wrote, "If such results can be achieved with a group of foreign children unleavened by the presence of English-speaking mates, what might we not expect if similar enthusiasm and equally efficient teaching methods were applied in schools where our foreign children have the added advantage of hearing English on the playgrounds and having associations with children skilled in the customs our schools must teach to our newer citizens?"[30] Later advocates of school integration would repeat Kendall's question.

Kendall viewed assimilation as the solution to the country's problems as well as those of the immigrants. The study clearly shows that Kendall and his dedicated staff worked for the betterment of their pupils, at least the betterment in terms of higher scholastic achievement. They discouraged expressions of Mexican culture and the Spanish language—expressions of biculturalism and bilingualism that many advocates of pluralism value in the 1980s—because they had judged that the road to success led through Anglo-American culture and the English language. Kendall was hostile toward the Mexican culture and language but not toward Mexican children. In true melting-pot rhetoric, Kendall implied that once rid of their national and linguistic baggage, immigrants would be just like everyone else.

Los Angeles educators also questioned the relationship between I.Q. scores and educational attainment. Teachers wondered why some students had successful school careers and others did not. In 1928, Winifred Murphy, a counselor at Belvedere Junior High, analyzed the problem to determine which factors led students to advance to senior high and which factors led only some of those to matriculate. Obviously Murphy was weighing the merits of educating masses of children beyond eighth grade, yet her study presents some interesting insights into her own sensitivities to cultural differences within the immigrant community. Her study shows an awareness that various criteria need consideration if patterns for school achievement are to be understood. She noted the influence of family expectations on continued schooling. Fifteen and sixteen year olds, for example, were expected to take care of their own needs, and this assumption led many to choose work over school. Murphy found that native capacity had little to do with whether or not students entered senior high, since the number of non-attendant pupils with low and high I.Q. scores formed a normal distribution curve. Moreover, correlations between I.Q. and matriculations were too low to be significant, as were age and grade marks. Correlations between effort and I.Q. and between cooperation and I.Q. proved insufficient also. The counselor had to conclude that since none of the criteria used correlated with each other, the test instrument was inadequate. Her remarks indicate the ambivalence that I.Q. testing had created, since test scores apparently gave little indication of a pupil's success or failure in senior high.[31]

The *Educational Research Bulletin* in 1928 also printed a study on the methods used to classify students into groups. Questionnaires were sent to all elementary schools: "regular," where the majority spoke English; "semi-neighborhood," where 30 percent were non-English speakers; and "neighborhood," where 50 percent were non-English speakers. In the neighborhood schools only, principals' and teachers' judgments received priority over test results in determining grouping. It is not possible to know how test scores influenced the decisions of principals or teachers, but placing the final responsibility for ability grouping or tracking with those educators most closely associated with immigrant children, clearly indicates that many in Los Angeles were aware and concerned about the unreliability of the testing program.[32]

A more comprehensive example of the growing suspicion about the adequacy of I.Q. tests as the means for classifying students appeared in a 1929 *Bulletin*. The studies conducted in 1926, 1927, and 1928 were based on over half of the elementary schools in the city. The results proved predictable. The percentage of mentally retarded—students with an I.Q. lower than 70—was highest in the neighborhood schools, those with over 50 percent immigrant children, and lowest in the regular schools, those with less than 30 percent immigrant children. The percentage of children scoring above 130 was highest in the regular schools and lowest in the neighborhood schools. McAnulty, the department's statistician, noted two factors that influenced her findings; the tests required a reading knowledge of English when a very large proportion of children in the city were foreign and a number of younger and brighter children had been promoted to senior highs, leaving the elementary schools in foreign neighborhoods bereft of their superior scores. McAnulty planned another study to determine to "what extent the use of group tests have failed to predict the intelligence quotient (as later determined by individual Binets) for the various groups (foreign and native) found in our schools."[33]

Another indication that the department found the testing results questionable appeared in a study done by McAnulty and Clara Schmitt in 1931. At this time they tested groups of eight- and nine-year-old Mexican and American students whose I.Q.s ranged between 60 and 69. The testers wanted to find out whether Mexicans failed the language test more often than Americans. They were not disappointed. American students succeeded 84 percent of the time, while Mexicans only 57 percent. On the nonlanguage sections, the results were very close. For example, Mexicans had success at counting from twenty to one 94 percent of the time, while the others succeeded 90 percent; Mexicans succeeded 88 percent of the time in finding likenesses, but the Americans only 72 percent. McAnulty and Schmitt concluded that the six Binet tests "may be a test of racial differences, but examination of the items indicate that they are the ones most affected by language."[34] They decided that Mexican children have a mental age at least a year higher than is usually computed for them.

In comparison to Mexican children, Blacks received less attention in the literature. For example, between 1923 and 1932 the *Bulletin* printed many studies of Mexican children and only one study of Black children.[35] One reason for their interest in Mexican children may have been the size of the Mexican population. Although the Black community grew during the 1920s, it never reached the proportions of the Mexican. Blacks, like other Americans, lured by the promises of temperate climate and economic opportunity, flocked to Los Angeles during the decade following the war. The census figures of 1910 reveal a Black population of 7,599; the 1920 numerations stand at 15,579, a more than 100 percent increase; and in 1930, 38,894 resided in the city. However, the Black community's major growth came during the next decades.[36]

Another reason the Blacks received less attention in the literature may be because educators found that they had few learning disabilities. Lawrence DeGraaf's study of Los Angeles's Black population indicates that until the 1930s, when poorer southerners migrated into the city, most of the Black residents were part of a nascent middle class.[37] Two earlier studies tend to confirm DeGraaf's analysis. In both studies Black children scored as well or better than their White counterparts. A *Bulletin* study, published in 1923, reported on a test given to five hundred Black children in five elementary schools. The results were compared to the results of other children from fifteen schools that the psychologists felt represented the city as a whole. Based on the scores of the National Intelligence Test, the Black children's median score was 104.7, while the median score of the "representative" schools was 106.0. Scores from achievement tests also compared favorably. Only on the sixty-word spelling test did Black children score almost a year below grade level, but as assistant supervisor Willis Clark noted, the situation was not materially different for the rest of the school population.[38] Ten years later, McAnulty promised another study of Black schoolchildren. It was part of a three-part study of Mexican, Japanese, and Black schoolchildren to determine whether these minorities "measured up to the norm." McAnulty reminded the reader that the standardized tests had been devised for White children. She failed to mention that it was devised for middle-class White children.[39]

Part of the study alluded to in the *Bulletin* may have been Hazel Whitaker's three-year survey of Los Angeles's Black population done in 1931. The first Black to receive a regular teaching assignment at a city high school, Whitaker used the files of the Department of Psychology and Educational Research where she found that Negro and White children from the same social and geographic area had similar I.Q.s. One difficulty Whitaker encountered was "to find one hundred gifted White children living in the community with Blacks."[40] Most of the whites were recent immigrants and poorer than their Black neighbors. They also scored lower on the tests.

Yet during those years Los Angeles began segregating Black students. The I.Q. tests played little or no part in their decision. There is ample evidence to prove the board bowed to community pressure and began deliberate segregation of Blacks during the late 1920s regardless of test scores. In the case of Jefferson High, and later of Jordan High, the board re-drew some school boundaries, and in others, school staff directed Black students into vocational education classes.[41]

The city's Japanese students, the only other sizeable nonwhite group, apparently posed no particular educational problems. Testers found the I.Q.s of Japanese students on a par with Whites. The January 1932 *Bulletin* showed that I.Q. test results for Japanese and whites averaged 105. McAnulty noted that the results appeared unusually high for both groups, but she did not question them further.[42]

Despite anti-Asian legislation in 1913 and 1924, there are no data to suggest that Japanese children were labeled defective. Teachers praised the scholastic aptitude of the Japanese pupils. A librarian from the Boyle Heights branch of the city library remarked, "The Japanese are not to be forgotten. We have many of them, and the Japanese children are great readers. The children are good students and make the most of their opportunities."[43] Yet at the same time that teachers and librarians commended Japanese students, other school administrators opened their facilities to the Anti-Asian League sponsored events. Nonetheless, the board refused to succumb to community pressure and did not segregate Japanese students.

By the mid-1920s, Los Angeles educators openly criticized the biases of the tests. Ethelda Drake, principal at Ann Street School, a tireless worker in Americanization, first at Ann Street and later at Ivanhoe, expressed her disapproval in the form of a satirical letter published in the *School Journal*. Drake, as keen an observer of human foibles as one can find, wrote:

> Dear Fellow-Principals:
>
> On the long stretch through the Indian Ocean I conceived the brilliant idea of giving mental tests to the children of the various countries wherein I might visit. Fortunately, I was supplied with samples both for group and for individual tests. Through the ship interpreter I have had them translated into the different languages—Chewrashee Tchukcha, etc., and have had the necessary numbers printed in each language. It is true that a translated test cannot be considered truly valid; yet it is analogous to the situation that confronts a foreign child in American schools, and we all know that test results under such circumstances are infallible.
>
> I have just finished with the children of Krasnovodka. It is difficult for me to write without sympathetic tears. Every child I tested is definitely feeble minded.
>
> Such a simple task as writing the word that makes the sentence comprehensible in "A ____ is made up of an engine and coaches"; "Mother _____ doughnuts," in every instance remained unattempted. Fancy a child, as I found out by subsequent questions, had never seen a train or a doughnut! It is sad in a way to think that actual mentality depends on such fortuitous circumstances. I shall continue this testing as I travel leisurely from country to country, for however disheartening it may be when one considers those benighted lands, it is wonderfully inspiring to know that American children have such measurably higher intelligence quotients than any foreigner can possibly have.
>
> Yours in the interest of research,
>
> Ethelda Drake[44]

Another indication that the testing movement was under assault came from Superintendent Susan M. Dorsey. Addressing the National Congress of

Parents and Teachers in Oakland in the spring of 1927, Dorsey stated: "In the first place, the test does not measure intelligence, but achievement. It does not measure brain matter nor brain capacity so much as brain opportunity. It is a test of mental experience, rather than mental ability. For example, a child born in the mountains, when questioned about wharves, piers, and fishing shacks, might display but little intelligence, but if the questions were directed toward forest trails and rangers, to mountain lakes and woodcraft, he might be found to be 100 percent intelligent."[45]

One of the more far-reaching statements appeared in the United States Office of Education *Bulletin* in 1933. Anne Reynolds, a teacher at Hollenbeck Junior High,[46] prepared a federal study of Spanish-speaking students in five southwest states. She called for specialized training for teachers who taught Spanish speakers and for an increase in the number of Mexican teachers within the schools. She noted that few Mexican children finished high school, and, therefore, few qualified for college training to become teachers. She also mentioned an experiment in New Mexico where children were taught Spanish for one period a day, and she noted that the preliminary results seemed encouraging.[47] Her remarks on I.Q. testing reflected the growing tendency of Los Angeles educators to question the test results, especially when they were applied to Mexican children. She called for all results to be interpreted in light of economic and social status and school attendance.

The data used in this study confirm that many teachers refused to accept test conclusions as infallible. Educators who worked with children of limited English-speaking backgrounds had seen some of the inadequacies of testing; they found the I.Q. tests to be inconclusive indicators of potential ability. They also began to change educational policy. When Kendall and his Lemona teachers disregarded I.Q. tests, used achievement tests, and, finally, incorporated enrichment programs to improve scores of their Mexican students, they were remaking policy. By rejecting standard I.Q. tests and publishing their results, the Lemona staff pointed in a new direction and hoped others would follow. Moreover, by using achievement tests and not relying exclusively on I.Q. tests, Los Angeles educators showed a basic disagreement with the hereditarians. Nevertheless, even though achievement tests measured cumulative learning rather than supposed innate ability, these tests, like the I.Q. tests, were firmly grounded in middle-class, English-speaking culture. Lower-class, non-English speakers' test scores reflected that bias. Too often the tests penalized poor children and justified holding them in remedial classes; those who were considered normal were channeled into vocational education. As a result, very few attended college, and fewer entered the professions.

The I.Q. testing program created more problems than its advocates had anticipated. Educators had hoped to solve the dual issues of reaching the slow learners and of enriching the curriculum for the gifted. They sought to overcome the dilemma of mass education and of children who were not conforming to their preconceived mold. They have been accused of using testing for exploiting Anglo-Saxon perceptions of superiority. Some undoubtedly thought that intelligence tests measured differences between races and nationalities, but others did not. For example, Whitaker's study of gifted Black students and the 1932 study of Japanese children refuted conventional notions that race played a part in I.Q. Yet the schools continued to rely on the tests to solve the problems imposed by mass education, immigration, and industrialization in the hope that tests would provide scientific answers to questions of educational efficiency. Educators would not abandon their beliefs in progress, clinging to their ideas that science would solve their problems with new labeling methods and specialized curriculum. Moreover, even though testing proved less efficient than expected, negating its value would be tantamount to refuting the wisdom of university schools of education, a thought repugnant to most of them.[48]

Los Angeles progressives developed an extensive testing program early in the 1920s. They hired experts to teach new methods and techniques, used standard I.Q. tests that had been translated into Spanish, and expanded the Department of Psychology and Educational Research. Mental testing became part of a reorganization of curriculum and part of a national preoccupation with scientific methods to solve problems. In this way progressives hoped to make schools more responsible to each child's needs. In some instances, educators used the tests to justify segregating students, but not always. None of the requests for segregating students by race mentions test results, and the board's decision to confine nonwhite pupils, particularly Blacks, to Jefferson High had little or nothing to do with I.Q. but, rather, with community pressure from White residents.[49] Moreover, Black children's scores differed little from Whites'.[50] Evidence also suggests that during the early years of testing, I.Q. may not have been used as much as a determiner for "tracking" or ability grouping among immigrant children as has been generally assumed since, according to the aforementioned 1928 *Psychology and Educational Research Bulletin* study, principals and teachers in predominantly immigrant schools had the final say over matters of placement.

The testing program developed a history and life of its own. While testing did not help much with education, it did affect unrelated aspects of schooling policy. The tests' value may have been slight for diagnostic and teaching purposes, but their use for unrelated purposes made them visible and the subject of continuing controversy.

Current thought stresses that placement of minority children, particularly Chicanos, depended exclusively on I.Q. tests.[51] Yet evidence from Los Angeles School Board publications indicates that teachers and supervisors, such as those at Lemona School, were highly sensitive to the shortcomings of the instrument and took a keen interest in the welfare of their students. By the mid-1920s, even though the Department of Psychology and Educational Research applied more pressure to the board to have students' classifications based exclusively on I.Q. scores, in neighborhood schools teachers and principals continued to exert the most influence on student placement; therefore, I.Q. tests as criteria for classification were used less in schools where most of the children were from immigrant homes. Of course, this does not mean that test results had no influence on decisions made by teachers and principals, or that tracking was not an essential ingredient of education. It does suggest, however, that criteria other than I.Q. scores entered the picture. Los Angeles educators did not rely as slavishly upon the supposedly scientific results of I.Q. testing as some would have us suppose.

NOTES

1. Hamilton Cravens, *The Triumph of Evolution: American Scientists and the Heredity–Environment Controversy, 1900–1941* (Philadelphia, 1978), 249–50; John Dewey, "Mediocrity and Individuality," *New Republic*, 6 Dec. 1922, 35; Walter Lippmann, "A Future for the Tests," *New Republic*, 29 Nov. 1922, 10. For a discussion of I.Q. testing by teachers and administrators in England, see Gillian Sutherland, "Measuring Intelligence: English Local Education Authorities and Mental Testing, 1919–1939," in *The Meritocratic Intellect: Studies in the History of Education Research*, ed. J. V. Smith and D. Hamilton (Aberdeen, Scotland, 1980), 79–95. Mental testing challenged English concepts of class, rather than race, at a time when England had few nonwhite residents.

2. David B. Tyack, *The One Best System: A History of American Urban Education* (Cambridge, Mass., 1974), 208–16; Tyack uses examples from a few testing programs, but he relies on the views of the schools' officials and not on those of classroom teachers. Clarence J. Karier, "Testing for Order and Control in the Corporate Liberal State," in Clarence J. Karier, Paul C. Violas, and Joel Spring, *Roots of Crisis: American Education in the Twentieth Century* (Chicago, 1973), 108–37; Karier relies on the work of well-known psychologists Lewis Terman, Edward R. Thorndike, Henry H. Goddard, among others, but does not consider what took place in the classroom. Paula Fass, "The IQ: A Cultural and Historical Framework," *American Journal of Education* 88(Aug. 1980):431–58; Fass criticizes I.Q. testing on a broad level but does not investigate a particular program. Gilbert Gonzales, "The System of Public Education and Its Function within Chicano Communities, 1920–1931" (Ph.D. diss., University of California, Los Angeles, 1974); Gonzales draws different conclusions from many of the sources. Ricardo Romo, *East Los Angeles: History of a Barrio* (Austin, Tex., 1983), 137; Romo writes that I.Q. tests were "generally administered in English to Mexican children," but he neglects to add that often the testers administered tests in Spanish.

3. A study of the New York City schools, by Leila Zenderland, presents complementary information. Leila Zenderland, "Psychological Expertise and Public Education: The Battle over Intelligence Testing in New York City, 1910–1915" (Paper presented at the Organization of American Historians Annual Meeting, April 1985).

4. Walton Bean and James J. Rawls, *California: An Interpretive History* (New York, 1983), 264; Robert A. Woods and Albert J. Kennedy, eds., *Handbook of Settlements* (New York, 1911), 153–57.

5. Judith Rosenberg Raftery, "The Invention of Modern Early Schooling: Los Angeles, 1885–1941" (Ph.D. diss., University of California, Los Angeles), 7–43. The theme of Robert Wiebe's *The Search for Order* is particularly applicable to the changing atmosphere of Los Angeles during these years. Robert Wiebe, *The Search for Order, 1877–1920* (New York, 1967).

6. The 1920 U.S. Census notes the number of Mexicans in Los Angeles at 21,653, an increase from 5,632 in 1910. Many scholars find these figures low, but they indicate the dramatic rise in Mexican population in the ten-year period. Bureau of the Census, *Fourteenth Census*, vol. 2, *Population* (Washington, D.C., 1920), 731, *Thirteenth Census*, vol. 1, *Population* (Washington, D.C., 1910), 855. See Albert Camarillo, *Chicanos in a Changing Society: From Mexican Pueblos to American Barrio in Santa Barbara and Southern California, 1848–1930* (Cambridge, Mass., 1979), 200–01. For a discussion of the agricultural interests recruiting Mexican workers, see Mark Reisler, *By the Sweat of Their Brows: Mexican Immigrant Labor in the United States, 1900–1940* (Westport, Conn., 1976). Los Angeles Board of Education Nationality or Racial Survey, 1938, Office of the Secretariat, Los Angeles Board of Education.

7. *Dictionary of American Biography*, Supplement 6 (1956–60), s.v. "Lewis Madison Terman." Lewis M. Terman et al., *Intelligence Tests and School Reorganization* (Yonkers-on-Hudson, N.Y., 1922); Los Angeles Board of Education, Department of Psychology and Educational Research *Bulletin*, Sept. 1928, 13. (Cited hereafter as *Bulletin*.) Sutherland had been brought from Yale University to become director of Psychology and Educational Research.

8. Daniel J. Kevles, "Testing the Army's Intelligence: Psychologists and the Military in World War I," *Journal of American History* 55(Dec. 1968):565–81.

9. The earliest work in achievement tests was done by E. L. Thorndike. Achievement tests ran the gamut: arithmetic, first introduced in 1908; spelling, 1910; handwriting and drawing, 1913; reading, 1914; and language ability, 1916.

10. Lewis Terman, *Intelligence of School Children* (Boston, 1919), 73. The concept of intelligence quotient had been used by the German psychologist, William Stern, but Terman introduced the term into the language. Daniel J. Kevles, *In the Name of Eugenics: Genetics and the Use of Human Heredity* (New York, 1985), 79.

11. Tyack, *One Best System*, 191. Tyack notes that experts hired to make school surveys published 67 of them between 1910 and 1919 and 114 between 1920 and 1927. His term "administrative progressives" aptly describes Los Angeles school people. Los Angeles Board of Education, *Minutes to the Board*, 18:399. Walter Jessup and Albert Shiels, *Report of the Advisory Committee to the Board of Education* (Los Angeles, 1915). In 1916 Jessup became president of the State University of Iowa.

12. Lawrence Cremin, *The Transformation of the School: Progressivism in American Education, 1876–1957* (New York, 1961), 200. In Cremin's opinion, Bobbitt typified the change in progressive education in the 1920s. Tyack, *One Best System*, 144, 163.

13. *Bulletin*, 4 Dec. 1922, 4, 20 Nov. 1922, 2.

14. *The Nation*, 17 Oct. 1928, cited in Daniel J. Kevles, *The Physicists* (New York, 1977), 174; Lawrence Cremin showed the relationship of progressive education to science when he wrote, "If science promised nothing else, it promised efficiency; this ultimately was the plum the educational scientists dangled before the taxpaying public." Cremin, *Transformation of the School*, 192.

15. Los Angeles Board of Education, *Reports* of the Board of Education, 1900–1901, 103.

16. Harlan C. Mines, "What Los Angeles Is Doing with the Results of Testing," *Journal of Educational Research* 5(Jan. 1922):45–47.

17. Ibid., 47.

18. *Bulletin*, 15 June 1925, 8.

19. Ibid. Rudolph Pintner authored several intelligence and performance tests, but in 1924 Raybold most likely administered the standard Pintner-Cunningham. Pintner had used his Pinter Non-language Group Test on foreign children and published the results in 1922. Pintner and Ruth Keller, "Intelligence Test of Foreign Children," *Journal of Educational Psychology* 13(Apr. 1922):214–22. In 1930 he published the Pintner Non-language Primary Mental Tests for use on deaf children in kindergarten through second grade with directions administered in pantomime, and he established the test's validity by correlations with the Stanford-Binet and the Pintner-Cunningham. Rudolph Pintner, *Non-language Primary Mental Tests* (New York, 1930).

20. Raybold expressed surprise that the San Fernando students understood more English than the counselors imagined, and yet, instead of taking this new-found information and using it in a constructive manner, the testers misinterpreted it. The children probably were what educators now call "limited English speakers," which means that they had an English vocabulary of about one hundred words.

21. *Bulletin*, 2 Oct. 1925, 12–15.

22. In 1935 Hershel T. Manuel, professor of educational psychology at the University of Texas, published his findings on the "Spanish and English Editions of the Stanford-Binet in Relation to the Abilities of Mexican Children" in the university's *Bulletin*. Manuel's interest in school performances of children of Mexican heritage in Texas had made him sensitive to some of the difficulties the children had in the often hostile environment of public schools. Manuel and his staff, including George I. Sanchez, one of the first Mexican Americans to criticize the conclusions drawn from conventional testing, had rejected the two commonly used Spanish translations of the 1916 Stanford Revision because neither fit the needs of their subjects. They felt that their translation closely followed the English version, but they allowed for some changes. Because the two languages were not always parallel, some of the idioms differed, and their translation better fit the dialect used by Mexicans living in Texas.

The Texas University staff administered the Spanish and English editions of the Stanford-Binet in 1931–32 to Spanish-speaking children in San Antonio. The findings reinforced the assumptions made by Los Angeles school people on the relationships among such factors as intelligence, language ability, socioeconomics, and years spent in school. In most cases, the Spanish version yielded higher mental ages and intelligence quotients than did the English edition. In grades two to five, the average I.Q. was 82.5 on the Spanish edition and 80.5 on the English.

After careful analysis, Manuel concluded that the lower scores represented a lack of training or experience. He speculated: "On account of their generally low cultural level and their retardation in school their experiences are greatly restricted. It is possible that this is reflected in such tests as the giving of differences between a president and a king and perhaps even in arranging the weights. . . . The parents of 10 out of 14 children in the fifth grade said that their children had never had toys such as blocks or puzzles." Hershel T. Manuel, "Spanish and English Editions of the Stanford-Binet in Relation to the Abilities of Mexican Children," University of Texas *Bulletin*, 22 Aug. 1935, 30.

23. *Bulletin*, 2 Oct. 1925, 13.

24. Ibid. Until at least 1931, the schools continued to use translated tests. See *Bulletin*, 5 Jan. 1931, 4.

25. In the *Bulletin* Heim stated, "language difficulty is often indicative of mental deficiency," *Bulletin*, 2 Oct. 1925, 13.

26. In the *Bulletin* Heim stated, "language difficulty is often indicative of mental deficiency," Dec. 1925, 9–12.

27. Ibid., Dec. 1926, 10–15.

28. Ibid., 13.

29. Ibid.

30. Ibid., 15.

31. Ibid., Feb. 1928, 13–15; for a discussion of matriculation of Italian and Jewish students in Providence, Rhode Island, public schools during this period see Joel Perlman, "Who Stayed in School? Social Structure and Academic Achievement in the Determination of Enrollment Patterns, Providence, Rhode Island, 1880–1925," *Journal of American History* 27(Dec. 1985):588–614.

32. *Bulletin*, Sept. 1928, 10–12.

33. Ibid., Mar. 1929, 6–8.

34. Ibid., Nov. 1931, 40–42.

35. Ibid., Mar. 1929, 8.

36. Bureau of the Census, *Thirteenth Census*, vol. 2, *Population*, 185, *Fourteenth Census*, vol. 3, *Population*, 125, *Fifteenth Census*, vol. 3, *Population* (Washington, D.C., 1930), 287, *Sixteenth Census*, vol. 2, *Population* (Washington, D.C., 1940), 132. The sixteenth census records the black population as 63,774.

37. Lawrence DeGraaf, "Negro Migration to Los Angeles, 1930–1950," (Ph.D. diss., University of California, Los Angeles, 1962); and idem, "The City of Black Angels: Emergence of the Los Angeles Ghetto, 1890–1930," *Pacific Historical Review* 39(Aug. 1970):323–52.

38. *Bulletin*, 12 Nov. 1923, 1–8; American Blacks sometimes, but not always, surprised the examiners. In a 1924–25 Massachusetts report, Black students scored higher than Portuguese children. As editor of *American Ethnic Groups*, Thomas Sowell noted that in Massachusetts schools with mixed ethnic populations of French-Canadians, Italian, Polish, and Portuguese, Blacks had the highest percentage of I.Q. scores over 120. Thomas Sowell, ed., *American Ethnic Groups* (Washington, D.C., 1978), 207–08.

39. Ibid., Sept. 1931, 65–70.

40. Wynn Commodore, ed., *Negro Who's Who in California* (Los Angeles, 1948) 128; Irving C. Hendrick, principal investigator, "Public Policy toward the Education of Non-White Minority Group Children in California, 1849–1970" (Unpublished Report, National Institute of Education Project No. NE-G-003-0082, University of California, Riverside, 1975). Whitaker recommended encouraging talented Blacks rather than dissuading them. She found the school's practice of admonishing bright Blacks against advancing academically one of the "most reprehensible . . . to be found among educators." Hazel G. Whitaker, "A Study of Gifted Negro Children in the Los Angeles City Schools" (M.A. thesis, University of Southern California, 1931), 82.

41. Some of the classes fitted Blacks into subservient occupations; for example, no other high school except Jefferson offered vocational training to become a maid. For a comprehensive account of Black school segregation see Hendrick, "Public Policy toward the Education of Non-White Minority Group Children in California," and Bessie Averne McClenahan, *The Changing Urban Neighborhood* (Los Angeles, 1929), 92. Community groups pressured the board through their petitions; see Los Angeles Board of Education *Minutes*, 21 July 1921, 433. Also see, David Ment, "Patterns of Public School Segregation, 1900–1940: A Comparative Study of New York City, New Rochelle, and New Haven," in

Schools in Cities: Consensus and Conflict in American Education, ed. Ronald K. Goodenow and Diane Ravitch (New York, 1983), 67–110.

42. Bulletin, Jan. 1932, 65–70; Bureau of the Census, *Fifteenth Census*, vol. 3, part 1, *Population*, 266. The Japanese community had grown from just a few at the turn of the century to over 35,000 in 1930.

43. High School Teachers' Association and Principals' Club, *Los Angeles School Journal*, 17 Jan. 1927, 30.

44. Ibid., 27 Apr. 1925, 34–35.

45. Los Angeles *Examiner*, 27 May 1927.

46. U.S. Department of Interior, Office of Education, "The Education of Spanish Speaking Children in Five Southwestern States," by Anne Reynolds, *Bulletin 7* (Washington D.C., 1933), 46–47.

47. Ibid., 46–47. Reynolds may have been familiar with the work of educators at the University of Texas.

48. Tyack, *One Best System*, 164, 180.

49. *Minutes* of the Board of Education, 31:433.

50. *Bulletin*, 12 Nov. 1923, 2, 3.

51. Gilbert G. Gonzales, "The System of Public Education and Its Function within Chicano Communities, 1920–1930" (Ph.D. diss., University of California, Los Angeles, 1974).

10

The Politics of Educational Retrenchment in Detroit, 1929–1935

Jeffrey Mirel

In 1930, Detroit was the nation's fourth largest city and one of the world's great manufacturing centers.[1] During the 1920s its schools had been transformed along Progressive lines and, by 1929, were considered among the best in the nation. The Great Depression, however, devastated the city's economy and plunged its schools into an unparalleled financial crisis. Detroit thus provides an excellent opportunity to investigate questions about the process of retrenchment under these conditions.

The City and the Schools in Good Times, 1917–29

During the years that stretched from America's entry into World War I to the stock market crash in 1929, Detroit stood as one of the jewels of the New Era. Sidney Glazer calls it the "boom city of all boom cities," its population growing from 993,678 in 1920 to 1,568,662 in 1930.[2] The city struggled throughout those years to provide services to a metropolis racing behind a motor driven economy.[3] In meeting those needs Detroit's bonded debt had increased to over $255 million by 1930, nearly ten times what it had been a decade before.[4] The city's tax levy jumped from $25.5 million in 1920 to $76 million in 1930.[5]

The form of municipal government that met the challenges of Detroit's dramatic expansion came into being in 1918 in a charter revision directed by the Detroit Citizens' League. The League was a "good government" organization whose leadership was generally composed of men from the upper reaches of the social and business worlds of Detroit.[6] In its quest for efficient and honest government it succeeded in expanding the powers of the mayor, reducing the forty-two person ward-based council to one of nine members elected at-large, and mandating nonpartisan city elections. As in many other cities where such Progressive reforms were instituted, their effect was to reduce the political strength of ethnic and working class voters while increasing the influence of groups like the Citizens' League.[7] The Detroit Bureau of Governmental Research (a semi-public organization created to "investigate local problems") and the Detroit Board of Commerce, for example, prepared annual analyses of the city budget and became particularly influential in fiscal matters.[8]

The growth of Detroit's public schools in the 1920s was perhaps even more remarkable than that of the city itself. In 1920, 122,690 young people were served by 3,750 public school teachers, supervisors, and administrators. By 1930, student population was 250,994 and the staff had reached 7,525.[9] At that time the city boasted an educational system that ran from kindergarten through graduate school, the Detroit Board of Education operating five colleges in addition to its K-12 program.[10] The building program that was initiated to handle the unprecedented growth was one of the most ambitious in the country.[11] The Board of Education's share of city tax revenue rose from almost $12 million in the 1920–21 school year to nearly $18 million in 1929–30.[12] In that year Detroit's school system was the single largest recipient of the city's tax revenue, receiving some 58 percent more than streets and roads, its nearest competitor.[13]

The Board of Education in the 1920s, like the new municipal government, was a product of Progressive Era reforms. Detroit provides a vivid example of the interrelatedness of political and educational changes in those years. The reform of school governance led the Progressive thrust in Detroit.

Like their civic counterparts, the main educational reformers were drawn from the city's social and business elite. Their primary objective was to eliminate the twenty-one member ward-based Board and replace it with a seven-member body elected at-large. In 1916, after a long struggle, the reformers placed their proposal before the people of Detroit, who voted overwhelmingly to institute the change.[14] The first Board elected under the new law represented a virtual takeover by Detroit's elite. Of the twenty-one members of the previous Board only one, Samuel C. Mumford, was listed in the city's social register.[15] All seven members of the new Board, which included Mumford, were listed in Detroit's blue book.[16] Where the old Board had had a sizeable number of clerks and tradesmen, the new Board was composed entirely of important businessmen, professionals, and, in the case of Laura Osborn, the wife of a prominent attorney.[17] During the next two decades three non-elite Detroiters were elected as school trustees, but the majority of the Board members from 1917 to 1939 were drawn from Detroit's "best families."[18]

The new Board member's plans for transforming Detroit's schools unfolded slowly over the next few years. They increased the powers of the superintendent and, in 1919, hired Frank Cody to fill the position.[19] Cody, who had risen through the Detroit system, remained superintendent for twenty-three years.[20] In 1920, Cody and the Board commissioned a major school survey to analyze almost every aspect of the city's public educational system. The findings of the survey had a far-reaching impact on the Board's educational policies for the next two decades. The survey was used to justify such fundamental changes as the imposition of a 6-3-3 form of school organization, the converting of all elementary buildings into platoon schools, and a commitment to comprehensive high schools.[21] Courses such as art, home economics, manual training, and physical education were increasingly emphasized on all levels but especially on the elementary where they were central to the platoon system. In addition, the Board created a psychological research bureau, greatly increased the scope of its testing program, and expanded extracurricular activities, particularly Scouting.[22] By the late 1920s successful adaptation of a wide range of "progressive" reforms had made the Detroit school system a national leader in education.[23]

THE DESPERATE YEARS, 1929–1933

Like the rest of the country, Detroit experienced the effects of the Depression slowly but irrevocably through late 1929 and the early months of 1930. By April, however, with over 90,000 Detroit workers unemployed, evidence of the economic collapse was unmistakable.[24] According to Sidney Fine, "Detroit was the hardest hit big city in the nation during the Hoover years."[25] The index of industrial employment that had reached 135 in February 1929 "averaged 87 for 1930, fell to 66 in 1931, and 56 in 1932, and ranged from 29 to 50 during the first four months of 1933."[26] In November 1932, it was estimated that over half of the city's approximately 690,000 workers were unemployed or working part time. Nearly 28 percent of the 400,000 auto-related jobs in 1929 had been eliminated a year later. By 1933, fewer than 30,000 out of an original 100,000 workers were still on the job at Ford's giant River Rouge plant.[27] Aggregate wages from industrial production dropped from $511,000,000 in 1929 to $218,000,000 in 1933. Retail sales in 1933 were 42 percent of what they had been in 1929.[28] Some of the most staggering declines were in the construction industry which did $183 million worth of business in 1926 and only $4 million worth in 1933.[29] In one area that most seriously affected the schools, tax delinquencies, Detroit led the nation. Unpaid taxes ran at a rate of 15 percent for 1930–31, 26 percent for 1931–32, and 35 percent for 1932–33—in every instance almost one-third higher than that of other major U.S. cities.[30] Every blow to Detroit's economy had impact on the public schools. School revenue from taxation fell from $17,885,000 in 1930–31 to $12,875,000 in 1932–33. At the same time, enrollment rose from 249,031 in November 1929, to 260,113 in November 1933. That growth came entirely in the high school section as teenagers unable to find jobs chose to remain in school; between 1929 and 1933 enrollment in Detroit's high schools jumped from 25,827 to 37,062.[31] Compounding the problem of declining revenue and a growing student population was the reduction of personnel through attrition. Between 1930 and 1933, 476 teachers and supervisors left their positions (through retirement, death, etc.) and were not replaced. Consequently, classes increased in size at every level, but particularly in the high schools where the median class size rose from 32.9 in 1929 to 37.2 in 1933.[32] The schools, together with the Michigan Children's Fund, set up a program of free lunches for children whose families were on relief. During the worst months of the Depression those lunches were, for many of the children, the only meals they ate.[33]

The public schools' response to the crisis was shaped not only by the economic collapse but by the city's political turmoil. Two features of Detroit's municipal government proved to have a profound effect on the public schools. The first was that the Board of Education did not have complete control over its revenues. The Progressives' attempt to "take the schools out of politics and politics out of the schools"[34] had been only partly successful in that the mayor and the Common Council had final approval over the total amount of tax money allotted to education. Although the school trustees retained control over how the money was to be spent, battles over the school budget (which annually stretched from December through April) were often fought more at City Hall than at the Board of Education. Even in the prosperous 1920s Board members had complained of tight-fisted councilmen.[35] In the midst of the Depression the struggle for the schools' share of tax revenues became one of the most heated political battles of the day.

The second factor that greatly influenced the schools in those years was the staggering relief burden borne by the city through its Department of Public Welfare. Unlike most American cities Detroit provided for its poor and unemployed through public funds rather than through private charities. As rising unemployment compelled greater relief expenditures the city was forced to borrow heavily from local banks and divert funds from other city departments. In fiscal 1931, the city spent almost $14 million on relief.[36] By 1933, the city's interest payment on loans was greater than the entire public school tax levy.[37] Until 1933, when the Reconstruction Finance Corporation (RFC) took over the bulk of Detroit's relief budget, and 1934, when the city refinanced its debt, the schools were engaged in a bitter contest with other municipal departments for a share of the dwindling tax revenues.

The schools' battles for funds were not, however, limited to conflicts with governmental officials. In December 1929, Ralph Stone, chairman of the board of the Detroit Security Trust Company, persuaded Mayor Charles Bowles (1929–30) to appoint a citizen's committee to advise the city on fiscal matters. The Committee on City Finance (generally known as the Stone Committee) was composed of representatives of the Michigan Manufacturing Association, the Detroit Real Estate Board, the Detroit Board of Commerce, the Business Property Association, the Woodward Avenue Improvement Association, the Detroit Automobile Club, the Detroit Bureau of Governmental Research, and the Detroit Citizens' League. Similar to other business-dominated "watchdog" organizations that appeared during the Depression to oversee public expenditures, the Stone Committee's power grew in relation to the increasingly desperate financial straits of the city.[38] When conditions worsened in Detroit, the city's requests for loans from local (and later New York) banks became contingent on the Stone Committee's approval. Demanding a balanced budget as the prerequisite for credit, the committee, and ultimately Stone himself, began to wield enormous power over city government. Members of Mayor Frank Murphy's (1930–33) staff called Stone the "Tenth Councilman," but Stone's power may well have exceeded the mayor's. Throughout Murphy's administration the mayor publicly denounced the growing control of "economic royalists" and "financial dictators," but the Stone Committee, in fact, had a stranglehold on the public purse. Invariably, the budget cuts Stone demanded primarily affected the two most costly areas of governmental service, welfare and public education.[39]

The seven members of the Board of Education who contended with the city government and the Stone Committee over school revenues included, besides Laura Osborn, three men listed in the city's social register. They were Dr. Burt R. Shurly, Dr. Angus McLean, and A. D. Jamieson, a vice-president of the Union-Guardian Trust Company.[40] Frank Gorman, a partner in an insurance company, and John H. Webster, a pharmacist, were in 1925 the first "non-elite" Detroiters to gain school board seats. Webster, in fact, had received the endorsement of the Detroit Federation of Labor (DFL) and Gorman was said to be "well thought of in labor circles."[41] Neither, however, disturbed the unanimity that marked most board decisions in the late 1920s. The most notable change on the Board came in April 1929, when Edward H. Williams, an insurance agent, ended Samuel Mumford's twenty-two years as a school trustee. Williams was the first avowedly pro-labor candidate to win a Board seat; the Detroit *Labor News* saw Williams's victory as a clear case of the people triumphing over the "interests."[42] Williams served until January 1935, when he resigned to become Wayne County auditor. He was replaced by Oscar Hull, an attorney, who, unlike Williams, was listed in Detroit's social register.[43] Except for that one change, the composition of the Board remained the same throughout most of the Depression decade.[44]

The Control of Retrenchment

Research into the social class composition of school boards has been an important feature of educational history and sociology for over sixty years. Beginning with the work of Scott Nearing and George Counts, such research has proceeded on the assumption that social class is the truest indicator of personal motives and the best predictor of educational policy. From that perspective, once elite control over a board of education is established the schools become, in essence, a functional appendage of powerful business and industrial interests.[45] The retrenchment controversies in Detroit offer an excellent opportunity to explore these assumptions.

The events that most readily shed light on those questions occurred in Detroit in 1930–31 and centered on issues of maintaining the teachers' salary schedule. On February 20, 1930, the Stone Committee issued a report calling on Common Council and the mayor to eliminate all raises from the 1930–31 budget. The Committee specifically demanded the deletion of

$732,000 in step increases for Detroit's teachers and more than $326,000 in step increases for city employees.[46] The Council, in contrast to the school board, was predominantly a middle-class body. Only one councilman was listed in the city's social register, while one had a trade union background (he was a bricklayer), and one had ties to the city's Polish community. The majority were businessmen; five of the nine were realtors.[47]

After a month of hearings in which the increases were hotly debated, Common Council voted to suspend the salary schedule for its own employees and to deny the Board of Education sufficient funds to grant the teachers their increases.[48] The Council's action was based on the belief, repeatedly voiced by several of its members and the Stone Committee, that the Board would not suspend its salary schedule willingly.[49] They had good reason for that fear. Throughout the hearings the Board strongly opposed suspending the schedule. At one point Board members even threatened to generate the money for the raises by shortening the school year if Council failed to appropriate the necessary funds.[50]

Throughout these months the Board was united in its efforts to protect its authority over the allocation of school funds and in "keeping faith" with its teachers. This commitment was highlighted dramatically in November 1930, during the bitterest of the debates over the teachers' raises. In September the Board had acceded to Stone's request and suspended the schedule;[51] but, with the receipt of an unexpectedly large state aid check in November, the Board found itself with enough money to grant the increase. The Stone Committee called on the Board to stand by its September decision. The Board instead chose to stand by its teachers, voting unanimously to grant the increases.[52] It maintained that position throughout the budget battle of the following year. In March 1931, the Board, again ignoring specific demands by the Stone Committee and the Board of Commerce, granted the teachers' raises for the 1931–32 school year.[53] It was supported in that decision by Mayor Murphy and by the favorable conclusions reached in a study of teachers' wages undertaken by a body of civic leaders. But, as the Board of Commerce's representative on the study noted in his minority report, the Board of Education stood alone among city departments in granting the increases.[54]

The Board of Education's defiance of the Stone Committee and the Board of Commerce did not go unanswered. At the first signs that the inspectors would not cooperate on the matter of salaries the Stone Committee urged the Common Council to review the laws pertaining to the school board's power over allocations.[55] In March 1930, Common Council requested that the city attorney "furnish an opinion on whether or not the Board of Education can use the funds appropriated for any other purpose than that specifically indicated [by the Common Council]."[56] After the attorney noted that in his opinion a 1927 revision of the school laws gave the Board complete authority over allocated funds, members of the Stone Committee began seeking a legislative solution to their problems with the Board.

The businessmen had discussed bringing the Board of Education under stricter control by the mayor and Council as early as February 1930, but nothing had come of the discussions. Following the Board's approval of the salary increases in November the idea once more seemed appealing. After the Board's decision, Stone declared, "[Granting the increases] is just another of those instances which furnished ammunition to those who believe the city budget and the budget of the Board of Education should be under one control and that control should be the Mayor and the Common Council."[57] Stone added that his committee was not yet ready to take legislative action, but the threat was clear. Several members of Stone's group were anxious to move in that direction. John L. Lovett, general manager of the Michigan Manufacturers' Association, and William P. Lovett of the Detroit Citizens' League were particularly vociferous in their calls for legislation to bring the Board of Education into line.[58]

Despite these threats, the Board did not alter its position on teachers' salaries or on its prerogatives in determining cutbacks. In March 1931, the Board's continued commitment to maintaining the salary schedule prompted the Stone Committee to appoint five of its members to "look into changes in the school laws which would curtail the expenditures of the present Board of Education."[59] The subcommittee included Divie B. Duffield, president of the Detroit Citizens' League; Dr. Lent D. Upson, director of the Detroit Bureau of Government Research; John L. Lovett, executive secretary of the Michigan Manufacturers' Association; G. Oliver Frick of the Downtown Property Owners' Association; and the executive secretary of the Detroit Real Estate Board. Their primary interest was the enactment of legislation to place the Board more firmly under the control of the mayor and the Council.[60] Lending force to the movement, Common Council voted in February 1931, to strip the Board of its authority to make unilateral property condemnations.[61] Three months later the City Controller formally requested the Board to refrain from acquiring any new property. At the meeting during which that request was read into the minutes, the Board voted unanimously to have its legal counsel draft legislation to give it complete financial autonomy from the city.[62]

Over the next few years neither the Board nor the Stone Committee made any progress in Lansing. Overwhelmed by the press of events the Board and the city became more concerned with sheer survival than with departmental autonomy.[63] The city's business leaders, who saw several important Detroiters break ranks over the issue of Council control over the Board,[64] also dropped the matter because by January 1932, the Stone Committee needed no legislation to gain its objectives regarding control of the school budget. The city's need for credit was so great and the Stone Committee's approval of the loans was so critical that neither Mayor Murphy, Common Council, nor the school board could have resisted Stone's demands, however much they might have wished to do so.

In the final analysis, the businessmen's failure to enact the school legislation is less important than the fact that it was proposed at all. The persistent demand by several of Detroit's most powerful social and business leaders for greater Council control over the school board flatly contradicts the assumption that a concert of elite interests determined Board policy, at least on the issue of teachers' wages. Indeed, there is a striking difference in the response to the Stone Committee by the middle-class Common Council and that of the elite-dominated Board of Education. Council acquiesced early in 1930 to the businessmen's demands while the Board unanimously defied those demands for almost two more years.[65]

If social class *was* a factor in determining the stand taken by Board members, it made itself felt in a very unexpected manner. The Board's resistance to the Stone Committee can, in part, be attributed to the failure of the trustees to be intimidated by the city's powerful business leaders. Social position in this case cancelled out social position. If we add to that the reawakened Progressive commitment to keep the schools free from political control and the legal framework designed for that purpose (including the trustees' staggered six-year terms and the Board's control over allocated funds) the picture of Progressive changes in Detroit's educational politics takes on new dimensions. The Board maintained its autonomy longer than any other city department. Throughout 1930 and 1931, it put what it believed were the best interests of its employees and its students ahead of the demands of city government and the Stone Committee. To a large extent its actions can be seen as a consequence of Progressive reform.

THE BATTLE OVER TEACHERS' SALARIES

Although the Board had stood firm on the issue of teachers' salaries in 1930 and 1931, the trustees knew that the schools would in some way have to share in the city's retrenchment. Once they settled who would have the greatest voice in determining school cutbacks, the Board members still faced the difficult choices of where and how much to cut. They faced a limited range of options. Additional revenue could have been raised by increasing fees and tuition in the system's night schools and colleges. School services such as the psychological clinic, the Children's Museum, and health programs (such as baths and visual education) could have been cut back or eliminated. Scheduled building construction could have been suspended and the maintenance of school property substantially reduced. The school program itself could have been curtailed through the elimination of what some called "fads and frills" courses. Finally, the salary budget could have been cut by a hiring freeze, layoffs, wage cuts or the shortening of the school year.

These options were constrained by the reality of the school budget. Fees and tuition, for example, accounted for less than 4 percent of the revenues. Sizeable cutbacks could be made only in three areas: construction, salaries, and programs. From 1929 to 1932 construction and capital costs averaged more than $6 million annually, over 20 percent of the Board's expenses. Salaries during those years averaged just less than 75 percent.[66] The programs that were most heavily criticized (art, home economics, music, manual training, and physical education) accounted for 10 percent of the budget with almost all of that in salaries.[67] From 1930 to 1935 the Board utilized nearly all of those options. Fees were raised, services and maintenance curtailed, a freeze was put on hiring, and construction costs reduced to a mere $91,200 by 1932–33.[68] Generally, the political repercussions stemming from these cutbacks were neither great nor prolonged.[69] By contrast, the question of cutting salaries and/or programs generated some of the fiercest political battles in Detroit's educational history.

From January 1930 to January 1933, the controversy centered almost exclusively on teachers' salaries. The issue was part of a larger argument over reducing government spending that many business leaders felt was crucial to ending the Depression. In an early version of "supply side" economics, businessmen argued that the tax cuts that would follow slashes in spending would stimulate investment and spur business recovery.[70] In Detroit, like much of the country, the school budget was among the largest of municipal expenses and thus was a natural target for those calling for cuts in government spending. Teachers' salaries made up the bulk of the budgets. It did not take the gift of prophecy to warn, as the *American School Board Journal* did in 1930, "When the war cry of retrenchment and economy comes it is going to be popular to strike at teachers' salaries without consideration of the character of service which teachers render."[71]

The battle lines over the issue were clearly drawn in Detroit in the first year of the Depression. The Stone Committee's call for educational retrenchment was enthusiastically supported by the "very conservative" Detroit *Free Press*, which, as early as February 1930, applauded the Committee's courage in attacking the "sacred cow" of teachers' salaries. The paper warned disgruntled teachers that there were plenty of applicants for their jobs.[72] Similarly, the Detroit Board of Commerce, which published its views in a weekly journal called *The Detroiter*, also lined up as an unrelenting advocate of large-scale school cutbacks, primarily in the area of teachers' salaries. A somewhat more disparate group opposed the calls for salary reductions. It was led by the Detroit *News*, a generally conservative, pro-business paper with the largest circulation in the city. The Detroit *Times*, which was owned by William Randolph Hearst and appealed to the city's "lower middle class and workingmen" also vigorously opposed most cutbacks in the education budget.[73] The most militantly anti-retrenchment mainstream paper was the Detroit *Labor News*, the weekly publication of the Detroit Federation of Labor. Basing its stand not only on unwavering support for public education but also on the belief that high wages and increasing demand were the only means to economic recovery, the DFL and the *Labor News* stood four square against almost all cuts in the education budget.[74]

The positions on school retrenchment crystallized in November 1930, over the Board's about-face in allowing the implementation of the 1930–31 salary schedule and in Mayor Murphy's refusal to veto the action.[75] The *Free Press* supported the Stone Committee's demand that the salary schedule be suspended and, in a series of editorials, attacked the city's teachers, the Board of Education, and Mayor Murphy. The tone of the final editorial was particularly bitter, congratulating the teachers on their raises "at a time when most people that experience any change of income are suffering decreases, and a good many people are trying to get along without any income at all."[76] The Detroit *News* and the *Times*, on the other hand, strongly defended the actions, the *Times* noting: "The board is to be congratulated and Mayor Murphy is to be congratulated on maintaining the credit of the school system in the face of the most powerful kind of opposition."[77] The *Labor News*, which had castigated its favorite, Edward Williams, when he supported the wage freeze, ultimately applauded Williams, the Board and Murphy for their refusal to knuckle under to "the Stone Committee and other reactionaries." The position taken by the newspapers and the organizations in November 1930 remained constant throughout the retrenchment battles to come, even as the arguments intensified.[78]

The salary issue, of course, could not be ignored as the city's economic decline continued unchecked.[79] In the last three months of 1930, Ford fired over 27,000 employees, almost 22 percent of its total workforce.[80] Apple vendors appeared on Detroit's street corners two months later, and the comment of the *Free Press* that the teachers got raises while others went without wages altogether must have galled many with its accuracy.[81] In its last meeting of 1930 the Board cut some $3.9 million from its 1931–32 budget request (primarily from maintenance and capital costs).[82] The Board of Commerce angrily and accurately described the cut as one that existed mostly on paper since much of the money was for *planned* expansion. An editorial in *The Detroiter* cautioned its readers not to be fooled into thinking taxes would go down and demanded real cutbacks in school spending.[83]

In January 1931, as the budget hearings approached, three separate committees filed reports on educational retrenchment that inflamed tempers and influenced decisions regarding teachers' salaries. The first study was prepared for Mayor Murphy by three leading businessmen drawn from Packard Motor Company, Chrysler Corporation, and the People's Wayne County Bank.[84] They recommended savings in the school budget of some 7 to 10 percent that included a one-week shortening of the school year (equaling a 2.5 percent cut in teachers' wages), fee hikes, curtailment of services, and minimal expenditures on construction. In addition, they urged major program changes, calling for a 20 percent slash in funds for kindergarten and a decrease in vocational education expenditures to make them "commensurate with the average cost for a student in high school"—approximately a 20 percent reduction.[85] School officials immediately denounced the report. Laura Osborn commented, "Of course those men know very little about the schools."[86]

Following that report was the annual budget analysis prepared by the Board of Commerce and the Detroit Bureau of Governmental Research. The education subcommittee, composed of John L. Lovett and G. Oliver Frick (both members of the Stone Committee), submitted its study on February 3, 1931. Lovett and Frick angrily accused Board officials of deliberately obfuscating elements of the budget, thus making it almost impossible to be precise about where savings could be made. They nevertheless recommended reductions similar to those suggested by the committee of three businessmen, especially regarding fees, services, and construction. Unlike the latter businessmen, however, they made no mention of programs and instead called for a major cut in teachers' wages. "With decrease in the cost of living," the sub-committee claimed, "it is apparent that a twenty percent reduction would leave them where they were a year ago."[87] Throughout February the Board of Education and the Board of Commerce waged a bitter war of words over the tone and substance of the report.[88] Superintendent Cody accurately pointed out that prices had not fallen even 10 percent; and, at one Board meeting, several trustees "dared" Board of Commerce officials to prove that their suggestions would not cripple the school system.[89]

The final report, and the one that had the greatest impact on the 1931 salary battle, came from a committee created by Mayor Murphy to study the issue. Composed of fourteen members, seven from the school system and seven representing various civic organizations, the Salary Schedule Committee presented its findings in a detailed report dated February 17, 1931. This study noted that Detroit's teachers were poorly paid when compared to teachers in other major U.S. cities, ranking twenty-first in elementary salaries, fifth in intermediate salaries, and thirteenth in high school salaries. Other boards of education across the country indicated to the committee that they were not planning to defer salary increases in 1931–32. In light of these facts the committee recommended that the salary schedule be maintained for the upcoming year. However, the mayor's committee acknowledged the severe financial distress of the city, and urged the Board to cut teachers' salaries 4 to 5 percent after the scheduled raises were granted.[90] Only two members dissented. The more notable dissenter was C. E. Rightor, who worked for the Bureau of Governmental Research and represented the Board of Commerce.[91] Frank Murphy and the Common Council (apparently convinced by the majority report) settled on a 3 percent cut in appropriations to the Board and left the matter of salaries entirely in the hands of the inspectors.[92]

The first opportunity to gauge popular reaction to these events came in the school board elections that took place on April 6, 1931. The re-election campaigns of John Webster and Frank Gorman coincided with the budget battle, and their stands in favor of the teachers' raises became a major issue.[93] Their main opponent, Dr. Albert Krohn, ran on a platform that called for suspension of the salary schedule and for additional school retrenchment.[94] The Detroit voters faced a clear choice and overwhelmingly returned Webster and Gorman to office (Gorman more than doubling Krohn's total vote).[95] The Detroit News and the Labor News took the election as a sign that the people did indeed support the Board and its recent actions.[96]

The popular will could not stem Detroit's economic decline, which by summer had become precipitous. In May, faced with growing tax delinquencies, the Board ordered fee hikes at all night schools and colleges, drastic cutbacks in summer school, and at last, a 3 percent cut in teachers' wages.[97] There were no protests, for the teachers probably appreciated that their wage cut was modest when compared to what other workers in the Detroit area were suffering. By April, Ford had laid off over an additional third of its employees, and half of those who still held jobs at Ford had had their wages slashed 40 percent.[98] Edmund Wilson reported that the auto plants in Flint had cut wages by 33 percent and Detroit's metal finishers, "the highest grade of skilled labor," had taken a staggering wage cut from $1.10 per hour to 15 cents.[99] "The enormous organism of Detroit, one of the vital organs of the country," wrote Wilson during these months, "is now seen, for all its Middle Western vigor, to have become partially atrophied. It is clogged with dead tissue and its life is bleeding away, and no one can do anything to stop it."[100]

In July, the city faced the first of many serious cash shortages. Ralph Stone wrote Murphy that it was time for "sharp retrenchment by the Board of Education."[101] The Board responded three weeks later with $445,000 worth of additional cuts in maintenance and services.[102] Those actions were merely stop-gap measures. Earlier that month the Board was informed that its share of the city's tax delinquencies would amount to some $2.5 million. The need for a more calculated long-range plan for retrenchment was apparent.[103]

On August 11, Board President A. D. Jamieson presented to his fellow trustees a lengthy analysis of the situation before them. He acknowledged that the Board's revenues were inextricably bound to those of the city. Detroit's municipal retrenchment, he stated, would have to be borne by all governmental departments, and the Board had pledged to the mayor and the controller that it would assume its share of the cuts.[104] But the means for achieving those reductions were still in the Board's hands, and Jamieson indicated how the reductions might be made. He underscored the system's commitment to "modern education—the education of the whole child." Chiding those who wished to "return to the little red school house," he declared that the schools should try to continue as much of their regular program as possible.[105]

Jamieson was less sanguine about maintaining the teacher's salaries. Although he defended the Board's past actions on the salary question, he noted that, salaries were the largest single expense of the Board, and "the obvious source of substantial economy." He added that the cost of living had fallen 13 percent in the past year, that private businesses had "readjusted" their wages, and that taxpayers who supported the schools were suffering wage cuts of their own.[106] Jamieson made no specific request for wage reductions, but the message was clear. Perhaps the one ray of light for the city's teachers was Jamieson's statement that the Board would attempt to retain all its employees.[107] At the close of the speech Jamieson presented a set of cost-cutting recommendations designed to save some $800,000, including a hiring freeze, leaves of absence for married women teachers, the elimination of paid sick leave, a centralization of the system's administrative offices, shelving of new building plans, and further fee hikes.[108] Jamieson's proposals were passed unanimously.[109]

Jamieson's speech proved to be a watershed in the making of Board policy.[110] It essentially defined the course of educational retrenchment for the next three years, first, by emphasizing the link between the city and the schools, and second, by assigning programs a higher priority than salaries. The latter was probably the most controversial financial decision the Board was to make. Within weeks it split the trustees into opposing factions. Edward Williams quickly emerged as a vocal advocate of program rather than salary cuts, and Laura Osborn began a lonely crusade against any reduction whatsoever in the school budget.[111] With Williams and Osborn in unrelenting opposition to the direction of Board policy the trustees never again voted unanimously on a major retrenchment decision in the Depression era. Despite the differences among the members, however, the debate over program elimination did not seriously concern the Board until the winter of 1933. For most of the 1931–32 school year the Board's attention was focused entirely on salaries.

In the months that followed Jamieson's speech Detroit's financial situation grew steadily worse. City officials spent much of the fall negotiating a series of short-term loans to cover what was an ever-widening city deficit caused by delinquent taxes.[112] By early December, unpaid taxes amounted to $13 million out of a total city tax bill of $76 million, and it was estimated that the delinquency would rise to $19 million before the fiscal year was up. Of the $57 million that Detroit would collect, almost a third was needed to apply to the city's massive debts.[113] What Sidney Fine described as "the twin nightmares of the cities in the Great Depression . . . the increasing burden of unemployment and the threat of financial bankruptcy" eventually forced Detroit's elected officials into an unequal partnership with the bankers whose lines of credit alone could keep the city from default.[114] Ralph Stone emerged as the final arbiter on all such transactions. His approval was vital to any loan, whether from a local or New York bank. It was based solely on a balanced budget. Stone delegated the tasks of checking on the city budget to Lent Upson and C. E. Rightor of the Detroit Bureau of Governmental Research, who were "in daily long conferences" with the city controller and budget director. By mid-December, William Lovett noted in a confidential memo "that Detroit's financial affiairs were being handled by Stone with the aid of Rightor, Upson and Divie B. Duffield, president of the Detroit Citizens' League."[115]

Faced with the demands of the bankers on one side and impending bankruptcy on the other, Mayor Murphy was forced into actions he had previously resisted. In December, he ordered the firing of some city workers and he sponsored a resolution ordering a substantial salary cut for city employees. A month later the Council adopted an ordinance that called for a 10 percent cut in all salaries and a 10 percent additional cut in salaries over $4,000 (known as ten-and-ten cuts).[116] It was obvious to most school trustees that this time the Board could not go it alone. With the schools' share of delinquent taxes exceeding $2 million, the Board voted, over the objections of Osborn and Williams, to adopt the ten-and-ten cuts. Because the Board's employees had already taken a 3 percent cut, the net effect of this action was to reduce wages by an additional 7 percent.[117] It was not enough, however.

On February 9, 1932, Stone wrote Murphy that deeper cuts in the city budget would be needed to wipe out a projected $6 million deficit. He computed the school board's share of the shortfall at $2.4 million. Stone suggested the sum could be trimmed if the Board eliminated the last month of the school year or instituted payless pay days to equal a one-month reduction.[118] Several days before, Murphy, in an informal meeting, apprised four Board members of the situation. At that time the trustees agreed to make substantial wage reductions equal to those of other city departments if the need arose. On February 9, after Stone's demands had been made official, the Board quickly voted "to contribute the same portion of payless days either through contributed service or by closing the schools as that contributed by city departments generally."[119] The February 9 resolution was a natural consequence of the retrenchment policies outlined by Jamieson six months before. School funds were now officially tied to the financial fortunes of the city government, and wage reductions were slated to be the major source of economy.

In the spring of 1932, Detroit's educators closely monitored the battles between Ralph Stone and Frank Murphy over the banker's demand for yet greater salary reductions for city employees. With $3.6 million (of a total $20 million package) in loans at stake, Stone demanded the equivalent of a one-month slash in city wages. Despite Murphy's fiery rhetoric, which included hints of debt repudiation, the outcome of the struggle was a foregone conclusion. As the city missed its April 15 and 30 payrolls and "welfare recipients were reduced to a ration of bread, flour and milk," Council voted a 50 percent pay cut for city workers for the months of May and June. It was now up to the school board to approve its share of the reductions.[120]

Stone had written Murphy in late March noting the Board's February 9 resolution as a positive sign of the trustees' willingness to cooperate.[121] The Board, however, proved itself to be an intractable body. In three extraordinary special sessions on May 3–5, with the city's loans hanging in the balance, the Board refused to conform to the ordinance. Its opposition this time was based entirely on what the members viewed as the inequity of the cutbacks as they affected teachers. Since teachers worked a ten-month year, the one-month cut cost them 10 percent of their wages whereas for most municipal workers, employed for twelve months, the loss was 8.3 percent. Hundreds of teachers crowded the Board room, booing and hissing as they heard city officials remind the Board of its February 9 commitment to share the wage reductions. Stone lashed out at the trustees, demanding that they live up to their pledge of salary cuts.[122] But the Board held firm. The resolution it passed on May 5 called for May and June cuts of 41.6 percent (amounting to 8.32 percent for one year) for teachers and promised to make up the difference in "other economies."[123]

The following months brought no relief to the financially beleaguered city. Sidney Fine described the situation in the summer of 1932:

> Detroit was certain to begin the new fiscal year with a deficit of about $6.3 million; the administration anticipated an additional deficit of $23.7 million by June 30,

1933, largely because of tax delinquency; the city was about $3.5 million short of the cash needed for July and August; all but $4,903,000 of the floating debt of $53,396,000 was to mature by August 5.[124]

In addition, the city was being challenged by a boisterous campaign for a charter amendment to limit the municipal budget to $61 million, a sum, its opponents argued, that would have brought most city services to a halt.[125] Faced with such desperate prospects Mayor Murphy called together a new committee of bankers and industrialists whose aid was needed to keep the city from defaulting on its debts. Their support in securing more credit, however, was contingent on an additional $7 million in retrenchments.[126] An article in *The Nation* accurately noted at the time, "[T]he city is today at the mercy of the banks."[127] Murphy agreed to the cutbacks and had the city controller inform the school board that its share of reductions would be $2,814,160. On July 26, 1932, the Board put the necessary economies into effect. It voted to end school on May 26, 1933, which resulted in a 12 percent cut in teachers' wages; and it instituted salary reductions of 14.5 percent for twelve-month employees (equal to those passed by the Council for twelve-month city workers).[128] That was the last salary reduction made by the Board in 1932. Combined with the larger municipal reductions the salary cut helped keep Detroit solvent over the next few months and probably contributed to the defeat of the $61 million tax limit at a special election in early August.[129]

The educational retrenchments of 1932 received far less editoral attention than had previous school cutbacks. This shift was probably due to the Board's decision to cut teachers' wages at the same rate that the city reduced the wages of its employees. With that action the schools became to the city's papers merely another municipal department caught in the larger struggle between "private capital and the public weal."[130] Only the *Free Press* commented regularly on the educational scene. Its criticisms of education were as shrill as they were wide-ranging. Attacking "the swollen condition of local school appropriations" in March, the *Free Press* editors turned on educators again in June, lashing out at them for trying to make the world subservient to their demands.[131] The paper's comment regarding the Detroit Board's decision to shorten the 1932–33 term was that the children would probably learn as much in nine months as in ten.[132] On the other hand, the usually pro-school papers, the *Times* and the *News*, rarely commented on the educational events of 1932. Even the *Labor News* was generally quiet on wage slashing, both municipal and educational, managing only an occasional swipe at Ralph Stone and his "payroll robbers."[133]

Most likely the lack of comment was due to the inescapable logic of events. Given the circumstances, severe salary retrenchment was probably the only means of keeping Detroit from bankruptcy. Even the schools' friends had to agree that the system needed to shoulder its share of the burden. But, the reduction of school funds had been severe. The total operating budget of 1932–33 was almost 29 percent smaller than that of 1930–31. At the same time school enrollments had grown by over 6,000; this increased student body was served by almost three hundred fewer teachers.[134] Many believed that the schools could not absorb further cutbacks and continue to perform functions deemed necessary. In the Winter of 1933, calls for additional reductions of the school budget reawakened the bitter contentiousness that had so marked the early politics of retrenchment.

In the Trough of Retrenchment

The winter of 1933 was undoubtedly one of the worst periods in American history. The November hopes raised by the election of Franklin D. Roosevelt withered during the following months in what one historian has called "the interregnum of despair."[135] The battered national economy hit bottom in February, beginning with the collapse of Detroit's two largest banking groups. Their failure set off a chain reaction of bank holidays that left only a handful of the nation's financial institutions open when FDR took office in March.[136] Detroit's economy was crippled by the closings. Lost savings and the shortage of "cash created a major economic crisis for most Detroiters and added significantly to the economic woes of the city."[137] The index of industrial employment fell from 49 in February 1933, "to 42 in March when unemployment in the city may have exceeded 350,000."[138]

Detroit's schools were inevitably caught up in the raging economic storm. Two million dollars in Board of Education funds were on deposit in the closed banks.[139] The teachers had received and most had deposited their paychecks on February 11, just days before the collapse.[140] Thereafter, like other workers, they received no wages until April 25, and then they were paid in scrip.[141] Although totally without funds, the Board was determined to keep the schools open. It sought in early March to secure credit for food and transportation for its employees but was successful only with the transit and oil companies. The grocery chains, already owed large sums by the city's welfare department, flatly refused the Board's requests. By late March the teachers joined thousands of other municipal employees in the relief lines.[142]

As serious as the bank crisis appeared to Detroit's school officials, it was, in retrospect, a minor problem compared to the long-range financial outlook for the district. In November 1932, Michigan's voters passed a constitutional amendment limiting property taxes to fifteen mills. Beginning in September 1933, Detroit's schools stood to lose over $2 million annually (more than 40 percent) of their state aid.[143] Over the long run, the fifteen-mill limit forced major changes in Michigan's public school finance. Its immediate impact on Detroit was felt as the Board wrestled with the 1933–34 budget. In December 1932, the Board announced that the ten-and-ten cuts would remain in effect as would the nine-month school year.[144]

Declining state revenue was not the Board's only problem, Mayor Murphy was once more under pressure to make further cuts in the school budget, and Ralph Stone continued to urge wage cuts for Board of Education employees.[145] As the various participants in the budget controversy prepared their cases,

Edward Williams launched a vigorous attack on the Board's retrenchment policies, demanding an end to "fads and frills" courses as an alternative to further salary cuts.[146] The ensuing debate was the most serious and critical of the 1930s discussions concerning educational retrenchment and the nature of public education in Detroit.

Edward Williams and Laura Osborn had distinguished themselves throughout 1932 by opposing every salary reduction the Board had approved. Osborn was almost indiscriminate in her casting of "no" votes, taking the position that teachers' wages simply should not be cut. She railed against "the reactionaries" who sought to cripple the schools and blasted "the bankers who have placed the city in receivership."[147] The only alternative she offered to salary cutting was that the banks, which held city of Detroit notes, cut their interest rates and "accept lower returns."[148] Williams, on the other hand, was an advocate of selective cuts. He had campaigned in 1929 on a platform that sought, among other things, to eliminate the system's platoon schools.

Williams' position on platoon schools was practically lifted from Upton Sinclair's *The Goslings*. Sinclair had denounced Detroit's platoon system as the "Fordization of infancy" designed to breed standardized factory operatives and cannon fodder. Sinclair, who deplored the lack of individual attention given the children, noted one teacher's remarks on the regular class changes, "If fatigue and inability to give attention are features of modern life, the children are certainly experiencing life."[149] In his 1929 campaign Edward Williams stated: "The Platoon system has taken away the human side of the educational system and has actually commercialized the teaching of children in the grammar grades. More individual attention should be given to reading, writing, arithmetic, etc. In many cases the children are physical wrecks due to the strain and nervousness inflicted upon them by the Platoon system."[150]

As the Depression worsened, Williams' attacks became focused specifically on the "enrichment" classes that were crucial to the operation of Detroit's platoon schools. When he voted against the ten-and-ten cuts in January 1932, he stated a view that remained unchanged throughout his term on the Board: "I vote no because I think it is highly unfair to assess this reduction at this time, that [sic] the Board should just eliminate Health Education, Cooking, Sewing, Art, Music, Manual Training, Children's Museum [and the] Psychological Clinic."[151] Williams routinely made similar objections at Board meetings and, on several occasions, presented them in speeches to parent and taxpayer groups.[152]

His most concerted attack on what he called the "luxury courses" came in two radio speeches delivered in late January 1933. The speeches were timed to coincide with the beginning of his campaign for Wayne County auditor and with the mayor's first hearings on the Board of Education budget. Williams' criticisms received front page coverage in the papers and generated a lengthy debate on Detroit's program of "modern" education. In both speeches he recited his list of expendable courses, adding elementary auditorium classes as well as calling for further reductions in administrative staff.

He argued that by eliminating the positions and classes the Board could save between \$3.2 and \$3.5 million, thus making it possible to retain a ten-month school year.[153] He reiterated his charges of waste and extravagance at the January 24 Board meeting, which was marked by several angry exchanges between Williams and Superintendent Cody. Although the meeting ended with none of Williams' notions even receiving a second, his "public" criticisms forced Detroit's educators to defend their Progressive innovations more vigorously and extensively than ever before.

Attacks on what Williams called "luxury courses" were a common feature of the retrenchment debates taking place across the country. A reporter describing the national battle of the "fads and frills" in a 1933 issue of *Harper's* remarked, "Art, home economics, manual training, physical education, trade and vocational classes, and even foreign languages are all being eliminated or curtailed."[154] According to historian Edward Krug, much of the drive to cut these courses was based on the simple fact that "academic subjects on the whole were cheaper, and more could be saved by cutting out the practical subjects."[155] In Detroit, however, school officials built their strongest case for retaining the "modern" courses precisely on the grounds of cost efficiency. Their argument rested on the centrality of those courses to the Detroit platoon schools.

Under the direction of Charles Spain, Detroit during the 1920s had adapted the platoon system to meet the needs of a rapidly growing elementary school population and the desire to introduce Progressive curricula. The students in each of the elementary schools were divided into two platoons of equal size, each of which used half the school's facilities for half the day. While one group studied traditional subjects in the home rooms, the second group was participating in the "enriched" program in special classrooms. This latter platoon was then subdivided, half of its students attending classes in literature, geography, music, art, manual training, domestic science and so forth; the other half taking physical (health) education classes in the gymnasium and playcourt and engaging in group activities in the auditorium. Each of those three classrooms accommodated twice as many students (eighty to ninety per room) as other classrooms in the school.

Operating the large classes concurrently with the other special subjects allowed almost one-third more students to use the buildings. In addition, the platoon schools needed two to three fewer teachers than traditional schools because teachers in the gym, playcourt, and auditorium were, in essence, teaching two classes at a time.[156] The key to the system was the rotating schedule that guaranteed that every classroom in the building would be used at all times during the day. The beauty of it, as far as Detroit's educators were concerned, was that it not only provided for more students in the same space, taught by fewer teachers, but also offered the "modern" curriculum as well. The nature of Detroit's platoon system, in fact, made these "modern" courses essential to the economical operation of the schools. Spain and Cody argued that the elimination of "frill" courses would not only diminish the schools educationally but would wind up costing the taxpayers more money.

Frank Cody had made precisely that point in early January 1933 when, as chairman of the White House Conference on the Crisis of Education, he told one subcommittee that Detroit would need nine hundred additional teachers if it eliminated art, music, and health from the school program.[157] Although this number appears to have been grossly exaggerated, Cody's general assessment of the situation was correct. The $3.2 million Williams sought to save by eliminating "frills" would have come entirely from salaries. Assuming that the special subject instructors would have been replaced by regular classroom teachers, very little savings would have been effected. Also, the resulting elimination of the platoon system on the elementary level which accounted for about 60 percent of the "frills" budget, would have forced the Board to hire between three hundred and four hundred fifty new teachers to make up for the loss of the oversized gymnasium, playcourt, and auditorium classes.[158] Cody and Spain, who took the initiative in responding to Williams, drove home those points at every budget hearing, in press releases, and in radio speeches.[159]

The heated debates over the nature and scope of additional educational retrenchment revived public interest and concern about Detroit's schools. The major papers once again began to editorialize regularly on educational issues. They were joined by a short-lived weekly, the Detroit *Leader*, published by the city's Socialist Party. Also during this time the publishers of *Detroit Saturday Night*, a weekly that "spoke for and to the city's upper income groups,"[160] began voicing their views on school matters. Quite apart from the newspaper attention, educational issues became the focus of concern of many political and civic organizations. Throughout 1933 Detroit's political alignments over the retrenchment issue though remaining much the same as in the previous years became more broadly based and more sharply defined than at any time during the Great Depression.

The "fads and frills" issue drew the initial fire of the controversy. The *Free Press*, which had attacked "practical subjects" as early as 1930, was the only major paper to advocate the elimination of the "modern" courses.[161] On January 29, 1933, in the midst of the debate over Williams' proposals, the *Free Press* blasted what it called the "Educational Despotism" and the "crowd of well-fed and well-paid professional educators who have fallen into the habit of considering luxury education necessary."[162] Teaching children to read, write, and do arithmetic problems was, they argued, all that was really necessary. These views were reiterated several weeks later during the city budget hearings. The *Free Press* praised one school district that had decided to go "back to the three R's" and argued that, in addition to cutting salaries and the school year, "an equally practical way to save is to cut from curriculums [sic] courses in music, art, manual art, domestic science, athletics and so forth, which in the aggregate create a considerable part of the expense of any school where they are given."[163]

The stand taken by the *Free Press* was voiced in several other prominent forums. At a December 1932 meeting of the Michigan chapter of the National Economy League (an organization noted for its prestigious leadership and its vigorous efforts to cut school budgets)[164] Thomas Conlin, an

Upper Peninsula newspaper editor, attacked the educational establishment that had over-burdened the taxpayers with "fads and frills" courses "that call for initial outlays for equipment and continual outlays in the way of added instructors."[165] Conlin's ideas were heartily endorsed by *Detroit Saturday Night,* which ran a front-page paean to "The Little Brown School." It reviled almost every educational innovation beyond the slate and waxed nostalgic for the past, when the three R's were more than enough.[166] Several months later two editorials in *Saturday Night* again applauded Thomas Conlin, who had called for a reduction of state school aid to levels that would enable systems to operate elementary and high schools, "stripped of all hangers-on, such as athletics, instrumental music, physical education, manual training, etc."[167] The editorials of the *Free Press* and *Saturday Night* reflected an attitude that combined conservatism regarding government spending with an intense anti-intellectualism.[168] The editorials were not, however, anti-education so much as they were anti-educators, particularly college professors, who, both papers believed, had foisted costly and questionable programs on a gullible public. The newspapers agreed wholeheartedly with the editor of the *Saturday Evening Post* who wrote in the January 14, 1933 issue, "Too long have we been at the mercy of the supereducators and the craze for novelties."[169] To eliminate the "frills" would not only save money but would help liberate the public from the snares of those educators whose real motive, as the Detroit papers saw it, was not education but their own personal aggrandizement.

The militant defenders of "modern" education had a decidedly Manichean vision of the issue as well. Educators argued that the same people who had wrecked the economy were now trying to wreck the schools.[170] In a radio speech sponsored by the Michigan Education Association (MEA) Laura Osborn declared that "reactionaries have seized this opportunity [the Depression] to become more active in their chronic opposition to modern education and are loudly advocating a return to the good old days of the three R's."[171]

Echoing these sentiments the Socialist *Leader* had no trouble identifying the reactionaries. A February 18 editorial argued, "The taxpayers of the city, now largely the banks and the insurance companies, still continue their drive against educational opportunities for the children of workers. For the past two weeks their campaign has been directed against the 'frills of educa-tion.' "[172] The Party's candidates for school board stated: "[W]ould these businessmen dare admit that what is good for their children is TOO good— or a 'frill'—for the worker's child?"[173] The fact that Edward Williams, the leading advocate of "fads and frills" retrenchment, was not a businessman but was rather the DFL's "man" on the school board did not trouble the Socialists. They regarded the DFL with suspicion believing it represented "labor's aristocracy," the skilled trades, and not the working class as a whole. Williams they dismissed as an unprincipled opportunist.[174]

Williams' "reactionary" stand did place the DFL in an uncomfortable situation. In December 1932, and early January 1933, the *Labor News* had supported the AF of L position paper at the White House Conference on the

Crisis in Education that defended the "modern" curriculum while denouncing the retrenchers who sought its elimination. Throughout 1933 the labor paper redoubled its determined defense of public education.[175] But in late January and February, the *Labor News* took no stand on the "frills" controversy in Detroit undoubtedly due to Williams' part in the debate. As a result of Williams' actions the DFL faced the difficult choice of either renouncing him or siding with its arch-enemies in supporting a move which could have led to the firing of perhaps 1,500 teachers. The *Labor News*, not surprisingly, chose to ignore the entire issue and simply supported Williams' candidacy for Wayne County auditor without reference to the "frills" controversy.[176]

The Detroit *News* faced no such dilemma. It strongly supported "modern" education against what it saw as misguided attacks by overly eager budget cutters. In two editorials, the *News* attacked those who wanted to return to "backwoods education" and defended the "frills."[177] In one widely reprinted editorial, "The Schools and the Average Citizen," the *News* editors cheered what they saw as a growing movement to oppose further educational retrenchment.[178] As if in answer to accusations of the *Free Press*, the *News* claimed, "Strange as it seems, the movement does not come primarily from educational authorities, eager to save their jobs and their income but rather chiefly from parents."[179]

As in 1931, the April school board election provided some clues as to public sentiment regarding the controversy over "fads and frills." When Burt Shurly and A. D. Jamieson kicked off their re-election drives in late February they attacked "the opponents of modern educational methods who would strip the schools of 'fads and frills' and limit education to the three R's, the curriculum of the little red school house of a bygone era."[180] Of their two opponents, Edward Kowalczyk, an insurance agent, campaigned on an antifrills platform. He recommended teaching "only the more fundamental subjects" such as "reading, writing, arithmetic, history" and advocated an end to "luxury courses" particularly "manual art, musical art, and domestic science."[181] Charles Lockwood, the other Board candidate, favored the "modern" curriculum. He ran on a platform that proposed changes in city and school finance (particularly refinancing of the debt). Attempting to make some political capital from the recent bank crisis, Lockwood also attacked Jamieson as a banker who, Lockwood claimed, was involved in a conflict of interest considering the city's ongoing battles with the financial institutions.[182] Both incumbents received the endorsements of the Detroit Citizens' League, the Detroit *News*, and the *Free Press*.[183] The *Labor News* attacked Shurly and Jamieson as the "bankers' fraction" on the Board but did not endorse either Lockwood or Kowalczyk.[184]

The results of the election must have been heartening to those who favored the "modern" curriculum. Shurly and Jamieson were re-elected and all three candidates who defended the "fads and frills" polled over 100,000 votes while Kowalczyk garnered only 55,536.[185]

The "fads and frills" debate was, in many ways, exemplary of the more wide-range response of educational retrenchment that took place in Detroit during 1933. A variety of organizations that had shown little interest in educational politics in the early Depression years now began to get active.

The state and local American Legion voted at its 1933 convention to aid in "preventing the breakdown of the educational system in Michigan."[186] In addition, the Twentieth Century Club (an elite women's group) took up the cause of the public schools, particularly regarding "enrichment" courses and social services. In December, representatives from a dozen women's organizations, including the American Association of University Women, the Detroit Federation of Women's Clubs, and the Wayne County League of Women Voters, formed the Detroit Council on Public Education to defend the schools and lobby in Lansing and at City Hall for increases in school aid.[187] Organized labor and the Socialist Party continued their passionate defense of public education. Eventually, during the Popular Front era the Communist Party also joined the ranks of staunchly pro-school organizations.[188]

The defenders of Detroit's public schools mush have had their worst fears confirmed in late March 1933, when the Board of Commerce issued its annual budget analysis. Although it supported Mayor Murphy's attempts to refinance the city debt, it also called for massive cuts in municipal spending including an additional 22 percent reduction of the school budget.[189] The sum the Board of Commerce recommended for the schools, just over $10 million, was lower than any amount appropriated for the school in fourteen years.[190]

When the dust of the budget battle settled the Board of Commerce had failed to get its way. The inability of the businessmen to force the city into deeper cuts of the school budget was due to several factors that coalesced in the spring of 1933. The outpouring of support for the schools in the newspapers and by so many social and political groups undoubtedly influenced Mayor Murphy and the Common Council. In addition, the demands by bankers and businessmen following the bank collapse seemed hollow when it was so apparent that they could not even keep their own financial houses in order.[191] During the budget hearings even Common Council lashed out at "the rapidly-growing dictatorship of Wall Street over the representative municipal governments of America" and eliminated interest payments from the 1933–34 budget.[192] Finally, it was obvious to most of Detroit's financial and political leaders that the refinancing of the municipal debt was the only way to save the city from ruin.

In March, Murphy began what would eventually be a successful refinancing process that continued until he left the city in May 1933 to become Governor-General of the Phillipines. In the end, the school budget was only trimmed some 5 percent, to $12,185,452, which was the lowest figure in a decade. The ten-and-ten cuts remained in effect as did the nine-month term. The 1933–34 school year, however, was the trough of the Depression for Detroit's public schools. The schools had hit bottom, and the educators began the slow work of recovery.

The year 1933 was a watershed in the history of education in Detroit. During its span Detroiters witnessed the most serious challenge yet directed against the schools' Progressive innovations. The successful defense of those programs set the course of educational policy for decades to come.[193] The year also marked the emergence of a broadly based movement to support the public schools against those who were calling for further educational retrenchment. The battle lines over school issues resembled the general political configurations of the New Deal years. Political liberals and moderates from diverse social backgrounds joined with advocates of social welfare and organized labor in opposition to political conservatives, powerful business and financial interests, and scions of established wealth. Only the issue of public relief for the unemployed polarized the city more clearly along these lines.

Aftermath

Between 1933 and 1940, the locus of educational politics largely shifted from Detroit to Lansing and, to a lesser degree, Washington, D.C. Retrenchment crises across the state and the devastating impact of the fifteen-mill property tax limitation spurred the effort to increase state aid to education in Michigan. By 1940, the state was providing $42 million in aid to local districts almost double the 1930 figure.[194] Detroit's share rose from $5.7 million in 1930 to $10.8 in 1939.[195] Those funds were instrumental in bringing Detroit's total school revenues back to pre-Depression levels.

Federal aid from such New Deal programs as the Civil Works Administration, Public Works Administration, and the Works Projects Administration also helped restore several important items to the school budget. Practically all the funds from these programs nearly $2.3 million in all, went toward construction of new buildings, additions to existing structures, or maintenance.[196] In light of the 1932 moratorium on school construction in Detroit these funds were a godsend. By mid-decade, with the schools moving toward financial stability as a result of the improved economy and state aid, the remaining area of greatest need was precisely that which the New Deal met; funds for capital improvements.

In 1935, the Board removed its hiring freeze and slowly began to replenish the depleted teaching staff.[197] Nevertheless, as late as 1937, Detroit still ranked well below other major U.S. cities in per capita instructional expenses.[198] Dismaying as such figures must have been, Detroit's school leaders had good reason to be proud of their handling of the retrenchment crisis. The school system's teaching staff and virtually all its major programs had been protected from the worst of the economic storm. In retrospect, even the controversial salary cuts which corresponded directly to the decline in the cost of living appear less harsh than they did at the time.[199] By 1940, the Detroit schools had recovered financially from the Great Depression. More importantly, they had maintained their status as one of the finest school systems in the nation.

CONCLUSIONS

During years marked by confusion, fear and despair Detroit's school officials fought on several fronts to preserve their institutions. They not only battled the fierce economic undertow but also powerful political and economic leaders who sought to weaken their financial autonomy, curtail their funds, and change their educational direction. The experience of the Detroit Board of Education in the Depression challenges some of the basic assumptions currently held by the educational historians.

If it is true, as some historians have argued, that during the Progressive era school policy was directed by a concert of business and educational interests, then events in Detroit in the 1930s point to the collapse of that "alliance" amid the pressures of the Great Depression.[200] Detroit's business leaders did not view the Board of Education as a reliable ally even in the early stages of the economic crisis. In fact, the relationship between the Board and the businessmen was regularly marked by antagonism and bitterness, not harmony. Even the elite social status of the majority of the Board members proved to be a double-edged sword. The elite Board members probably shared a general world view with members of the Stone Committee. They lived in the same neighborhoods and belonged to the same exclusive clubs. While these circumstances might have encouraged the Board to follow the lead of Stone and the businessmen, they also encouraged pride, independence, and faith in one's convictions. It is quite likely that the Board members would have recoiled at the suggestion that it was their duty to carry out the orders of Detroit's financial and industrial leaders. When Stone issued his demands, he was consequently confronted by a body that could not easily be intimidated. To a degree, the Board's defiance was a result of class conflict but in a way that highlights Weber's "paradox of consequences" much more than Marx's "theory of class interest."

Although social background may partially explain the Board's passionate defense of its prerogatives, a more important factor explains the members' response to the calls for retrenchment. The terms of Board members, who served unpaid, were six years long; and by 1933 all but one of the trustees were serving at least a second term. Having committed years of their lives to the schools, they were not about to see their work undone by anyone, regardless of social class or economic position. Long years of service to an institution can create a loyalty that transcends other powerful social influences. There is no doubt that most of Detroit's school board members were essentially conservative. Indeed, when the schools' survival was not at stake, as with such issues as denying Communist groups the right to hold weekend rallies in the schools, they readily agreed with conservative business organizations.[201] But on issues that involved the survival of the schools, the devotion of the Board members to their institution led them to defend it against all attackers.

The antagonism that developed between the Board and the businessmen erupted into several major confrontations. Detroit's battle over "fads and frills" brings into question another important argument concerning the schools as agencies for social control in a capitalist society.[202] The debate over "fads and frills" generally divided the city along class lines but in ways quite different from what some would have us believe. It was businessmen who called for curtailing kindergarten and vocational training. It was the city's most conservative newspapers that urged a return to the three R's. The anti-"frills" stand taken by Edward Williams, the "labor" member of the Board, smacks more of political opportunism than of far-sighted articulation of working class interests, particularly in light of the consistent strong support given the public schools by the Detroit Federation of Labor. The most passionate defenders of the "fads and frills" courses were Detroit's Socialists.

The major advocates of retrenchment were Detroit's business and financial leaders. If those men viewed the schools as an institution to "accommodate and deflect thrusts away" from the foundations of the capitalist economy it was not apparent in the worst years of the Depression.[203] Education was, for them, just another governmental function with a bloated budget. At no times was that attitude more apparent than in the awful winter of 1933. Detroit's business leaders demanded even greater cuts in the school budget amid an unprecedented political and economic crisis highlighted by the bank collapse and a series of Communist-led strikes in the auto industry.[204] The businessmen's ardor for educational retrenchment did abate as the decade wore on and by the end of the 1930s they even accepted the notion of increased state support for public education. But they invariable urged less revenue for education than practically any other group lobbying in Lansing. The Michigan Manufacturers Association, the Economy League of Michigan, the Detroit Board of Commerce, the Michigan Chamber of Commerce, the *Free Press* and *Saturday Night* fought almost every attempt to increase state school aid throughout the entire course of the turbulent decade.[205]

On the other side of the debate, the schools drew their support from organized labor, Socialists, Communists, academics, women's organizations, groups like the American Legion, as well as from political liberals and even the conservative Detroit *News*. While these groups held widely differing (and at times contradictory) views on public education they shared a sense that schools were valuable institutions. In some ways that informal coalition of public school defenders resembled the broad national coalition that was growing in support of the New Deal, much as opponents to increased school aid resembled those who became FDR's most vocal detractors. If the central question in American politics is *how much* government is necessary, then educational politics (based on a widely accepted belief that schooling is a necessary function of government) may be a bellwether of changing national moods and of emerging ideological conflicts. The battles over educational retrenchment in Detroit provide evidence in support of that proposition.

Few cities in the 1930s were more representative of national trends than was Detroit. Its early battles over social welfare and the role of government in the economic crisis foreshadowed similar struggles that marked the course of the New Deal. Its later transformation from an "open-shop paradise" to the bastion of industrial unionism was emblematic of changes in the American economy as a whole. The educational developments, though more subtle, were no less significant. There is no doubt that in the 1920s Detroit's schools were closely associated with the city's conservative business leaders. The economic collapse and the battles over educational retrenchment forced Detroit's school officials to reassess that relationship. The businessmen's attacks on the schools, the need for increased state aid, the desire for federal support all worked to shift the political alignment of public education. Similarly the strong support given the schools by organized labor and other left-wing groups, coupled with the growing strength of unionism in Detroit eased the school leaders, perhaps unwittingly, to the left. By the end of the Depression decade the schools were politically camped on the fringes of American liberalism.

NOTES

1. U.S. Department of Commerce, Bureau of the Census, *Fifteenth Census of the United States, 1930: Population*, v. 1, p. 18.
2. Sidney Glazer, *Detroit: A Study in Urban Development* (New York, 1965), p. 91; Arthur Pound, *Detroit: Dynamic City* (New York, 1940), pp. 244–47; Robert Conot, *American Odyssey: A Unique History of America Told Through the Life of a Great City* (New York, 1974), p. 260; Olivier Zynz, *The Changing Face of Inequality* (Chicago, 1982).
3. Sidney Fine, *Frank Murphy: The Detroit Years* (Ann Arbor, 1975), p. 97.
4. Ibid., p. 97.
5. Ibid., p. 97.
6. Ibid., p. 96.
7. Ibid., pp. 92–93.
8. Ibid., p. 96. The Detroit Bureau of Governmental Research was supported by the Community Fund. Detroit *Times* 2/18/31.
9. Detroit Bureau of Governmental Research, *Accumulated Social and Economic Statistics for Detroit* (Detroit, 1937), p. 15.
10. W. L. Coffey, "Detroit Has Five Municipal Colleges," *Michigan Education Journal* 8 (February, 1931):316; the colleges (City College, Teachers College, Law School, Medical School and Pharmacy School) were eventually merged into Wayne University.
11. Hoover Commission Report on Recent Educational Change quoted in Detroit *Labor News* 7/11/30. Schools accounted for approximately $63 millions; streets and roads, $47 millions; sewers, $44 millions; water supply, $17 millions; and hospitals, $15 millions.
12. *Detroit Teachers Association Executive Council Bulletin* (1940?), Detroit Council on Public Education Papers, Wallet #1, Miscellaneous Papers Folder, Burton Historical Collection, Detroit, Michigan, pp. 14–15.
13. Ibid., p. 14.
14. The vote was 61,806 to 11,342. See Donald Disbrow, *Schools for an Urban Society* (Lansing, Mich.), p. 228.
15. Detroit Board of Education *Proceedings*, 1916–17; R. L. Polk, *Detroit City Directory, 1917* (Detroit, 1917); *Dau's Blue Book for Detroit and Suburban*

Towns, 1917 (New York, 1917); Ruby Mervin (Ed.), *The Social Secretary of Detroit, 1930* (Detroit, 1930).

16. *Dau's, 1917*; Mervin, *Social 1930*, pp. 33, 35, 41, 82, 122, 126, 149.

17. Ibid., Laura Osborn Papers, Burton Historical Collection, Detroit, Michigan, Box 1, WDET Folder.

18. Of the eight people who served on the Detroit Board of Education from 1929 to 1939, five were listed in the social register.

19. Detroit Public School Staff, *Frank Cody: A Realist in Education* (New York, 1943), pp. 210–215.

20. Detroit *Free Press* hereafter DFP 6/22/42 in the Frank Cody Clipping File in the Burton Historical Collection, Detroit, Michigan.

21. Moehlman, *Public Education in Detroit* (Bloomington, IN, 1925), pp. 205–208.

22. Ibid., pp. 195–208.

23. William McAndrew, "A Word Portrait of Frank Cody," *Michigan Education Journal* 7 (January 1930):293.

24. Fine, *Detroit Years*, p. 201.

25. Ibid., p. 246.

26. Ibid., p. 245.

27. Ibid., pp. 97, 246–247; Conot, *American*, p. 260.

28. U.S. Department of Commerce, *Statistical Abstract of the United States, 1933* (Washington, D.C., 1933), p. 755; U.S. Department of Commerce, *Statistical Abstract of the United States, 1935* (Washington, D.C., 1935), p. 781.

29. U.S. Department of Commerce, *Statistical Abstract of the United States, 1931* (Washington, D.C., 1931), p. 871; U.S. Department of Commerce, *Statistical, 1935*, p. 789.

30. Fine, *Detroit Years*, pp. 298–299.

31. "School Finances, 1929–1933," Detroit Mayor's Papers, 1933, Board of Education Folder, Burton Historical Collection, Detroit, Michigan. *Detroit Teachers Associations Executive Council Bulletin*, pp. 8, 10.

32. *Detroit Teachers Associations Executive Council Bulletin*, p. 10.

33. Fine, *Detroit Years*, p. 283.

34. The slogan was used on Laura Osborn's campaign literature in 1917. Laura Osborn Papers, Box 19, Folder 1.

35. Disbrow, *Schools*, p. 225; Detroit *News* 12/28/28 in Detroit *News* morgue.

36. Fine, *Detroit Years*, pp. 202–203, 325.

37. *Detroit Teachers Associations Executive Council Bulletin*, p. 14.

38. Fine, *Detroit Years*, p. 206. Probably the most famous of those was the Committee on Public Expenditures (headed by Fred W. Sargent, president of the Northwestern Railroad) in Chicago. See Lyman Burbank, "Chicago Public Schools and the Depression Years: 1928–1937," *Journal of the Illinois State Historical Society* 64 (Winter, 1971):365–381.

39. Fine, *Detroit Years*, pp. 219–220; 299–300; 305, 314; Glazer, *Detroit*, p. 99.

40. Ruby Mervin (Ed.), *The Social Secretary of Detroit, 1932* (Detroit, 1932), pp. 92, 109, 123, 138. Frank Cody was also listed, ibid., p. 56. Frank Gorman was a member of two exclusive clubs listed in the register as well. Ibid., pp. 197, 216; Frank Cody, "Detroit's Board of Education," *American Schools Board Journal*, 82 (February, 1931), p. 57.

41. Detroit *Labor News* 3/20/25; 4/10/25.

42. Detroit *Labor News* 3/1/29; 2/29/29; 4/5/29; Leon S. Waskiewicz, "Organized Labor and Public Education in Michigan, 1888–1938" (Ph.D. dissertation, University of Michigan, 1939), pp. 325–326.

43. Ruby Brooks (Ed.), *The Social Secretary of Detroit, 1936* (Detroit, 1936), p. 91.
44. Angus McLean died in April 1929. He was replaced by Dr. Clark Brooks in June 1929. *Detroit Board of Education Proceedings*, 1938–39, pp. 336–439.
45. Scott Nearing, "Who's Who in Our Boards of Education?" *School and Society* 5 (January, 1917):89–90; George Counts, *The Social Composition of Boards of Education* (Chicago, 1927), pp. 82–97; Samuel Bowles and Herbert Gintis, *Schooling in Capitalist America* (New York, 1976), pp. 186–191.
46. Detroit *News* 2/20/30.
47. Mervin, *Social, 1930*, p. 82; Fine, *Detroit Years*, pp. 344–345.
48. Detroit *News* 2/22/30; 3/12/30; 3/13/30; 3/14/30; 3/25/30; 3/23/30; 3/24/30; Detroit *Free Press* 3/25/30; 4/4/30; Detroit *Times* 4/14/30; 4/13/30.
49. Detroit *News* 2/1/30; 2/20/30; 2/26/30; 3/13/30.
50. Detroit *News* 2/26/30; 3/11/30; 3/15/30; 3/25/30; Detroit *Free Press* 3/1/30 in Laura Osborn Papers, Box 5, Folder 4; Detroit *Labor News* 1/24/30; 2/21/30.
51. Detroit *News* 9/30/30 in Ralph Stone Scrapbook #16. Interestingly, it was Edward Williams who introduced the motion, *Detroit Board of Education Proceedings* 1930–31, p. 192.
52. *Detroit Board of Education Proceedings*, 1930–31; Detroit *News* 11/13/30; Detroit *Free Press* 11/13/30.
53. Detroit *Free Press* 2/22/31.
54. Detroit *News* 2/15/31; Detroit *Times* 2/20/31.
55. Detroit *News* 2/1/30; 2/20/30; 2/26/30.
56. Detroit *Journal of Common Council* 1930, v. 1, p. 425.
57. Detroit *News* 2/1/30; 2/20/30; 2/26/30; Detroit *News* 11/14/30 in Ralph Stone Scrapbook #16 in Ralph Stone Papers, Bentley Historical Library, Ann Arbor, Michigan.
58. Detroit *News* 11/14/30; Detroit *Free Press* 2/4/31. The two men did propose very different alternatives. John Lovett wanted the Board to be brought directly under council's control. William Lovett sought to have all Board members elected simultaneously rather than staggered terms. He believed that this would make the Board more responsive to the public's wishes.
59. Detroit *Free Press* 2/20/31.
60. Ibid. John L. Lovett and G. Oliver Frick had urged that the Board be placed under the Mayor and Council's control in their section of the Detroit Board of Commerce Governmental Committee Report on the City Budget, "Education Subcommittee Report," February 3, 1931, in Detroit Mayors Papers, Box 1, Board of Commerce folder.
61. Detroit *Journal of Common Council*, 1931, p. 196.
62. *Detroit Board of Education Proceedings*, 1930–31, pp. 642, 665. The Board continued its attempts at autonomy for at least another year. *Detroit Board of Education Proceedings*, 1931–32, pp. 427, 483; Detroit *Times* 4/27/32.
63. Board members stated that they would not seek to gain control over their funds until after the economic emergency was over. Detroit *News* 1/11/33.
64. Detroit *Times* 2/17/31; Detroit *News* 2/21/31; 4/17/31; Detroit *Free Press* 2/21/31; 3/20/31. Harvey Campbell, vice-president of the Board of Commerce, and Dr. Lent Upson, director of the Bureau of Government Research, particularly opposed the legislation, raising the fear that a "Tammany Hall" arrangement might emerge between the Council members and the 10,000

Board employees. The idea also drew fire from the Detroit *Times* and the Detroit *News*. On April 19, 1931 the *News* ran an editorial and cartoon that strongly defended the independence of the school board and warned that "the politicans must keep their hands off education, or they will feel the wrath of the people."

65. Edward Williams was the only Board member to break ranks vocally in the controversy regarding the wage freeze. He quickly switched sides after a harsh editorial attack from his otherwise main supporter, the Detroit *Labor News*. *Detroit Board of Education Proceedings*, 1930–31, p. 192; Waskiewicz, "Organized," p. 337.

66. *Detroit Teachers Associations Executive Council Bulletin*, pp. 6–7.

67. Detroit Board of Education, "Cost of Special Subjects—Salaries, 1932–33" (mimeo), Detroit Council on Public Education Papers, Wallet XI, Miscellaneous Papers Folder.

68. *Detroit Teachers Associations Executive Council Bulletin*, p. 6.

69. There were some protests, particularly over the raising of fees, but they never became an important political issue. Detroit *Free Press* 3/1931.

70. S. Alexander Rippa, "Retrenchment in a Period of Defensive-Opposition to the new Deal: The Business Community and the Public Schools, 1932–34," *History of Education Quarterly* 2 (June, 1962):75–78.

71. Quoted in Marilyn Cutler, "How the Schools Lived Through that Dread Depression of the Thirties," *American School Board Journal* (May, 1975):37.

72. Sidney Fine characterized Detroit's newspapers in *Detroit Years*, p. 201. Detroit *Free Press* 2/21/30. Today the *Free Press* is Detroit's liberal paper and the *News* the more conservative.

73. Ibid., p. 201.

74. For examples of the DFL stand, see Detroit *Labor News* 7/18/30; 9/26/30; 11/13/30.

75. The teachers' salary controversy was Murphy's first political crisis (he came into office in a special election in September 1930). Murphy's refusal to act as the Stone Committee recommended was the beginning of this three-year battle with Ralph Stone and the city's business leaders.

76. Detroit *Free Press* 10/1/20; 10/15/30; 10/20/30; 11/20/30.

77. Detroit *News* 11/18/30; Detroit *Times* 11/19/30.

78. Detroit *Labor News* 10/3/30; 11/14/30; 11/21/30.

79. Irving Bernstein, *The Lean Years: A History of the American Worker, 1920–1933* (Baltimore, 1960), p. 255.

80. Detroit *Labor News* 9/15/30.

81. Fine, *Detroit Years*, p. 269.

82. *Detroit Board of Education Proceedings*, 1930–31, pp. 438–445.

83. *The Detroiter* 1/5/31.

84. They were Hugh J. Ferry, treasurer of the Packard Motor Company; B. E. Hutchinson, vice-president and treasurer of Chrysler Corporation; and T. W. P. Livingstone, vice-president of the Board of Directors of People's Wayne County Bank. Detroit *News* 2/2/31.

85. Ibid. The twenty percent figure was obtained by using Cass Technical High School's average per pupil cost of $157 and the average non-technical high school cost of $126 per pupil. *Detroit Teachers Associations Executive Council Bulletin*, p. 9.

86. Detroit *News* 2/2/31.

87. Board of Commerce, "Education Subcommittee Report," February 3, 1931.

88. Detroit *News* 2/13/31; 2/14/31; 2/18/31; Detroit *Free Press* 2/17/31; 2/18/31; 2/22/31; Detroit *Times* 2/17/31; Detroit *Labor News* 2/20/31.

89. Cody's estimate was more accurate; prices between December 1929 and December 1930 had fallen nine percent. U.S. Department of Labor, "Changes in the Cost of Living in Large Cities in the United States, 1913–41," *Department of Labor Bulletin #1699* (Washington, D.C., 1941), p. 56; Detroit *News* 2/16/31; Detroit *News* 2/18/31; Detroit *Free Press* 2/17/31; 2/18/31; Detroit *Times* 2/18/31.

90. "The Report of the Salary Schedule Committee," February 17, 1931, Detroit Mayors' Papers, 1931, Box 1, Board of Education Folder #1; Detroit *Free Press* 2/24/31; Detroit *Times* 2/20/31. Even though Detroit's teachers *were* poorly paid when compared to teachers in other U.S. cities, those who reached the top of Detroit's salary schedule ranked among the upper third of all U.S. incomes received in 1929. Bernstein, *Lean Years*, p. 63.

91. The other opponent was Joseph A. Moross, a realtor. Detroit *Free Press* 2/24/31.

92. Detroit *Free Press* 4/3/31.

93. Detroit *News* 4/15/31; Detroit *Labor News* 3/20/31; 3/22/31; 4/3/31.

94. Detroit *News* 4/5/31; Detroit *Free Press* 4/6/31; Detroit *Labor News* 4/10/31.

95. Gorman received 92,581 votes; Webster 75,930; Krohn 45,371. Detroit *Times* 4/7/31.

96. Detroit *News* 4/19/31; Detroit *Labor News* 4/10/31.

97. Fine, *Detroit Years*, pp. 301–302; *Detroit Board of Education Proceedings*, 1930–31, p. 702.

98. Bernstein, *Lean Years*, p. 255.

99. Edmund Wilson, "Detroit Motors," *The New Republic* (March 25, 1931):149.

100. Edmund Wilson, "The Despot of Dearborn," *Scribner's Magazine* (July, 1931):25.

101. Stone to Murphy, July 7, 1931, Detroit Mayors' Papers, 1931, Box 3, Finance Committee Folder.

102. *Detroit Board of Education Proceedings*, 1931–32, p. 58; Detroit *Times* 7/29/31.

103. Detroit *News* 7/22/31; Detroit *Free Press* 7/29/31; Detroit *Times* 7/22/31.

104. *Detroit Board of Education Proceedings*, 1931–32, p. 77.

105. Ibid., p. 77.

106. Ibid., p. 78. Jamieson's figures were essentially accurate. Prices from June 1930 to June 1931 had fallen 13.5 percent. U.S. Department of Labor, "Changes," p. 56.

107. *Detroit Board of Education Proceedings*, 1931–32, p. 178.

108. Ibid., p. 79.

109. Laura Osborn, the only woman elected to city office, voted for the resolutions but immediately afterward protested the section that called for married women teachers to take leaves of absence. Ibid., p. 79. Detroit never forced its married women teachers to take the leaves, and very few did so voluntarily.

110. Angus McLean called the speech the most important he had heard in eight years on the Board. Detroit *Free Press* 8/12/31; Detroit *News* 8/12/31; 8/25/31; the Detroit *Free Press* praised the cuts 8/13/31.

111. Detroit *News* 8/28/31 in Detroit *News* morgue.

112. Fine, *Detroit Years*, pp. 313–314.

113. Detroit *Times* 12/2/31.

114. Fine, *Detroit Years*, p. 206.

115. Ibid., p. 314.

116. Ibid., p. 315.

117. *Detroit Board of Education Proceedings*, 1931–32, p. 283; Detroit *News* 12/30/31 in Detroit *News* morgue; Detroit *News* 1/13/32; Detroit *Times* 1/13/32.

118. Stone to Murphy, February 9, 1932, Detroit Mayors' Papers, 1932, Box 4, Finance Committee Folder.

119. *Detroit Board of Education Proceedings*, 1931–32, p. 319.

120. Fine, *Detroit Years*, pp. 317–319.

121. Stone to Murphy, February 23, 1932, Detroit Mayors' Papers, 1932, Box 4, Finance Committee Folder.

122. *Detroit Board of Education Proceedings*, 1931–32, pp. 405–413; DW 5/4/32; 5/5/32; 5/6/32; Detroit *Free Press* 5/4/32; 5/5/32; 5/6/32; Detroit *Times* 5/4/32; 5/5/32; 5/6/32.

123. *Detroit Board of Education Proceedings*, 1931–32, pp. 412–413. Osborn and Williams both voted "no" on the final resolution. The teachers eventually did get those wage losses restored in 1950 after a lengthy court battle initiated by the Detroit Federation of Teachers. Anna May Muffoletto, "Detroit Public School Teachers' Unions: Organization, Operation, and Activities" (Master's Thesis, University of Detroit, 1958), pp. 73, 99–105.

124. Fine, *Detroit Years*, p. 354.

125. Ibid., pp. 355–359.

126. Ibid., p. 354.

127. Mauritz Hallgren, "Grave Danger in Detroit," *The Nation* (August 3, 1932), p. 100.

128. *Detroit Board of Education Proceedings*, 1932–33, p. 21; Detroit *News* 7/27/32.

129. The $61 million campaign was led by a "front" organization of the Detroit Real Estate Board. Several of its major backers were developers who owed the city large amounts in delinquent taxes. Virtually every major newspaper and civic organization opposed the proposal. It was defeated 126,578 to 40,050. For a full description see Fine, *Detroit Years*, pp. 355–359.

130. The phrase appeared in Detroit *Labor News* 5/27/32.

131. Detroit *Free Press* 4/30/32; 6/18/32; 6/19/32.

132. Detroit *Free Press* 7/2/32.

133. Detroit *Labor News* 5/6/32.

134. *Detroit Teachers Associations Executive Council Bulletin*, pp. 8–10.

135. Jordan Schwarz, *The Interregnum of Despair: Hoover, Congress, and the Depression* (Urbana, IL., 1970).

136. Fine, *Detroit Years*, pp. 373–375; Conot, *American*, p. 306.

137. Fine, *Detroit Years*, p. 376.

138. Ibid., p. 376.

139. The Board eventually got that money back. Detroit *Journal of Common Council*, 1934, pp. 640–641.

140. *Detroit Board of Education Proceedings*, 1932–33, p. 216.

141. Fine, *Detroit Years*, p. 377. The scrip became another form of salary reduction as merchants around the city accepted it often at 20–30 percent discounts. Detroit *Saturday Night* 5/20/33.

142. *Detroit Board of Education Proceedings*, 1932–33, pp. 217, 226, 229, 235–236; Fine, *Detroit Years*, p. 377; Detroit *News* 3/30/33; Detroit *Times* 3/30/33.

143. *Michigan Educational Journal* 10 (September, 1932), p. 2.

144. Detroit *News* 12/7/32; 12/14/32; Detroit *Times* 12/7/32.

145. Ralph Stone to Lent Upson, January 18, 1933; Ralph Stone Papers, Box 1; Detroit *Free Press* 1/11/33; Detroit *Times* 1/16/33 in Laura Osborn Papers, Box 7.

146. Detroit *News* 1/24/33.

147. *Detroit Board of Education Proceedings*, 1932–33, p. 319; Detroit *News* 7/22/31; Laura Osborn Radio Speech, January 20, 1933, Laura Osborn Papers, Box 15, Manuscripts Folder.

148. Detroit *News* 7/22/31.

149. Upton Sinclair, *The Goslings* (Pasedena, CA., 1924), pp. 100–102, 186.

150. Detroit *Labor News* 3/1/29.

151. *Detroit Board of Education Proceedings*, 1931–32, p. 284.

152. *Detroit Board of Education Proceedings*, 1931–32, p. 123; *Detroit Board of Education Proceedings*, 1932–33, pp. 29, 284; Detroit *News* 8/28/31; 7/10/32.

153. Detroit *News* 1/24/33; 1/25/33; Detroit *Times* 1/24/32; 1/31/33.

154. Avis Carlson, "Deflating the Schools," *Harper's* (November, 1933):713–714. At the time, the most noted example of "fads and frills" retrenchment occurred in Chicago. In July 1933, the school board abolished all junior highs, the city's junior college, and all coaching and music positions. It reduced the number of physical education teachers, reduced kindergarten classes by 50 percent, and discontinued manual training and home economics in elementary schools. Burbank, "Chicago," pp. 373–374.

155. Edward A. Krug, *Shaping, of the American High School, 1920–1941* (Madison: University of Wisconsin Press, 1972), p. 214.

156. Charles Spain, *The Platoon School* (New York, 1924), pp. 43–100; Arthur B. Moehlman, *Public Education in Detroit* (Bloomington, IL: Public School Publishing Co.), pp. 195–198; Charles Spain, "Keep Frills—Save Money," *School Life* 18 (March, 1933):122.

157. Spain, "Keep," p. 122: Detroit *News* 4/1/33.

158. That number is based on two or three additional teachers in each of Detroit's approximately 150 elementary schools.

159. Charles Spain, "Economy and the Modern Curriculum," *Detroit Educational Bulletin* 16 (January–February, 1933):1–3, Detroit *News* 2/6/33; 4/1/33; Detroit *Free Press* 2/7/33; 3/26/33; Detroit *Times* 1/26/33; 2/6/33.

160. Fine, *Detroit Years*, p. 106.

161. Detroit *Free Press* 5/5/30.

162. Detroit *Free Press* 1/29/33. On that same day the *Free Press* ran a long article that was quite sympathetic to the plight of Detroit's teachers. It also presented the educators' views of the "modern" courses. Donald Disbrow quotes that article and assumes it represents the *Free Press*' editorial point of view on the issue. He is totally mistaken in that assumption. Disbrow, *Schools*, p. 236.

163. Detroit *Free Press* 3/11/33.

164. William Eaton, *The American Federation of Teachers, 1916–1961* (Carbondale, IL., 1975), p. 46.

165. Detroit *Free Press* 12/14/32.

166. Detroit *Saturday Night* 8/31/33.

167. Detroit *Saturday Night* 12/16/33; 12/23/33; 1/12/35.

168. For examples of their anti-intellectual attitudes see Detroit *Saturday Night* 12/2/33; Detroit *Free Press* 6/18/32.

169. Quoted in Edgar Knight, *Fifty Years of American Education* (New York, 1953), p. 361. Knight also mentions several other newspapers that shared the views of the Detroit *Free Press* on the "fads and frills" issue. They include the Atlanta *Constitution*, the Chicago *Tribune*, and the New York *Daily News*. Ibid., pp. 353–354.

170. See for example Charles S. Meek, Superintendent of Schools, Toledo, Ohio at the NEA Department of Superintendence meeting 1933, quoted in *Michigan Education Journal* 10 (April, 1933):371.

171. Detroit *News* 1/20/33 in the Laura Osborn Papers, Box 15, Manuscripts and Notes Folder.

172. Detroit *Leader* 2/18/33.

173. Detroit *Leader* 2/11/33.

174. Interview with Walter Bergman, 8/30/32.

175. Detroit *Labor News* 12/16/32; 12/30/32; 1/13/33; 5/26/33; 11/24/33: 11/15/33.

176. Detroit *Labor News* 3/3/33; 3/17/33; 3/31/33; 4/7/33.

177. "The 3 R's Not Enough," quoted in *Detroit Educational Bulletin* 16 (March–April, 1933):9.

178. "The Schools and the Average Citizen" was given full page coverage in the *Michigan Education Journal* 10 (February, 1933):267.

179. Detroit *News* 2/1/33.

180. Detroit *News* 2/22/33.

181. Detroit *News* 3/28/33. Kowalczyk had stated those positions as the essence of his platform in Detroit *News* 2/26/33.

182. Detroit *News* 4/1/33; Detroit *Times* 3/29/33.

183. The *Free Press* endorsement had less to do with the "frills" issue than with the other prominent issue of that election, the unionization and politicization of the school teachers, which Jamieson and Shurly opposed and Lockwood supported. Detroit *News* 2/26/33; 3/31/33; Detroit *Free Press* 3/29/33; 3/31/33; 4/1/33.

184. Detroit *Labor News* 3/31/33.

185. Shurly polled 154,221 votes; Jamieson, 132,346; Lockwood, 104,225; and Kowalczyk, 55,536. Detroit *News* 4/4/33. The frills issue did not disappear with Williams' departure from the Board. For example, in 1939 Michigan's Governor Dickinson called on Detroit to eliminate such "frills" as art, music, and playgrounds in order to reduce the amount of state school aid. Detroit *Times* 6/14/39 in Detroit Federation of Teachers 1939 scrapbook. Detroit Federation of Teachers Papers, Waller Rentuer Library, Wayne State University, Detroit, Michigan.

186. *Michigan Education Journal* 11 (October, 1933): 93; Russell Cook, "The Legion and the Schools," *Journal of the NEA* 22 (March, 1934):89–90.

187. "Constitution of the Detroit Council on Public Education" and "Minutes of the Detroit Council on Public Education, December 5, 1933." Detroit Council on Public Education Papers. Wallet #1, Folder #1. The Council lasted until 1946.

188. Robert Iversen, *The Communists and the Schools* (New York, 1959), pp. 17–20; Richard Frank, "The Schools and the People's Front," *The Communist* 6 (May, 1937):432–445; *The Michigan Worker* 5/1/33.

189. Detroit *News* 3/30/33; Detroit *Free Press* 3/30/33; Detroit *Times* 2/28/53; 3/30/33.

190. Detroit *Times* 4/3/33; Detroit Bureau of Governmental Research, *Accumulated*, p. 15.

191. Fine, *Detroit Years*, p. 375. Murphy had come out in opposition to "any cuts in the fundamental services of the schools" and he never changed that position. Detroit *Time* 2/5/33.

192. Ibid., p. 386.

193. Detroit did not phase out platoon schools until 1964. Disbrow, *Schools*, p. 230.

194. E. F. Shepard and William Wood, *The Financing of Public Schools in Michigan* (Ann Arbor, 1942), p. 26.

195. Detroit *Education News* 1/9/37.

196. Detroit *Teachers Association News* 2/6/34; 4/11/34; Detroit Board of Education "Financial Statements, 1936–1940; Detroit Board of Education" Cost Reports, 1937–1941.

197. Detroit *News* 2/27/35 in Detroit *News* morgue; Detroit *Labor News* 2/14/36.

198. Chicago and Baltimore were below Detroit in a ranking of the ten largest cities in the United States. *Detroit Teachers Associations Executive Council Bulletin*, p. 13.

199. Between June 1930 and June 1934 prices in Detroit fell approximately 25 percent. U.S. Department of Labor, "Changes," p. 56. According to Lester Chandler, the purchasing power of the dollar rose about 33 percent between 1929 and 1933, and people whose incomes fell by less than 25 percent "actually gained in real income." Chandler, *America's Greatest Depression 1929–1941* (New York, 1970), p. 33.

200. S. Alexander Rippa makes a similar point in "Retrenchment," p. 81.

201. *Detroit Board of Education Proceedings*, 1934–35, p. 250.

202. For examples of that position see Bowles and Gintis, *Schooling*, pp. 191–195; Michael Kali, *Class, Bureaucracy and Schools* (New York, 1971), pp. 120–123; Marvin Lazarson, *Origins of the Urban School* (Cambridge, MA., 1971), pp. x–xvii; Joel Spring, *Education and the Rise of the Corporate State* (Boston, 1972), pp. 149–150; Paul Violas, *The Training of the Urban Working Class* (Chicago, 1978), pp. 100–109, 124–143, 320–333.

203. Bowles and Cintis, *Schooling*, p. 5.

204. James R. Prickett, "Communists and the Automobile Industry in Detroit Before 1935," *Michigan History* 57 (Fall, 1973):193–208.

205. Examples of the business community's stand on school aid can be found in Detroit *News* 1/26/33; 6/15/33; *The Detroiter* 6/12/36; 12/18/33; 12/15/33; 1/8/34; 6/4/34; Detroit *Saturday Night* 12/2/33; 12/16/33; 12/23/22; 11/3/34; 1/12/35; Detroit *Free Press* 2/4/33; 2/7/33; 4/2/ 33; 11/4/34; Detroit *Free Press* 4/16/37 cited in George Male, "The Michigan Education Association as an Interest Group, 1852–1950" (Ph.D. dissertation, University of Michigan, 1952), p. 468. As late as 1940, Male argues, major Michigan corporations and the Michigan Chamber of Commerce were fighting for reduced state appropriations for education, pp. 476–484.

PART FOUR

THE POSTWAR ERA: 1945–1980

The decades following World War II were a time of momentous change in the United States. Despite fears of another depression, it was a period of expansive economic development and wondrous technological innovation. Perhaps the most important changes associated with this period, however, were social and political. It was a time of struggles over social and economic inequality, much of it revolving around the Civil Rights Movement, which focused national attention on racial discrimination and segregation, especially as they concerned schooling. Unlike earlier conflicts over urban education, these were struggles waged by large segments of the population directly served by public education. City schools came to stand at the center of conflicts over discrimination and unequal social status, particularly in urban neighborhoods where such issues were most plainly evident. The landmark 1954 Supreme Court decision in *Brown V Board of Education of Topeka*, declaring segregated schools unlawful, set the stage for these developments. It raised public awareness of inequity and social injustice to new heights, making it impossible for educators and policy makers to ignore them as they had in the past. It was the prelude to a period of dramatic confrontation and rapid transformation.

As noted in the introduction, the postwar migration of African Americans from the rural South to large cities in the North and West changed the demographic profile of many urban areas. Most city school districts outside the South did not formally segregate Black children, but allowed schools to segregate by degrees, as Whites abandoned the neighborhoods where Blacks arrived. The effects of this practice became known as "de facto" segregation, and by the end of the 1950s it had become a widely recognized problem in many large cities. Stark inequities often distinguished schools in Black and White neighborhoods, and it was not long before local civil rights organizations began to agitate for immediate remedies. By the early 1960s massive demonstrations occurred around these issues in some cities, and growing concerns about racial inequities in many others. Local school boards resisted efforts to desegregate urban schools, claiming impartiality in matters of race and social class, at least with regard to utilizing resources. But successful legal action by the NAACP and other civil rights groups eventually resulted in federal and state court-ordered desegregation, forcing school authorities to move children from one area of their cities to another. These rulings and the resulting bussing plans prompted a veritable storm of controversy, and contributed to the movement of middle-class Whites out of the cities to the suburbs, a process often labeled "white flight." These events were prominent features of urban education during the latter 1960s and 1970s. They also contributed to a growing political "backlash," which would shape public discourse over education in the 1980s and beyond.

The essays in this part of the book examine many of these issues as they were manifest in particular cities. The first is a study of the development of the Chicago public schools during this era. In many respects, Chicago represented a telling case of social and political conflict over unequal education. The schools were led by Benjamin Willis, a towering figure both locally and nationally among educators. Willis represented the conventional progressive mode of school leadership, as outlined earlier in this volume. Like earlier school leaders, he was a strong believer in efficient and orderly administration. On the matter of racial inequality he claimed to be colorblind, a stance he and many others believed to represent objectivity and fairness. He built new schools to accommodate the growing population of the city's Black wards, but segregation remained widespread, even if not formally dictated by Willis' administration or even recognized as such. This was not acceptable to Chicago's Black population, or others opposed to racial inequities. Protests mounted rapidly and eventually led to Willis' departure from Chicago. The uproar also helped to create an atmosphere of conflict and recrimination that took years to resolve. Even after all of the demonstrations, debate, and confrontations over race in education, Chicago today remains a highly segregated city, and still suffers from many of the problems that Willis and his generation of educators struggled to resolve. If he had been a little more adept at addressing them, perhaps a different set out outcomes might have been possible.

The second essay in this section deals with quite a different set of developments. Sociologist Joseph Tropea has examined the processes by which urban educators in the 1950s and 1960s dealt with the growing numbers of "problem" students they encountered in their classes. As Tropea pointed out in an earlier study dealing with the Progressive Era, city teachers became quite adept at finding informal mechanisms, or "backstage rules," for excluding students they did not want to teach. This included large numbers of immigrant and working-class children, who often were poorly prepared academically, did not speak English, or exhibited behavior problems. Some of the ways that teachers coped with these challenges was to send problem students to special classes for the slow, or to issue suspensions to the unruly. In this chapter Tropea extended his research to the postwar period, when a growing number of the children in urban schools were Black, Latino, or members of another minority group. This was especially true in the cities he chose to study: Washington, DC, Detroit, Baltimore, and Philadelphia. He argued that many of the same strategies for excluding students were utilized by urban teachers in the 1950s and 1960s, although they often were challenged by civil rights organizations representing the rights of students to a fair and equal education.

Tropea notes that such legal challenges did not fundamentally alter the response of teachers, however. Rather, they simply shifted their behavior so that it was less evident, and poorly documented, to avoid the possibility of litigation. The result was a pattern of teacher behavior quite similar to that observed during the Progressive Era: throughout this period urban schools dealt with poor and politically powerless children by systematically excluding large numbers of them from instruction. Obviously, this was not a strategy designed to improve academic performance, and as Tropea pointed out, it may have contributed materially to juvenile delinquency, a growing problem at the time. But it was a critical feature of urban education in many of the nation's largest cities, an artifact of institutional practice that contributed materially to inequality and the lack of achievement for many of the students in America's largest cities.

The section's final essay is Guadalupe San Miguel's compelling study of the development of an educational and social protest movement among Chicano youth in Houston during the 1960s and 1970s. San Miguel has done a remarkable job of capturing the atmosphere of anger and confrontation that often characterized the period, and describing its impact. The struggle in Houston was similar to others staged elsewhere, by African American students and Puerto Ricans in addition to Chicanos. A striking feature of many of these protests was that minority youth were in the forefront of campaigns to reform curricula, to hire teachers from the community, and to raise academic standards. They were deeply suspicious of traditional educators, and conventional school practices, perhaps because of exclusionary behavior of the sort that Tropea described in his study. And they wanted immediate change. Their primary concern was gaining high-quality education for themselves and their communities. It was a heady time, and campaigns like the sort that San Miguel describes in this study contributed to the major changes attributed to the period. This was yet another dimension of the Civil Rights Movement's impact on the educational system. On the other hand, events such as these eventually helped to provide fuel for a political backlash, which eventually took shape in the 1980s. Opportunistic politicians often incited this, but in the decades to follow the tenor of educational reform in the nation's cities would shift profoundly. This is a topic that will be taken up in Part Five of the book.

ADDITIONAL READING

There is a growing literature on urban education and related issues in the postwar era, even if historians have not devoted as much attention to this period as others (perhaps because it is still considered recent). For a survey of relevant literature, see John L. Rury and Jeffrey Mirel, "The Political Economy of Urban Education," in Michael Apple, ed. *Review of Research in Education* (Washington, D.C., AERA), 1997, 22, pp. 49–112. Perhaps the best overview of the period can be found in Harvey Kantor and Barbara Brenzel, "Urban Education and the 'Truly Disadvantaged': The Historical Roots of the Contemporary Crisis, 1945–1990" *Teachers College Record*

1992 94(2): 278–314; also see Harvey Kantor and Robert Lowe, "Class, Race, and the Emergence of Federal Education Policy: From the New Deal to the Great Society" *Educational Researcher* 1995 24(3): 4–11. On district leadership, see David B. Tyack and Elisabeth Hansot, *Managers of Virtue: Public School Leadership in America, 1820–1980* (1982) (cited earlier). For a comparative view of policies during this time, see Ira Katznelson and Margaret Weir, *Schooling for All: Class, Race, and the Decline of the Democratic Ideal* (1985) (cited in the previous section), and Harold Silver and Pamela Silver, *An Educational War on Poverty: American and British Policy-Making, 1960–1980* (New York: Cambridge University Press, 1991). On developments in urban Indiana, see William J. Reese, ed. *Hoosier Schools: Past and Present* (1998) (cited earlier), Ch. 7. A useful account of the great migration can be found in Nicholas Lemann, *The Promised Land: The Great Black Migration and How It Changed America* (New York: Knopf, 1991). There are a number of good books from the period itself, which though not written by historians can provide a great deal of valuable information. In this vein, see Robert J. Havighurst, *Education in Metropolitan Areas* (Boston: Allyn & Bacon, 1966), David Rogers, *110 Livingston Street: Politics and Bureaucracy in the New York City Schools* (New York: Random House, 1968), Ray C. Rist, *The Urban School: A Factory for Failure: A Study of Education in American Society* (Cambridge, MA: M.I.T. Press, 1973), and Raymond C. Hummel and John M. Nagle, *Urban Education: Problems and Prospects* (New York: Oxford University Press, 1973).

Many of the studies of this time by historians have taken the form of case studies of particular places. For example, a detailed and insightful examination of the experiences of several families in one city can be found in J. Anthony Lukas, *Common Ground: A Turbulent Decade in the Lives of Three American Families* (New York: Alfred A. Knopf, 1985). For additional studies of particular cities, though quite different from Lukas, see Jeffrey Mirel, *The Rise and Decline of an Urban School System* (1993) (cited in the previous section), William H. Chafe, *Civilities and Civil Rights: Greensboro, North Carolina and the Black Struggle for Freedom* (New York: Oxford University Press, 1980), Ronald P. Formisano, *Boston against Busing: Race, Class, and Ethnicity in the 1960's and 1970's* (Chapel Hill: University of North Carolina Press, 1991), John L. Rury and Frank Cassell, eds., *Seeds of Crisis: Public Schooling in Milwaukee since 1920* (Madison: University of Wisconsin Press, 1993), Alan B. Anderson and George W. Pickering, *Confronting the Color Line: The Broken Promise of the Civil Rights Movement in Chicago* (Athens: University of Georgia Press, 1986), Kevin Fox Gotham, *Race, Real Estate, and Uneven Development: The Kansas City Experience, 1900–2000* (Albany: State University of New York Press, 2002), Jack Dougherty, *More Than One Struggle: The Evolution of Black School Reform in Milwaukee* (Chapel Hill: University of North Carolina Press, 2004), and Jean Anyon, *Ghetto Schooling: A Political Economy of Urban Educational Reform* (1997) (cited earlier).

Another large body of literature about this period deals with the question of desegregation. While most of the studies cited above also address this issue, other works make it a central focus. Perhaps the best overviews can be found in Jennifer Hochschild, *The New American Dilemma: Liberal Democracy and School Desegregation* (New Haven: Yale University Press, 1984), and Gary Orfield, *Public School Desegregation in the United States, 1968–1980* (Washington, DC: Joint Center for Policy Studies, 1983). Among the better studies by historians with a case-study orientation, are Davison M. Douglas, *Reading, Writing, and Race: The Desegregation of the Charlotte Schools* (Chapel Hill: University of North Carolina Press, 1995), and Eleanor Wolf, *Trial and Error: The Detroit Desegregation Case* (Detroit: Wayne State University Press, 1981); also see Kevin Fox Gotham, "Missed Opportunities, Enduring Legacies: School Segregation and Desegregation in Kansas City, Missouri" *American Studies* 2002 43(2): 5–41, and Gary Orfield, "Lessons of the Los Angeles Desegregation Case" *Education and Urban Society* 1984 16(3): 338–353. Additional recent urban case studies include William Henry Kellar, *Make Haste Slowly: Moderates, Conservatives, and School Desegregation in Houston* (College Station: Texas A&M University Press, 1999), Gregory S. Jacobs, *Getting Around Brown: Desegregation, Development, and the Columbus Public Schools* (Columbus: Ohio State University Press, 1998), and Joseph Watras, *Politics, Race, and Schools: Racial Integration, 1954–1994* (New York: Garland Publishers, 1997).

The literature on Hispanic educational struggles in cities during this time is not vast, but it is growing. Guadalupe San Miguel's prize winning study, *Brown, not White: School Integration and the Chicano Movement in Houston* (College Station: Texas A&M University Press, 2001) is among the strongest, along with Ruben Donato, *The Other Struggle for Equal Schools: Mexican Americans During the Civil Rights Era* (Albany: State University of New York Press, 1997).

11

Race and the Politics of Chicago's Public Schools: Benjamin Willis and the Tragedy of Urban Education

John L. Rury

This essay examines the development of schools and educational policies in one city, Chicago, Illinois, during a time when its school system underwent a process of dramatic change. The Chicago schools were led by Superintendent Benjamin Coppage Willis from 1953 to 1966, one of the most widely acclaimed urban school leaders of his time. Public education in Chicago became something of a showcase under Willis' leadership, but it also ultimately came to exhibit many of the problems of racial inequity and discrimination endemic to the age, most of which he was quite reluctant to acknowledge publicly. Eventually, however, Willis was not able to avoid these issues, and he became embroiled in the growing storm of controversy over racial injustice in education following the historic 1954 Brown decision. The long-standing political arrangements that had guided big city school systems since the progressive era, and which had become so familiar and comfortable for him, proved inadequate to the task of governing urban public education in the era of civil rights. The challenges facing the school leaders of this period were further compounded by the process of suburbanization and the subsequent transformation of urban neighborhoods along the line of race and social class. As Whites left the city in ever-larger numbers, Chicago became a different city in the 1960s, and this presented a host of challenges that its educators had not faced before.[1]

There was considerable drama in these events as they unfolded in the nation's second largest school district. The story to follow outlines the social forces that made Benjamin Willis' task so difficult in the 1950s and sixties, and extends to the experiences of the school leaders and politicians who followed him and attempted to find solutions to the escalating problems of political conflict over education. As the title suggests, this is not an altogether cheerful tale, but it also is a portentous one for today's would-be reformers intent on rescuing urban public education. The condition of city schools today is the result of a long and difficult procession of historical developments. Taking account of the experiences of Willis and those who followed him, and the lessons of their era, would thus seem to be an essential consideration in any plan to address the contemporary problems of these vitally important institutions.[2]

THE CHANGING URBAN SCENE

During the past fifty years developments in public education in Chicago occurred in a rapidly changing social and economic context. Postwar demographic shifts and their social and economic consequences directly and dramatically affected the policies of public education. This is a story of the transformation of urban "space," a process necessarily wrapped up in perception and the lived reality of changing social and political relationships.

Much of this, of course, is well known. World War II had barely ended when a grand migration to suburbia began in most of the nation's largest cities. Pressured by severe housing shortages in the central cities and encouraged by public policies that stimulated road building and guaranteed cheap private transportation, Americans began flocking to newly opened developments on the fringes of the urban core areas. Between 1940 and 1960, the country's suburban population grew by about 30 million or more than twice the numerical increase in the population of central cities during the same period. As a result, the share of metropolitan area population living in central cities dropped from 62.6 percent in 1940, to 58.6 percent in 1950, and to 51.3 percent in 1960. This decline continued thereafter, and by 1980 only 40 percent of the country's metropolitan area population lived in central cities, with the rest in surrounding suburbs.[3]

Chicagoans participated in this movement to suburbia. While the city's total population increased by only 150,000 between 1940 and 1960, the suburban population boomed, growing by nearly 400,000 in the 1950s and by another million in the following decade. As a result, the city's share of the metropolitan area's population dropped from almost three quarters in 1940 to just over half in 1960. Thereafter the pace of change quickened; Chicago experienced a net population loss of nearly 800,000 between 1960 and 1990, while the suburbs gained almost 2 million. By 1990 the city held only about 40 percent of the metropolitan area's total population, just slightly better than half its 1940 share.[4]

Of course, migration from central cities was only one source of suburban population growth. But it was an important one destined to have significant impact on the cities and their educational systems. It was a process that altered the social landscape of Chicago and its environs, and it introduced a new spatial sensibility into calculations of social status and well-being. This was a series of changes that affected many aspects of life for all Chicagoans, perhaps none more than their schools.

Migrants from central cities were disproportionately young, middle class, and upwardly mobile. They also were overwhelmingly White. These were the persons who could afford to buy housing in the suburbs and whose jobs and earnings allowed them to spend the time and incur the costs involved in daily commuting. As a group, they were also allowed to move into these new burgeoning communities on the edge of the expanding metropolitan area. And as these people moved to suburbia, the populations of the country's central cities became older, poorer, and darker in complexion.[5]

This change was no less apparent in Chicago than elsewhere. In 1940, 90 percent of the city's total population of nearly 3.4 million was White. The proportion fell during the 1940s to 84 percent and to 70 percent by 1960. The volume of out-migration increased after 1960, and by 1990 Whites made up less than 40 percent of the city's total population of over 2.7 million. Overall, between 1940 and 1990 the city experienced a net loss of over 2 million Whites, nearly two-thirds of their number at the start of the period. This was the source of suburban population growth in metropolitan Chicago.[6]

At the end of this period a new spatial logic had been imposed upon the region, like many other large metropolitan areas in the late twentieth century. Predominantly White suburbs surrounding poor and largely "dark" urban population centers changed the relationship of central cities to the communities arrayed around them. Metaphorically, the term urban itself, the root of "urbane," became associated with social problems and loss of status; suburban residential enclaves became identified with idyllic refuges from the turmoil and danger of the city.[7] These were images invoked with particular urgency in connection with children and schooling.

This large-scale transformation of Chicago's population altered existing spatial accommodations in the housing market, in politics, and in education. The city's African-American ghetto expanded, pushing outward to the south and west, encountering bitter and often violent resistance from Whites every block of the way. By the mid-1960s, these and other racial struggles had given new meaning to the city's politics and new shape to its voting coalitions. The city's Democratic machine, earlier dependent on support from lower-income voters, especially Blacks, cast its lot with the White resisters on most integration issues, including education. By doing so, it created a new base of popular support, uniting Chicago's Northwest Side and Southwest Side Whites into a cohesive and highly mobilized voting coalition.[8] Battles over education and the spatial allocation of school resources played a significant role in this process.

At the same time that demographic change was underway, the city's economy shifted dramatically as well. With the overall loss of population in Chicago, the number of jobs in the city fell also. According to the Chicago *Tribune*, in the latter 1960s there were some 1,400,000 private sector jobs in the city itself. By 1983 that number had fallen by about 280,000 (or 20 percent). Of course, many jobs in the city were held by suburbanites, so these figures may understate the extent of job loss to Chicago residents during this period. Even more revealing, however, are data on the decline of industrial employment. In just 12 years, between 1970 and 1982, some 24 percent of Chicago's 8,000 factories closed or relocated outside of the city and hundreds more moved in the years that followed. Literally hundreds of thousands of manufacturing jobs, long the staple of employment for vast portions of Chicago's working-class population, were lost to the city. As the *Tribune* and a variety of other sources have documented over the years, the communities which have been hit hardest by these changes have been African American.[9]

What has been the impact of these changes? As William Julius Wilson, Douglas Massey, and others have suggested, it is the Black areas of the city that have borne the brunt of these massive shifts. In the past, while income has always been low in African-American neighborhoods, unemployment was relatively stable. In 1960, for instance, as Chicago's Black population was still expanding quite rapidly, Black unemployment stood at 11 percent (about double the White rate). In certain areas of Chicago, Black unemployment by the 1990s was twice that level, even with a buoyant economy.[10] Clearly, the process of suburbanization—and the associated loss of jobs and income—adversely affected many of Chicago's citizens. The new spatial logic of urban development in the late twentieth century dictated that there would be clear winners and losers in the distribution of social resources. And this inevitably gave shape to a new political order. Among the most critical of the resources at stake—and the object of much political conflict—was schooling.

THE EVOLUTION OF URBAN EDUCATION: CHICAGO'S GOLDEN YEARS

Changes in Chicago's public and parochial educational systems have mirrored these demographic and economic shifts. The modern history of the Chicago public schools clearly traces a line from reputed excellence in earlier times to allegations of "educational meltdown" in the 1980s. During the opening years of the century such celebrated figures as John Dewey, Jane Addams, Francis Parker, Margaret Haley, and Ella Flagg Young helped to shape a public school system that embodied many of the major innovations of Progressive educational reform.[11] The Chicago schools served an astonishingly diverse student population comprised in large part of children from impoverished, immigrant homes. The school system's apparent success in dealing with this diverse student population earlier in the century provides the counterpoint for questions about apparent failure in recent years.

It is important, of course, not to romanticize Chicago's educational past. Historically, the city's schools were beset with many problems, particularly as they struggled to provide seats to a rapidly expanding student body in the nineteenth century. Even in the heyday of progressive reform, many children in Chicago attended overcrowded, poorly lit, and inadequately ventilated schools. Thousands left school early to work in the city's many factories and sweatshops, particularly the children of non-English-speaking immigrant groups. Later, in the 1930s and 1940s, the schools were plagued by corruption and scandal. The city's political machine filled the educational system with patronage workers, and contracts were bought and sold with impunity. When the system was finally cleaned up in the latter 1940s, however, (under reform superintendent Harold Hunt) it seemed that Chicago's public schools would finally realize the promise they had exhibited a half century earlier. The arrival in 1953 of new superintendent Benjamin Coppage Willis, an energetic, progressive school leader from Buffalo, heralded a new era.[12]

It did not take long for things to get better. In many respects the decade of the 1950s was a golden age in Chicago public school history; that period offers the clearest reference point for contrast with recent times. It was a time of prosperity and growing public confidence in the schools. Under Willis' firm leadership, average class size across the system fell nearly 20 percent at the same time that enrollment grew at a rate of more than ten thousand new students each year (this was the era of the baby boom). Teachers' salaries increased, and financial incentives were created to reward advanced study for teachers. The numbers of such non-teaching personnel as nurses and psychologists in the system more than doubled. Curricula were liberalized, particularly in the system's high schools, and enrollment in summer and after-school programs climbed to nearly a quarter of the children in the system.[13]

Perhaps most telling of all, more than a quarter billion dollars in bond issues for school construction were approved by the public in five separate referenda (well over a billion in today's dollars). At the same time the district's operating budget more than doubled, with nearly two-thirds of its support coming from local property taxes. Altogether, Willis built or substantially expanded some 208 elementary schools and 13 high schools. In the popular media of the time he became known, among other things, as "Ben the Builder." It was a time of growth and Chicago's schools clearly were supported by the public. Given this, there can be little doubt that broad segments of the city's population believed the schools were doing a good job.[14] As a matter of perception, of course, this stands in stark contrast to public views of Chicago's schools in recent decades.

While in Chicago, Benjamin Willis became one of the most celebrated school superintendents of his day. Featured in the local and national press as a model of efficiency and competence, Willis projected a positive image for the city's public schools. His style of leadership, moreover, left little doubt about who was in charge. Willis represented a professional ethos of educational administration that highlighted the educational leader's role as expert and authoritative. In his view, the educator's responsibility lay outside the realm of politics, a particularly apt stance given Chicago's experience in the 1930s and 1940s, and above the court of public opinion.[15]

Shortly after arriving in Chicago, Willis contributed an especially revealing article to the *Chicago Schools Journal* entitled "The Need for Professionalism in Education Today." As he described it, professional authority resided with the expertise of the educator, just as the power of a doctor rested within his medical knowledge. "I know of no patient," he declared, "who upon entering a hospital, dictates to his physician concerning the program of medication."

"His family," he added, "does not either." For Willis, the control of education was properly a professional concern, and he expressed a particular disdain for popular views about educational issues. "Much of what is wrong with education today can be attributed to the fact that educators have abdicated from positions of educational leadership, and have permitted themselves to be swayed by the winds of uninformed public opinion." In this regard, Willis was a prototypical example of what David Tyack and Elizabeth Hansot have described as an administrative progressive in school leadership.[16] The views he expressed in 1954, it turned out, were a portent of controversies he would face in the future.

Like many schoolmen of his time, Willis firmly believed in the virtues of the neighborhood school. This, he maintained, was in keeping with the ideas of modern public education "which emphasizes the role of the school in community life," a notion he claimed was "subscribed to by leading educators over the years." Other considerations in the assignment of students to schools, he felt, were less legitimate. This was consistent with the school system's official stance of detachment from politics. If education was an activity bound by place and time, progressive educational principles—and long-standing school practice—dictated that it occur in close proximity to other facets of a student's life. To do otherwise, in his view, was to allow non-educational considerations to enter the picture.[17]

When confronted with questions of race, Willis claimed not to know how many Black or White students were enrolled in particular schools, since the district maintained "no record of race, color or creed of any student or employee." This, of course, was in keeping with his stance of non-involvement in political affairs. Given Willis' liberal progressive mentality, equality of educational opportunity meant race was irrelevant to the business of schooling. The Chicago Public Schools clung to this policy of color blindness until 1963 when the Illinois legislature required the system to collect data on the racial composition of its student body and teaching force. Even after such information was available, however, residence remained for Willis the only legitimate basis upon which to assign students to a particular school, especially for younger children.[18] This was a stand which tied the city's public schools directly to the new patterns of spatial differentiation then emerging in Chicago and to the rapidly evolving whirlwind of racial politics looming over American cities.

Like other progressive educational leaders, Willis claimed that achievement for all children was the goal of the Chicago schools. And although there was a great deal of variation in this respect across the system, achievement levels were considerably better than what Chicago schools exhibit today. Even as late as the early 1960s, when the system was already embroiled in controversy, there was evidence of solid achievement in the city's schools. Data from Robert Havighurst's 1963 survey of Chicago Public Schools indicated this. Looking at high schools (n = 39), Havighurst and his colleagues described as many as 14 (about a third) as "high achieving," all located in middle-class neighborhoods. They reported that more than half of the seniors in these schools planned to attend college, a high number for the time. These schools had roughly a third or more of their students in the top "three stanines on standard tests of reading." They also had low numbers of students in "Basic English" classes. On these two measures of achievement, about a quarter of the city's public high schools were doing quite well. Willis and his supporters had good reason to be proud of such institutions.

There were other sides to the achievement story, however. Another 15 schools were described by Havighurst as "common man schools," exhibiting achievement in the middle range, with as many as half their graduates planning to enter college. Twelve schools in this category had more than 20 percent of their students in the top three stanines in reading. This is better than what most Chicago Public Schools achieved in the 1990s, assuming that national norms from the two periods are comparable. On the other hand, one-third of the city's high schools were classified by Havighurst as "inner city," with achievement "well below averages," and with high drop-out rates (although these were not reported). Three-quarters of these schools were in African-American areas of the city and had student bodies that were 80 percent or more Black. Many were fed by overcrowded, under-funded grade schools.[19] Clearly, these schools represented a different extreme, and they were spatially differentiated from the city's more successful schools.

While this report pointed to serious problems, and contemporaries did not see it as altogether positive, it is an interesting benchmark. As the data indicate, in the early 1960s there was a sizeable portion of Chicago public high school students who were performing well by national standards—particularly among White students. By this measure, many of the city's schools appear to have been doing their job and thereby supported perceptions of competence which sustained confidence in the system. The very high degree of inequality in the district reflected the new pattern of spatial differentiation then emerging in Chicago and other large cities. The city's "good" schools, a vital resource to their immediate communities, helped to sustain a positive public perception of the system as a whole. The growing problem of inequality, however, threatened to change such perceptions, particularly as a battle over educational resources loomed in the wake of the emerging national civil rights movement.

THE NEW POLITICS OF SCHOOLING: WILLIS AND THE CRISIS IN URBAN PUBLIC EDUCATION

Not all of the public was pleased with Willis' performance. As suggested by Havighurst's data, there was great unevenness in the successes scored by Chicago's public schools in the 1950s and early 1960s. Schools in African-American neighborhoods were especially crowded as thousands of migrants from communities in the South poured into the city each year. And as the data above indicated, achievement levels were considerably lower in Black schools.

These disparities were well known by the time the Havighurst report was released. As early as 1957 an article in the National Association for the

Advancement of Colored People's magazine *The Crisis* found serious inequalities in Black and White schooling in Chicago. That article reported the average White elementary school enrolled fewer than 700 students, while the average for Black schools was greater than 1,200. Subsequent studies showed similar patterns. The Urban League, in a 1962 study, found that all but one of the city's largest elementary schools, those with more than 1,600 students, were in Black neighborhoods. By the early 1960s enrollments in some schools, particularly on the Westside, had exceeded 2,000. Children in these schools were placed on double shifts—one report held that more than 80 percent of the 20,000 children in the city on such shifts were African American. Overall, class sizes were 25 percent larger in Black schools. As a consequence, the Urban League study found that per-pupil expenditures in majority Black schools were only two-thirds of those in White schools.[20]

There were yet other dimensions of inequality. The Havighurst survey revealed that "inner city" elementary schools had the lowest proportion of "regular appointment" teachers, fewer than two-thirds, with the remainder being full time or temporary substitutes. The teachers in these schools also had considerably less experience than their counterparts in other schools, a median of 4 years compared to more than 12. The vast majority of Chicago's African-American children, more than 80 percent, attended virtually all Black schools (90 percent or more) simply because of long-established patterns of residential segregation. Willis' policy of making residential location the criterion of school assignment resulted in the well-documented inequalities observed in the early 1960s.[21]

In the immediate *post-Brown* phase of the Civil Rights Movement, sensitivities to racial inequality in schooling were quite high, particularly in the African-American community. But the inequities were real, and eventually they were irrefutably documented. The Urban League and others noted that some White schools had as few as 30 children to a classroom. Yet another Urban League report in the early 1960s counted some 382 empty classrooms in predominantly White schools. Findings such as these understandably led to considerable consternation and anger in the African-American community.[22] They helped to set the stage for a confrontation that would dramatically alter public views of the city's schools.

True to his stated philosophy of school leadership, Superintendent Willis refused to consider proposals for transferring children from Black schools to White areas of the city on a large scale. He did offer a largely ineffectual policy to allow children from schools with more than 40 students per classroom to transfer to those with under 30. But this affected fewer than two hundred students and was based wholly on class sizes without consideration given to race or other factors. In response to charges of segregation Willis repeatedly invoked the image of the "neighborhood school" which he argued was the best educational solution to the problems of inequality in education and to boosting achievement.[23]

This was a significant spatial metaphor, one that would be invoked repeatedly—by Willis and others—in the years to follow. It signaled that

Willis would not permit the schools to become an instrument for the transformation of the spatial relationships of power and privilege that defined Chicago's landscape. Instead, the resources of the system were poured into addressing well-documented inequalities in different areas of the city without changing the neighborhood school policy. Consequently, the Chicago Public School's (CPS) building program constructed more new schools in African-American areas (the South and West sides) than elsewhere. But the pace of this building only gradually closed the gap between Black and White schools with regard to overcrowding. It was not until 1964 that double shifts in many schools were ended, but even then disparities continued to be evident.[24]

When the Board of Education resorted to using temporary classroom structures constructed of corrugated steel to end double shifts instead of allowing Black students to attend majority White schools, most Blacks and many Whites were outraged. By the end of 1962 about 150 of these were in use, and there were 250 by 1964, more than 70 percent of which were used to house Black students. By then funds for new construction had been largely expended, and the Willis administration was reluctant to seek public approval of new bond issues in the wake of growing controversy over the schools. The building boom was ending and communities on the city's South and West sides still had over-crowded schools, even if the double shifts had ended.[25] If the rest of the city felt good about the public schools, Chicago's rapidly growing Black communities were increasingly restive about them.

The conflict which resulted from this set of circumstances, and which eventually led to Willis' departure from Chicago, was critical to the eventual fate of the Chicago Public Schools. The story of Black community mobilization around these questions has been told in considerable detail elsewhere. By 1961 the NAACP, the Chicago *Defender*, the Urban League, and other African-American community institutions were calling for Willis' dismissal. The next year saw the formation of a broad coalition of civil rights organizations, the Coordinating Council of Community Organizations (CCCO), led by former teacher Al Raby, which would be the focal point of Black mobilization around school issues for the next six years. Even the United States Commission on Civil Rights censured the Board and Willis for inaction on school integration. Unaddressed complaints led to confrontations and demonstrations in the years that followed. Sitins and boycotts, mass marches, and meetings with political leaders were the tactics employed in a four-year struggle to demand meaningful integration of the schools and the ouster of Benjamin Willis. In many respects the struggle against Willis and the Board provided the local civil rights organizations an opportunity to practice tactics of confrontation and exposure that they would use in future struggles. As in other cities, early battles over school desegregation provided an outlet for decades of anger and resentment in the Black community.[26]

Historians have divided this movement in Chicago into several phases, each culminating in a system-wide boycott of the schools—widely observed by Black and White students alike. Things first came to a head in 1963, as demonstrators set fire to a "Willis wagon" in August, and nearly three hundred thousand children—Black and White—boycotted school in October. At about the same time, Willis abruptly resigned, claiming that the Board was interfering with his administrative duties by ordering him to implement a transfer policy he had not approved. Shortly afterward, when the Board voted to refuse that resignation, another mass boycott of the schools followed, along with a demonstration by eight thousand adults, circling city hall with pickets and placards. The sense of outrage in the city's Black community became palpable. Finally, when Willis' contract was approaching an end in 1966, the Board began to search for a successor, although the demonstrations and public acrimony over desegregation and equity in education continued.[27]

The conflict also led to the appointment of a special commission to study racial inequalities in the public schools, headed by Phillip Hauser, chairman of the University of Chicago's Sociology Department. The Hauser report reproved Willis, calling him "a giant of inertia, inequity, injustice, intransigence and trained incapacity." Willis, not surprisingly, refused to acknowledge the report (even though it was written by "experts") and was steadfast in his refusal to broach any interference in his own management of the public schools. This was partly a response to the long history of corrupt political manipulation of the schools in Chicago; but it was also emblematic of the professional culture Willis had championed throughout his career. Schools were supposed to be managed by expert professionals, without external influences to distract them. As a consequence of this stance, or perhaps in spite of it, Willis became a symbol of resistance to school desegregation in Chicago. To African Americans he became an object of vilification, and for years afterward the temporary classroom buildings sometimes set up outside public schools were referred to as "Willis Wagons" in Black neighborhoods.[28]

On the other hand, for many Whites—particularly those who felt threatened by encroaching Black neighborhoods—Willis became a champion of resistance to the very idea of integration. Small White counter-demonstrations began to appear in 1963, usually to protest the prospect of school integration or housing reform. Bogan High School on the city's Southwest side, a flashpoint for conflicts over neighborhood integration, was the site of considerable turmoil in the wake of demands to bus children to relieve overcrowding in Black schools. Willis met privately with a group of Bogan demonstrators, something he had not done with civil rights protestors, and shortly thereafter he removed Bogan from a list of schools eligible to receive voluntary transfer applications. This resulted in a storm of protests from civil rights groups, but it also helped to make him a champion to White opponents of school desegregation. In the wake of the Hauser Report and other calls for desegregation, Whites in neighborhoods across the city began to organize. Willis' unwillingness to consider plans for integrating the schools abetted their own hostility to such ideas and provided them with time to mobilize in anticipation of desegregation efforts to come.[29]

Although he may not have recognized his predicament in these terms, Benjamin Willis found himself ensnared in the early stages of a massive struggle over the spatial distribution of educational resources in Chicago. In keeping with his training and professional proclivities, he focused much of his energy on building new schools in the city's most crowded neighborhoods to keep up with demand. But Willis does not appear to have recognized the larger political and cultural dimensions of the problems he faced. In the extant literature on this period in Chicago we have a detailed—if sometimes poorly focused—account of mobilization in the African-American community in response to perceived inequality and injustices in education. No corresponding picture exists for the city's White communities.[30] This is critical to comprehending what later occurred in the history of Chicago public education. The process of spatial differentiation in the city's school system began to accelerate in the 1960s. And as much as Benjamin Willis may have wanted to ignore the issue of race, it threatened to overwhelm the school system he had worked so hard to build.

SCHOOL POLITICS AND THE CHICAGO MACHINE

It is an open question how much Willis' stance on school desegregation was influenced by the mayoral administration of Richard J. Daley. For his part, Daley maintained an assiduous distance from school affairs, largely because the lessons of the 1940s scandals were still fresh in the public mind. When he did speak, however, he consistently expressed support for "what the people want," and for neighborhood schools. In one frequently noted comment he stated that children ought to be able to eat lunch at home and tell their mothers about school, invoking an image that intimately linked home and school. There is also Daley's well-known confrontation with United States Commissioner of Education Francis Keppel over the disposition of federal funds under the Elementary and Secondary Education Act, which were withheld because of a CCCO petition in 1965. Appealing directly to the White House, Daley succeeded in defusing what promised to be an effective challenge to Willis' policies of abetting segregation.[31]

But more than anything else, it was Daley's silence on the question of desegregation and the outspokenness of his machine functionaries against it that probably was most telling in the Chicago school crisis. The response of the Chicago Public Schools to race issues under Willis' leadership, after all, was consistent with many facets of Democratic machine politics in the city during this era.[32] As many historians have noted, the elder Daley relied heavily on Black votes through much of his early career—they provided him the crucial margin of victory in the critical and very close 1963 election—so it is little wonder that Daley did not attack desegregation outright. Daley did not believe there was competition for Black votes, on the other hand, so he felt no obligation to respond to Black community demands. As long as Black machine politicians including legendary Black Congressman William L. Dawson—delivered support there was no need to heed demands for improvements in the schools or other community services. Indeed, there is evidence that the Dawson forces worked to undermine desegregation efforts early on.[33]

Daley and his machine allies were worried about White votes, however. Fearful of losing support in the city's White ethnic neighborhoods, where he had lost to Benjamin Adamowski in 1963, Daley quickly learned to resist civil rights measures—outside of symbolic gestures toward housing reform—that would upset Whites and contribute to further suburbanization or a successful challenge to his power in the machine. Given this, in the confrontation that unfolded between Chicago's Black communities and the Willis administration, there can be little question about where the Mayor's sympathies lay, especially in the period following the pivotal year of 1963 when Daley was narrowly reelected and Willis faced his first crisis of authority. To maintain power, the Chicago Democratic machine had to uphold the existing spatial distribution of status and privilege in the city. It was not that equity in education for African Americans ran contrary to the mayor's principles; rather it was the fact that he had so few principles—apart from remaining in power—that allowed the crisis to go forward. In the end the mayor did not care enough to try to save the city's schools. They too were expendable if that was the price of power. A quote from a former mayoral aide was telling on this point: "The more Blacks picked on Willis, the more popular he became among Whites. If Daley gave in, the Whites would have been mad. He figured he'd always get the Black vote, but the Whites had already shown that they would go for someone else when they went for Adamowski. Besides, Willis was useful to Daley. If the civil rights people kept after Willis, it kept the heat off Daley."[34]

It is possible, in that case, that Benjamin Willis, the consummate progressive school executive, was simply a dupe for Chicago's wily mayor. Daley certainly was cognizant of the shifting spatial dynamics of Chicago's political system. And since Daley appointed each member of Chicago's Board of Education, the body that Willis reported to, he presumably could have moved Willis out of the picture if he felt the superintendent was an impediment to progress. But Daley was willing to let Willis take "the heat." In this respect Willis may have been a hapless victim, even if he contributed a great deal to his own increasingly difficult dilemma. But the structural feature of public school administrative culture that made this situation possible was the self-imposed isolation of educational leadership from political affairs. The legacy of the administrative progressives, reinforced by Chicago's unhappy history of corruption and educational malfeasance, meant that Willis was largely unprepared for the challenges posed by the social, demographic, and political changes that altered the face of urban public education. Without access to the mechanisms of political power, Willis may have felt there was little he could do to resolve the situation. As a man of firm principles, however, it is also clear that the superintendent was steadfast in his refusal to change course because of political pressure, regardless of its source.[35]

CHICAGO SCHOOLS IN THE POST-WILLIS ERA

Willis finally left Chicago in 1966, and his successor—James Redmond—was committed to achieving desegregation through such measures as voluntary transfers and establishing magnet programs to attract and hold White students. While these policies allowed Black students to attend a much wider range of schools, Daley's Board of Education implemented them haltingly and only after protests.[36] Specifically, Redmond's plans to target certain White communities on the Northwest and South sides of the city for relatively modest, incremental bussing plans, led to immediate, vociferous, and sometimes violent resistance on the part of Whites. Consequently, these plans never got off the ground, and he never succeeded in achieving a meaningful level of desegregated enrollment.

Redmond left Chicago in 1975 and was followed by Joseph P. Hannon, who proposed a series of plans to provide transportation to Black students who wanted to transfer to predominantly White schools, although it was still a voluntary plan. White reaction again was swift and extreme. By this time there was a growing national movement opposed to bussing, and "neighborhood schools" had become a rallying cry among opponents to desegregation. Local organizations, with names like "Save Our Schools," and "Mothers for Neighborhood Schools, American Style," sprang up to lead demonstrations against Hannon and the Board's policies. White protesters—mostly mothers—picketed, shouted at incoming Black students, even threw eggs at them in some instances. Although only about 17,000 students (3 percent of the total) were involved in Hannon's "Access to Excellence" program it provoked a very strong reaction. Under pressure from the federal government to achieve meaningful desegregation, Hannon was preparing to implement a second, more ambitious plan, when he abruptly resigned in 1979 as the school system headed into its most serious financial crisis to date.[37]

The effect of battles over the various desegregation plans of the 1970s was an accelerating rate of White flight from the system. Chicago's public schools had a slight Black majority when Willis left, but there were more than 200 schools with enrollments more than 90 percent White. Within just six years, the number of such schools had dropped by half, and by 1980 there were less than ten. In the same time frame, the White proportion of the public schools' student population fell from roughly half to less than 20 percent. Faced with the prospect of desegregation across the system, white Chicagoans abandoned the public schools altogether.[38]

By and large, the ethnic profile of the city's public school population changed considerably faster than the pace of suburbanization, or "White flight" from the city itself. While Chicago's White population fell by about half between 1960 and 1980, the number of White students in the public schools plummeted by almost 80 percent. Although the change in public school enrollment patterns was largely due to the loss of middle-class White families to nearby suburbs, in some areas parochial and other private schools became an alternative to the public schools for White families, particularly so-called "White ethnics." In an unpublished paper, James Lewis of the Urban League has noted a shift to these schools by Whites with the onset of desegregation. Private schools were largely White throughout these years, and by the 1980s nearly two-thirds of the White students in the city attended these schools.[39] Either way, White families with sufficient resources chose not to send their children to public schools in the city. By the 1970s Chicago's public schools, like those of other large northern cities, had come to be seen as embattled institutions, struggling to serve a clientele which was increasingly poor and racially isolated. This was a dramatic change from less than two decades earlier.

It is within this context that political conflicts have occurred over education in Chicago. Following Willis' departure the public schools clearly ceased to enjoy the same level of public confidence evident in the 1950s. Indeed, the 1970s, with increasing public acrimony over school issues in Chicago, a growing fiscal crisis driven by rapidly rising payrolls (partly a consequence of collective bargaining), and stagnant revenues, offer a virtual reverse image of the 1950s.[40] In the wake of continuing battles over questions of equity, public confidence in the schools was deeply shaken. The decade following Willis' departure saw the Chicago Public Schools begin a steep descent into the condition that William Bennett encountered—and commented on so emphatically—in the latter 1980s.

The key to understanding this entire process of change appears to be the Willis years. It was that period, after all, which set the stage, and determined the tone, for what followed. There can be little doubt that Willis' refusal to consider desegregation efforts encouraged resistance to change in the public schools in White neighborhoods. In a revealing passage, Paul Peterson notes that the Redmond administration was taken aback at the speed with which resistance was mounted to the very first desegregation proposals—modest as they were—undertaken in 1968. Redmond, who spent an early part of his career in Chicago as Herald Hunt's assistant, had been superintendent of the New Orleans schools during the bitter desegregation battles of the latter 1950s and early 1960s in the South. A veteran of protracted conflicts over race and inequality, he certainly was not naive about the situation he faced. But he was unprepared for the level of mobilized resistance he encountered in Chicago.[41]

Political scientist Jennifer Hochschild has argued that school desegregation was most likely to succeed in settings where civic and educational leaders were supportive of change and played a leading role in quieting irrational fears and racial animosity. In this regard there was virtual silence in Chicago, despite valiant efforts on the part of certain civic groups and individuals and the roles of leading academics—Robert Havighurst and Phillip Hauser in particular—who issued reports pointing to the need for integration. It is also important to note that all of the city's major daily newspapers supported the neighborhood school policy in their editorials. Several, most notably the *Tribune*, were supporters of Willis virtually to the end of his tenure in Chicago. Apart from civil rights groups, Black community publications such as the Chicago *Defender*, and a handful of liberal academics there were few advocates for desegregation.[42] Even if the pace of change in the loss of Whites from the system was faster in the 1970s, the Willis years—particularly his latter years—created the atmosphere for continuing racial conflict over public education in Chicago.

By the time a desegregation plan was offered by the Redmond administration the lines of resistance across the city were clearly drawn and had already hardened. They proved impossible to surmount by the city's school system alone. Redmond succeeded in piecemeal reforms, but in the latter 1970s Chicago still did not have a comprehensive plan for desegregating its public schools.[43] By the time the State of Illinois and the United States Justice Department began to pressure the system to develop one, the number of Whites in the schools had declined precipitously. As a rear-guard action to slow the pace of change, resistance to desegregation both within the Board of Education itself and in White communities across the city had succeeded. As a matter of social policy, on the other hand, it resulted in a school system that was largely impervious to court-mandated desegregation, simply because there were so few Whites left in the public schools.[44] During the 1980s the ethnic composition of the city's school population continued to change, and education remained an important political issue. The number of White students in the public schools continued to decline, dropping to under 12 percent of the total by 1990; the number of Black students declined slightly as well, dropping to 58 percent of the student population; while Hispanics increased from about 18 percent to 27 percent. Confidence in the public schools appeared to weaken further as business leaders expressed frustration with the quality of recent graduates. It was at this point that William Bennett selected Chicago as his educational whipping boy, declaring its schools "the worst in the nations" to score points with the Reagan administration's largely suburban Republican constituency.[45]

THE POLITICS OF LATE TWENTIETH-CENTURY URBAN SCHOOL REFORM

This atmosphere of crisis eventually gave birth to the Chicago school reform movement. Although much of the initial leadership was provided by Harold Washington's administration, a wide array of disparate interests eventually gave shape to the reform which was implemented in 1989.[46] In many respects, the first wave of Chicago school reform represented a step toward turning the schools back to a process of reform through popular political action and an end to making schools instruments of state and federally mandated social policy. Ironically, in a new context where desegregation was no longer the overriding issue, the neighborhood school—and local control of school policies— emerged as a *new* ideal, the key to educational reform. As Jeffrey Mirel has pointed out, just ten years earlier such a slogan would not have been a viable instrument of reform. This is how dramatically the spatial logic of school reform has changed in Chicago since the failure of desegregation.

Now, with changes brought about by the administration of Paul Vallas, and the 1995 Chicago school reform legislation, it appears that the public schools have become the instruments of city hall. Indeed, it might be accurate to say that Chicago's current mayor, Richard M. Daley, is working to undo some of the damage that the short-sighted and ultimately destructive policies of his father—and his father's generation—had wrought on the city and its schools.[47] In any case, the old progressive saw that the schools must be kept out of politics is increasingly honored only in the breach today. Perhaps this is a positive development, at least for the time being. As the Willis era demonstrated, an unyielding belief that the educational system is above politics was both naive and misguided and ultimately left school leaders impotent when faced with explosive political crises.

But what of the questions of inequality and the new spatial distribution of resources that so clearly marks Chicago and other late twentieth-century American metropolitan areas today? Clearly, the process of racial change that the city's public schools underwent in the decades following 1960 reflected the emergence of a new social order; by the 1990s Whites represented a minority of the city's somewhat smaller population. In recent years, despite positive press reporting of new waves of local school reform and the work of the Paul Vallas administration, Chicago's largely Black and Latin schools continue to be compared unfavorably with predominantly White suburban institutions. The spatial distribution of ethnic groups in the metropolitan area has changed dramatically, but the geographic differentiation of educational resources has remained intact, even if the geography or inequality has also shifted somewhat since the Willis years. Despite recent indications that the White population of the Chicago Public Schools has increased incrementally while the Black population has fallen, the spatial logic of exclusion and inequity that Willis struggled unsuccessfully to mediate still haunts the city schools.[48] This is the tragedy of urban education in the latter twentieth century and the single greatest challenge for the next generation of school leaders.

NOTES

1. Chicago *Tribune*, November 7, 1987, 1.
2. For an influential statement on the state of urban education in the 1980s and 1990s, one that accepts the proposition of urban school inferiority, see Jonathan Kozol, *Savage Inequalities: Children in Americas Schools* (New York: Harper, 1991), passim. On the low state of public opinion regarding big city school systems, particularly regarding perceptions of bureaucratic control, see Dan A. Lewis and Kathryn Nakagawa, *Race and Educational Reform in the American Metropolis: A Study of School Decentralization* (Albany: State University of New York Press, 1995), Ch. 2.
3. These figures are calculated from data in Bureau of the Census, *Historical Statistics of the United States: Colonial Times to 1970* (Washington: Government Printing Office, 1975), Ch. A; and Idem., *1980 Census of Population, Volume 1, Characteristics of the Population, Chapter A, Number of Inhabitants, Part I, United States Summary* (Washington: Government Printing Office, 1983), 227; also see Kenneth Fox, *Metropolitan America: Urban Life and Urban Policy in the United States 1940–1980* (New Brunswick: Rutgers University Press, 1985), 51. On the urban–suburban migration at this time and its effect, see Jon C. Teaford, *The Twentieth Century American City*, Second Edition (Baltimore: Johns Hopkins University Press, 1993), passim; also see Kenneth T. Jackson, *The Crabgrass Frontier: The Suburbanization of the United States* (New York: Oxford University Press, 1985), Ch. 12.

4. These figures are from Irving Cutler, *Chicago: Metropolis of the Mid-Continent*, Third Edition (Dubuque: Kendall/Hunt Publishers, 1982), Ch. 5, and Chicago Fact Book Consortium, *Area Fact Book: Chicago Metropolitan Area, 1980* (Chicago: University of Illinois at Chicago, 1984), xvi, xvii; For a discussion of early trends, see Otis Dudley Duncan and Beverly Duncan, *The Negro Population of Chicago: A Study of Residential Succession* (Chicago: University of Chicago Press, 1957), Ch. VIII; also see Paul Kleppner, *Chicago Divided: The Making of a Black Mayor* (DeKalb: Northern Illinois University Press, 1985), Ch. 2; and Ann Durkin Keating, *Building Chicago: Suburban Developers and the Creation of a Divided Metropolis* (Columbus: Ohio State University Press, 1988), passim.

5. Fox, *Metropolitan America*, Ch. 2; Jackson, *Crabgrass Frontier*, Ch. 15; Arnold Hirsch, "With or Without Jim Crow: Black Residential Segregation in the United States," in Arnold R. Hirsch and Raymond Mohl, eds., *Urban Policy in Twentieth Century America* (New Brunswick: Rutgers University Press, 1993), 65–99; and Andrew Hacker, *Two Nations: Black and White, Separate, Hostile and Unequal* (New York: Charles Scribner's Sons, 1992), Ch. 1.

6. Gregory D. Squires, Larry Bennett, Kathleen McCourt, and Phillip Nyden, *Chicago: Class, Race and the Response to Urban Decline* (Philadelphia: Temple University Press, 1987), Chs. 2 and 4.

7. On race in the changing structure of North American metropolitan areas, see George C. Galster and Edward W. Hill, "Place, Power and Polarization: Introduction" in Galster and Hill, eds., *The Metropolis in Black and White*, 1–18; for the social meaning of "urban" in the latter twentieth century, see Michael B. Katz, "The Urban 'Underclass' as a Metaphor of Social Transformation," in Katz, ed., *The Underclass Debate: Views from History* (Princeton: Princeton University Press), 3–23.

8. For changes in the 1950s, and conflicts over changing housing patterns, see Arnold Hirsch, *Making the Second Ghetto: Race and Housing in Chicago, 1940–1960* (New York: Cambridge University Press, 1983), passim. On subsequent years, see Kleppner, *Chicago Divided*, Chs. 2, 3 & 4; William J. Grimshaw, *Bitter Fruit: Black Politics and the Chicago Machine, 1931–1991* (Chicago: University of Chicago Press, 1992), Chs. 5 and 6. Also see Gary Rivlin, *Fire on the Prairie: Chicago's Harold Washington and the Politics of Race* (New York: Henry Holt, 1992), Ch. 1.

9. Chicago *Tribune, The American Millstone: An Examination of the Nation's Permanent Underclass* (Chicago: Chicago Tribune Publishing, 1986), Ch. 5.

10. On this point see William Julius Wilson, *When Work Disappears: The World of the New Urban Poor* (New York: Alfred A. Knopf, 1996), Ch. 1; also see Wilson's earlier book, *The Truly Disadvantaged: The Inner City, the Underclass and Public Policy* (Chicago: University of Chicago Press, 1987), Chs. 2 and 4; and Douglas S. Massey and Nancy A. Denton, *American Apartheid: Segregation and the Making of the Underclass* (Cambridge: Harvard University Press, 1993), Ch. 4.

11. On the development of the Chicago Public Schools in the early twentieth century, see John David Hogan, *Class and Reform: School and Society in Chicago, 1880–1930* (Philadelphia: University of Pennsylvania Press, 1985), Chs. 1 and 2; and Julia Wrigley, *Class, Politics and Public Schools: Chicago, 1900–1950* (New Brunswick: Rutgers University Press, 1982), Chs. 1 and 2. Also see Mary Herrick, *The Chicago Schools: A Social and Political History* (Beverly Hills: Sage Publications, 1971), Ch. 4.

12. On dropouts, see Hogan, *Class and Reform*, Ch. 3; On corruption and its resolution, see Herrick, *The Chicago Schools*, Chs. 14 and 15.

13. For an overview of the system under Willis' leadership in the 1950s, see Herrick, *The Chicago Schools*, Ch. 16. On Willis' building campaign and growth in the system, see Cynthia Ann Wneck, "Big Ben the Builder: School Construction, 1953–66" (Ph.D. diss., Loyola University—Chicago, 1989), Chs. III, IV, and V.

14. On the passage of referenda and budget growth, see Herrick, *The Chicago Schools*, 309–310.

15. For a capsule portrait of Willis, his major accomplishments and personality, see Larry Cuban, *Urban School Chiefs Under Fire* (Chicago: University of Chicago Press, 1976), 1–8. For Willis' somewhat rocky relationship with the press, see Thomas Foster Koerner, "Benjamin C. Willis and the Chicago Press" (Ph.D. diss., Northwestern University, 1968), Introduction.

16. The quote can be found in Herrick, *The Chicago Schools*, p. 425. For Tyack's characterization of urban school leaders, see David Tyack and Elisabeth Hansot, *Managers of Virtue: Public School Leadership in America, 1820–1980* (New York: Basic Books, 1982), Part II.

17. The quotes are from remarks made to the press on September 6, 1961, in the Benjamin Willis Papers, Box 3, The Paul Hanna Collection, The Hoover Institution Archives, Stanford, CA (hereafter cited as "Willis Papers"). Willis was also quoted in 1961 as saying that "there is no question that an elementary school which serves pupils who live in the immediate area around the school is best able to involve community and parents in a quality program of education for their children." A little later he declared, "The life and comprehension of the child within its known and explorable neighborhood provides the emotional security required for his wholesome development." These quotes are provided in Cuban, *Urban School Chiefs Under Fire*, 11.

18. The quote is from "Statement on September 6, 1961 to Television Reporters and Press," Box 3, Willis Papers. On Willis' professed ignorance of racial composition of the Chicago Public Schools' students and staff, see Alan B. Anderson and George W. Pickering, *Confronting the Color Line: The Broken Promise of the Civil Rights Movement in Chicago* (Athens: University of Georgia Press, 1986), 77. On Willis' opposition to bussing and other alternatives to the neighborhood schools, see Wneck, "Big Ben the Builder," Ch. VII.

19. Robert J. Havighurst, *The Public Schools of Chicago: A Survey for the Board of Education of the City of Chicago* (Chicago: Chicago Board of Education, 1964), Ch. X. Havighurst reports the correlation between socio-economic status and achievement levels as .8. My own calculations show the relatiosnhip between race (percent black) and achievement to be slightly weaker and negative at −.72. Interestingly, socio-economic status was positively associated with college plans (−.71), and negatively associated with remedial reading enrollments (−.54). Black enrollment was positively correlated with remedial reading (.86) and negatively with socio-economic status (−.47). Clearly, race and socio-economic status worked together in Chicago's high schools to produce two quite different patterns of achievement. On current levels of achievement in Chicago schools, see The Chicago Assembly, *Educational Reform for the 21st Century* (Chicago: Harris Graduate School of Public Policy, 1998), 36, and the background report prepared for the Assembly by Melissa Roderick, "Educational Trends and Issues in the Region, the State and the Nation." The Chicago Assembly report indicates that only about 20 percent of Chicago eleventh grade students scored above national medians in reading and math during the early 1990s. Roderick documents the low achievement levels in contemporary Chicago Public High Schools: by 1990 only

about 10 percent of Chicago public high school students scored in the top quartile in mathematics and reading achievement on nationally normed tests (54).

20. "De Facto Segregation in Chicago Public Schools," *The Crisis* 65 (February 1958), 87–95, 126–127; Herrick, *The Chicago Public Schools*, pp. 310–312; Anderson and Pickering, *Confronting the Color Line*, Ch. 3. Chicago, of course had a long history of racial inequality in education, and this also may have contributed to heightened sensitivities on these questions. See Michael W. Homel, *Down From Equality: Black Chicagoans and the Public Schools, 1920–1941* (Urbana: University of Illinois Press, 1984), passim, and Judy Jolley Mohraz, *The Separate Problem: Case Studies of Black Education in the North, 1900–1930* (Westport: Greenwood Press, 1979), passim.

21. Havighurst, *The Public Schools of Chicago*, Ch. VII; Herrick, *The Chicago Public Schools*, 313. Herrick notes that these findings were upheld by the U.S. Commission on Civil Rights, which found that the Chicago Public Schools' policies created unfair disadvantages for Black students. For a detailed account of this case, see Anderson and Pickering, *Confronting the Color Line*, 85–90. Also see Cuban, *Urban School Chiefs Under Fire*, 10.

22. The best account of this is in Anderson and Pickering, *Confronting the Color Line*, Ch. 3. For an overview of issues of racial inequity in Chicago's schools in the latter 1950s and 1960s, see William A. Vrame, "A History of School Desegregation in Chicago since 1954" (Ph.D. diss., University of Wisconsin, 1971), passim.

23. Herrick, *The Chicago Schools*, 314–321; also see Wneck, "Big Ben the Builder," Chs. VI and VII.

24. Wneck, "Big Ben the Builder," Ch. VII. Havighurst noted that Black children in schools built since 1951 outnumbered White children in such schools by nearly a 4 to 1 ratio in 1963. See *The Public Schools of Chicago*, Ch. XI.

25. Ibid. Anderson and Pickering note that a construction bond referendum was defeated in April 1962, marking a historic turn in public support for the schools. See *Confronting Color Line*, 98. Also see Herrick, *The Chicago Schools*, Ch. 17.

26. These events are described in fulsome detail in Anderson and Pickering, *Confronting the Color Line*, Ch. 3. Also see Herrick, *The Chicago Schools*, Ch. 16; Cuban, *Urban School Chiefs Under Fire*, Ch. 1; and James R. Ralph, Jr., *Northern protest: Martin Luther King, Jr., Chicago and the Civil Rights Movement* (Cambridge: Harvard University Press, 1993), 14–25.

27. Anderson and Pickering, *Confronting the Color Line*, Ch. 3; Cuban, *Urban School Chiefs Under Fire*, 14–20.

28. Roger Biles, *Richard J. Daley: Race, Politics and Chicago* (DeKalb: Northern Illinois University Press, 1996), 100; Herrick, *The Chicago Schools*, Ch. 17; Cuban, *Urban School Chiefs Under Fire*, 21–29.

29. Thomas F. Koerner, "Benjamin C. Willis and the Chicago Press," 225–230. Hundreds of Bogan parents came to Board of Education meetings to protest voluntary transfer plans, including Willis', but cheered Willis loudly and carried signs saying "We Support Dr. Willis." Koerner suggests that Willis realized his support came from Whites, and that this made him responsive to their demands. Also see Cuban, *Urban School Chiefs Under Fire*, 17. For a somewhat abstract analysis of community mobilization around education issues in this period, see Joseph Weres, "School Politics in 33 Community Areas in Chicago" (Ph.D. diss., University of Chicago, 1971), 57, 149, and 173. Weres notes that opposition to school integration was already highly organized in the period immediately following Willis' departure.

30. The best account of mobilization in the Black community and among civil rights organizations is Anderson and Pickering, *Confronting the Color Line*, particularly Chs. 4, 5, and 6. Referring to the 1963 controversy over Willis, Anderson and Pickering note that "organized white neighborhood groups, such as the Bogan parents, became outspoken in his behalf," but they offer no details of how widespread such a movement was. See 117–118. On white community mobilization over housing issues, see Hirsch, *Making the Second Ghetto*, Ch. 4; and Eileen M. McMahon, *What Parish are You From? A Chicago Irish Community and Race Relations* (Lexington: University Press of Kentucky, 1995), passim.

31. The best general account of Daley's participation in the early 1960s Chicago school crisis can be found in Biles, *Richard J. Daley*, Ch. 4; on the question of Keppel and Daley's handling of the threatened withdrawal of federal funds, see 115–116. also see Cuban, *Urban School Chiefs Under Fire*, 16–17.

32. Anderson and Pickering, for instance, note that Alderman James Murray spoke out forcefully against voluntary transfers, helping to incite and agitate Bowen demonstrators. See *Confronting the Color Line*, 117. Even Black alderman, long loyal to the Mayor, spoke in favor of Willis. See for instance, Koerner, "Benjamin C. Willis and the Chicago Press," 126 and 257. For an especially adroit analysis of how the Daley Mayoral administration dealt with school politics in this period, see Paul E. Peterson, *School Politics Chicago Style* (Chicago: University of Chicago Press, 1976), Chs. 4 and 7.

33. On Daley's reliance on Black votes, see Kleppner, *Chicago Divided*, Ch. 4; also see Crimshaw, *Bitter Fruit*, Ch. 5. On Dawson, see Anderson and Pickering, *Confronting the Color Line*, 77.

34. Daley, of course, won the 1963 mayoral election because of support from the city's Black wards. The quote was originally found in Mike Royko's account of Daley, and is cited in Biles, *Richard J. Daley*, 99. Also see the discussion of Daley's response to the school crisis, 100–102.

35. There also can be little question that Willis' forceful personality and tempermental disposition also contributed to his dilemma. Perhaps the most detailed account of this can be found in Koerner, "Benjamin C. Willis and the Chicago Press," Ch. 1. It is also worth noting that even at the height of the schools controversy, in 1963 and 1964, most of the local press in Chicago supported neighborhood schools and Willis' positions, even if some of them called for his departure. This, along with the support of White communities and members of the local political machine, probably accounts for much of the superintendent's obstinance. On local press support, see Koerner, 158.

36. On the "Redmond Plan," see Peterson, *School Politics Chicago Style*, Ch. 7; and Christina Hawkins Stringfellow, "Desegregation Policies and Practices in Chicago During the Superintendencies of James Redmond and Joseph Hannon" (Ph.D. diss., Loyola University Chicago, 1991), Ch. II. Also see Kleppner, *Chicago Divided*, 53–54, and Anderson and Pickering, *Confronting the Color Line*, Ch. 12.

37. Kleppner, *Chicago Divided*, 55–60; Stringfellow, "Desegregation Policies and Practices in Chicago," Ch. 3.

38. These figures are taken from James H. Lewis, "Choice and Race: The Use of Private Schools for Public Purposes." Unpublished paper presented at School Choice Forum, Social Science Research Institute, Northern Illinois University, November 1997.

39. Ibid. Interestingly, some Catholic leaders suggested that parochial school enrollments would insure neighborhood stability, a way of avoiding White flight.

See John T. McGreevy, *Parish Boundaries: The Catholic Encounter with Race in the Twentieth-Century Urban North* (Chicago: University of Chicago Press, 1996), 240–241; Peterson, *School Politics Chicago Style*, 168; Kleppner, *Chicago Divided*, 55.

40. On collective bargaining see Peterson, *School Politics Chicago Style*, Ch. 8. On the labor difficulties and the schools' financial crisis, see Kleppner, *Chicago Divided*, 122–123.

41. Peterson, *School Politics Chicago Style*, 165–173; on Redmond's experiences in New Orleans, see Alan Wieder, *Race and Education: Narrative Essays, Oral Histories, and Documentary Photography* (New York: Peter Lang, 1997), Ch. 6. Of course, there had been considerable conflict over housing issues in the period immediately prior to the school crisis. See Hirsch, *Making the Second Ghetto*, Chs. 1, 2, 3, and 7. Hirsch makes no reference to school issues, but it is clear that in some areas of the city—such as the Southwest side—they were clearly connected. On this point see Kleppner, *Chicago Divided*, 55.

42. Jennifer Hochschild, *The New American Dilemma: Liberal Democracy and School Desegregation* (New Haven: Yale University Press, 1984), Ch. 5. On newspaper support for neighborhood schools, see Koerner, "Benjamin C. Willis and the Chicago Press," 98–99, 119, and 143. On support for Willis, see 151, 161, 236 and 278.

43. Stringfellow, "Desegregation Policies and Practices in Chicago," Ch. 4.

44. Stringfellow, "Desegregation Policies and Practices in Chicago," Ch. 4.

45. For an overview of change in the Chicago Public Schools during the latter 1970s and 1980s, see Jeffrey Mirel, "School Reform, Chicago Style: Educational Innovation in a Changing Urban Context, 1976–1991," *Urban Education* 28:1 (January 1993): 116–149. The Bennett quote is from the *Chicago Tribune*, November 7, 1987, p. 1.

46. Ibid.; also see G. A. Hess, Jr., *School Restructuring, Chicago Style* (Newberry Park: Corwin Press, 1990) passim; Maribeth Vander Weele, *Reclaiming Our Schools: The Struggle for Chicago School Reform* (Chicago: Loyola University Press, 1994), passim; and G. A. Hess, Jr., "Introduction: School Based Management as a Vehicle for School Reform," *Education and Urban Society* 26:3 (May 1994): 203–219.

47. See Kenneth Wong, Robert Dreeben, Laurence E. Lynn, Jr., and Gail L. Sunderman. *Integrated Governance as a Reform Strategy in the Chicago Public Schools: A Report on System-wide School Governance Reform* (Chicago: University of Chicago Department of Education, 1997), Passim.

48. Ibid. On patterns of inequality in the Chicago region, see The Chicago Assembly, *Education Reform for the 21st Century*, 37. As indicated in this report, Chicago schools enroll more than 70 percent of the low-income children in the region, and more than 60 percent of children from minority ethnic groups, even though they serve only about a third of the total metropolitan student population. For a national perspective on persistent educational inequities, see William L. Taylor, "The Continuing Struggle for Equal Educational Opportunity," in John Charles Boger and Judith Welch Wegner, eds., *Race, Poverty and American Cities* (Chapel Hill: University of North Carolina Press, 1996), 463–489.

12

Bureaucratic Order and Special Children: Urban Schools, 1950s–1960s

Joseph L. Tropea

The character of the urban school has been shaped by the processes of democracy, law, bureaucracy, professionalism, and the market. These identify important but very different rule regimes, each with its own "action logic."[1] The concurrent exercise of these diverse regimes—not moderated by a common culture—implies conflict in the urban school's organizational evolution. Other difficulties are implied by the heterogeneity of the common school and job market transformations as well as by political pluralism.

The common school suggested an ideal organizational form for a democratic society. Yet a disjuncture between its democratic beliefs and practical organization resulted from turn-of-the-century compulsory attendance laws, which effectively compelled pupils into its domain. This problem was mitigated by joining professional rhetoric with bureaucratic action to produce "special rooms" and "special curricula" for "special children."[2] These changes mark the beginning of an evolution in the segregation of pupils and in lowered performance and curriculum standards, which became increasingly important to the organization of the urban school.

The negative consequences of segregation and lowered standards were lessened by their moderate use and, especially, by the affected pupils' early exit, often from school to work, during this century's first few decades. These practices may have seemed innocuous, compared to the task of assimilating pluralist youth into industrial society. However, the school's increasing reliance on pupil segregation and lowered standards, coupled with the market's decreasing need for common labor and its need for more skilled and disciplined labor, produced a young population whose development and productive role were problematic. This problem was manifest during the depression, moderated by World War II, then evolved as a major American crisis during the decades following the war. Historical research can contribute to understanding the urban school's organizational evolution and such consequences; in particular, it can shed light on how bureaucracy, law, democracy, professionalism, and the market produced dilemmas for school actors and how the latter responded, especially to groups of difficult pupils.

Previous work argued and demonstrated the evolution of "backstage" understandings and actions that developed in the urban schools consequent to turn-of-the-century compulsory attendance laws.[3] This backstage organizational order evolved because school actors could not restructure dominant, legitimate, rule regimes, at the same time they needed practical rules and procedures for dealing with problems, particularly groups of difficult pupils. That work covered the period from the 1890s to the 1940s. It showed how special classes, special curricula, and lowered promotion standards buttressed informal strategies that evolved to maintain school order after the passage of the turn-of-the-century attendance laws. It illustrated how professional standards and rhetoric that supported the "interests of the child" legitimized and facilitated these backstage organizational developments. The article demonstrated that neither formal programs nor professional standards and rhetoric supplanted those backstage understandings and actions that continuously allowed administrators and teachers to adapt formal mandates, programs, and rationales into mechanisms for preserving school order.

The 1890s-to-1940s evolution of backstage rules for dealing with difficult pupils, from selective use of exclusion to increasingly indiscriminate segregation and lowering of performance expectations, helped shape urban school policy; for example, progressive pedagogy and professionalization of pupil diagnosis aided in removing children from the regular classroom; staff offices mitigated the enforcement of labor and attendance laws vis-à-vis older, more difficult students; debasement of promotion standards enhanced bureaucratic "efficiency" and moderated the costs of "laggards" in the schools.

The debilitating, long-term, social consequences of these organizational arrangements became evident during the Great Depression when growing numbers of older youths remained in the schools' increasingly custodial-like programs. World War II provided some respite to the schools through lowered enrollment rates and increased work for youth. However, the postwar period's demographic shifts and swelling enrollments refueled challenges to the school's organization. During this period the urban school's backstage rules and procedures became even more important and entrenched. This resulted in the amplification of exclusionary practices—whose consequences spilled out into the streets of the American cities. This article takes up the development and consequences of informal strategies for dealing with difficult pupils during the 1950s and 1960s.

DIAGNOSTIC EXCLUSION

Problems of urban school order in the United States were exacerbated after World War II by such factors as increasing enrollments, problems in family organization, racial integration, decreasing opportunities for urban youth to participate in the labor market, and decline in teaching authority.[4] These many factors made controlling difficult pupils and organizing effective classrooms very difficult in many school systems. At that time, in other societies, "where secondary school attendance was a privilege instead of compulsory, administrators and teachers did not worry about the constant trouble maker. They just expelled him."[5] This response to the difficult or "exceptional" pupil was reminiscent of nineteenth-century practices, described by a Philadelphia school administrator: "The pupil who . . . seriously interfered with the regular work of a class, tended to drop out, or to be forced out, of school and the problem of the exceptional child disappeared with him."[6] However, by the 1950s, expulsion of pupils from public school systems in the United States was largely precluded by law; American school authorities then had to resolve classroom problems within the organization of the school.

Notwithstanding the law, almost 50 percent of American teachers and principals polled in the mid-1950s supported the early expulsion of misbehaving children as a means to resolve problems of classroom order.[7] Indeed, there were indications that "school staff is inclined to relieve itself of the inadapted or delinquent pupil by early rejection or dismissal."[8] Yet "rejection" or "dismissal" does not denote the organizational and systemic character of informal rules and procedures that developed to deal with difficult children. Cultivated for over five decades amidst legal and cultural conditions that compelled attendance, these backstage rules, procedures, and understandings enabled school authorities to transform the use and meaning of formal programs and mandates, particularly in removing difficult pupils from the regular classroom. Exclusionary responses to difficult, "exceptional," or "special" children had become integral parts of urban school bureaucracies.

Exclusionary practices had become commonly exercised options, particularly by teachers who had pupils they were unable or unwilling to control in the regular classroom. The decades-long practice of segregating difficult pupils from the regular classroom through placement in special classes had become organizationally honed and exercised with great alacrity. This method for removing pupils from the regular classroom was legitimized by the use of a staff office, commonly entitled "Pupil Personnel Services"; its predecessor was the "Psycho-Educational" clinic of the 1920s and 1930s. This office usually included guidance and counseling, group measurement, and child and youth study divisions. Teachers were provided a standardized form to request from this office an evaluation of students they considered particularly troublesome in the classroom, behaviorally or academically. This evaluation of students, often conducted by a "Child and Youth Study Division" of pupil personnel services, was ostensibly for "the development and welfare of the pupil."[9]

Depending on the recommendation made by pupil personnel, a student could be placed in a special classroom. This request-diagnosis-prescription process illustrates a formal professional-administrative procedure that had been transformed by backstage understandings and rules: it could serve the order of the regular classroom by removing difficult pupils. Indeed, by the 1960s this process had become ensconced as a backstage procedure for preserving the order of the regular classroom in urban school systems where teachers experienced the greatest difficulties.[10]

Because selected populations were disproportionately removed from the regular classroom, many school systems were legally challenged in the 1960s. These challenges were often made on the basis of the disproportionate presence of lower-class and nonwhite pupils in special programs. Successful legal challenges often mandated organizational changes; fortuitously, these provide evidence illustrating how backstage rules had transformed the request-diagnosis-prescription process to serve school order. An example is provided by the case of *Hobson v. Hansen* which culminated in a successful challenge to the District of Columbia public school system's use of a special academic program, entitled "Basic Track." The court's decision in this case prohibited the continued use of that program.[11]

The "Basic Track" program was officially for students who had academic problems. It was also the main repository of students removed from the regular classroom. It is not surprising, then, that most District of Columbia teachers cited academic problems as the major reason for requesting evaluations of their pupils—prior to the judge's decision. Nor is it surprising, consequent to their evaluation, that staff recommended, in the main, that these pupils be placed outside of the regular classrooms—prior to the judge's decision. In sum, before the court's intervention, teachers' reasons for requesting evaluations ("academic") and staff's recommendations for placement outside of the regular classroom ("special") were consonant with an institutional willingness and ability to place students in "Basic Track."

The court's decision changed these relationships by eliminating "Basic Track." This decision, effective school year 1967–68, devastated the school system's formal capacity to satisfy teachers who, by citing academic reasons, sought the removal of difficult children from their regular classrooms. The court did not confront the understandings and backstage rules that supported exclusionary practices to preserve classroom order. In this sense, it eliminated a formal option, not an informal strategy. Consequently, removal of difficult pupils from the regular classroom did not stop with the court's stricture.

After the legal decision, in order to remove pupils from their classrooms, teachers had to relabel the pupils' behavior. For the years prior to the court's decision the majority of pupils had been cited as "academic" problems in justifying pupil evaluation requests. However, for 1967–68, the school year the court decision was binding, there was a stark transformation of this majority into "behavioral" problems.

This change in the reasons for requesting pupil evaluations was a consequence of the loss of the "Basic Track" program, officially for pupils with "academic" problems. It had served as a major vehicle for ridding the regular classroom of difficult pupils. After the court's elimination of this "academic" program, if teachers wanted difficult pupils removed from their classrooms, they could not accomplish this end by citing "academic" reasons for requesting evaluations. The court did not preclude placement outside of the regular classroom for "behavioral" reasons; it only eliminated a special academic program that had a disproportionate share of lower-class, nonwhite students. After the court's decision, teachers continued to want difficult pupils removed from their classrooms and continued to share backstage understandings and informal rules that supported exclusionary practices for classroom order. So, they simply relabeled the pupil's "problem" to get relief after the court's decision; they changed the difficult pupil from an "academic" to a "behavioral" problem in 1967–68.

This change in the labeling of pupils illustrates how informal understandings and rules worked to preserve school order. The "condition of the child" was interpreted within a backstage framework that allowed exclusionary practices after the court's stricture. The scale and abruptness in redefining pupils' behavior affirm how deeply entwined the request-diagnosis-prescription process was with backstage understandings and rules for preserving school order. In corroborating this interpretation, a District of Columbia teacher characterized the "Request for Personality Investigation" form as the "get-rid-of-the-kid form."[12]

Professional staff as well as teachers were ensconced in the informal order of the schools. Ostensibly, diagnosticians exercised their professional skills and judgment in evaluating pupils and making recommendations. Yet the recommendations of the diagnostic staff, like teachers' reasons for requesting pupil evaluations, abruptly changed. Prior to the court's elimination of "Basic Track," the diagnostic staff had recommended many more "special" placements, compared to "regular" placements; that is, their prescriptions placed pupils outside of the regular classroom. Officially, these recommendations were predicated on professional training and the interests of the child. This view belied staff's accommodations to problems of classroom order, specifically to teachers' interests in removing difficult children from the regular classroom. When the court eliminated "Basic Track," it reduced the diagnostic staff's ability to accommodate teachers' interests by recommending "special" placements.

Administrators as well as staff and teachers knew the importance of backstage rules for preserving school order. Consequently, with the loss of "Basic Track," administrators accommodated to exclusionary practices by developing a new program into which pupils could be placed from the regular classroom— a program implemented in the school year the court's decision was effective. This program was entitled MIND, an acronym for Meeting Individual Needs Daily. This title provided a benevolent rhetoric for outside consumption, which served the order of the schools. This program, for students who had behavioral or emotional problems, accommodated to teachers who had, by and large, changed their reasons for requesting pupil evaluations from "academic" to "behavioral" or "emotional." MIND was not only implemented the first school year the school system lost "Basic Track" but within one year reached a capacity more than equal to the number of pupils referred for evaluation prior to the court's intervention.

These events illustrate how interrelated exclusionary practices were, how integral they had become to urban school order, and how elusive they were vis-à-vis outside control. Because of this, they appear more insidious. Yet teachers and staff were not entirely treacherous or arbitrary in describing their pupils as behavioral or academic problems. Obstreperous behavior and poor performance are often consequences of a common condition: teaching authority's inability or unwillingness to control pupils and organize the classroom effectively. Thus, teachers under duress in organizing their classrooms were not entirely dishonest in relabeling the "condition of the child." Yet reliance on these particular exclusionary practices for maintaining the order of the regular classroom, with the consequent large proportion of minority and lower-class pupils in special programs, made them more visible and questionable to the outside world and resulted in closer scrutiny and monitoring by the courts. However, there were other backstage exclusionary practices that compensated for those lost or lessened through legal and political decisions. Suspending students was one such practice.

Suspensions: Policy, Law, and Subterfuge

There were three basic ways to suspend students. One way was approved by a central office, usually the same "Pupil Personnel" office that tested, diagnosed, and placed pupils. During the 1960s the use of this centrally approved, formal suspension increased dramatically, more than doubling in Detroit and Baltimore. However, the reported number of these suspensions gave only a conservative indication of actions taken, as demonstrated in the following Washington, D.C., school report:

> Suspensions and emergency exclusions from school of pupils of compulsory school age for disciplinary reasons are still a problem. Attendance officers' reports show that they worked on 152 suspension cases. However, the number of suspensions reported to this department as authorized by the Superintendent's Office or staff or on which authorizations were requested total 46. The suspensions which are without authorization are a serious matter in that established procedures approved by the Superintendent to protect the pupils' welfare have been ignored.[13]

Three years later this same office discovered 752 unreported suspension cases.[14] Also, the number of formal suspensions does not indicate their duration. For example, in one system in which it was stated that, "a one, two or three month delay is a normal period for this kind of individual case assessment," there were cases reported of up to twenty-seven months duration on suspension.[15] This lengthy period of time for processing suspension cases suggests administrative collusion in the extended exclusion of difficult pupils. A former teacher corroborated this by pointing out that bizarre and threatening depictions of students' behavior were most effective in securing central approval.[16]

The magnitude of the schools' reliance on suspension as an exclusionary method was evidenced in the District of Columbia schools, when efforts were made to clarify or limit its use. When, in May 1969, the Washington, D.C., school board ordered that suspensions cease until policy was clarified, the teachers staged a walkout. The teachers did not walk out because of the limitation on formal suspension; only eighty-seven had been reported for the school system the previous year. These centrally approved suspensions were relatively insignificant, compared to those exercised and approved at the local school level. Teaching authority was much more reliant on the school-level suspension. Teachers walked out because school-level suspensions were threatened.[17]

Principals had authority, statutory and administrative, to approve school-level suspensions. Law typically circumscribed these by specifying a maximum number of days a pupil could be suspended. The school-level suspension was usually exercised by the principal or assistant principal in cooperation with the classroom teacher. Data on this type of suspension normally were not provided by school systems in the 1960s. However, an internal survey was conducted by the Baltimore school system on the use of these suspensions for school year 1968–69. As a result, figures for school-level suspensions for part of that school year in Baltimore were produced. This allowed a comparison of those suspensions centrally reported with those exercised at the school level. Baltimore's annual report listed 841 formal suspensions for school year 1967–68, while the number of school-level suspensions reported for the following eight-month school period was over 11,000.[18] This survey reported the number of suspensions principals were able or willing to acknowledge. There were, of course, other suspensions that were not sanctioned by law or formal policy.

These latter suspensions were mainly exercised at the teacher level and were not recorded. Good data on these have not been found. However, an administrator in the Detroit system, which reported in one year 1,827 formal suspensions, estimated, based on his experience, that all kinds of suspensions for that same year totaled around 100,000.[19]

The extent of the use of these different suspensions in the 1960s generated a number of problems for the schools. Suspensions had become as much a source of instability as stability. Suspended pupils were increasingly coming into contact with the police, and the latter were exerting public pressure on the schools to do something about this situation. Further, suspension was not much of a punishment for young people who were unwilling students; indeed, it was more of a reward. One school report recognized that suspension "seems to place a premium on objectionable behavior in the classroom." Junior high school principals stated that, "It's a vacation for them" and "Suspension is like throwing B'rer Rabbit in the briar patch."[20]

The increasingly public and problematic nature of suspensions generated political and legal problems for the schools, which culminated in highly publicized studies on the excessive use of suspensions and a Supreme Court decision.[21] The use of suspension had become visible, controversial, and ineffective. Yet other backstage exclusionary practices compensated for the constraints imposed on the schools and the notoriety they received for suspensions. Toleration, even acceptance, of nonattendance moderated some of the organizational problems created by restrictions on the use of suspensions.

Uncompelling Compulsory Attendance

A school system's responsibility for investigating nonattendance is spelled out in statute; for example, in the District of Columbia, in the 1960s, two full days or four half days of unexcused absences occurring within a school month had to be reported.[22] Such reports were made through a request-for-investigation-of-absence form. Consequently, the number of requests for investigation relative to absences in the schools provides an indication of efforts to control nonattendance. This measure suggests how rigorously schools complied with compulsory attendance laws or, conversely, how the backstage order mitigated enforcement. School systems that complied with the law should show a constant number of requests for investigation relative to absence. On the other hand, school systems that relied on nonattendance as a means of exclusion would reflect a decreasing number of investigations relative to absences. Data, from Washington, D.C. and Detroit illustrate the decrease in investigations relative to absence during the 1960s, and Philadelphia exhibited a similar pattern for the 1950s and 1960s. These data suggest how toleration of nonattendance steadily increased during the 1950s and 1960s.

Such system-wide trends are conservative indicators of the reliance on the toleration of nonattendance as an informal means of exclusion. These patterns indicate attendance in "homeroom" and do not reflect nonattendance subsequent to that period. For example, during a two-week period in school year 1968–69, when one District of Columbia junior high showed a homeroom attendance rate of 76 percent, the principal reported that "easily 50 percent" of these students left the school sometime after the homeroom period; if the principal was accurate, a full-time attendance rate of less than 40 percent was indicated.[23]

There is another reason why such "official" data are unreliable: teachers may not have reported the absences of particularly troublesome students. Because such absences were not reported to the principal's office, they were not recorded on the general absence sheet which was forwarded to central administration and, consequently, would not appear as absences in system-wide data. One junior high school teacher stated that failure to report students whose presence was undesirable was accepted procedure; "everybody does it," she said.[24] This teacher provided absence sheets from her school for twenty-five consecutive days in the fall of 1969. One indication of the extent of non-attendance is suggested by students from this junior high who were absent five days (20 percent) or more during that twenty-five-day period. One study lists such pupils from a random selection of seventh, eight, and ninth grade homerooms. Some of these students may have been ill, may have been enrolled in another school, or, particularly for the ninth graders, may have been over age sixteen and, thereby, not compelled by law to be in school. However, in the ninth grade homeroom of the teacher who provided the absence sheets there was one pupil who had missed twenty-two out of twenty-five days. Yet this boy was under sixteen, properly enrolled, not incarcerated, and in good health. The teacher had not reported his absence to the attendance office because he was particularly difficult to control.

Still, official reports can be used to illustrate the relationship between difficult pupils and the toleration of their nonattendance. This is suggested by the officially reported attendance rates of Detroit's schools for behavioral problems in the late 1960s, ranging from 57 percent to 84 percent. These data are particularly striking when it is understood that many, if not most, of the students who were enrolled in those special schools would have been on probation from the juvenile court; one condition of probation is invariably regular attendance at school.

There are other dimensions of exclusion through the toleration of non-attendance that suggest how ingrained a part of the school's organization it had become. In Detroit there was a sharp decrease in the number of attendance officers and a decrease in their daily efforts, comparing the late 1920s with the late 1950s. Further, investigating truancy had changed from visits to the family and community to the use of the mail service and the telephone. This is illustrated by the Baltimore system whose "Home Visits" decreased from 83,730 in 1952–53 to 46,332 in 1968–69, while the use of the mail and telephone more than doubled in a comparable period of time.

The professionalization of attendance officers provided ideological support for enforcement inactivity by articulating a less compulsive, more clinical, posture:

> Traditionally, the function of the attendance service was conceived as solely compulsory in character. The duty of an attendance officer was considered to be that of receiving from principals lists of the children who failed to appear at school from day to day and making sure that such children did appear. Another duty was to seek out truants upon the streets or in loitering places and to take them directly to school. Modern attendance operates on a higher professional plane.[25]

This professional "plane" is suspect in the context of attendance officers' actions or inaction. For example, in the District of Columbia public school system during the 1960s there were efforts made to change job titles, reduce hours in the workday, and increase salary but not to "seek out" truants. Indeed, memoranda were forwarded that instructed attendance officers not to transport truants in their cars or even to approach groups of known truants in the streets. Also, there were major sex differences, comparing the students referred to pupil personnel with the attendance officers; there were well over two males for every one female in the student population referred to pupil personnel, recommended for placement in behavioral classes, and requested to be suspended, while there was less than one male for every four females among the attendance officers.[26] These officers' timidity vis-à-vis truants may be explained, in part, by these sexual differences, in part, by costs in liability insurance, but also, by their consonance with backstage rules and procedures for exclusion.

The lack of enforcement rigor in the attendance office does not suggest independent organizational malfeasance. Rather, it was a part of backstage interrelationships that were organizationally functional. The schools' lack of rigor in reporting absences and the attendance office's ineffectiveness in investigating them were reciprocal consequences of an informal organizational development. Indeed, this reciprocal ineffectiveness indicates that backstage exclusionary rules were effective. Rhetoric, relationships, and actions—or inaction—associated with the attendance office are consonant with the evolution of informal practices for dealing with difficult pupils. However, the backstage strategy of exclusion that served school authority for much of the century came back to haunt urban schools in the 1960s.

Coming Home to Roost

As the depression made exclusionary practices less effective organizationally, so too, suspensions and the toleration of nonattendance in the 1960s did not always rid the schools of difficult pupils. Because students did not attend classes, this did not mean that they were absent from the schools. They were in and around schools in large numbers. The population of nonattending youth who frequented the schools had become so common that a generic term "outsider" was applied to them. However, these so-called outsiders were, in large part, pupils who were officially enrolled in the schools but not attending the classrooms. This was confirmed in testimony before U.S. Senate hearings in 1969: "On this particular day I had five youths from another school, (by) which I do not necessarily mean to say they are outsiders, because they are insiders from another school, they are just in the wrong school."[27]

Outsiders were truants. They were suspended students. They were students "put out" in the halls for disrupting class. They were students who were cutting classes. In brief, they were pupils school authorities had excluded from the classroom because of the difficulties they posed. The institution that had been unable to control these pupils' classroom behavior had to face their more blatantly deviant, or delinquent, behavior. These students were joined by the true "outsider," the person not enrolled in the school system. Together these groups of young people amplified problems for urban schools in the 1960s.

The problems outsiders posed ranged from frightening students during playground activities to the more serious activities of stealing, extortion, fighting, carrying weapons, and selling drugs. Outsiders entered the schools, used school bathrooms, roamed the halls, disrupted classes, and attacked teachers. Schools attempted to deal with these problems in different ways; for example, in some schools teachers appeared in the hallways at a signal; in others, students were stationed by classroom windows to give warnings of activities in the halls; in one junior high, a vocational teacher and his male students ran into the hall at a signal and chased persons discovered in the halls; many teachers simply covered their classroom windows to keep persons in the hall from disrupting their classes; in many schools, doors, auditoriums, and bathrooms were locked to keep out the intruders. The phenomenon of the outsider became a formidable problem for school authorities; one principal stated it simply: "I cannot handle an outsider."[28]

Implicit in the analysis of the backstage rules of the urban school is the process of amplifying deviant behavior. Exclusion and lowering performance expectations served immediate interests in classroom order. These practices, in turn, encouraged school reliance on backstage procedures, particularly where and when classroom authority was most problematic. Then, the depression made apparent the deviation-amplifying consequences of this evolving institutional order with its custodial approach to controlling older pupils, which poorly prepared them for industrial society. Yet World War II, by productively engaging many youths, offered the schools some respite and moderated the ill consequences of their organization. However, by the 1960s the organization of urban schools not only effected poor performance and discipline problems but delinquency as well.

During the 1960s the adverse consequences of school organization became most apparent to the police. Truants tended to spend time where stores were located; for example, 76 percent of truants reported by the District of Columbia police in 1968–69 were from the downtown shopping area. Because of shoplifting, the police had to take action. For example, in 1969 in Baltimore, because of similar problems in their downtown commercial area, school administrators released memoranda informing principals that "any child of obvious school age found during school hours in the area of the Central Police District is subject to questioning by a police officer." In Los Angeles, when the police launched an experimental crackdown on truancy, they reduced daytime burglaries and auto thefts by 30 percent and daytime thefts from autos by 75 percent. Suspension exacerbated these problems. For example, the school board in the District of Columbia recognized that the use of suspension in their system contributed to delinquency; in Baltimore in school year 1968–69, the police began to hold suspended students in their detention center until a parent or guardian came to pick them up while the school system developed a special facility to hold suspended students.[29]

During the 1960s the schools increasingly turned to the police to resolve their problems. Yet, when the schools called the police, they could take little action in many instances because of the delay in the time of their arrival or the lack of educators' will to prosecute. Under these conditions the police could not justify continuing to respond to the schools' calls. Consequently, measures were taken to rationalize police intervention. For example, Washington, D.C., installed special telephones that provided the schools a direct line to the police, the so-called "hot line," that enabled a more rapid response. The Washington, D.C., schools, however, had to be willing to pursue a formal complaint in cases when they called the police; this was guaranteed by obligating school authorities, effective school year 1968–69, to sign an "unlawful entry" complaint. More than 800 complaints were issued in the first year of implementing this approach; also, the very high frequency of complaints at the middle school levels indicates another consequence of backstage practices: difficult pupils did not achieve senior high status.

Similar measures were taken in other jurisdictions. For example, in Oakland, California, the police enforced a law prohibiting students or outsiders from loitering in the vicinity of a school during school hours, expedited school-police communications, established prosecuting procedures, and exercised surveillance through selective patrolling of school areas.[30] Many cities also introduced police personnel directly into the schools; for example, in the late 1960s Chicago had a paid force of 420 off-duty policemen patrolling 200 of its 500 schools; Los Angeles had 102 "security agents" armed with revolvers and the power to arrest; Baltimore had a "security division" with a force of 33, mostly former policemen in the junior high schools; New York had uniformed police in 40 of its secondary schools and 170 unarmed "security guards" in particularly troubled schools; Philadelphia had a force of 500 "non-teaching assistants" whose original purpose was to relieve teachers of non-teaching tasks but whose main function became keeping order.[31]

The U.S. Senate conducted a study, held hearings, and produced a report in which trends were cited; it was reported, comparing 1964 to 1968, that assaults on teachers increased from 25 to 1,801, assaults by students on students from 1,601 to 4,267, crimes by non-students from 142 to 3,894, and students expelled for incorrigibility from 4,884 to 8,190. Significantly, the report said, "The chief troublemaker in many schools is the drop-out who returns to his old school to destroy it because he harbors a deep fury against the school which, through lack of discipline or lack of interest, has rejected him."[32]

CONCLUSION

This article and its predecessor showed that law, bureaucracy, and professionalism, as well as their rhetorics, did not identify urban school authorities' guides for action in dealing with difficult pupils. These articles argued and documented the evolution of backstage organizational rules, procedures, and understandings that commenced around the turn of the century and continued through the 1960s. This backstage order constituted an integral part of urban schools' organization. It enabled teaching authority, which lacked sufficient power, organization, resources, or will, to deal with difficult children. However, this backstage order created, perpetuated, and amplified a class of "special" children. It lowered expectations vis-à-vis difficult pupils and then allowed their exclusion in the 1950s and 1960s when segregation within the school itself became problematic. This backstage organizational order provided school actors with guides to action amidst the public rules and rhetorics of bureaucracy, law, professionalism, democracy, the market, and the common school. In relation to these legitimate rule regimes the school's backstage order was more dialectical than diabolical.

In retrospect, order within the urban schools was secured at the cost of future deviance and conflict. Lowered performance expectations, segregation in special classes, and exclusion generated poor performance, negative school experiences, and limited future possibilities. Processes such as these, as is often noted, served to reproduce stratified society by marginalizing many youths. In this sense, the "sorting machine" may be an appropriate metaphor for the school for the first half of the century. However, the postwar elaboration of these school practices and the flight of capital from urban areas served not only to marginalize the economic future of many youths but to contribute to their criminalization as well.

Social conflicts involving the courts and schools, race and pupil performance, and school disturbances and the police were not unrelated to some of the negative consequences of the backstage order. In the 1960s social reformers used law, curricular reform, federal monies, and technology to limit some of the exclusionary consequences of the schools' backstage order but did not confront the actual rules and rationales that produced them. As a result, social reform produced some unanticipated and unwanted consequences. For example, reform effectively affirmed equal treatment through heterogeneous classes and elimination of segregation and exclusion from the regular classroom. This had the effect of increasing the importance of lowering performance standards as a backstage strategy for classroom order.

This research, by documenting the decades-long evolution of interrelationships among policy, legal change, and backstage rules and procedures, should increase our understanding of the organizational bases of poor performance. It should also enable us to anticipate likely consequences of reform efforts. For example, the impact of "back to basics" efforts, as with reforms commencing with the turn-of-the-century attendance laws, will be transformed by the actual rules guiding school actors. If the history of urban schools' backstage order documented in this research is accurate, then new or old forms of segregation and exclusion would accompany efforts to raise performance norms—if the common school, its teaching authority and bureaucracy are not restructured.

NOTES

1. Tom R. Burns and Helena Flam, *The Shaping of Social Organization: Social Rule System Theory with Applications* (London, 1987).
2. Joseph L. Tropea, "Bureaucratic Order and Special Children: Urban Schools, 1890s–1940s," *History of Education Quarterly* (Spring 1987): 29–53.
3. Ibid.
4. Gerald R. Leslie, *The Family in Social Context* (New York, 1967), 586, 602; Paul H. and Lois N. Glasser, eds., *Families in Crisis* (New York, 1970), 35; "Teacher-Opinion Poll," *National Education Association Journal* 53 (Sept. 1964): 25; "Major Problems of Teachers," *National Education Association Research Bulletin* 49 (Dec. 1971): 105; Bennet Harrison, "Education and Underemployment in the Urban Ghetto," in *Problems in Political Economy: An Urban Perspective*, ed. David M. Gordon (Lexington, Mass., 1971), 185; United States Department of Labor, Bureau of Labor Statistics, Middle Atlantic Regional Office, *The Working Age Population: Initial Findings* (New York, 1969), 2.
5. Lawrence E. Vredevoe, "School Discipline, Third Report on a Study of Students and School Discipline in the United States and Other Countries," *National Association of Secondary-School Principals Bulletin* 49 (Mar. 1965): 215–26, 218.
6. *Philadelphia School Report* (Philadelphia, 1909), 58.
7. "Teacher Opinion on Pupil Behavior, 1955–56," *National Education Association Research Bulletin* 34 (Apr. 1956).
8. William C. Kvaraceus, "The Urban Schools and Juvenile Delinquency," in *Social Maladjustment: Behavior Change and Education*, Proceedings of the Fifth Annual Invitational Conference on Urban Education (New York, 1966), 60.

9. *Baltimore Board of School Commissioners Annual Report* (Baltimore, 1934); Public Schools of the District of Columbia, *Pupil Personnel Services Annual Report, 1967–68,* foreword.

10. In many school systems the use of these procedures was consonant with professional and administrative goals; for example, see data reported in Mary Alice White and June Charry, eds., *School Disorder, Intelligence, and Social Class* (New York, 1966).

11. *Hobson v. Hansen,* 269 F. Supp. 401 D.C.D.C. (1967).

12. Behavioral Systems Research Group, Program in Policy Studies in Science and Technology, George Washington University, "The Development and Implementation of a Behavioral/Systems Approach for the Prevention and Control of Delinquency and Crime," Third Report (submitted to National Institute of Law Enforcement and Criminal Justice [Grant No. NI-023], Nov. 1970), 25.

13. *Pupil Personnel Services, 1962–63,* 8.

14. Ibid., 1965–66.

15. Memorandum, "Factors That Influence the Length of Time a Pupil Remains on Suspension," Division of Special Services, Baltimore City Public Schools, 1968.

16. Interview with author. This teacher had been assigned to a social adjustment class, a class of behavioral problems. She had requested an evaluation of a thirteen-year-old girl, innocently seeking professional help because she had heard this girl was involved with a group of shoplifters. The immediate and unintended consequence of this request was an administrative suspension.

17. Herbert H. Denton, "Forty Eliot Teachers Walk Out," *Washington Post,* 9 May 1969; and "Teacher Walkout Grows," ibid., 10 May 1969; *Pupil Personnel Services, 1967–68,* 24; "The Development and Implementation of a Behavioral/Systems Approach for the Prevention and Control of Delinquency and Crime," Second Report, Dec. 1969, 20.

18. "Informally Suspended Students," Baltimore City Public Schools Circular No. 244, Series 1968–69 (27 Mar. 1969).

19. Joseph L. Tropea, "Family, Productive Organization, Formal Authority, and the Generation of Deviant Youth: Toward a Social Structural Theory of Social Control and Socialization" (Ph.D. diss., George Washington University, 1973), 235.

20. Baltimore Schools Circular, No. 245, Series 1968–69 (1 Apr. 1969) and No. 89, Series 1969–70 (15 Oct. 1969); *Pupil Personnel Services, 1963,* "The Development and Implementation of a Behavioral/Systems Approach for the Prevention and Control of Delinquency and Crime," Second Report, Dec. 1969, 12.

21. Children's Defense Fund, *School Suspensions: Are They Helping Children?* (Washington, D.C., 1975); *Goss v. Lopez,* 419 U.S. 565, 95 D. Ct. 729 (1975). *Goss v. Lopez* established hearing procedures for public school discipline cases.

22. *D.C. Code Ann.,* paragraphs 31–37 (1967).

23. Tropea, "Family, Productive Organization, Formal Authority, and the Generation of Deviant Youth," 243.

24. Ibid., 244.

25. Ibid., 249.

26. *Pupil Personnel Services, 1965–66, 1967–68.*

27. U.S. Congress, Senate, Hearings before the Public Health and Education, Welfare, and Safety Subcommittee of the Committee on the District of Columbia, Crime in the National Capital, Part 5 (Washington, D.C., 1969), 1645.

28. Ibid., 1573–81; "The Development and Implementation of a Behavioral/Systems Approach for the Prevention and Control of Delinquency and Crime," Second Report, Dec. 1969, 32–34.

29. "The Development and Implementation of a Behavioral/Systems Approach for the Prevention and Control of Delinquency and Crime," Second Report, Dec. 1969, 43; Baltimore Schools Circulars No. 245, Series 1969–70 and No. 89, Series 1969–70; Robert Kistler, "Campaign on Truancy Cuts Crime," *Washington Post*, 13 Feb. 1971.

30. Kistler, "Campaign on Truancy Cuts Crime."

31. Peter Milius, "Police, Security Aides Patrol Many U.S. City Schools," *Washington Post*, 10 Jan. 1970.

32. "Study Cites Surge in School Violence," *Washington Post*, 13 Jan. 1970.

13

"The Community is Beginning to Rumble": The Origins of Chicano Educational Protest in Houston, 1965–1970

Guadalupe San Miguel, Jr.

"The Mexican American community is beginning to rumble," noted Ben Canales, an official with a Mexican American community group by the name of United Organizations Information Center.[1] This comment was made at a committee meeting before the Houston board of education in October 1969 and aptly reflected the Chicano community's growing dissatisfaction with the local school district's unwillingness to improve the conditions under which Mexican American children were educated.

The rumbling in the community noted by Canales referred to the growing restlessness among middle and working-class Chicanos over the neglect by government institutions of their political interests and special needs. Since 1960, Mexican Americans in Texas, especially middle-class individuals who were members of existing organizations such as the League of United Latin American Citizens (LULAC), the American G.I. Forum, and the Political Association of Spanish-speaking Organizations (PASO), had worked hard to elect liberal politicians, to enact federal legislation aimed at meeting the educational and vocational needs of Mexican American children, and to ensure the passage of important civil rights measures. Despite their involvement in the political process, Mexican Americans continued to be neglected by authorities and agencies at all levels of government.[2]

Failure to bring about any significant changes in the treatment of Mexican Americans laid the groundwork for further radicalization and political mobilization. The Farmworkers' strike and its brutal suppression by the Texas Rangers and state police as well as the Minimum Wage March of the summer of 1966 unleashed a series of new organizations with different ideological notions of ethnic identity, political culture, and social change. These organizations began to mount a vigorous campaign against all forms of inequalities in American institutional life. Public education was one of those institutions that increasingly came under attack.[3] Canales's statement was in reference to this complex process of ideological fermentation, organizational development, and political mobilization that was occurring in the Chicano community in Houston and throughout the state. The shift in emphasis and tactics in the struggle for adequate education reflected a pivotal change of focus in community activism—from negotiating limited political and cultural change to demanding a broad restructuring of the larger society.

EARLY EFFORTS AT EDUCATIONAL REFORM

Chicano efforts to promote school reform which aimed at eliminating discrimination and at improving school performance emerged gradually during the 1960s. Several forces fueled the broader movement by Mexican Americans for equality and justice in the United States during this period—the material conditions of the 1960s, the national and international political climate, and the continued efforts by African Americans to eliminate racial discrimination.[4] These same forces inspired an increased involvement in education, as men and women of different ages and social classes and with multiple ideologies and perspectives worked together or in tandem to change the schools so that they could better serve the Mexican American population.

Although Mexican Americans had a rich legacy of activism in the schools by the early 1960s, it was subdued and narrowly focused. Activism in the schools focused on three areas of activity. First, sporadic efforts were made to improve the treatment of Mexican American children in the schools and the quality of their education. For instance, in the summer of 1961, parents from the Clayton Homes area met to discuss conditions in their local schools. They set up committees to find ways of improving the quality of the school facilities provided for their children. Although it is unclear what happened to these recommendations or what further actions the Clayton Homes tenants took, the establishment of these committees indicated a deep concern for quality education for their children.[5] At times, specific incidents of discrimination were challenged. One such incident occurred in early 1960 when the school board was engaged in a debate over the need for free lunches in the schools. One school board member remarked that "Mexican American children did not need free lunches because they would rather eat 'pinto beans.' "[6] This remark incensed the community and led to the study of and support for a free lunch program in the Houston Independent School District (HISD). This study was sponsored by three Mexican American organizations: LULAC, the American G.I. Forum, and the Civic Action Committee.[7]

The second major focus of Mexican American activism during this early period occurred at the University of Houston. In 1963, Mexican American students at the University of Houston founded a branch of the PASO on campus to promote awareness of their community's needs and to endorse candidates who the group felt best represented the community's interests.

Under the leadership of Samuel S. Calderon and Manuel Crespo, the UH-PASO conducted voter registration drives, awareness of the community's needs, get-the-vote-out campaigns, and analysis of political campaigns. For several years, this organization was an important instrument of political change on campus.[8]

Third, and probably most important, was the promotion by LULAC of the Little Schools of the 400 concept, a specific educational innovation aimed at improving the scholastic achievement of Mexican Americans. This concept was the brainchild of Felix Tijerina, a Houstonian and national president of LULAC for four consecutive terms from 1956 to 1959. During the Texas legislative session in 1959, he and LULAC had lobbied on behalf of state support for the Little Schools of the 400 concept. Throughout the following year, Tijerina was feverishly promoting the Little Schools of the 400 program throughout the state. This project was Tijerina's approach to improving the education of Mexican American school-age children and reflected his personal philosophy toward underachievement. Felix Tijerina believed that the lack of facility with English in the early years of child development was at the heart of the high failure rates of Mexican Americans in the schools. The solution to this problem of underachievement was English-language instruction at the preschool level. His strategy for improving academic achievement thus was to change the child, not the school. In 1957, he established the Little Schools of the 400 with this objective in mind. The primary objective of this educational project was to teach Mexican American preschool children 400 essential English words that would assist them in completing the first grade of school and thus in advancing throughout the grades.[9]

The state legislature agreed to fund this project in 1959 and to implement it during the summer of 1960. Tijerina and LULAC promoted, publicized, and helped implement this educational innovation. The success of this promotional campaign was apparent when, on June 1, 1960, the first 614 schools opened their doors to 15,805 Spanish-speaking children. For the next several summers, the number of children and school districts participating in the preschool instructional program increased significantly so that by 1967, when it expired, over 150,000 Spanish-speaking children had gone through the program.[10]

The program was relatively successful in increasing school achievement among Mexican American school-age children entering the first grades.[11] Despite its apparent success it was heavily criticized by prominent scholars such as George I. Sanchez, Herschel T. Manuel, and others. This program, noted the critics, ignored the positive role that the children's native language played in their intellectual and psychological development. It also was based on unsound educational assumptions about language teaching and learning.[12] This criticism, coupled with the development of similar and new federal programs such as Title I and Project Head Start in the mid-1960s, contributed to its diminished importance in the community and to its expiration by 1967.

In addition to his support of the Little Schools of the 400, Tijerina also ran unsuccessfully for the school board in 1960. He ran on an independent platform and promised to represent all his constituents "fairly and honestly." He said nothing about his ethnicity and, despite his promotion of the preschool English program for Mexican Americans, promised no significant changes in education if elected to the school board.[13]

During the first part of the 1960s, then, Mexican American activism in education was subdued and narrowly focused. By the mid-1960s, however, Mexican American activism in education began to increase and assume different forms. Educational activism increased due in part to the tremendous historic changes taking place in the nation. The passage of important domestic legislation at the federal level and the Black civil rights movement were especially significant. Antipoverty legislation and federal aid to education brought to the forefront issues of poverty, employment, education, housing, and local community organization. The Black civil rights movement, among other things, raised the issues of racial discrimination in American life and introduced a variety of unorthodox methods for attacking inequality such as sit-ins, protest marches, and confrontation tactics. The continuing neglect of the linguistic, cultural, and academic needs of Mexican American children by local officials also encouraged activists to seek school changes.[14]

THE RISE OF THE CHICANO MOVEMENT

In the years from 1965 to 1968, most of the increased activism was by existing organizations in the community such as LULAC and the American G.I. Forum. These organizations took advantage of the new federal legislation and developed innovative educational and work training programs for the community's benefit. One such program was the Jobs for Progress sponsored jointly by LULAC and the G.I. Forum. The idea of a job placement referral service originated in Houston's LULAC group during the spring of 1964, in the context of a national war-on-poverty program. The national LULAC office endorsed this idea in February 1965. Two months later, in April, LULAC Council #60, one of Houston's most active chapters, opened the first Jobs for Progress placement office. In June of the following year, the concept of Jobs for Progress received federal funding.[15] It provided education to adults and helped place them in meaningful jobs.[16]

These educational efforts by LULAC and the American G.I. Forum did not go far enough, however, in bringing about change in the schools or in the society. They were based on changing the individual rather than changing the society and its discriminatory practices. During the next several years, varied groups with different ideologies emerged to challenge both the political direction of established community organizations and the lack of institutional responsiveness to the needs of Mexican Americans. Of particular importance was the emergence of youth, and especially students, as a powerful force for change in the Mexican American community. Mexican American youth approached educational and social change from a radically different perspective than did the older members of the "Mexican American Generation." Although there were significant differences among youth groups, for the most part they rejected the ideology and identity of the Mexican American Generation. The older generation's identity was based on a complex mixture of cultural, political, and individual beliefs. As Mexican Americans, they viewed themselves as a recent immigrant group with a Spanish background on its way to absorption into the great American melting pot, and as victims of poverty and powerlessness. This view also encompassed a noncritical appreciation for United States institutions and a cautious approach to social change.[17]

The youth, most of whom came from working-class backgrounds, rejected these assimilationist, laudatory, and accomodationist views and adopted a new one that they called Chicanismo. This new consciousness comprised a complex set of racial, cultural, and political ideals and behaviors that were internally contradictory or inconsistent. These ideologies developed at different points in time and with different intensities or emphasis among the youth groups.[18]

The components comprising the ideology of Chicanismo were nationalism, a critical perspective of United States society, and a militant approach to change. Whereas the members of the Mexican American Generation accepted assimilationist thought, the emerging Chicano identity rejected it and replaced it with a nationalist one. This nationalist ideology had two major components. First, it was based on a non-white and predominantly indigenous identity. The youth began to view itself, not as another white immigrant group in American society undergoing the pains of assimilation and integration, but as members of an oppressed indigenous group. Mexican Americans, the youth declared, were members of an indigenous "Bronze race" who had been dispossessed of their lands, exploited by greedy economic interests, and whose cultural identity had been trampled upon by ethnocentric Anglos.[19] Second, this nationalist ideology required that the youth actively assert its cultural identity through the establishment of alternative "Chicano-based" institutions, ideals, and behaviors, through the maintenance of Spanish as a primary language, and through the promotion of Chicano cultural traditions.[20]

Chicanismo also rejected the Mexican American Generation's view of United States institutions and ideals. Whereas the older group praised American "democracy" and the ideals of "equality," "opportunity," and "freedom," the Chicano generation condemned them. The youth looked to developing Third-World countries and their revolutionary ideals or to its indigenous ancestors for spiritual guidance. Blind allegiance to United States institutions or ideals was not a cherished value among the majority of youth. For instance, the Houston Chapter of the Mexican American Youth Organization—the single most important youth organization in Houston— viewed capitalism as "an exploitative system" that needed to be overthrown and replaced with socialism. It also viewed the police as "pigs," the United States as imperialistic and "the great enemy of mankind," the American social and political system as structurally inhumane, the Church (especially the Catholic church) as an oppressor of the poor, and the law enforcement system as racially discriminatory. In their view, there was little in the American way of life worth salvaging.[21]

Finally, the youth rejected the older generation's cautionary approach and nonviolent means to socio-educational change. For the most part, the younger generation of activists were in basic agreement with the reformist goals of increased representation and institutional responsiveness to their community's needs, goals espoused by the Mexican American Generation and the more moderate middle-class organizations.[22] However, they opposed the older generation's circumspect approaches to social and educational change. Like their white and black counterparts elsewhere in America and Europe, Chicano youth willingly embraced militant approaches and actively promoted the use of unorthodox methods, including protest, confrontation, and violence, in their quest for social justice and equality.[23]

Armed with a new consciousness and an increased commitment to militant social change, Chicano youth in Houston and elsewhere began to mobilize against all forms of inequalities and against discrimination in American institutional life. Public education was one of the institutions that these youths attacked.

MEXICAN AMERICAN YOUTH AND EDUCATIONAL ACTIVISM

In Houston, the Mexican American youth began to speak out and organize in 1967. In this year, for instance, a number of students founded the League of Mexican American Students (LOMAS) at the University of Houston.[24] LOMAS sought to increase awareness of Mexican American issues among students and worked to formulate an intellectual foundation for the emerging activism by students. In late 1968, the group changed its name to the Mexican American Youth Organization (MAYO), an organization initially founded in San Antonio, Texas.[25] Sometime during the 1968–69 school year, junior and senior high school students organized a new group called Advocating Rights for Mexican American Students or ARMAS. The purpose of this group was to bring about school changes that would increase the achievement of Mexican American students.[26]

Mexican American youth also organized outside of education. The most important and vocal of these groups to emerge was the community chapter of MAYO. This organization became key in increasing the awareness and involvement of Mexican American youth in educational and social change.

These new youth groups came together in the spring of 1968. In April of that year, several youth, under the direction of Joseph Rojo and George Rivera, planned and hosted a Raza Unida Conference. ("Raza Unida" meant "United People," and an ethnic-based third party was later launched under this name.) The purpose of this conference was to bring together leading activists from across the city and to agree on goals and tactics for increasing social change. One of the major outcomes of this highly publicized meeting was the collective call for a "peaceful revolution" for Mexican Americans in Houston and for aggressive action on behalf of "la causa" or the cause.[27] Several months later, in June 1968, a new group calling itself Las Familias

Unidas de Segundo Barrio took up the "revolutionary" cause by protesting the inadequate city services that were provided in the Second Ward barrio.[28] The era of youthful protest had begun in Houston.

In public education, the era of protest in Houston began during the 1968–69 school year. Although it was initiated by ARMAS, the context for their actions was shaped by militant developments in other parts of the state. Of particular importance was the walkout by students in South Texas. In the fall of 1968, 192 Mexican American students walked out of Edcouch Elsa High School in Hidalgo County because the school board refused to listen to a list of 15 demands. Sixty-two of the students were expelled and the newly formed Mexican American Legal Defense and Education Fund (MALDEF) filed suit charging that the expulsions were unconstitutional and violated the students' right to protest. MALDEF and the students won the suit in December of the same year.[29] In that same month, the United States Commission on Civil Rights (USCCR) held several days of hearings in San Antonio, Texas. These hearings focused national attention on the invidious discriminatory practices utilized by most social institutions against Mexican Americans. A multitude of school policies and practices, especially no-Spanish-speaking rules and tracking, came under sharp criticism at these hearings.[30]

Youth in Houston supported and publicized these events.[31] In December, for instance, one of the youth, Raul Gutierrez, wrote in support of the Edcouch Elsa boycott in the first community newspaper established by young people during this period—the *Compass*. Gutierrez complained that "nada [nothing] is being done in Houston" although conditions such as those at Marshall Junior High School were bad. According to Gutierrez, at Marshall the principal failed to meet on time with parents, there was an intimidating presence of "police protection" at parent meetings with the principal, and the school ignored parental demands, especially those concerning a teacher who was molesting young women. Marshall did not have a Parent–Teacher Association nor a student council. Gutierrez urged that militant action be taken to correct these injustices. The recent walkout at Edcouch Elsa, he noted, was a reminder for the youth in Houston to "do our share."[32]

Several months later, ARMAS decided to take action on problems in the Houston schools. The actions ARMAS took during the next two years marked their entry into the local Chicano movement of that era and reflected an increasing militancy among youth. Student activism moved beyond the politics of accommodation and integration which had been shaped by the Mexican American Generation and the community's middle-class leadership.

The first action taken by ARMAS occurred in March 1969 after the school board forced cuts in the free lunch program that affected 4,000 Mexican American children. Mexican American parents protested this action and demonstrated in front of the school administration.[33] ARMAS supported the parents and passed out leaflets in some of the schools. These leaflets asked everyone—"Mothers, high school students, office workers, [and] laborers . . ."—for their support.[34] Although additional funds for the lunch

program were eventually provided, the issues of discrimination in the schools
and inferior education were not addressed by local officials. This prompted
ARMAS to take more radical action. Sometime during early September
1969, ARMAS drafted a list of demands that it planned to present to the
HISD administration. This list reflected the new consciousness of historical
oppression based on race and of cultural pride. It specifically demanded fair
treatment for Mexican Americans, the inclusion of Mexican American history
and culture in the schools, and the hiring of Chicano counselors "who understand the special problems of Chicanos in high school."[35] In order to gain
support and publicity for their demands ARMAS planned a demonstration
and a general walkout from the schools.[36] These actions would take place
on *el 16 de Septiembre*, a traditional holiday celebrating the anniversary of
Mexico's independence from Spain. On this day, Chicano students, symboli-
cally speaking, would celebrate their independence from Anglo America.[37]
On Tuesday, September 16, 1969, over 100 students demonstrated in front
of Jefferson Davis Senior High School at 1200 Quitman. The principal,
J. Paul Rodgers, requested that they not trespass on school property. The
demonstrators complied with this request but only after they had read their
list of grievances and demands.

List of Demands Made by Advocating Rights for Mexican American Students (ARMAS), September 16, 1969

1. Initiation of courses on Chicano history and culture, taught by Chicanos, into the regular school curriculum.
2. Stopping the practice of "push-outs"—that is, when counselors whose main concern is to keep order in the school advise students who are disciplinary problems to drop out of school.
3. Hiring of more Chicano counselors, who understand the special problems of Chicanos in high schools, who understand why only 2% of the students at the University of Houston are Chicanos while they comprise over 14% of the city's population.
4. Elimination of the "pregnancy list" at Davis High School, a publicly posted list of all girls who have left school because of pregnancy—a vicious form of personal degradation.
5. Lengthening the 20-minute lunch break allowed at Marshall. All other schools get at least 30 minutes.

Source: Richard Atwater, "Chicano Students' Walkout," *Space City News* 1, no. 7 (Sept. 27–Oct. 11, 1969), in Gregory Salazar Collection, Houston Metropolitan Research Center, Houston Public Library.

ARMAS members then encouraged students from Jeff Davis to join them as
they moved their demonstration off school property. About 100 students
walked out of Jeff Davis.

Students in support of the ARMAS demands also walked out of other
schools. At Marshall Junior High School the student newspaper reported
that approximately 75 students walked out although the principal locked the
gates so no one could leave. An additional 40 students left Hogg Junior High

School, 20 walked out of Sanjacinto Senior High School, and 20 left Booker T. Washington Junior-Senior High School. A few brave souls from Reagan High School also walked out.[38] They all met at Moody Park for a rally to discuss the success of the walkout and to plan for the future.

The principals and faculty at these schools reacted in various ways, most of them negatively. Some principals threatened all the students participating in the walkout with expulsion. A few teachers also threatened to use physical force to keep the students in class and viewed the students' demands as unworthy of consideration. At Sanjacinto High, uniformed and plainclothes police "were everywhere, shouting insults at the students and spoiling for a fight," noted one observer. Some of the teachers grabbed students and shoved them back into class while others tried to intimidate them by taking down the names of those who were walking out. Other schools, namely Reagan High and Marshall Junior High, were locked up completely and nobody was allowed to go outside.[39] "The students who did escape, however, marched around the high schools encouraging those in sympathy to join them," reported one journalist. Although most students were intimidated by the administration's threats as well as by teachers, many of them expressed verbal support for the walkout.[40]

The walkouts were considered by local activists to be well planned and executed.[41] They also helped ARMAS attain one of its primary goals: to gain support from other students for its demands. According to one source, more than 500 students walked out in all and many others showed their support by staying home that day.[42] But the student strike failed to have any significant impact on the schools or on the community as did other walkouts in different parts of the state or the Southwest. In Los Angeles, for instance, the student strikes of 1968 resulted in significant political developments beyond the issues of school reform and contributed to the further development of community organizations. They also acted as the catalyst for the formation of a Chicano student movement as well as the larger Chicano movement of which it became the most important sector.[43]

The Houston walkout did not serve as a catalyst for any further school reforms. Lack of publicity and parental support as well as neglect by school officials probably limited the walkout's potential impact, which was confined largely to the junior and senior high school students themselves. One observer believed that the students learned an important lesson from this action: that "if they act together, they can force the administration to acknowledge their demands and respect their Mexican American heritage."[44] This statement was misleading, however, since the school board essentially ignored the issues raised by the boycott. Punitive actions were taken against the leaders and followers by expelling or suspending some of them but nothing was done to acknowledge or address their demands.[45] The walkout did, however, have some limited effect on community political mobilization. Perhaps its greatest effect was to increase parental participation in school affairs and to encourage several middle-class leaders to raise questions about the schooling of Mexican American children.

PROTEST FROM THE COMMUNITY

A month after the walkout, a few Mexican American community leaders went before the local school board and leveled charges of inferior education and discrimination against HISD. On Wednesday, October 1, 1969, Leonel Castillo, local director of Services, Employment, and Redevelopment, a federally funded "manpower" training agency, went before the school board's compensatory education committee. He charged that Mexican American students were getting an inferior education in Houston. Castillo's comments were based on his experiences with Mexican American students who participated in a college-bound summer school program. These youngsters, who came from several junior high schools including Hogg, Marshall, Edison, and George Washington, had been identified by several educators involved in the summer school program as potential college material and selected to participate in this all-male program. Upon their arrival, however, the organizers of the program found that the reading level of these students was so low that the curriculum had to be revised downward. A majority of the approximately 120 participants were reading at either a second- or third-grade level.[46] These boys, noted Castillo, "had received their education, since the first grade, in the Houston public schools." He also charged that the administrators had a bad attitude toward the Mexican American students, had no desire to improve educational programs for them, and did not want to motivate them to learn.[47]

Ben Canales, an official with United Organizations Information Center (UOIC), a relatively new community organization, charged that in some schools, such as Jeff Davis and Sanjacinto high schools, Mexican American students were constantly harassed by teachers.[48] He added that the Mexican American community was fed up with the local officials' neglect of the students' needs. "We know that principals and teachers in schools with predominantly Mexican American enrollments are inferior to their counterparts in Anglo schools and they wouldn't make it in Anglo schools."[49]

Canales's charges were based on the legacy and current practice of school discrimination against Mexican American children. In Houston, the origins of unequal schooling for Mexican children originated at the turn of the century when a handful of Spanish-speaking children enrolled in the old Rusk Elementary School in the city's Second Ward. By 1920, there were over 529 Mexican children attending city schools primarily at Rusk, Dow, Jones, Hawthorne, and De Zavala Elementary Schools. These segregated schools in many cases were older than those provided for Anglo children, had less space and amenities than the Anglo schools, and were generally uncomfortable. Few Mexican American children were adequately educated in these deplorable facilities. Not only were the schools segregated and unequal but the cultural heritage of the students as well as the parents themselves were constantly disparaged by local school officials, administrators, and the teachers. The practice of segregated and inferior schools, which continued unabated, had a detrimental impact on the students and led to a pattern of poor school performance. A decade before Canales's complaint, for instance, 90 out of

238 Mexican American pupils at Hawthorne Elementary School were one year behind in school; an additional 57 students were two years behind. As noted by Canales, Mexican American children continued to be victims of inferior educational opportunities in the 1960s.[50]

Students in general, and ARMAS in particular, were conspicuously absent from this hearing before the board's compensatory committee. It is unclear whether the students declined to participate or whether the board only invited selected "leaders." Despite their absence, the issues of discrimination and underachievement raised by ARMAS in their boycott were again presented to the school officials by the Mexican American community representatives.

As part of their presentations, community leaders made specific recommendations for school reform. These recommendations reflected a mixture of new and old ideologies pertaining to language and culture in the schools—a compensatory view of language as a "handicap," an emerging pluralist notion of language as asset, and a civil rights perspective of language as an instrument of discrimination. Antonio Criado, vice-president of UOIC, recommended three changes. He proposed that school officials (1) recognize a language barrier as a handicap, "just as deafness and blindness are handicaps," and take steps to help students with this, (2) alter history and other courses that make Mexican American students feel inferior and ashamed of their heritage, and (3) recognize that Mexican Americans cannot be treated like Anglo-Americans in measuring ability by testing. This latter recommendation was most likely based on the emerging view among Mexican Americans that there were inherent cultural and language biases in standardized evaluation instruments.[51]

Ben Canales also added that the district should hire Mexican American principals, counselors, and teachers in those schools with large numbers of Mexican American students. Additionally, he stated that the professional staffs of these schools should be sensitized to the feelings and needs of Mexican American students through in-service programs.[52]

Probably because of the seriousness of the charges, the general superintendent of HISD, Glenn Fletcher, agreed to call a meeting between the Mexican American community leaders and the principals, assistant principals, and counselors of some schools with large numbers of Mexican American students to discuss these problems. HISD also invited additional community representatives, mostly non-Hispanic, to participate in the meeting. "We recognize that problems exist and we are working on them," he added.[53]

A NEED IGNORED

On October 13, 1969, top personnel from 25 Houston public schools and their community representatives met with a panel of Mexican Americans. Although it was intended to be a meeting, there was no discussion of the issues. The group of educators merely heard the Mexican American leaders level charges against the school district. Jose Rojo, an attorney with the Houston Legal Foundation, presented a position paper prepared by the UOIC. He argued that there was a pattern of discrimination and harassment against Mexican Americans in the school district. More specifically, he argued that the general feeling by students was that Mexican Americans were fair game for mistreatment or different treatment by teachers and administrators "without fear of retribution." Corporal punishment was administered too frequently against Mexican Americans and without sufficient reason. Some teachers had a negative or hostile attitude toward Mexican American students and called them names. One junior high school coach, for example, called Mexican American students "hoods" and "punks." Teachers, principals, and counselors also were insensitive to Mexican American problems.[54]

In addition to evidence of discrimination Rojo provided data indicating the low median years of schooling for the Mexican American population and especially the high rates of student dropouts. According to him, 89 percent of the Mexican American pupils in Houston dropped out without finishing high school. This, he said, proved that the district's educators were not doing an adequate job.[55] He recommended the establishment of a task force of educators, parents, student leaders, and others to investigate these charges.[56]

The HISD administrators did not immediately respond to these charges at the meeting, but one of HISD's token Mexican American representatives did. Rosemary Saucillo, a Houston school district graduate who had earned a law degree, disagreed with Rojo's charges and blamed the parents of Mexican American pupils rather than the school administration for the problems of underachievement and high dropout rates. She said heavier penalties should be dealt parents who permitted their children to be absent from school. "Let's do something about the dropout rate even if we have to put the parents in jail," she said. A good number of the HISD-appointed parents, staff, and administrators at the meeting heartily applauded her remarks.[57]

Several days later, the HISD administration responded to the charges of discrimination and harassment. The staff vehemently denied the charges of inferior teachers. J. Paul Rodgers, principal at Jeff Davis, stated that teachers at his school had to have the same requirements and qualifications as teachers in other schools. Ken Mueller, principal at Sanjacinto, said, "If anyone can cite one instance of discrimination I will personally apologize to the students." "It's too bad the critics don't see what we are doing here before complaining," noted Rodgers.[58]

A select group of Mexican American student leaders at several of the mentioned schools also denied the charges leveled against HISD by community leaders. Ramiro Marin, 17, senior class president at Jeff Davis, for instance, said he had never been discriminated against in the Houston public schools. Robert Casares, 16, junior class president at Jeff Davis, said no junior had ever complained to him about discrimination and harassment. "I feel I'm getting a good education. I respect the school," he noted. Christina Uride, 18, a senior and president of the Future Teachers Association at Sanjacinto, said she knew of no harassment or discrimination. "I think I'm getting a good education here," she said. Jose Garza, 17, president of the Spanish Club at Sanjacinto, said, "I think the teachers here are good and would teach anywhere." Gracie Soliz, 17, a National Honor Society member at Sanjacinto, said she had received encouragement from the teachers. Finally, Delia Salas, 17, secretary of the Spanish Club at Sanjacinto and student council representative for the past two years, said that Mexican Americans got a good education at the school.[59]

Principals Mueller and Rodgers also noted how they had tried to institute special courses aimed at Mexican American students. Sanjacinto had a Texas history course that emphasized the contributions of "Spanish-speaking citizens" and recently had tried to start a Spanish-language business education course but could not locate a bilingual teacher. Jeff Davis had bilingual courses in Latin American and Mexican history.[60]

School administrators also noted how, during the current school year, HISD had begun a pilot program in bilingual education in six elementary schools. Both Ben Canales and Antonio Criado maintained that these efforts were not enough. "They are trying pilot programs when they should be trying mass programs," Criado said. "The dropout rate for Mexican American students is a crisis and the school administration doesn't recognize it," he added.[61]

Despite the seriousness of these charges, no specific measures were taken to address them by either the board of education or the superintendent. The request made by Rojo on October 16 for the establishment of a task force of educators, parents, student leaders, and others to investigate these charges likewise was ignored. Community leaders found out that local officials were not genuinely interested in addressing the issues of underachievement and discrimination in the schools.

Although ignored, community leaders continued to organize and mobilize against discrimination in the schools. For instance, several months later, on February 13, 1970, a new community group—Barrios Unidos—decided to press the case for school reforms again. It charged HISD with discrimination, inferior education, and insensitivity toward Chicanos. Barrios Unidos also presented the local board with 13 demands for improving the education of Mexican Americans. Unlike the one drawn up by ARMAS, this list was more comprehensive in proposing changes, including taking punitive actions against school staff having "negative attitudes toward Mexican American students," eliminating the no-Spanish-speaking practices, and opposing the possible "integration" of schools with students who were Mexican American and African American.[62] The demands for school reforms "were not presented for the purpose of gaining any type of publicity," noted *El Yaqui*, the newsletter for Barrios Unidos, "but because our children are recipients of very poor quality education, and are the subject of the worst discriminatory practices on the part of teachers, principals, and other students. . . . Barrios Unidos," it continued, "fully intends to pursue this issue until a balanced educational attitude and program has been developed that will enable the Chicano student to receive quality education, and the treatment and dignity to which he is entitled."[63] But, as in prior cases, the local board refused to acknowledge these demands or to address them. Once again the community was ignored.

Despite the protestations by students, parents, and community groups, local school officials remained indifferent to their concerns. Their refusal to recognize and tackle the problem of discrimination in the schools increased the Chicano community's disillusionment with public school officials and laid the groundwork for its further radicalization and mobilization. All that was needed was a catalyst to begin the process of mass mobilization against educational discrimination. The federal court decisions on integration during the summer of 1970 provided this catalyst. These federal decisions set the stage for a vigorous response by the Mexican American community in Houston that would last for the next two decades. Local school district intransigence and insensitivity served to sustain the new activism motivated by these unjust federal court rulings. The rumbling of the Mexican American community during the 1960s, in some respects, was a prelude to the coming explosion of political activism. The cataclysmic events of the 1970s would mobilize the community into a political force to be reckoned with.

NOTES

1. "Education of Latins Called Inferior," Houston *Chronicle*, October 2, 1969.
2. Arnoldo De Leon, *Ethnicity in the Sunbelt: A History of Mexican Americans in Houston* (Houston: Mexican American Studies, University of Houston, 1989), 163–170.
3. For a history of the Chicano movement's rise and decline in Houston see De Leon.
4. See De Leon, especially 163–184.
5. Houston *Post*, July 27, 1961.
6. Thomas H. Kreneck, *Del Pueblo: A Pictorial History of Houston's Hispanic Community* (Houston: Houston International University, 1989), 151–152.
7. The CAC had been founded in 1958 to promote Mexican American involvement in the political process. Roy Elizondo, Alfonso Vasquez, E. P. Lean, and Dr. Alfredo Hernandez played key roles in the evolution of this organization. Kreneck, 151–152.
8. Kreneck, 153.
9. Guadalupe San Miguel, *Let All of Them Take Heed: Mexican Americans and the Quest for Educational Equality in Texas, 1910–1981* (Austin: University of Texas Press, 1987), 141. For a history of the Little Schools of the 400 see *ibid.*, 139–163; also Guadalupe Campos Quintanilla, "The Little School of the 400 and Its Impact on Education for the Spanish Dominant Bilingual Children of Texas" (Ph.D. diss., University of Houston, 1976).
10. This program expanded in size between 1960 and 1964 and served close to 150,000 Mexican American children before it expired in 1967. San Miguel, 156–160.
11. For data on the success of this program in improving school achievement, see Texas Education Agency, *Report on the Preschool Instructional Program* (Austin: Texas Education Agency, 1962). See also San Miguel, 155–157.
12. San Miguel, 158–159.
13. De Leon, 164.
14. De Leon, 163–184.
15. Kreneck, 155.

16. The city of Houston under the Welch administration in 1967 also developed a program similar to Jobs for Progress. Mayor Welch's program, entitled Houston City Job Fair, targeted Mexican American neighborhoods. It involved Mexican American volunteers who assisted residents, particularly youth, in finding summer employment and in encouraging them to further their education. Kreneck, 155.

17. The "Mexican American Generation" was comprised of both middle and working-class individuals who were born or raised in the United States. Community leaders from this group embraced a liberal version of cultural pluralism and a politics of cautious activism. Mario T. Garcia, *Mexican Americans: Leadership, Ideology, and Identity, 1930–1960* (New Haven: Yale University Press, 1989), 13–22.

18. For one recent history of the Chicano student movement and its ideological development, see Carlos Munoz, *Youth, Identity, Power: The Chicano Movement* (New York: Verso, 1989).

19. One of the first documents written by youth was *El Plan Espiritual de Aztlan*. Its opening sentence states, "In the spirit of a new people that is conscious not only of its proud historical heritage, but also of the brutal 'gringo' invasion of our territories, We, the Chicano inhabitants and civilizers of the northern land of Aztlan, from whence came our forefathers, reclaiming the land of their birth and consecrating the determination of our people of the sun, Declare that the call of our blood is our power, our responsibility and our inevitable destiny." *El Plan*, written in March 1969 in Denver, Colorado, is stapled to an undated Mexican American Youth Organization (MAYO) document in the Luis Cano Collection, Houston Metropolitan Research Center, Houston Public Library.

20. *El Plan* reiterated this sentiment throughout. Point number one of *El Plan* noted that nationalism was the key to organization and the "common denominator that all members of La Raza can agree upon." Another one of the *Plan*'s points under the heading of culture reaffirms this position: "Cultural values of our people strengthen our identity and the moral backbone of the movement . . . We must insure that our writers, poets, musicians, and artists produce literature and art that is appealing to our people and relates to our revolutionary culture . . ." *The Program of El Plan Espiritual de Aztlan*, points #1 and #3, Crusade for Justice folder, Gregory Salazar Collection, Houston Metropolitan Research Center, Houston Public Library.

21. MAYO Positions (undated document), 1–4, Barrio Programs folder, Salazar Collection.

22. In the early 1970s, a fringe group of Mexican American youth did advocate drastic or fundamental change in the socioeconomic and educational structures of the society. But, for the most part, both the youth and the older generation wanted pluralist reforms and militant changes in the society, not significant or revolutionary ones. For a history of the political ideologies of students in the broader Chicano movement of the late 1960s see Juan Gomez-Quinones, *Chicano Politics: Reality and Promise, 1940–1990* (Albuquerque; University of New Mexico Press, 1990).

23. Munoz; Gomez-Quinones.

24. LOMAS was influenced by Tatcho Mindiola, Ramon Villagomez, Al Perez, Ninfa Zepeda, George Rangel, Susie Quintanilla, and others during its early years. See Kreneck, 157.

25. Kreneck, 157.

26. De Leon, 143.

27. Kreneck, 156.

28. Kreneck, 152.
29. MALDEF, *Diez Anos* (San Antonio: MALDEF, 1978); "Chicanos Boycott High School," *Compass* 2, no. 9 (December 1968): 1.
30. USCCR, *Hearings Before the United States Commission on Civil Rights, San Antonio, December 9–14, 1968* (Washington, D.C.: Government Printing Office, 1968).
31. On the South Texas boycott see, for instance, "Chicanos Boycott High School."
32. Raul Gutierrez, "Mexican Americans Boycott Elsa High School—Greater Houston—Uneasy?," *Compass* 2, no. 9 (December 1968): 2.
33. This picket at HISD to protest funding cuts was organized by Abel Alvarez, who argued that the need was for more, not less, funding of the free breakfast program as a way to improve school performance among Chicano children. See "An Example from Houston?" *Compass* 3, no. 3 (March 1969): 6.
34. ARMAS, undated handout, Salazar Collection.
35. Richard Atwater, "Chicano Students' Walkout," *Space City News* 1, no. 7 (Sept. 27–Oct. 11, 1969), Salazar Collection.
36. As early as December 1968, community members and students had been discussing the need for "a revolution of walkouts, sit-ins, or stay outs," as a way of pressuring school officials to improve the schools for Mexican Americans. See Gutierrez, "Mexican Americans Boycott Elsa . . ."
37. "Latins Demonstrate at Schools to Mark Mexican Holiday." Houston *Post*, September 17, 1969.
38. "Latins Demonstrate . . ."
39. David M. Yeager, principal at Marshall, said he did not lock the front or side entrance gates to the school or any doors to prevent a walkout as reported in the newspaper. He said that most decided not to participate. See "Latins Demonstrate . . ."
40. Atwater, "Chicano Students' Walkout"; unidentified newspaper clipping, Salazar Collection.
41. ARMAS also distributed many leaflets and articles from their newspaper. These leaflets were passed out to gain student support and also to announce the demands made by ARMAS. Atwater, "Chicano Students' Walkout."
42. *Ibid.* In another part of the article, Atwater noted the biased and inadequate coverage of the walkout by the mainstream media. He said that it printed distorted versions of the walkout and omitted most of the facts. The *Chronicle*, for instance, reported that only 32 students walked out at Jeff Davis yet according to one eyewitness there were at least 130.
43. Munoz, 66, 70–71.
44. Atwater, "Chicano Students Walkout."
45. Some student leaders, especially those at Sanjacinto, were expelled the day after the walkout but by the end of the week all students were back in class. Atwater, "Chicano Students Walkout."
46. This program was held at the Strake Jesuit Preparatory School during the summer of 1969. Most of the students were headed into the seventh and eighth grades. Their reading level was determined after they were given a battery of recognized achievement tests. See "Education of Latins Called Inferior," Houston *Chronicle*, October 2, 1969.
47. *Ibid.*
48. According to De Leon, UOIC was founded in 1966 or 1967 to "develop, promote, and encourage, by the preparation and distribution of literature,

pamphlets, magazines, periodicals, tokens, and otherwise to act as a clearing house of information." De Leon, 181.

49. "Education of Latins Called Inferior."

50. Luis Cano, "A History of Segregation and the Chicano Movement" (unpublished book manuscript, Houston, 1977), Chapter 6, 2–10.

51. For one scholar's analysis of linguistic and cultural biases in the testing of Mexican American children in the public schools, see Blandina Cardenas, "Defining Equal Access to Educational Opportunity for Mexican American Children: A Study of Three Civil Rights Actions Affecting Mexican American Students" (Ph.D. diss., University of Massachusetts, 1974).

52. "Education of Latins Called Inferior."

53. *Ibid.*

54. "Latin dropouts, Low Achievement Talked," Houston *Post*, October 14, 1969.

55. *Ibid.*; "Mexican-American Schooling Held Worse Than Negroes'," *El Sol*, October 17, 1969.

56. "Latin dropouts . . ."

57. *Ibid.*

58. Ken Sheets, "Latin Student Harassment in City Schools Denied," undated newspaper clipping, Salazar Collection.

59. Sheets, "Latin Student Harrassment . . ."

60. *Ibid.*

61. *Ibid.*

62. "Chicanos Too: Students Are Not All Black and Anglo," *El Yaqui* 2, no. 2 (Febrero 1970): 5, Cano Collection. It is unclear why Barrios Unidos began to oppose the integration issue at such an early date, since it did not take place until later in the year. In August 1970, the Fifth Circuit Court of Appeals directed HISD to undertake racial integration of Houston's elementary schools by busing, using predominantly Mexican American schools to provide the "white" students. Community protest led to a long-term boycott of the public schools, the development of alternative schools within the community, and the establishment of several effective community activist groups.

63. *Ibid.*

PART FIVE

URBAN SCHOOL REFORM IN THE LATE TWENTIETH CENTURY

The turmoil of the 1960s and 1970s gave way to a new period in the history of American urban education during the 1980s and 1990s. It was a time of political reaction, urban decline, and continued suburban development, along with considerable anguish among educators in the nation's major cities. The era of mass protests and desegregation orders gave way to a conservative response in national politics that led to the election of Ronald Reagan in 1980, creating a new atmosphere in federal policy. The Reaganite Republicans cut funding to the social programs of the 1960s and 1970s, and rolled back federal aid to urban schools. Even if less draconian than many had feared, these developments came to demarcate a major change in policy. Education remained an important issue, but the publication of *A Nation At Risk* in 1983 helped to shift the national agenda from equity and social justice to the issue of academic achievement. Urban schools, of course, had long exhibited problems in the academic performance of their students. But in the new political context of the 1980s, educators in the cities could no longer look to Washington for assistance. New approaches were called for—a different reform paradigm.

In the meantime, many of the older cities in the United States began to realize dramatic changes in their collective social and economic fortunes. Suburban development continued apace, drawing middle-class families and economic resources away from the central cities. Perhaps even more significant, however, was an accelerating movement of industry out of urban centers, taking jobs and infrastructure investment away as well. While these trends had been evident since the 1960s, they assumed crisis proportions in the 1980s. As a consequence, ever-larger numbers of urban residents found themselves falling into poverty, most of them members of racial and ethnic minority groups who did not have the option of moving to the booming suburbs. While rates of household destitution increased, in some cases transforming entire communities, the social environment of many cities deteriorated. Family structures shifted in the face of widespread unemployment, and ever-larger numbers of single parent households became commonplace in the most distressed neighborhoods. These were developments with profound implications for the schools. Extreme poverty and shifting family structures compounded the problems that urban educators had long faced. Coupled with the downward spiral of fiscal resources, and the changing political scene in Washington, these factors helped to make the 1980s a very difficult time for city schools.

In the wake of deindustrialization, fiscal decline, and growing deprivation, educators in the nation's largest cities looked in new directions for ideas in the 1980s and 1990s. One of the most popular critiques of large urban districts during the 1960s and 1970s concerned their reliance on centralized administrative structures and a correspondingly inflexible bureaucratic culture of leadership. Benjamin Willis in Chicago had personified this problem. Critics had come to characterize district administrators as unresponsive and inefficient, if not noisome and corrupt. Consequently, a growing number of reformers, both in the cities and in various academic centers, came to the conclusion that urban schools needed to be released from the constraints of bureaucratic oversight and regulatory authority. Decentralization became the watchword of the day. Many observers were influenced by the success of magnet schools, desegregation-era institutions established to help retain high achieving middle-class students. Reformers wanted to give schools the freedom to develop innovative and demanding academic programs, to hire teachers without reference to archaic rules, and to involve parents and community members in decision making. Some looked to private institutions for models of success, particularly the Catholic schools in older cities. By the start of the 1990s, however, there was growing impatience with the pace of change. Decentralization did not produce dramatic results, and the largest districts seemed mired in procedural and political inertia. Meanwhile, the term "school choice" had become the new reform slogan across the country, and was especially influential among those intent on fundamentally changing urban education. This gave impetus to a movement to establish "charter schools" in cities across the country, institutions organized outside of traditional district regulations, often designed to meet the needs of their communities. It also helped to launch the first voucher plans in certain cities, programs to provide eligible families with stipends to send their children to private schools. Altogether, it was a time of dramatic changes in the way that problems in urban education were thought about, resulting in correspondingly radical proposals for making the schools more responsive to the needs of urban children.

The chapters in this section examine issues of educational change in major cities that reflect the various themes of this period. The first is an essay by Jeffrey Mirel describing changes in Detroit during the years following 1980. As he has pointed out, Detroit represented an extreme case of deindustrialization and urban decline, perhaps the most severe in the nation. It also was beset with political problems stemming at least in part from an administrative apparatus that was unresponsive to the educational problems of the district and its critical fiscal condition. Mirel examined the events leading up to an election in 1988 that swept a reform coalition into positions of power on the city's school board. This group immediately set about making changes in the way that schools were run, instituting reforms to allow educators greater flexibility in designing curricula, changing work rules, and encouraging greater involvement by parents and the community. It was a heady time in Detroit, and with additional financial assistance from the state, it seemed as though positive changes might be possible. Before long, however, the new reform regime ran afoul of the powerful Detroit Federation of Teachers, which was concerned that changing expectations for the system's teachers would undermine their status. Teachers also worried about the role of parents and other non-educators in educational reform, and whether these groups would gain greater authority at the expense of teachers. Detroit was a strong labor town, and the opposition of the union dealt a serious blow to the reform effort. Mirel has suggested that this represents a cautionary tale: educational reform, no matter how carefully conceived or well intended, must always take heed of the people who actually deliver instruction. Without the support of urban teachers, meaningful and effective school reform simply is not possible, no matter how innovative a proposed change may be. This is an insight that many would-be reformers lose sight of all too often.

The second chapter in this section concerns the nation's first voucher plan in a major urban school district. The city was Milwaukee, and the essay by John Witte is a summary of an evaluation study that he conducted to assess the program's implementation and impact. The idea of vouchers as a method of changing education had a long history when the first proposals for establishing plans in urban districts appeared in the 1980s. First articulated by the fabled economist Milton Friedman, the concept had been supported by a relatively small but highly vocal band of supporters for several decades. Some believed that it represented a "magic bullet" reform, one that promised to transform urban schools by making them responsive to the needs of the families and communities that utilized them. As Witte pointed out, the Milwaukee plan was launched in 1990 to test this proposition. It was started as a relatively small experiment, involving a limited number of students and a handful of schools. Because of potential legal challenges, Catholic schools were not involved at first. Still, hopes were high that even a limited voucher plan would highlight the advantages of private education for students who traditionally could not afford the cost of these schools.

Witte's study offered a detailed look at the effects of the plan in a variety of realms, including student achievement, parental satisfaction, and its impact on the city's public schools. These were aspects of education that voucher proponents had claimed would improve under the plan. Witte reported, however, that the results from his study of Milwaukee were mixed. By and large, the impact on student achievement was negligible, at least in the areas of reading and mathematics, the two subjects tested most regularly. Parent satisfaction with the private schools was quite high, but the impact of the program on the public schools was difficult to discern. Altogether, in that case, the evidence that Witte reported does not seem to provide support for the most stalwart proponents of vouchers as a reform strategy in public education. While the voucher plan did not harm most of the children who participated, it also did not result in significant improvements in academic achievement. While still an interesting reform possibility, in that case, the evidence seems to suggest that vouchers do not represent a dramatic solution to the many problems faced by the urban schools.

The final chapter concerns yet another major reform effort in American urban education, the case of Chicago. In 1988 the Chicago Public Schools underwent a major reorganization, similar in certain respects to the reform described in Detroit above. In Chicago, a coalition of reformers, educators, and neighborhood organizations conceived a new system of organization for the city's schools, placing authority in the hands of "local school councils" (or LSCs) for a wide range of matters, extending from curricular decisions to the appointment of principals. Parents were the dominant group represented on these councils, but they also included teachers and community representatives, along with principals as ex-officio members. The theory guiding the reform held that these governing bodies would chart new directions for individual schools, making them more responsive to community interests and boosting parent involvement in public education. Following a period of intense public interest in Chicago school reform, however, the level of community involvement in LSCs began to decline. Five years later, researchers found that while about a third of the schools had elected active and effective councils, some of them accomplishing major change, another third exhibited little change, and other schools actually registered academic declines following the implementation of reform. System-wide, following an initial jump in achievement, additional advances in the academic performance of the city's schools were modest at best. While some schools clearly benefitted from the reforms of 1988, the effect on the entire district was clearly not as dramatic.

This was the situation that preceded an intervention by Chicago Mayor Richard M. Daley in 1995, refocusing reform efforts in Chicago at the district level and introducing a vigorous accountability regime to identify schools with problems. This new approach to urban school reform was the subject of Brian Jacobs' chapter, titled "High Stakes in Chicago." While the new reform regime under Daley left the LSCs in place, it made the schools accountable to performance measures promulgated by the system's central office, led during the first phase of reform by Paul Vallas, Daley's former chief financial officer. As Jacobs points out, this was a dramatic change from the tenor of the earlier reform, but it also had the effect of focusing educators across the system on the importance of academic achievement in a way that the earlier reforms had not. Jacobs presented evidence that achievement gains under the new accountability system have been significant, and he suggested that it was because teachers and other educators have been given clear goals and tangible consequences. Chicago's new system gained widespread attention following its implementation in 1995, and accountability has become a watchword in educational reform in the years hence. Jacobs even has argued that it was a critical precursor to the federal "No Child Left Behind Legislation." While still controversial, the Chicago approach to school improvement has managed to show results. It is important to note, however, that Jacobs is among its more positive evaluators. The jury is out on whether these gains can be sustained, and if Chicago's teachers and other educators will fully embrace this approach to reform in the long run.

ADDITIONAL READINGS

There is a vast literature on urban education and related issues in the past 25 years. On the question of deindustrialization and urban change, see William Julius Wilson, *When Work Disappears: The World of the New Urban Poor* (New York: Knopf, 1996), also see Wilson's earlier work, *The Truly Disadvantaged: The Inner City, The Underclass, and Public Policy* (Chicago: University of Chicago Press, 1987), Carter A. Wilson, "Restructuring and the Growth of Concentrated Poverty in Detroit" *Urban Affairs Quarterly* 1992 28(2): 187–205, John D. Kasarda, "Urban Industrial Transition and the Underclass" *Annals of the American Academy of Political and Social Science* 1989 (501): 26–47, John D. Kasarda, "Entry-Level Jobs, Mobility, and Urban Minority Unemployment" *Urban Affairs Quarterly* 1983 19(1): 21–40, and Lee Sigelman and Jeffrey R. Henig, "Crossing the Great Divide: Race and Preferences for Living in the City versus the Suburbs" *Urban Affairs Review* September 2001 37(1): 3–18. For historical perspectives on this development, see Michael B. Katz, ed., *The "Underclass" Debate: Views from History* (Princeton, NJ: Princeton University Press, 1993), and Thomas J. Sugrue, *The Origins of the Urban Crisis: Race and Inequality in Postwar Detroit* (Princeton, NJ: Princeton University Press, 1996).

On urban education in this period, dealing with particular cities, see Jean Anyon, *Ghetto Schooling: A Political Economy of Urban Educational Reform* (1997) (cited in previous sections), Michael B. Katz, *Reconstructing American Education* (1987) (also cited earlier), Marion Orr, *Black Social Capital: The Politics of School Reform in Baltimore, 1986–1998* (Lawrence: University Press of Kansas, 1999), Gary Orfield and Carole Ashkinaze, *The Closing Door: Conservative Policy and Black Opportunity* (Chicago: University of Chicago Press, 1991), John L. Rury and Frank Cassel, *Seeds of Crisis: Public Schooling in Milwaukee Since 1920* (1993) (cited earlier), Allan C. Ornstein, "Urban Demographics for the 1980's: Educational Implications" *Education and Urban Society* 1984 16(4): 477–496, Nathan Glazer, "The Real World of Urban Education" *Public Interest* 1992 (106): 57–75, and Paula D. McClain, "Thirty Years of Urban Policies: Frankly, My Dears, We Don't Give a Damn!" *Urban Affairs Review* 1995 30(5): 641–644.

There is a growing literature on the politics of urban schooling and social inequality. See for instance, Clarence N. Stone, Jeffrey R. Henig, Bryan D. Jones, and Carol Pierannunzi, *Building Civic Capacity: The Politics of Reforming Urban Schools* (Lawrence: University Press of Kansas, 2001), Clarence N. Stone, ed., *Changing Urban Education: Studies in Government and Public Policy* (Lawrence, University Press of Kansas, 1998), Jeffrey R. Henig, Richard C. Hula, Marion Orr, Desiree S. Pedescleaux, *The Color of School Reform: Race, Politics, and the Challenge of Urban Education*

(Princeton: Princeton University Press, 1999), Kenneth K. Wong and Francis X. Shen, "Big City Mayors and School Governance Reform: The Case of School District Takeover" *Peabody Journal of Education* 2003 78(1): 5–32, Stefanie Chambers, "Urban Education Reform and Minority Political Empowerment" *Political Science Quarterly* 2002–2003 117(4): 643–665, and G. Alfred Hess, Jr., "Community Participation or Control? From New York to Chicago" *Theory into Practice* Autumn 1999 38(4): 217–224.

Regarding urban schools and inequality, see Doris R. Entwisle, Karl L. Alexander, and Linda Steffel Olson, *Children, Schools, and Inequality* (Boulder, CO: Westview Press, 1997), Howard A. Glickstein, "Inequalities in Educational Financing" *Teachers College Record* 1995 96(4): 722–728, Jeannie Oakes, "Two Cities' Tracking and Within-School Segregation" *Teachers College Record* 1995 96(4): 681–690, Marta Tienda and Haya Stier, "Generating Labor Market Inequality: Employment Opportunities and the Accumulation of Disadvantage" *Social Problems* 1996 43(2): 147–165, Rick Ginsberg, Henrietta Schwartz, George Olson, and Albert Bennett, "Working Conditions in Urban Schools" *Urban Review* 1987 19(1): 3–23, James E. Rosenbaum, Marilynn J. Kulieke, and Leonard S. Rubinowitz, "White Suburban Schools' Responses to Low-income Black Children: Sources of Successes and Problems" *Urban Review* 1988 20(1): 28–41, and Gary Orfield, "Public Opinion and School Desegregation" *Teachers College Record* 1995 96(4): 654–670.

On the question of school choice in cities, see John F. Witte, *The Market Approach to Education: An Analysis of America's First Voucher Program* (Princeton: Princeton University Press, 2000), Ellen Goldring, Claire Smrekar, "Magnet Schools: Reform and Race in Urban Education" *Clearing House* September–October 2002 76(1): 13–15, Natalie Lacireno-Paquet, Thomas T. Holyoke, Michele Moser, Jeffrey R. Henig, "Creaming versus Cropping: Charter School Enrollment Practices in Response to Market Incentives" *Educational Evaluation and Policy Analysis* Summer 2002 24(2): 145–158, and Jeffrey R. Henig, "Race and Choice in Montgomery County, Maryland, Magnet Schools" *Teachers College Record* Summer 1995 96(4): 729–734. For a pro-voucher perspective, see Paul E. Peterson, Jay P. Greene, and Chad Noyes, "School Choice in Milwaukee" *Public Interest* 1996 (125): 38–56. For other views, see Frederick M. Hess and Patrick J. McGuinn, "Muffled by the Din: The Competitive Noneffects of the Cleveland Voucher Program" *Teachers College Record* 2002 104(4): 727–764, Jeffrey R. Henig, *Rethinking School Choice: Limits of the Market Metaphor* (Princeton: Princeton University Press, 1994), Jim Ryan, "School Choice and the Suburbs" *Journal of Law & Politics* 1998 14(3): 459–468, and Stephen L. Percy, and Peter Maier, "School Choice in Milwaukee: Privatization of a Different Breed" *Policy Studies Journal* 1996 24(4): 649–665.

There also is a substantial literature on Chicago school reform. For an overview and progress reports, see Anthony S. Bryk, Penny Bender Sebring, David Kerbow, Sharon Rollow, and John Q. Easton, *Charting Chicago School Reform: Democratic Localism as a Lever for Change* (Boulder, CO: Westview

Press, 1998), G. Alfred Hess, Jr., *Restructuring Urban Schools: A Chicago Perspective* (New York: Teachers College Press, 1995), Jeffrey Mirel, "School Reform, Chicago Style: Educational Innovation in a Changing Urban Context, 1976–1991" *Urban Education* July 1993 28(2): 116–149, Anthony Bryk and others, "The State of Chicago School Reform" *Phi Delta Kappan* September 1994 76(1): 74–78, and Melissa Roderick, Brian A. Jacob, and Anthony S. Bryk, "The Impact of High-Stakes Testing in Chicago on Student Achievement in Promotional Gate Grades" *Educational Evaluation and Policy Analysis* Winter 2002 24(4): 333–357. For a somewhat different perspective, see Michael B. Katz, Michelle Fine, and Elaine Simon, "Poking Around: Outsiders View Chicago School Reform" *Teachers College Record* 1997 99(1): 117–157, Michael B. Katz, *Improving Poor People: The Welfare State, the "Underclass," and Urban Schools as History* (Princeton: Princeton University Press, 1995), Dorothy Shipps, "The Invisible Hand: Big Business and Chicago School Reform" *Teachers College Record* 1997 99(1): 73–116, Pauline Lipman, "Making the Global City, Making Inequality: The Political Economy and Cultural Politics of Chicago School Policy" *American Educational Research Journal* Summer 2002 39(2): 379–419, and her book, Lipman, *High Stakes Education: Inequality, Globalization, and Urban School Reform* (New York: Routledge Falmer, 2004).

Finally, there is a growing literature on the "new" immigrants in American cities, and the educational fortunes of their children. On these questions, see Alejandro Portes, Rubèn G. Rumbaut, *Legacies: The Story of the Immigrant Second Generation* (Berkeley: University of California Press, 2001), Rubèn G. Rumbaut and Alejandro Portes, eds., *Ethnicities: Children of Immigrants in America* (Berkeley: University of California Press, 2001), Alejandro Portes and Dag MacLeod, "Educational Progress of Children of Immigrants: The Roles of Class, Ethnicity, and School Context" *Sociology of Education* October 1996 69(4): 255–275, Carl L. Bankston III, Min Zhou, "Being Well vs. Doing Well: Self-Esteem and School Performance among Immigrant and Nonimmigrant Racial and Ethnic Groups" *International Migration Review* Summer 2002 36(2): 389–415, and Lamar P. Miller and Lisa A. Tanners, "Diversity and the New Immigrants" *Teachers College Record* 1995 96(4): 671–680. For an international perspective on these issues, see Marta Tienda and William Julius Wilson, eds., *Youth in Cities: A Cross-national Perspective* (New York: Cambridge University Press, 2002).

14

AFTER THE FALL: CONTINUITY
AND CHANGE IN DETROIT,
1981–1995

Jeffrey Mirel

In 1988, a group of reformers—blacks and whites, Democrats and Republicans, business and labor—forged a well-financed and apparently powerful political coalition to take control of the Detroit Board of Education. Running as the HOPE coalition (the anagram made up of the first letter of the last name of the three candidates: Hayden, Olmstead, and Patrick for Education), these reformers promised to change the Detroit schools in ways that were quite similar to those the "new Progressives" had implemented in other cities. Upon their election to the board, the HOPE candidates worked diligently to place the school system on a firm financial footing, to run it in a more efficient manner, to establish closer ties with the city's business community, to decentralize the district by empowering principals and local schools, and to create schools of choice that would enable parents to have alternatives to neighborhood schools. Despite some notable successes in these areas, in 1992, the HOPE initiatives abruptly ended as voters turned most of the reformers out of office following a series of bitter confrontations and crises.

Analyzing what led up to the HOPE campaign, what contributed to its rapid demise, and what its legacy appears to be can provide something of a cautionary tale about the prospects for educational reform in large cities and, importantly, about the challenges facing the new "Progressive" mayors. Certainly, the most lasting change and, for a time, the crowning achievement of the old Progressives was their transformation of urban public education. Unless the "new Progressives" find some way to reform urban schools, not merely by changing their structure but also by dramatically improving the quality of education, then their impact on major cities and the prospects for a revitalized American politics based on their efforts will be far less impressive and far less important than their current press notices imply. In this regard, Detroit has much to tell us.

CONTINUING CRISES AND CALLS FOR CHANGE, 1981–1988

Until quite recently, little seemed to have changed in Detroit since the disastrous 1970s. A reporter for the *Toronto Star* who visited the city in 1993 described it as "a ghost town. The utter desolation takes your breath away. There's no way to adequately prepare for what you see in Detroit . . . It's a city of broken glass, abandoned buildings, wind whistling through empty skyscrapers, tall grass blowing in empty lots and seagulls feeding on the debris of America." The reporter described large sections of the city as decaying into wilderness. In the 1980s, the city issued almost 42,000 more permits for the demolition of buildings than permits for new construction. As many as 40 percent of the buildings in the city were abandoned. There were reports of people seeing coyotes prowling through the streets of what once had been thriving neighborhoods. Detroit, one urbanologist stated, was "past the point of no return."[1]

During the 1980s, the city's population continued the precipitous decline that had begun four decades earlier. At its peak in 1950, Detroit had almost 1.9 million people. Over the next 40 years, the city lost almost 47 percent of its population, registering just over 1 million inhabitants in the most recent census. One consequence of that massive population loss was the increasing racial and social class homogenization of the city. Due to the almost unrelenting exodus of whites since the 1950s, by 1990 over three-quarters of Detroit's inhabitants were African American, most of whom lived in racially isolated neighborhoods. According to sociologists Reynolds Farley and William Frey, in 1990 Detroit ranked as "the most segregated" of the forty-seven cities in the United States with populations of a million or more.[2]

Detroit remained not only racially segregated but also overwhelmingly poor. Since the 1970s, the city has become a classic case of deindustrialization with a massive loss of manufacturing jobs. Not surprisingly, it has suffered from chronically high rates of unemployment. As late as 1992, unemployment in the city stood at over 15 percent, more than double the United States average. Due in large part to the growing national economy, in 1997 the jobless rate in Detroit fell to under 8 percent, still comparatively high but a considerable improvement over the past. Despite such improvements the long-term effects of deindustrialization have been slow to disappear. A recent report by New Detroit, Inc., a civic organization formed in the aftermath of the 1967 riot, noted that despite improvements in employment "[p]er capita income of Detroit residents is less than one-half that of surrounding suburbs."[3] No group was affected more profoundly by the deterioration of the city than Detroit's children. According to a study done by the Children's Defense Fund, in 1990 over 46 percent of Detroit's children were living in poverty, one of the highest rates in the nation. Ominously, that figure represented an almost 50 percent *increase* over what it had been ten years before.[4]

Throughout the 1980s, educators in Detroit struggled to find ways to provide a decent education for the children who entered the public schools.

Following the 1981 election that ended eight controversy-filled years of decentralization, the schools were run by an eleven-member board of education, seven members elected from districts and four elected at-large. That board, however, did not have full control over the schools for most of the decade. Due to the *Milliken v. Bradley* desegregation case the system remained under the supervision of a federal judge until 1989, at which time the experiment with court-ordered busing quietly ended. Yet the divisiveness of the busing controversy left a lasting legacy on the Detroit schools. As numerous commentators have pointed out, busing was a key factor behind white flight from the city and the subsequent steep drop in school enrollments. In 1966, when the system hit its peak enrollment, the Detroit Public Schools served almost 300,000 students who were about evenly divided between blacks and whites. Twenty-four years later, enrollment had fallen to 170,000, approximately 90 percent of whom were African American. Most of these children, over two-thirds according to recent estimates, came from families living below the poverty line.[5]

Despite difficult circumstances, there were some positive educational developments in the post-decentralization era-elementary students, for example, gradually improved their performance on the California Achievement Test and the Michigan Assessment of Educational Progress tests.[6] Similar gains, however, did not occur in the high schools which remained deeply troubled institutions. Despite some exceptions (notably Cass Tech and Renaissance High), students in Detroit high schools performed at a level that the chair of the federal court monitoring commission called "deplorable." Throughout the 1980s, the high school drop-out rate ranged from 41 to at times 57 percent. Yet, even graduating seniors lacked the basic reading and math skills necessary to succeed in the modern workplace, a situation attested to by the abysmal scores of Detroit students on the American College Test (ACT). In 1987, the average ACT score in Detroit was about 14, more than four points below the national average. A *Detroit News* survey found that Detroit high school students had the lowest average ACT and SAT scores of the ten largest school districts in the nation.[7] Contributing to the on-going failure of the high schools were chronic problems of order and discipline declining academic standards. The problem of disorderly, often violent schools began in the late 1960s and continued almost unabated into the 1980s. A 1984 study by the federal monitoring commission found that fatal shootings or stabbings in or around schools, assaults on students and teachers, and a ready supply of weapons and drugs on school grounds all remained frighteningly common in Detroit high schools. The study reported that in the previous year 1,287 assaults or batteries, 943 weapons confiscations, and 384 drug incidents occurred in Detroit schools. Three years later another survey found that over half of Detroit teachers reported that violence was a "frequent—if not daily" part of their school experience.[8] The consequences of this climate of violence for education were inevitable. The 1987 survey of teachers noted that "the victims of the troubled system are the vast majority of good students who are denied a quality education because a few create an atmosphere of danger and disorder."[9]

Declining academic standards had become a chronic problem since the end of World War II as increasing numbers of white working class and black high school students in Detroit were routinely and disproportionately placed in the general track and fed a steady diet of watered-down academic and personal development courses. This pattern did not change when the school system became majority black in the 1960s. As the nation began to raise graduation requirements in the late 1970s, Detroit followed suit, increasing the total credit hours for graduation from 160 to 200 and increasing the number of academic courses needed to graduate (e.g., the math requirement rose from one to two years). At the same time, however, school leaders doubled the credit hours granted for a host of non-academic courses which to some extent neutralized the impact of the increases in academic subjects. Moreover, the system created a number of new "academic" courses that focused mainly on very basic skills and knowledge. For example, Detroit students could take a four-year math sequence—Freshman Math, Junior Math, and Math Competency 1 and 2 which amounted to simply four years of general math. In 1983, the system did put into place a basic skills competency test which when passed allowed students to graduate with an "endorsed," but not a regular, high school diploma.[10]

While the continuing violence and academic problems provided much of the impetus for the late 1980s reform movement in Detroit, as in the past, the single most important factor contributing to calls for change were fiscal crises. During the 1980s, the financial and political woes that had brought the system to the brink of bankruptcy in the early 1970s—a shrinking tax base, the continuing exodus of manufacturing jobs and middle-class families, declining state and federal aid, and increasing costs for salaries and other necessities—now combined with several additional elements to create a new series of dire fiscal emergencies.[11]

First, the severe recession of the early 1980s—in which "the US auto industry experienced an economic slide unparalleled since the Great Depression"—had a devastating impact on the local and state economies. Unemployment rose to double-digit levels in Detroit and remained at those levels into the 1990s. As in the Great Depression, these conditions put severe strains on the ability of the school system and the state to provide adequate funds for education.[12]

Second, the board's ability to address its financial problems remained severely constrained. This was due in part to the continued monitoring of the system by the federal court and the increasing power of the state over local educational decisions. Moreover, during the 1980s, the Detroit Federation of Teachers (DFT) gradually emerged as the single, most important interest group in educational politics in the city. As in the late 1960s and 1970s, teachers continued to see the DFT as an island of stability and as a source of protection in the turbulent educational environment of the Detroit school system. Rank-and-file teachers were generally united behind union leaders, a fact that gave those leaders considerable influence in the political arena. While the DFT did not win *all* its battles with the board, it became increasingly clear that nothing could be accomplished either financially or educationally without the commitment of the union.

Third, the nature of racial politics in the city, region, and state changed in subtle but significant ways. In 1981, John Elliot took over as the president of the DFT, becoming the first African American to hold that position. From that point on, virtually every major figure involved in local educational politics—the school board president, the superintendent of schools, the union president, and the mayor—was African American. That change in leadership reflected the new political reality of Detroit. Since the mid-1970s, African Americans had become a voting majority in the city, a fact that had a dramatic impact on leadership and more generally on politics in the city. For example, millage elections that often had pitted whites against blacks in the 1960s and 1970s became calmer and quieter affairs in the 1980s. Not only did the elections become less contentious, they also became more predictable. Black Detroiters had consistently supported higher taxes for the schools since the 1940s and that support did not waiver as the century wore on. Consequently, between September 1977 and November 1985, Detroit voters approved eight out of nine requests by the board for tax renewals or tax increases. The only defeat, of an August 1980 request for a 3.5 mill tax increase, was reversed three months later when it reappeared on the November ballot.[13]

These changes in leadership and politics did not mark the end of the financial problems of the schools. Nor did they mean that race had disappeared as a factor in the issue of school finance in Detroit. They did, however, indicate that the influence of race on educational issues had become less overt than in the 1960s and 1970s. Whites still controlled powerful institutions such as the Greater Detroit Chamber of Commerce, the two daily newspapers, indeed almost every major media outlet in the city. Above all, whites played a dominant role in state government. The power of all these institutions *especially* in the area of school finance was considerable. During the 1980s, for example, the state government provided between 50 to 60 percent of the total budget of the Detroit Public Schools, a situation that gave state-level political and educational leaders enormous leverage over the school system particularly during periods of financial crisis.[14]

Unfortunately for Detroit, in the 1980s all these factors came into play, as the school system suffered from a series of chronic financial problems. Beginning in 1978, the system began running annual budget deficits. They ranged from a low of $10 million in mid-decade to a high of almost $160 million in 1989. All of the factors noted earlier combined to create the financial emergency. The deteriorating economic situation in the city and state in the early 1980s led to reduced property values, lower local tax revenues, and less state aid. The board was hampered in its ability to respond to this situation by the limited amounts of money it could raise through tax increases (and the negative consequences of those increases) and by the power of the unions in regard to which policies and actions it would support.[15]

In 1982, for example, the board attempted to reduce a $37 million deficit by asking the unions to accept salary and fringe benefit concessions. The DFT rejected the request stating that the board should not expect teachers to bear the full burden of reducing the deficit. Following fruitless negotiations, the teachers walked off the job for 17 days to preserve their contract. Following binding arbitration, the DFT agreed to $20 million in concessions set up as a loan to the board. These concessions, however, failed to end the deficit, causing the board to freeze salaries for the 1983–84 school year. Unfortunately, even that freeze did not reduce the shortfall which by August 1984 was estimated at over $43 million. The only solution to the problem was another tax increase.[16]

In November 1984, Detroit voters approved a 4-mill increase in their school taxes, the third increase in seven years. The benefits of this boost in revenues, however, were short-lived. Having made salary concessions to the board during hard times, concessions that had caused the salaries of Detroit teachers to slip further behind those of suburban teachers, DFT leaders were in no mood to compromise when they sat down to negotiate the 1985–86 contract. Seeing the funds raised by the tax increase as money that would bring them closer to parity with suburban teachers, the DFT threatened to strike again unless Detroit teachers got substantial raises. This was not a frivolous demand. DFT leaders realized that unless Detroit teachers received salaries at least equal to those in the suburbs, it would be increasingly difficult both to attract and to retain talented teachers. Why would good teachers come to Detroit if they could find better working conditions *and* far better salaries in the suburbs? Such arguments and the unity displayed by the teachers behind their leaders, ultimately compelled the board to grant a 10-percent increase for 1985–86 and a 7-percent increase for 1986–87. Rather than being magnanimous in victory, however, DFT president John Elliot declared, "We got every dime they had."[17] These raises made it virtually impossible for the board to reduce the deficit without major layoffs or school closings, actions it was unwilling to take.

Over the next two years the deficit gradually rose, a trend that set the stage for an even more serious confrontation between the union and the board in the fall of 1987. In many ways 1987 seemed like a replay of all the developments of the previous five years. Now facing a $27 million shortfall the board announced a no-raise budget and called for other concessions from the teachers in order to pay off the debt. Carol Thomas, vice president of the DFT, angrily responded that "[t]he board's priorities are misplaced. The teachers should come first on that budget and everything else next." Negotiations with the board went nowhere, and on September 2, the DFT set up picket lines. The strike lasted three weeks and ended with a contract that gave the teachers a 6.5 percent raise for 1987–88, 7 percent for 1988–89, and the promise of 6 percent for 1989–90.[18]

This time, however, several new factors entered the political mix producing the most volatile political situation the schools had faced in two decades. First, throughout the strike, the school board was dogged by allegations of malfeasance and misuse of funds. Since the early 1970s, board members had been criticized for their use of chauffeur-driven cars and exorbitant travel expenses which often included first-class air fares, criticism that sharpened during the 1986 school board election. As the 1987 financial crisis worsened, these criticisms grew into howls of protest particularly after a front page exposé in the *Detroit News* reported that the chauffeurs made more than the average Detroit teacher, that the board had spent nearly $500,000 on chauffeurs in the previous seventeen months, and that board members had spent $70,000 in out-of-state travel during the 1986–87 school year. These expenses symbolized for many Detroiters a board that was more interested in perks and privileges for its members than in rescuing the financially strapped school system from its plight. The president of New Detroit, Inc., declared that "It appears that the board members place their own well being ahead of the children. The trips and chauffeured cars, in the face of layoffs are outrageous."

Several board members utterly rejected this assessment and charged that the criticisms were racially motivated. They argued that when whites controlled the board no one questioned the expenses. Board member Alonzo Bates, defended his first-class travel declaring, "We as blacks don't have positions young people aspire to. We have blacks in sports as performers but we don't have managers or executives. I want young people to see me traveling first class and say 'This is a position I want to be in.' "[19]

More important than these battles over symbolism (eliminating the travel expenses would hardly have made a dent in the deficit) was the fact that the board simply could not pay for the raises it had granted the teachers. Within days of announcing the new contract, school leaders warned that the agreement would lead to a $50 million deficit by June 1988. A year later, they projected that the deficit would surpass $150 million, equal to about 20 percent of the system's operating budget. With an impending financial catastrophe looming, the board began to look at layoffs, school closings, and another tax increase, actions that only further outraged parents and community leaders. In October 1987 angry Detroiters began circulating petitions to recall all eleven board members.[20]

In desperation, the board asked the state to approve the sale of a series of short-term bonds to keep the system afloat. This request, however, created new problems. In a scenario reminiscent of the confrontation in the 1930s between the board and the Stone Committee (when a group of bankers and business leaders had demanded budgetary cutbacks from the school board before approving loans to the city), state treasurer Robert Bowman refused to approve the sale of the bonds until the board brought its travel policies in line with those of state employees and ended its use of chauffeurs. Board members responded angrily to what they saw as an attempt by the state to usurp their prerogatives. They were, after all, elected officials. Nevertheless, they ultimately accepted Bowman's terms.[21] Amid this growing crisis the mood of large numbers of Detroiters and leaders of major civic organizations coalesced into a powerful movement for change, the HOPE campaign.

THE HOPE YEARS, 1988–93

In many ways the coalition that formed to take control of the Detroit school board in 1988 supports Peter Beinart's thesis that a new form of Progressivism is emerging in America's great cities. Like the Progressive Era consensus that shaped educational politics in Detroit in the 1920s, the HOPE campaign had the backing of a wide variety of interest groups including the Greater Detroit Chamber of Commerce, the Metropolitan Detroit AFL-CIO, the Detroit Federation of Teachers, civic organizations such as New Detroit, Inc., and a number of grass-roots community organizations. The HOPE candidates received the endorsement of both daily newspapers and all the other major media outlets. The leading contributors to the campaign were a prominent local Republican who donated $1,000 and the DFT which contributed $5,000.[22] Moreover, the themes the HOPE candidates stressed in their campaign echoed those that dominated Progressive politics in Detroit in the 1910s and 1920s—the moral integrity of the reformers, their desire to restore public confidence in the school board through their commitment to the wise stewardship of funds, their ability to get the school system's fiscal house in order, their promise to run the schools more efficiently and effectively, and their plans to introduce corporate structural and management innovations.

The backgrounds of the HOPE candidates represented the remarkable diversity of the coalition. The HOPE group included Frank Hayden, an African-American city employee who served as chair of the School-Community Relations Organization; David Olmstead, a white corporate attorney and former member of the Michigan School Finance Commission; Lawrence Patrick, a black Republican and an attorney who was co-chair of the Group of Organized Detroiters for Quality Education (GOOD); and Joseph Blanding, an African American who worked as an international representative of the United Auto Workers. Several of them had been active in groups that for some time had sought to develop an interracial coalition to take over the school board and to introduce dramatic reforms into the system.[23]

The 1988 school board campaign was one of the most highly publicized in the history of the school system. Mayor Coleman Young supported the incumbents who included Alonzo Bates and Clara Rutherford, two veteran board members. While the most pressing problems facing the system were the financial crisis, the continuing violence, and the poor performance of the students, much of the attention in both the primary and general election campaigns, as in the Progressive Era, was focused on the moral character of the board members and their challengers. The HOPE group denounced the profligate spending of the incumbents on chauffeurs and travel, repeating allegations that such spending showed an utter lack of conmiitment to fiscal responsibility. The incumbents responded by stressing the challengers' lack of experience and accusing them of being tools of white suburbanites, the media, and business interests.[24]

The election did provide a clear choice to the voters. The incumbents ran on their records rather than on proposals for change. They responded to the looming deficit by presenting the voters with a "financial rescue plan" that included a 6-mill tax increase and a $160 million bond issue. These proposals appeared on the same November ballot as the school board election. In contrast, the HOPE group offered an "education revolution" as they put it. Although vague in terms of how they would address the deficit, the HOPE group assured the voters that they unquestionably could do a better job than the incumbents. Moreover, their promises to bring financial stability to the system was strengthened by the support they had received from the business community, from David Olmstead's experience with school finance on the state level, and from their image as outsiders unsullied by allegations about misspent funds.[25] The major educational components of HOPE's "revolution," empowering local schools and creating schools of choice, received considerably less attention during the campaign than did the budget problems. At the time, that lack of attention did not appear to be troublesome. Eventually it would play an important role in the problems the HOPE team faced in implementing its reforms.

The election was a stunning success for the HOPE candidates. All of them received over 100,000 votes, 20,000 more than the closest incumbent. The voters did not merely vote the incumbents out of office; they sent a strong message of disgust with the system by rejecting the incumbents' financial rescue plan, defeating both the 6-mill tax increase and the $160 million bond issue. In all, as the *Detroit News* education reporter put it, "The defeat of four incumbents combined with the defeat of the tax increase and bond issue was the biggest shake up of Detroit school leadership in at least two decades."[26]

Despite their apparent mandate and Lawrence Patrick's election as president of the school board, the HOPE team's first six months in office were tumultuous. Early on they made some serious political blunders such as first agreeing to place another tax increase on the ballot and soon after deciding to remove it. In addition, during these months they had to address a series of demands from state officials to cut the budget and appoint a new superintendent in order to keep state loan money flowing. Accompanying these demands were repeated threats that the state would take over the school system if the board did not get its fiscal house in order. Joining the chorus of criticism, Mayor Coleman Young called for the abolition of the school board altogether and demanded that the system be brought under the direct control of the mayor's office.[27]

By August 1989, these initial crises were resolved. Bowing to state pressure, the reformers appointed John Porter as interim school superintendent. Having served as the president of Eastern Michigan University and as state superintendent of schools (the first African American to hold that position), Porter proved to be an inspired choice. He quickly fashioned a plan for rescuing the system from its chronic financial problems, built a strong political coalition behind that plan, and negotiated a new contract with the DFT.[28]

Porter's plan to rescue the school system from its financial crisis was quite similar to the one that the previous board had offered the voters in November 1988, namely a 6-mill tax increase to pay for operating expenses (particularly raises promised to the teachers) and a $150 million bond issue (equal to another 1.5-mill tax increase) to pay off the deficit. The difference, of course, was that, first, the public had no confidence in the ability of the previous board to use that new revenue wisely and, second, Detroiters continued to believe that the new HOPE-led board, despite its early missteps, would use the funds to make positive changes in the system. This renewed public confidence was reflected in the about-face that a number of leading civic organizations made on the issue of tax increases. The Greater Detroit Chamber of Commerce, the Detroit Association of Black Organizations, Black Parents for Quality Education, and New Detroit, Inc., all had opposed the November 1988 measures but now backed the increases on the September 1989 ballot. Both measures won with over 60 percent of the vote, a fact that convinced the HOPE team that the public was solidly behind its leadership and reform efforts.[29] As a result of this election, the Detroit schools were fiscally stable for the first time in a decade, and with that stability came the opportunity to plan for educational reform without the fear that changes would be overwhelmed by recurring budget crises.

The HOPE team advocated two major reform efforts: "empowered schools" and "schools of choice." Supporting school empowerment, initially viewed as a form of school-based management, was one of the key terms which the DFT had agreed to in its 1989 contract.[30] Implementing empowerment, however, took longer than expected. The delay was because of the time the board spent wrestling with financial problems and because the HOPE team still needed time to consolidate its power. Eventually, the HOPE group gained control of 10 of the 11 board seats, and from that position of strength, it started its quest for dramatic educational change. Efforts began in earnest in July 1991 when the board replaced John Porter as superintendent. (Porter had declared early on that he did not want his position as interim superintendent to become permanent.) In his place, the board appointed Deborah McGriff, deputy superintendent from Milwaukee, a strong supporter of both empowered schools and school choice. McGriff was the first African-American woman to serve as superintendent of the Detroit schools and the first "outsider" to take the permanent position of general superintendent in over two decades.[31] Secure in their control of the board and led by a superintendent who fully backed their reform efforts, in 1991 the HOPE team began a major push for empowered schools and schools of choice.[32]

Few aspects of HOPE's reform agenda more clearly embodied the spirit of the new, urban Progressivism than their plan for school empowerment. In their 1988 campaign literature, the HOPE team described empowered schools as ones that receive "greater decision-making authority through a process in which the principal establishes regular and meaningful opportunities for representatives of students, parents, community administrators, instructional and non-instructional staff to have input into the selection of areas and/or problems which are addressed and to suggest the solutions and strategies to be used." Ultimately, this concept of empowered schools went beyond simply shifting authority from the central administration to local schools. Uniting ideas from corporate restructuring, site-based management, privatization, changes in union-management work rules in the auto industry, and the experiments in educational decentralization then underway in Chicago, Miami, and Rochester, the Detroit reformers fashioned one of the most dramatic plans for restructuring urban education in over a century.[33]

Once the principal, 75 percent of the teachers, 55 percent of the support staff, 55 percent of the parents, and 55 percent of the students voted in favor of their school becoming "empowered," the board allocated 92 percent of the district's per-pupil allocation (about $4,000 in 1992) to the school for it to spend as it wished. Non-empowered schools received only about 70 percent of the per-pupil allocation. Run by a School Empowerment Council composed of the educators and parents, empowered schools were free to determine such things as faculty assignments, how funds should be spent, how classes and schedules should be configured, the nature of the curriculum, even the length of the school year, indeed virtually every aspect of providing education for their students.

The relationship between the schools and the central administration also changed. The central administration expected to monitor the empowered schools to insure they maintained a balanced budget and met district-wide achievement standards but beyond that the empowered schools were free from any mandatory involvement with the central administration. For example, unlike other schools in the district, the empowered schools did not have to get their services from the central office. If cheaper or better suppliers could be found in private industry, empowered schools could contract with them. The central administration became simply one of many vendors for such things as school supplies, building materials, maintenance services, even in-service training for teachers and staff. The HOPE team was convinced that this arrangement put school-level policy and financial decisions into the hands of those people who knew best how to make them—the people who actually worked with students. Moreover, the HOPE team was convinced that this arrangement would transform the central school bureaucracy itself by forcing it to become competitive with private industry in terms of quality and efficiency or, failing that, by forcing it to close down operations that could not compete.[34]

The second initiative, creating schools of choice, was equally bold. Expanding on the success of the two city-wide magnet high schools, Cass Tech and Renaissance, the HOPE team sought to expand choices for younger children by creating a series of magnet elementary schools across the city. Ideally these schools would function to stimulate competition for students throughout the city, competition that ultimately would lead to improved schools throughout the system. By 1993, a number of different models existed for these schools of choice including professional development schools that had partnership agreements with area universities, schools modeled after James Corner's successful reform projects in New Haven, Connecticut, and several Afrocentric academies. Of these, the most successful in terms of implementation and the most nationally visible during the HOPE years were the Afrocentric academies—the Marcus Garvey Academy, the Malcolm X Academy, and the Paul Robeson Academy. These schools still operate as magnet elementary schools and offer a highly structured, African-centered education. Parental involvement with the schools is required, dress codes are mandatory, fighting and chronic disciplinary problems in the schools are not tolerated, and a committed teaching staff sets high academic and behavioral standards for all students. Like the magnet high schools, Cass Tech and Renaissance High, almost since their inception these choice schools have led the district in standardized test scores.[35]

Despite this success and the intriguing possibilities that these initiatives opened up, both the schools of choice and the empowered schools became controversial. The first conflict erupted over the Afrocentric academies that the board had initially designated as all-male institutions. According to Detroit's leading proponents of the all-male schools, Clifford Watson and Geneva Smitherman, the "underlying rationale" for these schools was "that a unique school program is necessary to address the unique problems of urban males." The American Civil Liberties Union and the National Organization of Women disagreed with that premise and filed a successful lawsuit claiming that black girls were as deserving and as in need of unique educational efforts as were black boys. A federal judge eventually ruled that prohibiting girls from attending the schools constituted gender discrimination, and the board was forced to grant them admission. Despite that federal court order, the schools have continued to serve a largely male student body.[36] Settling the conflict over the all-male status of the academies, however, did not end criticism of the schools of choice. Community activists and parents from across the district increasingly argued that these "boutique schools," as they called them, were elitist and that the board was diverting funds from neighborhood schools to support them.[37]

As contentious as were the debates about the all-male academies and the other schools of choice, they were nothing in comparison to the outcry that began in late 1991 over the empowered schools. Unlike the responses to the Afrocentric academies, initially there was little controversy about empowerment. Observers believed that all fifteen of the newly empowered schools (about 6 percent of those in the district) had gotten off to promising starts. Nevertheless, throughout the 1991–92 school year, opposition to this reform grew. In December 1991, with thirty more schools ready to vote on empowerment, the union issued an "embargo" on empowerment, in essence forbidding its members to continue the process of empowering schools. The problem emerged when the board tried to get the union to move beyond its earlier commitment to empowerment by demanding that it agree to a set of policies that would give empowered schools greater flexibility in operating. These policies included the right to waive provisions of the union contract without seeking the approval of the union, providing higher salaries to "lead teachers" in the empowered schools, and authorizing the schools to select their own teachers. Such policies ran directly into long-standing DFT concerns about decentralization, arbitrary dismissals of teachers, and the sanctity of their union contract. In 1973, similar fears had precipitated the worst strike in the history of the school system. In this case, the DFT was joined by every union in the system in lashing out at empowerment mainly because of concerns about "job security, privatization of some school services, and [the] transfer of staff."[38]

Negotiations between the DFT and the board broke down just before school was scheduled to start, and on August 31, 1992, the union again went on strike. Empowerment was the key issue in the walkout. Arguing that granting waivers to empowered schools would essentially "gut the contract in those schools," DFT president John Elliot declared, "We will not even allow that possibility." Elliot explained that the DFT opposed empowerment because the teachers preferred a centralized school system in which work rules and procedures were uniform. Moreover, he argued that teachers in empowered schools would have no protection from "vindictive administrators" who might transfer them for personal or arbitrary reasons and once transferred these teachers had no guarantee they would be placed in another school. Such an outcome in essence eliminated tenure.[39]

The DFT received strong support from the Organization of School Administrators and Supervisors (OSAS), the administrators' union, which argued that forcing principals to deal with such issues as purchasing supplies and negotiating with contractors reduced their ability to be educational leaders. Helen Martelock, president of OSAS declared, "I'm not certain that paying the light bill, buying toilet paper, and arranging for garbage pickup and snow removal has a whole lot to do with schools." OSAS also feared that empowerment would lead to a form of outsourcing which would enable the board to cut supervisory jobs in the central office. Like the DFT, OSAS questioned the effectiveness of school-based management generally, noting accurately that the practice had not produced great results in other school systems. Indeed, both the DFT and OSAS blanketly dismissed empowerment as "a management strategy, not a tool for improving education."[40]

Faced with such determined opposition the HOPE team desperately tried to convince the unions and the public that its proposals were neither anti-union nor impractical. David Olmstead dismissed the DFT's allegations about gutting the contract and the loss of job security as "a parade of imaginary horribles." Rather than being anti-union, he argued that the board's proposals were akin to those that the United Auto Workers had agreed to in which the union still negotiated wages and other large, systemic issues with central management but allowed each local to negotiate work rules at individual plants. Olmstead declared, "I truly believe this board is more strongly in favor of teachers than the union is." This dispute, he declared, was "about whether the union or the teachers will be in control." Lawrence Patrick was more blunt. Pointing out that the board was not *mandating* any reforms, that the decision to seek empowerment was entirely voluntary on the part of administrators and teachers, Patrick questioned whether John Elliot really spoke for his members. "If nobody wants to do it," he asked, "then what is he afraid of?"

In response to union arguments that teachers preferred the traditional centralized system and that these reforms were just a "management strategy," one ally of the board stated bluntly that the old system had failed and that new strategies had to be tried, declaring "bureaucracy has not worked which is exactly why the board wanted empowerment." Critics of the DFT and OSAS noted that the unions were offering nothing more than business as usual, a situation that had made the Detroit school system one of the worst in the nation.[41]

The ensuing strike dragged on for twenty-seven days punctuated by increasingly angry exchanges between the board and the union, especially after the board went to court and obtained a back-to-work order, an order that the teachers overwhelmingly ignored. The contract to which the board finally agreed was an almost complete victory for the union. It contained a face-saving provision for the board to increase the number of empowered schools to forty-five but the terms of empowerment were minimal—the contract provisions that empowered schools could waive were only in "non-controversial" areas such as parent–teacher conferences, selecting textbooks, and choosing testing materials. The contract also included salary increases for the next two years that again threatened to throw the district's budget out of balance.[42]

The agreement and the return to work by the teachers did not reduce tensions between the union and the board. The four HOPE board members were running for re-election in November, and the emotions and controversies that had raged during the strike continued without pause in the campaign. Unlike 1988 when the Detroit AFL-CIO and the DFT had strongly supported the HOPE candidates, in 1992 the unions actively campaigned against them, tarring them as anti-labor. Put simply, the unions accused the board of using empowerment as a tool for "union-busting." Joining organized labor in their opposition to the HOPE group were community activists who denounced the HOPE candidates as elitists who tried to stratify education in Detroit through the promotion of the schools of choice.[43]

The board members tried to put the strike behind them and run on their record—four years of a balanced budget, test score improvement, and a lower dropout rate. "For people to judge us based on what happened [during the strike] would be unfair to us," Frank Hayden declared, "and to what we accomplished." The voters rejected those appeals. As David Olmstead noted "[b]eing called anti-union is the political curse of death in this town." In the November election three of the four HOPE candidates were defeated. Of the original HOPE team, ironically, only Lawrence Patrick, the black Republican, was re-elected.[44]

Despite the losses, allies of the HOPE team still had a 7–4 majority on the board, and they were committed to pushing on with the reforms. Indeed some of their efforts began paying dividends after the November defeat, for example, the announcement that the Skillman Foundation would provide $17.5 million to encourage the development of Comer model schools.[45] Nevertheless, the wind was very much out of the reformers' sails by 1993. A parents' organization began a recall effort against four of the remaining pro-reform board members. Progress on even the scaled-back version of empowered schools was painfully slow largely due to both an embargo placed on the process by OSAS and by budget cuts (due in part to the new contract) that eliminated $1.3 million set aside by the board to keep the process going. In October, Deborah McGriff, whose term as superintendent had been marked by almost continuous conflict and whose reappointment was uncertain, announced her resignation to accept a position with the Edison Project. David Snead, the principal of Cass Tech, and a veteran Detroit educator replaced her. Many commentators saw Snead's appointment as a signal that the old order had returned to power and that the HOPE period had come to an end.[46]

AFTERMATH

The failure of the HOPE reform effort raises a number of interesting questions. First, why did what seemed to be a promising and widely supported reform movement fail so quickly? Second, what are the implications of that failure for the prospects of a revitalized urban politics? Third, and most important for those of us concerned about urban education, what does this failure say about the possibilities for truly improving urban public schools?

In regard to the first question, the corpse of the HOPE movement was barely cold before critics began dissecting its demise. The critiques were as wide ranging as they were contradictory. Some observers such as Thomas Bray, editor of the *Detroit News*, argued that the reformers moved too slowly on their educational revolution. He claimed that they squandered their electoral mandate by focusing too much of their initial attention on the budget and not enough on choice and empowerment. Other critics took the exact opposite position, claiming that the HOPE team and Superintendent Deborah McGriff moved too quickly on the educational changes and did not give teachers and administrators enough time to accommodate to them. As one board member who supported the HOPE team put it, "We all pleaded with them to slow down. It was not what they wanted to do. It was how they did things, not the mission, where the reform group split up on the board." Other critics, particularly community activists, were less disturbed by the pace of reform than they were by the reforms themselves. These activists branded the HOPE team as elitists committed to schools of choice at the expense of neighborhood schools.

Still other detractors placed the HOPE efforts in a larger context claiming that their initiatives were too closely tied to corporate-style restructuring efforts and to Republican educational policies to have had any hope for success in a city so strongly committed to unionism and the Democratic

Party. The president of OSAS, for example, dismissed the entire reform process as a "Bush initiative." Mayor Coleman Young initially agreed, referring to empowered schools as a "concept from conservative circles" whose ultimate purpose he believed was to "privatize" the schools. Young, however, went further, characterizing the whole movement as an effort by white suburbanites to take over Detroit institutions.[47]

Certainly many of the factors cited by critics had a significant impact on the failure of the movement. But several other aspects of this situation seem to have played as large or larger a role. As noted earlier, the HOPE reformers drew some of their inspiration for empowered schools from the decentralization and school-based management experiments in Chicago, Miami, and Rochester. But the HOPE initiative differed from these experiments in one very important way—unlike them it did not draw its power or authority from a stable, dependable base. The Chicago reforms were "top-down," mandated by the state legislature, while those in Miami and Rochester were "bottom-up," initiated mainly by the union. The Detroit reformers, on the other hand, had drawn their power and authority from more volatile sources, namely the coalition that supported them in the 1988 election, and the voters who put them in office. In essence, the HOPE team believed that they could build reform upon the broad-based political support they had received and on their convincing electoral victory. That belief was flawed in two ways.

The initial error appears to have been in how the HOPE team interpreted its electoral mandate. The issues that had dominated the 1988 election were the financial crisis and the allegations of profligate spending by the incumbent board members. While the HOPE candidates promised an educational revolution and passed out literature describing school empowerment, voters were much more fixed upon the financial issues than on the promised changes. Certainly, many Detroit voters and the organizations that joined the HOPE coalition agreed with the HOPE candidates that the system needed to be changed; but it is far less certain that either a majority of the voters or the various groups in the coalition supported the specific changes the reformers introduced. By relying on their coalition and their electoral victory rather than on more stable forms of change such as revisions of state law, the reformers constructed their revolution upon a very shaky foundation.

Even more serious than this initial error was that the HOPE team underestimated the power of the DFT and overestimated the union's commitment to change. Since 1973 when the DFT shut down the system in protest against the powers granted to the decentralized, regional school boards, it was clear that no educational changes could be introduced in Detroit without DFT support. By the 1990s, the power of the DFT was probably greater than it had been at any time in the history of the school district. After the 1992 strike, one Detroit church leader declared, "I think probably the strongest influence on the Detroit Public Schools system is the teachers union . . . they've demonstrated that they're in charge. The system is in the hands of the professionals, the unions."[48]

On first glance, however, the HOPE teams' expectations that the union would support empowerment seemed quite reasonable given the strong endorsement the DFT had given the group in the 1988 election. Moreover, the reformers had reason to believe that the union agreed at least in principle to the idea of empowered schools. After all, American Federation of Teachers (AFT) president Albert Shanker was a strong supporter of the idea, other AFT locals in Miami and Rochester had led the movement for school-based management, and the DFT itself had agreed to support empowerment in the first contract they signed with the HOPE-dominated board.

The events of the early 1990s, however, revealed that the DFT was not interested in following the lead of its visionary national president, its fellow locals, or its original commitments. From a strictly economic perspective, one could interpret the union's support for the HOPE team as simply a strategy for restoring public confidence in the school board, a development that the union saw as a necessary first step in restoring the financial health of the system. Without such confidence, union leaders may have reasoned, the public would have continued to defeat tax increases which would have eliminated future raises and would have made the disturbing prospect of a state takeover of the system more likely. From that perspective, once the HOPE team resolved the system's financial problems, the DFT had no further use for them and their proposed educational changes. Even if one takes a more multifaceted view of the union's actions, that the DFT had genuinely supported school-based management at first but became disillusioned with the reforms when it appeared that they threatened the contract and job security, one still has to question why it responded so militantly to issues that clearly had been resolved in other cities engaged in decentralization efforts.[49]

Part of the reason for the failure of the union and the board to find common ground has to do with the context in which these events occurred. As the birthplace of industrial unionism and as a city with a proud but often violent history of labor relations, Detroit has developed what one business leader termed a "dysfunctional civic infrastructure." "People don't know how to talk with one another on the basis of the problem." This individual continued, ". . . the civic language of Detroit is the old style of labor negotiations. I mean in your face, side deals, don't trust anybody, you know, what can I get for myself, and the only way I can get for myself is by pushing somebody else down—very, very win-lose, very dysfunctional."[50] Seen from within the old, labor–management paradigm, John Elliot's claim during the strike that Detroit teachers opposed empowerment because they were comfortable with a highly centralized system makes more sense. Such an arrangement enabled the union to interact with the board much like the United Auto Workers might interact with Ford. But like other aspects of the factory model of schooling that remain so deeply entrenched in large urban systems, one wonders whether it may have outlived its usefulness. David Olmstead characterized the actions of the union in opposing empowerment as the "antithesis of professionalism."[51]

However, Olmstead and his fellow reformers did not totally discard the old paradigm either. By dismissing as "imaginary horribles" the union's concerns about the possible loss of tenure and the potential for arbitrary dismissals of teachers (the very issues that set off the long and deeply divisive 1973 strike), the board ignored very legitimate fears that restructuring—whether in industry or school systems—would mean job losses and weakened unions. Moreover, as the process developed, the HOPE reforms looked increasingly like a "top-down" initiative that the board was trying to impose on the union and the teachers. Regardless of whether teachers unions are strong as in Detroit or weak as in other parts of the country, it is clear that no major reforms can be implemented without the support of teachers. Given this fact and given the approach the board took to reform, the failure by the board to bring large numbers of rank-and-file teachers into the process was a serious political error. In the end, however, *none* of the educational leaders, neither those on the school board nor those in the union, shifted the terms or categories of the debate to make improving the quality of education in Detroit the preeminent concern. Rather both sides faced each other as representatives of labor and management locked in a bitter struggle in which ultimately the union had the upper hand.

Good public schools are vital for livable cities, and teachers' commitment to improving educational quality is crucial for positive changes to occur in big city school systems. However, teachers unions, as the Detroit case demonstrates, are often quite resistant to change. Yet maintaining the *status quo* is untenable. Unless big city teachers' unions become more flexible and teachers themselves assume greater professional responsibility, there is every possibility that they will be subject to a series of actions that will certainly weaken if not destroy them. More ominous is the fact that African Americans, particularly in large cities, are becoming increasingly strong proponents of educational choice. A 1993 poll, for example, found over 60 percent of African Americans supporting choice and a more recent local study found similar percentages among black Detroiters.[52] Teachers' unions and other supporters of public education cannot blithely dismiss these data as evidence of conservative political mischief or right-wing plots against the schools. Urban schools are the worst in America and black parents seeking better educational alternatives for their children are hardly dupes of conservative political or educational leaders. Unless urban schools improve, the pressure from poor and minority families for options that will allow them to move their children to other schools will only increase. Given the centrality of teachers to the success of any educational reform, teachers unions must be part of, if not the leaders of, efforts to improve urban schools.

All this leads to one final question. Assuming that teachers and teachers' unions commit to the kinds of reforms the HOPE team advocated, would things necessarily improve in urban public schools? The answer to that is, I think, only a qualified "yes." Certainly many of the reforms the HOPE team advanced and advocated are desperately needed in urban education. Stabilizing—and if possible increasing—the flow of funds to urban schools to enable educational leaders to have a more predictable future and some discretion in how they might pursue changes are fundamental prerequisites to urban educational improvement. Urban school systems cannot thrive if they continue to lurch from funding crisis to funding crisis.

But they also cannot thrive if money continues to be spent in traditional ways. As the economist Eric Hanushek has argued we must shift from asking if money makes a difference in education to questioning *where* money makes a difference and, once we have identified those areas, direct funds to them.[53] Decentralization can be an important part of that process since it both brings "front-line" educators into the process of determining where new funds might be spent and gives them the ability to address immediate problems.

Yet, as important as are stabilizing and improving funding, directing money to where it can have the best effect, and granting administrators and teachers greater control over their schools, ultimately these are insufficient for improving urban public education. They reflect what might be called, with apologies to David Tyack and Larry Cuban, our passion for "restructuring toward utopia." Since at least the Progressive Era, educational reformers have been committed to the idea that if we can only find and implement the right structure for urban schools they will improve on their own. Yet the fact is none of the restructuring in the last three decades—moving from highly centralized to highly decentralized school systems—has dramatically improved the quality of urban education.

What we have ignored in this process is curriculum and teaching, the basic stuff of educational life. As important as changing urban educational politics and economics surely are, our preoccupation with these efforts tend to overwhelm discussions of what goes on in classrooms. Yet such discussions are essential for improving the quality of urban education and insuring genuine educational progress. Even well-funded, restructured, schools will not improve urban education if teachers have not mastered the material they are supposed to teach, if what is taught in the classrooms is low level and undemanding, and if teachers believe that urban children cannot master rigorous academic content. Urban school reform must begin with teachers who know their material, with substantial changes in curriculum, with the firm belief that urban children can meet high curricular standards, and with appropriate strategies to help students meet these standards.

Such reforms are crucial largely because they focus on classrooms and students. Structural changes whether they involve better funding or decentralizing invariably concentrate on the adult components of the educational process providing, for example, better salaries or more authority for educators. We cannot assume that positive steps in these areas alone will translate into better educational outcomes for children. Curricular changes (reforms that address both content and methods) deal directly with students and for that reason are essential components for success.

Here again, the Detroit experience offers an example and a glimmer of hope. I have not given the story of curricular reform in Detroit in the 1980s and 1990s because the events described above pushed such developments

out of the public eye. Yet stepping back from the great battles over restructuring one finds steady and in some ways impressive changes in this area. By
going "back to basics" on the elementary level and toughening requirements
for high school graduation (areas that the board, administrators, and teachers
did find common ground on), in 1993 the scores of Detroit students on the
Michigan Assessment of Educational Progress (MAEP) tests began to rise.
For example, in 1992 only 19.2 percent and 16.5 percent of Detroit's fourth
graders scored in the satisfactory level of the math and reading MAEP tests
respectively. In 1995, these percentages had climbed to 40.5 and 36.3 percent
respectively. Similar increases also could be found in those two areas among
seventh graders. Indeed, in almost every grade, test scores rose although the
increases on the high school level were usually smaller than those in the lower
grades. While the percentages of Detroit students scoring at the Satisfactory
level remains far below what they should be, the trends are in the right direction. Since these test scores show that even modest curricular change can
make a difference in achievement, shifting the debates about urban education
by bringing questions of educational quality and curriculum to the fore
might inspire new, positive changes.[54]

CONCLUSION

The decline of urban education may be the greatest educational disaster of
this century. Political events in education in Detroit in the last fifteen years do
not give great reason for hope that things will change for the better any time
soon in that school system. Nevertheless, the political changes that seem to
be taking place in other major cities leave open possibilities that new alliances
and coalitions can be formed that may well improve urban life. Moreover, in
some cities (including Detroit) modest curricular and coursetaking reforms
have produced important, positive changes in achievement and outcomes.
These are not insignificant developments and they make me more hopeful
today than four years ago. The damage that has been done to our great cities
and to their schools is serious but it is repairable. Creating urban schools that
offer all their students access to the best possible education, to brighter
futures, will not be easy but it is at least possible.

NOTES

1. Linda Diebel, "Devolution of Detroit" *Toronto Star* (July 11, 1993), p. Fl.
2. Sidney Glazer, *Detroit: A Study of Urban Development* (New York Booknian,
   1965), p. 129; Southeast Michigan Council of Governments, "Community Profile
   for Detroit" (Detroit, 1997), p. 3; Wilbur C. Rich, *Black Mayors and School
   Politics: The Failure of Reform in Detroit, Gary, and Newark* (New York, 1996),
   p. 21; Reynolds Farley and William H. Frey, "Changes in the Segregation of
   Whites from Blacks during the 1980s: Small Steps Toward a More Integrated
   Society" *American Sociological Review* 59 (February), pp. 23–45.
3. Wes Smith, "Detroit Builds for a Revival" *The Chicago Tribune* (July 23, 1997),
   Sec. 1, p. 1; Barry Bluestone and Bennett Harrison, *The Deindustrialization of*

America (New York, 1989), p. 184; Fred Siegel, *The Future Once Happened Here: New York, DC, L.A. and the Fate of America's Big Cities* (New York, 1997); New Detroit, Inc. "The Face of Difference" *The Coalition* 1:1 (Spring 1997), p. 1. The aggregate unemployment figures mask how devastating the problem was for black youth whose jobless rate in the 1980s may have been as high as 50 percent. Martha Hindes, "Major Firms' Employment Down in '83" *Detroit News* (January 8, 1984), p. 1D; Joseph Radelet, "Stillness at Detroit's Racial Divide: A Perspective on Detroit's School Desegregation Court Order, 1970–1989" *The Urban Review* 23: 3 (September 1991), p. 189.

4. The Children's Defense Fund study is cited in Valerie E. Lee, Robert G. Cromnger, and Julia B. Smith, "Parental Choice of Schools and Social Stratification in Education: The Paradox of Detroit" *Educational Evaluation and Polity Analysis* 16:4 (Winter 1994), 438.

5. Don Tschirhart, "Election will revamp Detroit's school board" 28 (1982), p. 4B; Radelet, "Stillness at Detroit's Racial Divide," pp. 173–190; New Detroit, Inc., "The Face of Difference," p. 1. Busing was not the only reason that the Detroit schools lost enrollment. The poor quality of the education in most of the city schools also had an impact. Indeed, a 1990 survey conducted by the *Detroit Free Press* found that 14 percent of all African Americans in Detroit (and 25 percent of blacks with incomes over $20,000) sent their children to private or parochial schools. The figure was 43 percent for white Detroiters. Brenda Gilchrest, "A Choice that is Academic: Education System's Curriculum Drives Students Away" *Detroit Free Press* (December 17, 1990), p. 1A.

6. According to school leaders, the improvement of scores by elementary students was due mainly to teachers emphasizing the mastery of basic skills. See, Mike Wowk, "Students' Test Scores on the Rise" *Detroit News* (December 6, 1982), p. 1A; "Students Raise Scores in State Test" *Detroit News* (December 21, 1985), p. 1B; Earl Eldridge, "Reading and Math Scores Up in Detroit" *Detroit News* (December 19, 1987), p. 1B.

7. Renee D. Turner, "Renaissance High: Detroit's Beacon of Achievement" *Ebony* 63: 10 (August 1988), pp. 64, 66, 68; Mike Wowk, "Panel Rates Detroit School Gain 'Medium'" *Detroit News* (June 15, 1982), p. 12D; "Dropouts Join 'Underclass' at Alarming Rate" *Detroit News* (June 13, 1985), p. 1A; Laurie Bennett, "41% of Detroit's Pupils Drop Out" *Detroit News* (May 20, 1987), p. 1B; Mike Wowk, "Executive Says Grads Lack Skills" *Detroit News* (February 11, 1986), p. 4A; Editorial, "A City at Risk" (April 7, 1987) *Detroit News*, p. 8A. The ACT/SAT survey data are reported in William Snider, "In Backing Tax Proposals, Voters Endorse School Reforms" *Education Week* (September 20, 1989), pp. 1, 12. A 1988 poll found that only 14 percent of the people surveyed believed the graduates of the Detroit schools "were well-prepared to enter careers," while 73 percent disagreed. See, "Detroit Casts 'No' Vote on Direction of Schools" *Education Week* (November 16, 1988), p. 12.

8. On the commission's report see, Robert Ankeny, "City Schools Called Lax on Discipline" *Detroit News* (December 12, 1984), p. 3A. The survey of teachers is described in Ron Russell, "Amid Disorder, Education Fails" *Detroit News* (June 7, 1987), pp. 1A, 1SA. For additional examples see, Ron Russell, "Promising Teacher Gives Up After Students Beat Him Twice" *Detroit News* (May 10, 1984), p. 1B, 2B; "Six Shot at Detroit [High School] Ballgame" *Detroit News* (October 19, 1985), pp. 1A, 3A. Editorial, "Toward Better Schools: Discipline," *Detroit News* (May 20, 1987), p. 14A. The mother of a student wounded in a 1984 shooting at

Southeastern High School, the third shooting that week in a Detroit high school, summed up the situation, "Things are pretty bad when you send him to school not knowing if he'll come back alive in the afternoon." Don Tschirhart and Linda LaMarre, "Another Detroit Student Shot" *Detroit News* (October 25, 1984), pp. 1A, 9A.

9. "Panel Gives Schools 'F' in Discipline" *Detroit News* (February 24, 1983), pp. 1B, SB; Ron Russell, "Schools 'Tolerate Violence,' Commission Says" *Detroit News* (July 20, 1983).

10. For more detail on this see David Angus and Jeffrey Mirel, *The Failed Promise of the American High School* (New York, 1999).

11. Don Tschirhart, "New Education Board to Face Old Problems" *Detroit News* (August 12, 1982), p. 6B.

12. The quote on the auto industry is from Joe T. Darden, Richard Child Hill, June Thomas, and Richard Thomas, *Detroit: Race and Uneven Development* (Philadelphia, 1987), p. 27.

13. Robert J. Richards, "School Tax Elections" *Detroit News* (October 30, 1987), p. 4B.

14. In 1984–85, for example, Detroit received 55.2 percent of its revenue from the state, 34.3 percent from local taxes, and 10.5 percent from the federal government. By 1991–92, the schools were getting 60.1 percent of their funds from the state, 28.6 percent locally, and 11.2 percent from the federal government. National Center for Education Statistics, *Digest of Education Statistics 1988* (Washington, DC, 1988), pp. 88–89; National Center for Education Statistics, *Digest of Education Statistics 1993* (Washington, DC, 1993), p. 100. See also, Don Tschirhart, "Detroit Teachers Shun Concessions" *Detroit News* (August 13, 1982), p. 3A; Darrell Dawsey, "School Budget Allows no Pay Raises" *Detroit News* (July 2, 1987), p. 3B.

15. Laura D. Varon, "Red Ink" *Detroit News* (June 21, 1988), p. 1B. Between 1974 and 1984, for example, the Detroit schools had fallen from 61st to 119th in per pupil expenditures and from 49th to 135th in average teacher salaries. Ron Russell, "Per-pupil Spending Drops" *Detroit News* (March 28, 1984), p. 1A; Ron Russell, "Inequities in Schools Growing" *Detroit News* (April 16, 1985), p. 1A.

16. Tschirhart, "Detroit Teachers Shun Concessions"; Peter Lochbiler, "Teachers Walk Out in Detroit" *Detroit News* (September 13, 1982), p. 1A; Don Tschirhart, "Pupils in Class as Strike Ends" *Detroit News* (August 13, 1982), p. 1A, Don Tschirhart, "Detroit Teachers' Vote Highlights Weak Law" *Detroit News* (August 13, 1982), p. 1A; Ron Russell, "Budget Freezes Pay for Teachers" *Detroit News* (July 2, 1983), p. 1A; Mike Wowk, "4-Mill Tax Hike Urged for Schools" *Detroit News* (August 24, 1984), pp. 1A, 7A.

17. Mike Wowk, "Immediate Results Seen from School Millage Hike" *Detroit News* (November 8, 1984), pp. 1D, 8D; Mike Wowk, "Detroit Teachers Get 10% Pay Raise" *Detroit News* (August 27, 1985), p. 1A.

18. Dawsey, "School Budget Allows no Pay Raises"; Ron Russell, "No Money for Raises, Teachers are Told" *Detroit News* (August 1987), p. 3B; Ron Russell, "Teacher Strike Hits Detroit" *Detroit News* (September 2, 1987), p. 1A; Ron Russell, "School Can't Meet Costs of Contract" *Detroit News* (September 19, 1987), p. 1B.

19. Ron Russell, "School Board Recall Urged as Classes Resume" *Detroit News* (September 22, 1987), p. IA; The president of New Detroit is quoted in Rich, *Black Mayors and School Politics*, p. 38; Bates is quoted in Fred Girard and

Norman Sinclair, "School Boards' Junkets, Chauffeurs Rile Teachers" *Detroit News* (September 2, 1987), pp. 1A, 5A.

20. Ron Russell, "Detroit School Deficit Put at $50 Million" *Detroit News* (September 24, 1987), p. 1B; Ron Russell, "School Woes Lure Many 'Mr. Fixits' " *Detroit News* (June 21, 1988), p. 1B; Ron Russell, "School Cutback Talk Fuels Recall Drive" *Detroit News* (October 16, 1987), p. 1A; Brenda Ingersoll Gave, "Groups Launch School Recall" *Detroit News* (October 18, 1987), p. 1B; Ron Russell, "Schools to Lay Off 500, Seek Tax Hike" *Detroit News* (October 29, 1987), p. 1B.

21. Charlie Cain, "Rules Set for Loan to Detroit Schools" *Detroit News* (October 20, 1987), p. 1B; Ron Russell, "School Board Bows to State on Chauffeurs" *Detroit News* (May 17, 1988), p. 1B.

22. Ron Russell, "Vote Called 'Repudiation' of Board" *Detroit News* (August 4, 1988), p. 3B; Ron Russell, "Detroit Teachers' Union Backs 4 School Challengers" *Detroit News* (September 30, 1988), p. 4B; Editorial, "HOPE for School Board" *Detroit News* (October 16, 1988), p. 22; Rich, *Black Mayors and School Politics*, pp. 39–40.

23. Editorial, "HOPE for School Board"; Ann Bradley, "Crusaders in Detroit Fight to Keep Board Seats" *Education Week* 12:7 (October 21, 1992), pp. 1, 10; Rich, *Black Mayors and School Politics*, pp. 39–40.

24. N. Scott Vance, "Young Backs School Millage, Incumbents" *Detroit News* (October 8, 1988), p. 1B; "Candidates Deny Funding Charges" *Detroit News* (October 12, 1988), p. 3B; Rich, *Black Mayors and School Politics*, pp. 41–45.

25. Joshua Ravitz, "School Board Panel Favors Tax Boost, Bond Measure" *Detroit News* (September 2, 1988), p. 1B; On the campaign pledge to bring about an education revolution see N. Scott Vance and Ron Russell, "Young Again Suggests City Control of Schools" *Detroit News* (January 6, 1989), p. 3B.

26. Ron Russell, "Detroit Schools Plan no Big Cuts Despite Defeat of Millage Hike" *Detroit News* (November 3, 1988), p. 1B; Rich, *Black Mayors and School Politics*, p. 43; The education reporter is quoted from Russell, "New School Board Hopes to Fix Financial Mess Without State Help," p. 1B.

27. Ron Russell, "Patrick Heads School Board" *Detroit News* (January 11, 1989), p. 1B; Ron Russell and Dennis B. Mulqueen, "School Official Wary of State Takeover" *Detroit News* (January 12, 1989), p. 3B; Mark Hornbeck, "State Superintendent Calls on City Schools to Solve Deficit" *Detroit News* (January 24, 1989), p. 3B; Ron Russell, "New School Chief or No Loan" *Detroit News* (March 3, 1989), pp. 1B, 7B; Russell, "New School Board Hopes to Fix Financial Mess Without State Help," p. 1B; Vance and Russell, "Young Again Suggests City Control of Schools," p. 1B; Editorial, "Detroit School Discontent . . ." *Detroit News* (May 5, 1989), p. A14; Ron Russell "Schools Cancel Tax Vote Plans" *Detroit News* (May 17, 1989), p. 1B.

28. None of these accomplishments came easily. See, for example, Liz Twardon, "Porter Gets Interim Job Offer" *Detroit News* (May 10, 1989), p. 1A; William Snider, "Detroit Officials See Belt-Tightening Moves as First Steps Along Road to Recovery" *Education Week* (August 2, 1989), pp. 1, 27; Rich, *Black Mayors and School Politics*, pp. 48–49.

29. Ron Russell, "Teachers Agree to 6 Percent Pay Raise" *Detroit News* (July 14, 1989), pp. 1A, 6A; Ron Russell, "School Tax Vote Called Test of Porter" *Detroit News* (July 16, 1989), p. 1B; Snider, "Detroit Officials See Belt-Tightening Moves as First Steps Along Road to Recovery"; Snider, "In Backing Tax Proposals, Voters Endorse School Reforms."

30. Russell, "Teachers Agree to 6 Percent Pay Raise," p. 6A; Snider, "In Backing Tax Proposals"; Richard C. Hula, Richard W. Jeier, and Mark Schauer, "Making Educational Reform: Hard Times in Detroit, 1988–1995" *Urban Education* 32:2 (May 1992), pp. 211–214.

31. Isabel Wilkerson, "Can Deborah McGriff Save Detroit Schools?" Ms. 2:1 (July/August 1991), pp. 98–99; Rich, *Black Mayors and School Politics*, pp. 49–50.

32. The HOPE team did pursue other initiatives besides empowerment and choice. One of the most interesting was the Detroit Compact in which school and business leaders worked together to aid high school graduates who had followed a rigorous, prescribed course of study in going to college or entering the workforce. While the HOPE team strongly supported this initiative, I have not included it as part of the overall HOPE strategy, as others have, because much of the groundwork for the Compact had been completed before the HOPE team took office. On the compact see, Ron Russell, "School Board Gets Scolding" *Detroit News* (September 22, 1988), p. 3B; Marion Orr, "Urban Regimes and School Compacts: The Development of the Detroit School Compact" *The Urban Review* 25:2 (1993), pp. 105–122; Hula et al., "Making Educational Reform," pp. 207–211.

33. The HOPE literature is quoted in Rich, *Black Mayors and School Politics*, p. 41; Ron Russell, "New School Board Hopes to Fix Financial Mess Without State Help" *Detroit News* (January 1, 1989), pp. 1B, 4B; Hula et al., "Making Educational Reform," pp. 207–217. Actually, HOPE's empowered schools initiative was something of a compromise between the Chicago and Dade County efforts. Unlike Chicago it did not make parents and community members the key policy makers in the schools and unlike Dade County it did not explicitly make teachers partners with administrators in setting school policy. On the different forms of urban school decentralization in the 1980s and 1990s see, John L. Rury and Jeffrey E. Mirel "The Political Economy of Urban Education" in Michael Apple (ed.) *Review of Research in Education* (Washington, DC, 1997), pp. 89–98.

34. Lynn Olson, "Detroit Board Set to Vote on Plan 'To Empower' Schools" *Education Week* (March 18, 1992), p. 4; Hula et al., "Making Educational Reform," pp. 211–214, 231.

35. "Detroit's African Centered Academies" *Black Issues in Higher Education* V. 2 (February 24, 1994), pp. 18–21; Karen Houppert, "Establish Afrocentric, all-male academies" *Utne Readers* (January/February 1994), pp. 83–85; Kevin Bushweller, "Separate by Choice" *The American School Board Journal* 183 (October 1996), pp. 34–37.

36. Clifford Watson and Geneva Smitherman, "Educational Equity and Detroit's Male Academy" *Equity and Excellence* 25:2–4 (Winter 1992), p. 90. "Update" *Education Week* (November 13, 1991), p. 3; Jawanza Kunjufu, "Detroit's Male Academies: What the Real Issue Is" *Education Week* (November 20, 1991), p. 29; Arthur S. Hayes and Jonathan M. Moses, "Detroit Abandons Plan for All-Male Schools, Citing Bias" *Equity and Excellence* 25:2–4 (Winter 1992), p. 92.

37. On the "boutique schools" criticism see Bradley, "Crusaders in Detroit Fight to Keep Board Seats," p. 10; Hula et al., "Making Educational Reform," pp. 220–222; Rich, *Black Mayors and School Politics*, p. 50.

38. The 1973 strike was not the only walkout in which these types of issues played a role. Indeed, the issues of giving teachers greater power and demanding greater

accountability from them as a result was part of the 1987 strike as well. In that case also the DFT adamantly opposed the proposals. Ron Russell, "Teachers Offered Raise Tied to New Funds" *Detroit News* (September 11, 1987), p. 9B; Hula et al., "Making Educational Reform," pp. 211–212; see also Ann Bradley, "Teachers in Detroit Strike over Proposal for Flexible Schools" *Education Week* (September 9, 1992), pp. 1, 21; Bradley, "Crusaders in Detroit Fight to Keep Board Seats."

39. Elliot is quoted in Bradley, "Teachers in Detroit Strike over Proposal for Flexible Schools," pp. 1, 21.

40. Martelock is quoted in Bradley, "Crusaders in Detroit Fight to Keep Board Seats," p. 10.

41. Olmstead, Patrick, and the board ally are quoted in Bradley, "Crusaders in Detroit Fight to Keep Board Seats," p. 10.

42. Ann Bradley, "Detroit Teachers Defy Court's Back-to-Work Order" *Education Week* (September 30, 1992), p. 9; Ann Bradley, "Contract Accord in Detroit Ends 27-Day Teacher Strike" *Education Week* (October 7, 1992), p. 13; Bradley, "Crusaders in Detroit Fight to Keep Board Seats," p. 11.

43. Bradley, "Crusaders in Detroit Fight to Keep Board Seats," p. 11; Hula et al., "Making Educational Reform," p. 221; Rich, *Black Mayors and School Politics*, p. 50.

44. Hayden is quoted in Bradley, "Crusaders in Detroit Fight to Keep Board Seats," p. 10. Olmstead is quoted in Peter Schmidt, "Voters Oust 3 Reformers From Detroit Board" *Education Week* (November 11, 1992), p. 5; Hula et al., "Making Educational Reform"; Rich, *Black Mayors and School Politics*.

45. Meg Somerfield, "Grant to Implement Comer Model in Detroit Schools" *Education Week* (July 13, 1994), p. 3; Hula et al., "Making Educational Reform," pp. 215–216.

46. "Detroit Parents Launch Effort To Recall Reformers on Board" *Education Week* (January 20, 1993), p. 2; Ann Bradley, "Detroit School-Empowerment Plan Suffers Setback" *Education Week* (April 21, 1993), p. 5; Ann Bradley, "Detroit Superintendent To Join Edison Project" *Education Week* (October 20, 1993), p. 10; "People" *Education Week* (November 11, 1993), p. 3; Hula et al., "Making Education Reform"; Rich, *Black Mayors and School Politics*.

47. Thomas Bray, "Is HOPE Dead?" *Detroit News* (1989). The unnamed board member is quoted in Hula et al., "Making Reform Work," p. 218; Young is quoted in Rich, *Black Mayors and School Politics*, p. 53.

48. The unidentified church leader is quoted in Hula et al., "Making Reform Work," pp. 220–221.

49. Moreover efforts at creating new union-management relationship similar to those developed by the United Auto Workers and General Motors in the Saturn Corporation (which in part inspired the HOPE team's efforts) continue to make news as delegations from both the American Federation of Teachers and the National Education Association (NEA) have toured the Saturn plant, the most recent being led by NEA president Bob Chase in the fall of 1997. See, Jeff Archer, "A Different Kind of Union: What an Innovative Car Company Can Teach Educators about 'New Unionism' " *Education Week* (October 29, 1997), pp. 27–31.

50. The unidentified business leader is quoted in Hula et al., "Making Reform Work," p. 202.

51. Olmstead is quoted in Schmidt, "Voters Oust 3 Reformers From Detroit Board," p. 5.

52. Deborah L. Cohen, "Americans Say Family Life Worse, Survey Find" *Education Week* (December 15, 1993), p. 6.

53. See for example, Eric A. Hanushek, "The Impact of Differential Expenditures on School Performance" *Educational Researcher* 18 (May 1989), pp. 45–62; *ibid.*, "Measuring Investment in Education" *Journal of Economic Perspectives* 10:4 (Fall 1996), pp. 9–30.

54. Michigan Department of Education, "MEAP District and School Proportions Report, 1995: Detroit Public Schools" (Lansing, 1996).

15

THE MILWAUKEE VOUCHER EXPERIMENT

John F. Witte

The Milwaukee voucher program was enacted by the Wisconsin State Legislature in the summer of 1990. Beginning that August, it allowed students to attend private schools with public vouchers for the first time in the United States. This article provides a summary of the results of the first five years of that program. I begin with a brief discussion of the theoretical and research issues—brief because these issues have been thoroughly aired many times (Cookson, 1994; Henig, 1994; Smith & Meier, 1995; Wells, 1993; Witte & Rigdon, 1993). Following a description of the initial program and subsequent changes, I outline who participated in the program—including characteristics of students and families and schools. I then describe the results in terms of the effects on families and students and on schools. I conclude with a discussion of the implications of this type of program and more open-ended voucher programs.

For those holding extreme positions on this controversial issue, there will be both ammunition and frustration, for the results contain both positive and negative elements. The mostly quantitative results presented conform to perceptions revealed by five years of observation and case studies of the private schools, as well as analysis of the Milwaukee Public Schools over the last decade. The quality of both the public and private schools, and student outcomes, varies within and among schools, and that variance is more extreme than in middle-class or wealthy communities. Some schools are excellent, and families fight to get in them and stay in them. Some are so bad that they fail and, if they are private, cease to exist—often in mid-year. The general results of the voucher program follow that pattern: Some results are clearly positive, some can be interpreted either way, and others are negative.

THEORETICAL AND RESEARCH ISSUES

At an abstract level, educational vouchers represent an approach to the provision of a collective good that challenges the dominant public good approach to American education. The market model on which vouchers are based assumes a set of private choices by families and providers, which in the extreme would be unfettered by government interference or regulation. As such, it deviates considerably from the public provision of education— controlled democratically and heavily regulated by local, state, and federal rules, statutes, and constitutional provisions. It also assumes a very different approach to accountability, with public schools held accountable through external promulgation and review of results, while the market model bases accountability on consumer (family) satisfaction. Arguments for and against these models have been discussed at length in a literature that need not be reiterated here (Chubb & Moe, 1990; Cookson, 1994; Coons & Sugarman, 1978, 1992; Friedman, 1955; Hannaway & Garner, 1980; Henig, 1994; Hoffer, Kilgore, & Coleman, 1982; Manski, 1992; Smith & Meier, 1995; Wells, 1993; Witte, 1992; Witte & Rigdon, 1993).

The general issues associated with the public or private provision of collective goods apply directly to educational vouchers. The first, often stressed by philosophers and political theorists more than economists, has to do with the intrinsic value of individual choice. Certainly one could argue quite forcefully, given the world events of the last decade, that individual choice is intrinsically valuable in terms of personal satisfaction, motivation, responsibility, and so on. Supporters of vouchers, especially those advocating income-targeted vouchers, make a strong claim that vouchers will provide opportunities for a set of families who now are limited to public school options.

On the other hand, the debate over the public or private provision of collective goods invokes concerns and questions over the equity of both opportunities and results. Those favoring private provision emphasize the equal opportunity that vouchers might provide. Opponents stress that vouchers might exacerbate already unequal opportunities and further erode differences between relevant social and racial groups in terms of educational results.

A third consideration is the overall efficiency of public-versus-private approaches to collective goods. Which schools produce the best results at the lowest cost? Will vouchers improve or decrease cost effectiveness? More specifically, will vouchers drive costs toward the currently lower cost of private schools, or will vouchers allow private schools to raise prices to more closely match expenditures by public schools?

The way an individual assesses the trade-off between the values of choice, equity, and efficiency often determines his or her position on educational vouchers. One might concede that vouchers add to family opportunities but still fear the effects on equity would be too great. A fiscal conservative might understandably applaud the increased choice, downplay the equity concerns, but fear that vouchers will simply inject more public money into a system that already spends too much. Thus, honorable people can easily disagree on the normative merits of vouchers.

Because of program constraints, the Milwaukee voucher experiment provides modest evidence on this general set of issues. However, those issues do provide the framework for a series of research questions, which have driven this study over the last five years. First, can a program be developed that will provide increasing opportunities for poor students who currently cannot avail themselves of "better" options in terms of either public or private schools? Or will such a program inevitably "cream off" the best students and families? Second, will a voucher system improve the educational environment for families and students? Are families more satisfied with the education their children are receiving? Is there evidence of improvement in educational achievement and other outcomes? Third, does a voucher system improve the provision of services? Do schools get better? Do more schools, of higher quality, emerge? Is there a reduction in costs for the same quality of service? The Milwaukee voucher program provides some information on all of these questions. However, because of the constraints involved in the program and in the research situation that emerged, generalizations should be considered with caution.

Because Milwaukee's is the first voucher program in the United States to incorporate private schools, there is no directly relevant prior empirical literature to guide this study.[1] However, there have been numerous studies of achievement and other comparisons between public and private schools that have been summarized numerous times (Henig, 1994; Witte, 1992, 1996). The results remain controversial, with some studies arguing for a private school advantage (Bryk, Lee, & Holland, 1994; Chubb & Moe, 1990; Hoffer & Coleman, 1987; Hoffer, Kilgore, & Coleman, 1982; Hoxby, 1996), while others have either found public school advantages or no differences (Driscoll, 1993; Gamoran, 1996; Goldhaber, 1996; Plank et al., 1993). Throughout these studies, the issue of unmeasured selection bias looms as a problem, and the potential methodological solutions are also often challenged. This problem will be discussed below.

What is consistent in these studies is that those who currently attend private schools are much more likely to be White and upper middle class than those attending public schools. Also, religious schools dominate the private sector, with well over 80% of the students attending religiously affiliated schools. As I will note in the conclusion, these facts are not irrelevant in long-term discussions of educational vouchers.

THE MILWAUKEE VOUCHER PROGRAM[2]

The Milwaukee Parental Choice Program (its statutory title) can be categorized as a limited and targeted voucher program. In contrast with more or less open-ended voucher proposals, such as those proposed and defeated in referendums in Colorado and California, the Milwaukee program was initially designed to create an experimental program to provide an opportunity for some poor children to attend private schools. The program was enacted at the initiative of Republican Governor Tommy Thompson and Democratic Assemblywoman Annette (Polly) Williams. There are a number of detailed specifications that are relevant for understanding what happened in the program.

The Initial Program

The Milwaukee Parental Choice Program allows students living in Milwaukee and meeting specific criteria to attend private, *nonsectarian* schools located in the city. For each Choice student, in lieu of tuition and fees, schools receive a payment from public funds equivalent to the Milwaukee Public Schools (MPS) per-member state aid ($2,500 in 1990–91; $4,373 in 1996–97). Students must come from families with incomes not exceeding 1.75 times the national poverty line. New Choice students initially could not have been in private schools in the prior year or in public schools in districts other than MPS. The total number of Choice students in any year was limited to 1% of the MPS membership in the first four years, but was increased to 1.5% beginning with the 1994–95 school year.

Schools initially had to limit Choice students to 49% of their total enrollment. The legislature increased that to 65% beginning in 1994–95. Schools must admit Choice students without discrimination based on race, ethnicity, or prior school performance (as specified in Section 118.13, Wisconsin Statutes). Both the statute and administrative rules specify that pupils must be "accepted on a random basis." This has been interpreted to mean that if a school were oversubscribed in a grade, random selection is required in that grade. However, a 1990 court ruling exempted the private schools from having to enroll all types of disabled students. In addition, in situations in which one child from a family attended the school, a sibling was exempt from random selection even if random selection was required in the child's grade.

The New Program

The legislation was amended as part of the biennial state budget in June 1995. The changes were dramatic. The principal changes were (a) to allow religious schools to enter the program; (b) to allow students in grades kindergarten through grade three, who were already attending private schools, to be eligible for the program;[3] (c) to increase the number of students allowed in the program over three years to a maximum of 15,000 students (from approximately 1,500 allowed prior to 1995); (d) to allow 100% of students in a school to be Choice students; and (e) to eliminate all data collection and evaluations, specifying instead that the Wisconsin Legislative Audit Bureau file a report in the year 2000. Because of court challenges to the new program, parochial schools were not allowed in the program until the Wisconsin Supreme Court ruled 4–2 in favor of the new, expanded program in June 1998. Voucher-receiving students attended parochial and nonsectarian private schools for the first time in the fall of 1998.

The evidence reported in this article is based on the initial program, with modifications in 1993. Thus, this policy experiment is far from a test of a universal voucher program. And neither the positive nor negative findings should be generalized to programs without income limits on families and to wider sets of schools that may also be unconstrained in their ability to select students.

RESEARCH AND DATA

The study on which this report is based employs a number of methodological approaches. Surveys were mailed in the fall of each year from 1990 to 1994 to all parents who applied for enrollment in one of the Choice schools. Similar surveys were sent in May and June of 1991 to a random sample of 5,474 parents of students in the Milwaukee Public Schools. Among other purposes, the surveys were intended to assess parent knowledge of and evaluation of the Choice Program, educational experiences in prior public schools, the extent of parental involvement in prior MPS schools, and the importance of education and the expectations parents hold for their children. We also obtained demographic information on family members. A follow-up survey of Choice parents assessing attitudes relating to their year in private schools was mailed in June of each year.[4] Finally, beginning in the fall of 1992 and continuing through 1995, brief mail and/or phone surveys were completed with the parents of students who did not continue in the program.

In addition, detailed case studies were completed in April 1991 in the four private schools that enrolled the majority of the Choice students. An additional study was completed in 1992, and six more case studies in the spring of 1993. Case studies of the K-8 schools involved approximately 30 person-days in the schools, including 56 hours of classroom observation and interviews with nearly all of the teachers and administrators in the schools. Smaller schools required less time. Researchers also attended and observed parent and community group meetings and board of director meetings for several schools.

The research includes analysis of four or five years of outcome measures including data on achievement test scores,[5] parental attitudes, parental involvement, attrition from the program, and the effects of the program on private schools. In accordance with normal research protocol, and with the agreement of the private schools, to maintain student confidentiality, reported results are aggregated, and schools are not individually identified.

The most appropriate comparison group to the Choice families, on most measures, is the low-income MPS sample. That group, which includes about two-thirds of Milwaukee students, is defined as qualifying for free or reduced-price lunches. The income level for reduced-priced lunches is 1.85 times the poverty line; free lunch is 1.35 times the poverty line. Almost all low-income students qualify for full free lunches and thus would have qualified for the Choice Program. The full MPS sample is included because one might wish to anticipate expansion of the Choice Program to the full population of MPS students. If that were to occur, comparison and generalization of results to the complete random sample would be appropriate.

Some analyses include data on "nonselected" Choice applicants, but the outcome results do not. These are students who were randomly rejected from the program. Initially, this group was of great interest because it provided a potential control on unmeasured selection bias. Unmeasured selection bias assumes that there are unmeasured factors that distinguish "choosing" families from "nonchoosers" and which affect student achievement. Randomly rejected students should theoretically possess these unmeasured characteristics to the same degree as those selected into the program, thus providing the opportunity to analyze a natural experiment in student achievement. Unfortunately, as will be discussed below, it is my opinion that for reasons beyond the control of the program or the research, this sample of students is completely unreliable as a control on selection bias. A more detailed paper on this subject has been presented earlier and is forthcoming in a book on vouchers in America (Witte, 1997, 2000). Others hold a contradictory opinion (Green, Peterson, & Du, 1996; Rouse, 1997).

FINDINGS

Enrollment in Choice

Because most people assume that private schools provide superior education to public schools, it is usually assumed that demand for vouchers would exceed supply and that the issue would be the generation of new schools. However, evidence from the Milwaukee Choice Program indicates that this assumption is too simplistic. The program has not included religious private schools, which have always been the mainstay of private education in the United States. Without religiously affiliated schools being eligible for vouchers, there appear to be both supply and demand problems.

Supply and Demand in the Choice Program

Enrollment in the program increased steadily but slowly, never reaching the maximum number of students allowed by the law. September enrollments were 341, 521, 620, 742, and 830 from 1990–91 to 1994–95. The number of schools participating was: 7 in 1990–91, 6 in 1991–92, 11 in 1992–93, and 12 from fall 1993 to 1995. The number of applications also increased, with again the largest increase in 1992–93. In the last two years, however, applications leveled off at a little over 1,000 per year. Applications exceeded the number of available seats (as determined by the private schools) by 171, 143, 307, 238, and 64 from 1990–91 through 1994–95. Some of these students eventually filled seats of students who were accepted but did not actually enroll.

The number of potential schools in the program was an obvious limitation. Only 22–23 secular private schools existed in Milwaukee during this period. That compared to close to 100 religious private schools. Of the secular schools, more than half chose not to participate in the Choice Program. We contacted those schools in the third year of the program. The reason for nonparticipation varied. Several schools concluded it was too costly for the school (the voucher would not match tuition); others were devoted "contract" schools with MPS;[6] others were wary that this program was established by African Americans—primarily for African Americans.

However, the limited supply was not much of a constraining factor because applications were far from the avalanche that Choice supporters often tout. The number of seats available consistently exceeded the number of students enrolled, but primarily because not enough seats were available in the most desirable schools. It is difficult to determine how many more applications would have been made if more schools participated and more seats were available. In 1992–93, when the number of participating schools increased from 6 to 11, applications rose by 45%. From fall 1993 to 1995, however, seats available increased by 22% and 21% but applications increased by only 5% in 1993–94 and declined in the last year.

During the Choice experiment, there was a parallel privately funded "scholarship" program that clearly affected the demand for vouchers—and possibly the supply of schools as well. This program, Partners Advancing Values in Education (PAVE), provided half of the tuition (up to $1,000) for free-lunch-eligible students and allowed them to attend any private school. Nearly all of the PAVE scholarship students attended parochial schools. The draw of religious schools was clear in that almost three times the number of students applied for PAVE scholarships as applied for vouchers, yet families were required to come up with half of the tuition for PAVE schools (Beales & Wahl, 1995; Wahl, 1994). Because many parochial schools had vacancies, the program also probably deterred new private schools from opening.

Who Applied for Vouchers?

Vouchers raise concerns about both equal opportunity and equality of results. The opportunity concerns surrounding voucher programs can be broken down into two separate issues: (a) Without any program limits or eligibility requirements, who would use vouchers to attend private schools? And (b) can a targeted voucher program be created that will increase opportunities for students currently unable to attend private schools? The Milwaukee voucher program provides little evidence on the former question, but considerable evidence on the latter. However, given the political inclination to move this program from a targeted to an open-ended voucher program, the former issue is of ultimate importance and will be addressed in the conclusion of the article.

Based on survey responses sent to parents of Choice applicants, the picture of parents applying to the targeted Milwaukee Program is very clear. Five years of survey data, for five separate family cohorts, are extremely consistent. The demographic profile was quite stable over each of the five years. Both applicants, and students who ultimately enrolled in Choice, were from very-low-income families, considerably below the average MPS family and about $500 per year below the low-income (free-lunch-eligible) MPS family. Blacks and Hispanics were the primary applicants to the program, both being over-represented compared with the MPS control groups. Asian students essentially did not apply, and White students were considerably underrepresented. Also, Choice students were considerably less likely to come from a household in which parents were married (25%) than their counterparts in MPS (35% for low-income and 51% for all MPS families).

In contrast, however, Choice mothers reported considerably more education than did mothers in MPS. Fifty-two percent of applicant parents and 55% of enrollees reported some college. This contrasted with 30% and 40%

for the two MPS samples. Finally, there is also evidence that Choice families were small, averaging about 2.5 children in contrast with 3.24 and 2.95 for the MPS samples.[7] There are four separate dimensions of parental involvement, all of which have very good scaling properties and produce dramatic and highly statistically significant results in comparison with either MPS control group. For all forms of parental involvement—contacts with schools, organizational involvement, or home involvement—Choice parents reported considerably greater involvement than MPS parents.

Finally, there was evidence that Choice parents were very dissatisfied with their former (MPS) schools; there may have been good reason for it, as indicated by test scores taken in MPS prior to students enrolling in Choice. In terms of attitudes, the judgment of Choice parents of their child's prior public school was especially harsh in contrast with the MPS control groups. As is apparent from the means of the scales, Choice parents viewed their prior public schools much less favorably than the MPS control groups. The two items that elicited the greatest alienation were "the quality of education" and "discipline" (Witte, Thorn, Pritchard, & Claibourn, 1994; Witte & Thorn, 1996). Prior test scores of Choice students provided further evidence supporting parent dissatisfaction with their children's prior schools. Choice students were achieving considerably less than MPS students and somewhat less than the low-income MPS students. For the national population, normal curve equivalents (NCE)s have a mean of 50 and a standard deviation of 18, and it is apparent that for all students, they are below national averages. Choice students were statistically significantly below (at the .05 level) the full MPS sample each year on both tests and below the low-income sample on three of the eight prior tests.

Choice applicants were also asked why they applied to the Choice Program. "Educational quality" led the list, eliciting an 89% "very important" response. That was followed by "teaching approach and style," 86%; "discipline," 75%; "general educational atmosphere," 74%; and "classroom size," 72% (Witte, Thorn, & Sterr, 1995, Table 3). Although this list is not surprising, it is relevant that several of the top categories—"educational quality" and "discipline"—were also the most alienating issues in Choice parents' assessment of their prior public schools.

The portrait of Choice students and families is thus complex and not simple to interpret. On one hand, the program clearly demonstrated that a program could successfully be targeted on poor families who have had bad experiences in their prior public schools. Thus, the program created the type of equalizing opportunity that was intended. On the other hand, one could also argue that the program is depriving the public schools of families who have more educated parents and who are actively involved in their children's education— in short, the type of parents who could potentially aid in reform efforts.

Outcomes: Effects on Families and Students

Outcomes are broken down simply into effects on families and students and then on schools. In each set of results, there are outcomes that most people would interpret positively and negatively. Given the complex normative issues surrounding vouchers, as outlined above, I let the reader reach his or her own judgment. I count among the positive results positive parental attitudes toward Choice schools (in contrast to prior public schools), positive attitudes toward the program, increased parental involvement, and some benefits for most of the private schools. More critical results, certainly as interpreted by foes of vouchers, include similar test score gains for Choice and MPS students, seemingly high attrition from the program, and the collapse of three private schools in mid-year.

Attitudes and Parental Involvement

Too often, outcomes of experiments in education are reduced to their effects on "achievement." Although any sensible conceptualization of "achievement" would extend well beyond standardized test scores, the vast majority of evaluations of educational programs focus, often exclusively, on test score results. That is not the case in this study. Parents of Choice students were surveyed as they applied to the program and at the end of each subsequent year. Thus, we are able to ascertain their attitudes toward their prior schools and compare them to their attitudes toward the Choice private schools. And all of those attitude comparisons are extremely positive.[8]

Satisfaction of Choice parents with private schools was just as dramatic as dissatisfaction was with prior public schools. As noted in the last section, Choice parents were much less satisfied with their public schools than either the average MPS parent or the low-income group. Exactly the reverse occurs when parents respond to the same questions for private schools. The results were a dramatic reversal—high levels of dissatisfaction with prior public schools, but considerable satisfaction with private schools. There were eight questions in the school satisfaction scale. The four-point Likert ratings ranged from *very satisfied* to *very dissatisfied*. Thus, 13.6 meant that most parents were from very to somewhat satisfied on all measures. Interestingly, the two measures on which parents were least satisfied in the public schools—"educational environment" and "discipline"—were the areas of greatest satisfaction in the private schools.

These results were consistent with several other indicators of satisfaction. On both pre- and post-surveys, parents were asked to grade their schools on an *A-to-F* scale. The comparative results from prior schools again indicated much greater satisfaction with the private schools. On a 4.0 scale, the average grade for prior schools for both Choice applicants and those who enrolled was 2.4, while the grade for private schools was 3.0. This compared to an average grade for the MPS control groups of 2.8 (Witte et al., 1994, Table 7; Witte et al., 1995, Table 7).

There was also, in each year, overwhelming support among participants that the Choice Program should continue. The positive responses averaged 98%, even in the first year, when a school went bankrupt and almost 90 students ended their year in MPS schools. Those parents overwhelmingly supported the program (Witte et al., 1994, p. 20).

Finally, parental involvement, which was clearly very high for Choice parents before they enrolled in the program, increased while their children were in private schools. Comparing the prior involvement of parents of students who enrolled in Choice (fall) to private school involvement, parental involvement increased on all dimensions. The differences were statistically significant at the .05 level on school contacts and organizations, but not on involvement at home. Part of the reason for this increase may have been that some of the private schools required participation and made parents sign parental involvement agreements. However, these were involved parents from the beginning, and at best, the contracts would have been a marginal incentive.

Achievement Test Scores

Extensive analysis of achievement results, with all the glorified technicalities, are presented elsewhere (Witte, 1997, 2000). However, the results of the more complex presentation do not alter in any way the conclusions drawn from the core data. The general conclusion is that there is no substantial difference over the life of the program between the Choice and MPS students, especially the low-income MPS students. On a positive note, estimates for the overall samples, while always below national norms, do not substantially decline as the students enter higher grades. This is not the normal pattern in that usually inner-city student average scores decline relative to national norms in higher grades. That these students held their own is a positive result for the city as whole.[9]

The year-to-year change scores indicate the general pattern, which does not change dramatically with subsequent, much more complex analysis. They apply to students who had valid tests in both years. For Choice students, five of the eight change scores do not significantly differ from zero, while three do—one negative reading score and one positive and one negative math score. For the low-income MPS sample, the results are similar. Two of the eight scores differ from zero—one positive math score and one negative math score. Adding the change scores across the four years, results in the following: Choice ($R = -2.6$; $M = +1.7$); low-income MPS ($R = +0.2$; $M = +0.9$); MPS ($R = +0.5$; $M = +1.0$). The Choice advances in math are solely determined by the third-year gains, and the MPS positive math scores by the first-year gains.

Various multivariate models were utilized to extend the analysis, and all have relevance in evaluating program success. Policymakers certainly would be interested in understanding the overall effect of a program intervention. However, they might also be interested in the trend in the program. Does it show variance from year to year, or are the results stable over time? Finally, we would also be interested in a learning curve or trend effect for individual students. It could be that students need time to become acclimated to the different approaches applied in the private schools, and thus achievement gains might be delayed. It could also be that as initial enthusiasm with a new school wears off or a student fails to adjust to a different educational style, achievement could drop.

The basic results mirror the descriptive statistics. With some complexities, which will be described, the general conclusion is that there were no consistent differences between Choice and MPS students in value-added achievement scores using any of these modeling approaches. The first analysis, which includes more students but fewer control variables, indicates that the control variables all act as anticipated.[10] The two prior tests are always highly significant, with a much larger coefficient on the matched prior test (i.e., reading for reading). Test grade always has a negative sign, but it is only significant for math. Girls do better on reading, but not on math. Minority students do less well than Whites, and low-income students less well than non-low-income students. And with all of these variables controlled, none of the Choice variables is significant, and only the second year reading score even approaches significance (-1.2 with a t value of 1.6).

A second analysis, with more variables included, tells a similar story, but the reading result is now significant and favoring the MPS students. Again, the control variables are almost all in the expected direction, with some less significant and some more significant than in the prior analysis. Of the new variables in this treatment, "income" and "mother's education" are in the direction expected. Some parental involvement scales seem to be counter to expectations, which indicates that the prior involvement may have been connected to difficulties of their children or their frustration with prior schools. Negative signs on parent involvement at home, which are significant for math, are unclear.

The results of the Choice indicator variables are in the same directions as in the first analysis and are generally not significantly different from zero. The one exception is the negative Choice effect on reading, which is about 1.5 points lower than in the first analysis. It is statistically significant at the .01 level. However, when we look at the year effects, it is quite clear that the entire effect is driven by a bad second year in the Choice schools. The reason it may be significant in this analysis is the inclusion of "mother's education," which is higher in Choice families, thus setting up higher expected scores. As will be discussed below, the reason for the effect in this single year is probably connected to attrition from the program.

The trend over time in student performance has been a very controversial aspect of the Choice Program. Several other authors have claimed a trend effect favoring Choice students. Specifically, they argue, using rejected Choice students as a control, that third- and especially fourth-year Choice students make remarkable gains in math, but (with little explanation) no statistically significant gains in reading (Greene, Peterson, & Du, 1996).[11] That result has been addressed in subsequent research, and the problems will be briefly summarized below.

The final analyses provide trend data in comparison to the MPS control group. Because the data indicate trends for each of the four years, only student record database variables are included. Sample sizes, especially of

Choice students, would be very small if survey variables were also incorporated. Inclusion of those variables tended to reduce the levels of significance
of the findings because of inflated standard errors.

The results again tend to support the conclusion that there is no consistent
pattern in achievement score differences across the different tests and years.
For reading scores there is only one significant coefficient: a −2.45 NCEs
disadvantage for the second-year Choice students in the second year of the
program. This result reinforces the pattern indicated in the second analysis,
where the negative reading result seems to be completely the result of the
second program year. As will be discussed below when analyzing attrition,
that negative result is not repeated in subsequent years for this first-year
(1990) cohort. The only other score in the table that approaches statistical
significance is the second year cohort's +1.99 points in the third year
(1993). It appears that this Choice cohort (1991) was made up of better
students. This result carries over to math scores.

Consistent with the descriptive results described above, there appears to
be a positive Choice effect for math in the third year for all Choice students.
The results for second- and third-year Choice students in 1993 were
statistically significant at the .05 level. However, again reinforcing the no-
consistent-difference conclusion, these results are not repeated in the fourth
year of the program. In that year, nothing approaches significance except the
newly admitted Choice cohort, and it does worse than MPS students
(−2.23 NCEs).

Thus, combined with the reading results that are in the opposite direction,
these results confirm the general conclusion that there is no consistent
difference between the Choice students and the control group. This is true
for the descriptive statistics, mean effects, program effects, and student
trends. And what significant results did emerge will be at least partly
explained by attrition from the program as described below.

Why does this analysis not include the reject students? As noted above,
Greene et al. (1996), relying exclusively on the Choice/reject comparison,
claimed a large and significant difference favoring Choice students in math
scores for students remaining in the Choice Program for three or four years.
I question the Choice/reject math results based on two major problems:
(a) The rejects who remained in the experiment were not a random sample of
rejected students, and (b) small sample sizes and outlier effects produced the
large result in math.

In subsequent research, I looked at selection and samples size problems in
two ways. First, I analyzed the differences between all students who applied
and were not selected and those on whom we had subsequent test data. That
test data had to come from MPS. Therefore, rejected students who did not
enroll in MPS or were not tested essentially dropped out of the experiment.
Because most rejects were very young, there was little prior test data on
them. However, all applicants were sent surveys, so information exists on
both those who later returned to MPS and those who did not. When we
initially compared *all* rejects with Choice enrollees, we found few differences

among the groups. The most notable were that rejected students were more likely to be Black and their parents had lower educational expectations for their children than parents of selected students (Witte et al., 1994, Table 20). Those differences may, of course, indicate selection biases for all rejects, and they would likely bias reject scores downward.

However, the major problem was with those rejects who, in effect, left the experiment. Both descriptive statistics and a logistic regression indicated that the rejected students who remained in the study were (a) poorer, (b) in higher grades, and (c) from families whose parents were likely to be less educated and were less involved in their children's education than students who disappeared from the program. This makes sense. Rejects were looking to leave MPS in the first place. If not selected for Choice and if they had the means (and especially if their children were young), they left for private schools, either on their own or with the help of privately funded vouchers, or they went to another public school district. Thus the reject "control group" that remained behind in MPS was hardly a random sample of those who applied and were rejected. And all indications suggest those remaining in the experiment were likely to be an educationally weak representation of the initial group (Witte, 1997, 2000, chapter 6).

Small samples were a second problem with the Choice/reject comparison, especially when the results focus on one or two years. In such a situation, the scores of a few students could influence the general results. And that is exactly what happened. My prior research more or less reproduced the third- and fourth-year effects (in math only) that favored Choice students and were so widely circulated in the unpublished paper by Greene, Peterson, and Du (1996). However, I then analyzed more carefully the scores of the two sets of students. As one might anticipate from the selection problems outlined above, low reject scores created the difference. For the most significant fourth-year effect, there were only 27 reject students who tried to enter the Milwaukee Parental Choice Program in 1990 for whom there were test scores four years later. Of those rejects, 5 students (18.5%) received a score of 1 on the math test. A 1 NCE is the lowest recorded score on the Iowa Test of Basic Skills. It often results from a student *simply not filling in the dots* on the test form. There were no similar 1 scores in the Choice schools.[12] The lowest Choice score (of 85 in the fourth year) was 4.

To test the sensitivity of the models, I re-estimated the results, taking out the students from both groups who had scores less than 5 NCEs. The results were quite extraordinary. First, the reading estimates were unaffected—still no differences between Choice and rejects. For math, the coefficient representing the big fourth-year effect was reduced by 40% and was no longer significant by conventional standards. And these results were accomplished by eliminating only seven students who scored the lowest scores on the math test (Witte, 1997, 2000, chapter 6).[13] Thus, unfortunately, the natural experiment, which would have controlled for selection bias, was hopelessly contaminated by systematic attrition from the reject group, and the results were dramatically affected by outlier cases because of small samples.

Attrition from the Program

A final concern, as both an outcome measure and as a methodological issue, is the level of attrition from the program. For whatever reasons, the attrition rates from the Choice schools were quite high, although they declined over time. Attrition is defined as leaving a school before a terminal grade is reached. Because students only had to submit to lottery conditions once, subsequent leaving was the result of either family or school choice. Because the program did not require schools to list non-readmitted students (and they do not have to readmit Choice students), we cannot distinguish between these reasons. For whichever reason, the numbers are, in one sense, substantial.

Annual attrition averaged 33.4% for all Choice schools, and 30.2% if we exclude alternative schools in the Choice Program. The numbers are substantial in the sense that if the Choice Program is to have a major impact for a number of students, those students would have to remain in the Choice schools—and few do. For example, of the initial class of 341 in 1990, four years later, in spring 1994, there were only 57 students left—and very few "had graduated" (Wisconsin Legislative Audit Bureau, 1995, p. 28).

Is attrition itself a measure of Choice school failures? The answer is probably no. Although the numbers appear high, they seem to be in line with the attrition rates in the public schools for the elementary grades. Given data reporting problems on who is in what school in the first month of school, the range of attrition for K to eighth graders was estimated at 22% to 28%, which is close to that in the Choice Program (Witte et al., 1994, p. 22). Thus, attrition appears to be a common problem in inner-city school districts, regardless of the type of school.

Who was likely to leave and for what reasons? The characteristics of leavers varied from year to year, but the four-year profile is interesting and suggestive. The general characteristics of continuing compared to leaving students indicate that Whites and Blacks were somewhat more likely to leave than Hispanics, and boys more likely to leave than girls. Also, students living farther away were more likely to leave.

Perhaps more important, however, it appears that leavers were underachievers in every sense: lower prior scores, lower post scores, and lower change scores. This was reflected in a considerably lower opinion of the private school among leaving parents than those who stayed. This latter difference is as large as the differences were between Choice applicants and MPS parents in appraising their prior public schools. The combination of results makes sense to either explain family choices to not return—the hoped-for educational improvement did not occur—or schools not readmitting lower achieving and non-improving students.

The four-year pattern of attrition masks important year-to-year variations. Year-to-year data indicate that leavers in the first two years were very different from one another. After the first year, the program was very much up in the air in that the courts had not yet decided its validity and the closing of Juanita Virgil Academy had put political pressure on the program. A number of high-achieving students left that year, presumably pulled out by parent choice. The next year, with the program stabilized, the exact opposite occurred, and this was at least in part induced by the schools not readmitting some of the underachieving and non-improving students.[14]

The Test Score Means Verify These Differences

There was an extraordinary difference in spring test scores between leaving and returning students in the two years. In the first year, leaving students outperformed returning students by 3.7 NCEs in reading and 2.5 points in math. In the second year, leaving students were 3.0 NCEs worse than returning students in reading and 2.0 points worse in math.

This difference in attrition is undoubtedly linked to the sharp decline in reading scores in the second year, following an increase in reading in the first year. The decline in 1992 is mostly the result of second-year students—those who were indulged for the first year. In the following two years, the remaining students from that first cohort do better in reading, but essentially the same as MPS students. The same phenomenon may well account for the remarkable change in math scores for this cohort. In 1992, the second-year students have an estimated effect compared to MPS of -1.58 NCEs in math. In 1993, that coefficient changes to a positive (and significant) $+2.66$ NCEs. Again, and consistent with the reading results, attrition after the second year could account for this sharp improvement.

These attrition levels suggest several other methodological cautions. First, the small sample sizes among Choice students allow for unique selective actions—such as one or two schools changing re-admission decisions—to have quite dramatic effects. Second, the overall attrition of Choice students indicates that if a similar attrition did not occur among the Milwaukee sample, the achievement test results could be biased in favor of Choice students. Clearly, over the four-year period, lower achieving students left the Choice Program. A subsequent analysis, correcting for attrition from both samples, indicated that reading differences (which favored MPS) were probably not significant.[15] But the general lesson is that program attrition is a major problem both in terms of policy conclusions and in terms of subsequent evaluations of similar programs.

Several final questions concerning attrition are: Why did students not return? And where did they go? The characteristics of leavers described above indicate that they were not doing as well as students who continued and were much less satisfied with Choice schools. Follow-up survey data tend to confirm that conclusion, although it is far from perfect data. Because those who left were not known until the September following the close of school in June, it was extremely hard to track down nonreturning families. The response rates to mailed and phone surveys were only 38%. We must assume that the largest bias in these responses was missing families who moved out of the Milwaukee area. Telephone searches were impossible for that group.

Parents were asked two open-ended questions: Why did your child leave the Choice Program school? And where is he/she going to school now?

Of the reasons parents gave for leaving, only 15% of the responses (and they could give more than one) indicated child- or family-specific reasons— including moving. This category is clearly underestimated, however. Almost all of the remaining responses were critical of some aspect of the Choice Program or the private schools. The leading problems with the program were the lack of religious training, school transportation problems, and difficulties in reapplying to the program (including references to not being readmitted). Within-school problems most often cited were unhappiness with the staff— usually teachers—dissatisfaction with the general quality of education, and per- ceptions that discipline was too strict. The lack of special programs, which might have been available elsewhere, was also cited in 6% of the responses (Witte et al., 1994, Table 19). Thus, survey responses fit in with the factors that seem to distinguish attrition students from those who remain—distance and transportation problems, less achievement success, and resulting dissatisfaction with the private schools.

Finally, where did the students go? Survey data were very consistent with later efforts by the Wisconsin Legislative Audit Bureau to track leaving students back to MPS. Survey data indicated that approximately half of the students who left after the second and third year (57%) enrolled in MPS schools, 26% in other private schools in the area (often for religious reasons), with the remaining 16% going to MPS contract schools, home schooling, or schools outside Milwaukee. The Legislative Audit Bureau confirmed that 51.5% of the students had enrolled in MPS (Wisconsin Legislative Audit Bureau, 1995, p. 35).

Outcomes: Effects on Schools

Effects on Public Schools

Ideally, an analysis of a voucher program would include a study of the impact of vouchers on both private and public schools. Choice supporters argue that competition will improve all schools, including those in the public sector. There are, unfortunately, several research problems that make such a study difficult if not impossible in the Milwaukee case and possibly for a much larger and less targeted voucher program as well. First, in the case of Milwaukee (and now Cleveland), the program was simply too small to have discernible direct effects on the school system. There was no doubt that with the hundreds of media presentations about Milwaukee, usually prefaced by anguished examples of failures of the public schools, the program provided a bully pulpit for public school critics. This may have had indirect effects on MPS. However, given that the number of students enrolled barely reached 1% of the MPS enrollment, direct competition for students was not likely.[16]

The problems of determining the effects of vouchers on public schools are not only a question of size, however. Large inner-city school districts are constantly reforming, experimenting, and reorganizing their schools and sys- tems. The effect is that change is ongoing, and trying to causally distinguish "routine" changes from those specifically tied to the onset of a voucher program will be very difficult if not impossible.

Effects on Private Schools

Some would argue that publicly subsidizing the improvement of private schools is far from a positive outcome. Others may believe that maintaining and improving all options makes sense in what everyone agrees is a difficult educational environment. Whatever normative spin the reader wants to assume, improvement in many of the surviving Choice schools did occur.

Of the initial seven schools in the Choice Program in 1990, one was a very small, highly regarded, upper-class Montessori school that enrolled only several Choice students. One was a school for extremely-at-risk students (on the verge of dropping out), and the other five were kindergarten-through-eighth-grade schools. Of those, one, Juanita Virgil Academy, with initially 90 students, went bankrupt and closed abruptly in February 1991. The other six survived and remained in the program for the entire five years of this study.

However, two of the surviving schools were on the verge of bankruptcy when the program began. One had declared its intention to close when the program was enacted, and another was in an extremely difficult financial position. It went through three principals in the first year and probably only survived because of an infusion of money and support from a powerful neighborhood community center. These two schools today enroll over 700 children. The school taken over by the community center has managed to build a new and quite beautiful 11-room school attached to the community center. As of this writing, building was beginning on eight more classrooms. Although clearly, the Choice Program alone was not responsible for that new school, it played a role.[17]

The other schools, while their stories are not as dramatic, also improved their facilities, expanded their programs (one adding an additional preschool site), and improved turnover and diversity in their faculty. Turnover and new personnel rates declined substantially over the life of the program. Undoubtedly, this was due to increasing teacher salaries and benefits, but precise data were unavailable. Certification figures are less clear because of the types of certifications available, but the number of teachers with no certification clearly declined.

Correlated with the decline in turnover, the seniority levels of teachers also increased, although they remain well behind average seniority in public schools. Two important facts to note are that after the first year, there were no teachers hired *during* the year (as indicated by the 14% with zero years in 1990–91). Also, in 1990–91, there were only 24% of the teachers with more than four years in the schools. After the Choice Program was created, 52% of the teachers had four or more years of experience.

With 1990–91 as the base year (the teaching force was more or less set before the program was finally enacted), over the course of the program, there was racial and gender diversification among teachers in the schools. Although these schools were primarily minority schools (with one exception), the teaching force was not. One of the reasons for this was that MPS had an aggressive affirmative action program, and minority teachers could easily find much higher paying jobs in the public schools. Over the life of the program, while the trend is not uniform, there was a decline in White teachers from 75 to 62%. This was approximately matched by an increase in males from 11% to 24%.

Finally, continual visits to the schools also confirmed the positive impact of the Choice Program among the major schools. From the beginning, the voucher amount was considerably higher than tuition (more than double) for the three largest schools (accounting for over 80% of the students). These schools fought hard to keep the program going and lobbied extensively for the first round of program expansions.[18] Teachers and principals went out of their way to express their gratitude to influential politicians and were consistently positive in hundreds of media contacts.

Private School Failures

A full understanding of the impact of the Choice Program would be incomplete without mention of three Choice schools that went out of existence in mid-year. The first occurred in the first year; the last two in 1995–96. The first case, which was the only one researched for this study, was a case of bankruptcy preceded by very inadequate instruction and administration. By the time the school actually went bankrupt in February 1991, more than half of the students had already quit and returned to MPS (Witte, 1991). The later failures were of one school that was in the program for two and one half years and one school that began in 1995. In both cases, the founders, who were also the directors, are under various criminal charges, including but not limited to mishandling and embezzlement of public funds. Three hundred fifty-six students were in these schools, and the state lost an estimated $390,000 in funds that were paid for education that never occurred (*Education Week*, February 21, 1996, p. 3; *Milwaukee Journal Sentinel*, February 21, 1996, p. B1).

Thus, as with the effects on students and families, school effects of the Milwaukee voucher experiment are mixed. For most schools, the program was a welcome source of support. In a minority of schools, not only were public moneys wasted, but also precious months of children's education. To assume that vouchers will not be subject to some corruption and abuse and that simply pumping money into private schools will automatically enhance education and create great schools is hopelessly naive. But these problems are offset by the enhanced opportunities provided for families who otherwise could not afford a private school alternative.

CONCLUSIONS

Although somewhat frustrating, the mixed results of the Milwaukee voucher program are what we might anticipate from a very controversial program applied to an inner-city educational system. Controversy exists for a reason. Studies comparing public and private school achievement have reached varying conclusions. And claims favoring private schools were often questioned because of the problem of unmeasured selection bias. So why, in a program that required random assignment, would one assume that the private schools would work miracles that the public schools could not? And given that vouchers were provided to schools with no requirements other than being registered private schools, why would one assume that the quality of these schools would be uniformly high? More realistic assumptions would be that educational results and the quality of schools would vary, and that is what our research found.

One final point must be addressed. This study is of a targeted and limited voucher program. But the Milwaukee program also exemplifies the tendency to expand vouchers to a much wider population. The 1995 expansion, which has just been approved by the Wisconsin Supreme Court, expanded the program to include religious schools, many more students, and students already in private schools.[19] If that becomes law after an appeal to the U.S. Supreme Court and later just a few more words were removed from the statute, the result would be an open-ended voucher program. The mayor of Milwaukee, John Norquist, has already proposed removing all income limits on the program (*Milwaukee Journal Sentinel*, August 5, 1998, p. 5A). In that case, the outcomes presented here might look very different.

The strongest argument for vouchers in this article is equal opportunity. The program clearly provided an opportunity for some poor families, whose children were not doing well in public schools, to obtain an alternative education that it is unlikely they could have afforded on their own. Would an open-ended voucher program produce the same results? We do not know. However, we can be quite confident that at least in the short term the students likely to benefit from vouchers would differ considerably from those who received them in the Milwaukee Parental Choice Program. Without income constraints or random selection, and given that most students attend private schools for religious purposes, it is reasonable to assume that the current private school population would be a good guide to those who will benefit under an open-ended voucher program. And they are not poor, minority families. In Milwaukee, based on 1990 census data, they are quite the opposite. The average private school family made over $42,000 a year compared to $25,000 for the average public school family. In terms of race, 84% of private school children in Milwaukee were White, whereas only 33% of the public school children were White (Witte & Thorn, 1995). To open this program up to everyone, which certainly is the direction of change, would undoubtedly produce a very different program with very different consequences.

Notes

1. A planned voucher experiment in the early 1970s, the Alum Rock experiment, in a small district near San Jose, California, never included private schools. They were to be included under the original experimental design, but were eliminated at the insistence of the local teachers association (for details, see Witte & Rigdon, 1993). A number of other countries subsidize private schools in many ways. However,

those systems vary considerably in terms of public school arrangements. Also, no other country has the unique characteristic of almost total nonregulation of private schools because of the separation of church and state that has developed because of our First Amendment to the Constitution.

2. Information in this section comes primarily from Witte and others (1994, 1995).

3. This change is extremely important because most students were admitted to the Choice Program in those grades. Private schools, in general, prefer to limit lateral entry at higher grades and therefore have a grade structure with more students in the lower grades.

4. The average response rates for the first (fall) Choice surveys were 44%; the second (spring) surveys were 46%; the rate for the MPS sample was 32%. Although the response rates were low relative to face-to-face interviews with national samples, they were higher than the approximately 20% response rates that MPS reported for its usual surveys. Independent measures of race and qualification for free lunches existed from the Milwaukee student record database for both the random sample and the Choice students. Thus, it was possible to assess sampling bias and construct weights to offset that bias. For MPS, the only statistically significant sampling bias was for race, where we had a less-than-expected response for African Americans, oversampling of Asians and Whites, and a slight undersample of low-income families. For Choice students, there was a disproportionately high response from African Americans and a low response from Hispanics. The results presented in this article are for unweighted samples.

   Scales and demographic variables were also analyzed using three weights: a weight based on expected race, a weight based on expected low/non-low income, and a weight combining both race and income. The combined race and income weight is the most accurate because for the MPS respondents, the sampling bias for race was considerably larger than income; the income-weighted analysis produced no significant differences except on the income variable itself. The race/income analysis produced only one marginally significant difference on attitude scale means. It also produced significantly different effects for household income, percent of female parents on Aid to Families With Dependent Children (welfare), and the percentage of single-parent families. Analysis of the weighted Choice sample produced no differences that approached significance at the .05 level.

5. Comparative standardized test data were only available during the first four years because MPS ceased giving most Iowa tests after 1994. They were replaced by required state tests.

6. Wisconsin allows school districts to contract with secular private schools to educate preschool and at-risk students. The contracts are yearly and average about 80% of the per-member cost in the public school district. A number of independent private schools that had a history of contracting unsuccessfully fought the voucher program, advocating instead expansion of contracting options. Most of them later refused to enter the Choice Program.

7. This difference is statistically significant at the .01 level. Whereas it may appear to be quite small substantively, in terms of long-term demographic trends, this difference in fertility would be very substantial.

8. Surveys of Choice parents, conducted in June of each year, were returned by an average 46% of the parents. All surveys, pre- and post-, were sent twice. It is difficult to determine biases in the responses. Would more pleased or angry parents be more likely to respond? Even if the response bias favors more favorably disposed parents, the reported differences between pre- and post-attitudes are extremely large.

9. It is not as clear that the Choice students held their own as it is for the MPS students. The reason is that the original MPS sample was unchanged, except for attrition, whereas new students entered the Choice Program each year. Because Choice students were admitted in the very lowest grades, the MPS sample "aged" more than did the Choice sample.

10. The results in Tables 5 and 6 (in the original article) are stacked, and thus, a student may appear more than once in different years. This could violate the ordinary least squares (OLS) assumption of independence of error terms. The standard correction for this is to use the Huber/White corrections to recompute standard errors of the estimators. Application of that correction had no appreciable effect, and therefore, ordinary OLS estimates are reported (see Huber, 1967; White, 1980).

11. Large differences among groups in math with no differences in reading are highly suspect given that math and reading scores are very highly correlated for large populations.

12. The data do not contain the original answers to each question so it cannot be determined if students missed all of the questions or large blocks—which would be indicative of not filling in the dots. However, adding to the speculation that these students simply did not do the test is that those same five students scored an average of 31 on their math tests in the prior (1993) year.

13. Eliminating 2 Choice students raised the average on math of the remaining 83 students' 1994 post-tests by only 0.9 NCE. However, eliminating 5 reject students raised the average of the remaining 22 students by 6.5 NCEs.

14. The author had a conversation to this effect with the principal of one of the largest schools. He said, "We were very lax the first year because we knew these kids needed readjusting to our style. However, by the end of the second year, it was clear they were not working out and we let a number go."

15. MPS also experienced attrition and did not test every student each year. In a detailed study of achievement scores, the regressions were rerun inserting a Heckman correction for attrition (Heckman, 1979). The Mills ratio was significant, and the re-estimated reading difference between Choice and MPS proved to be insignificant because of inflated standard errors (Witte, 1997).

16. During the first years of the program, the reverse may have occurred. MPS was overcrowded, and very early in the semester in each of the first two years, the MPS administration wanted lists of students enrolled in Choice private schools because a number of those students had also signed up for MPS schools. The administration wanted to release seats of Choice students and give them to other students.

17. The new school cost approximately $3.2 million, not including donated labor. Of that, $1.7 million came in the form of a HUD grant to the community center, and $1.6 million was raised in the community, primarily from corporations and wealthy donors. Two retired businessmen led the fundraising efforts, and a Democratic congressman was influential in securing the HUD grant.

18. Their position on expanding to parochial schools in 1995 is not unified, however. The original sponsor of the legislation, Rep. Polly Williams (D-Milwaukee), whose district includes the two biggest schools, has subsequently introduced legislation to drop parochial schools and return to the original program.

19. The 1995 changes in the statute seem to match Governor Thompson's original intent. In legislation he proposed in 1989, a program limited to free-lunch-eligible students would have included parochial schools and students already in those schools (in grades K-6). There was no limit on the total number of students, and all of Milwaukee County, not just the city, would have been included.

REFERENCES

Beales, J., & Wahl, M. (1995). Private vouchers in Milwaukee: The PAVE program. In T. Moe (Ed.), *Private vouchers* (pp. 41–73). Stanford, CA: Hoover Institute.

Bryk, A., Lee, V., & Holland, P. (1994). *Catholic schools and the common good.* Cambridge, MA: Harvard University Press.

Chubb, J., & Moe, T. (1990). *Politics, markets and American schools.* Washington, DC: The Brookings Institution.

Cookson, P. W., Jr. (1994). *School choice: The struggle for American education.* New Haven, CT: Yale University Press.

Coons, J., & Sugarman, S. (1978). *Education by choice: The case for family control.* Berkeley, The University of California Press.

Coons, J., & Sugarman, S. (1992). *Scholarships for children.* Berkeley: Institute of Governmental Studies Press, University of California.

Driscoll, M. (1993). Choice, achievement and school community. In E. Rasell & R. Rothstein (Eds.), *School choice* (pp. 147–172). Washington, DC: Economic Policy Institute.

Friedman, M. (1955). The role of government in education. In R. A. Solow (Ed.), *Economics and the public interest* (pp. 123–144). New Brunswick, NJ: Rutgers Press.

Gamoran, A. (1996). Student achievement in public magnet, public comprehensive, and private high schools. *Educational Evaluation and Policy Analysis, 18*(1), 1–18.

Goldhaber, D. (1996). *Public and private high schools: Is school choice an answer to the productivity problem?* Unpublished manuscript.

Greene, J., Peterson, P., & Du, J. (1996, August–September). The effectiveness of school choice in Milwaukee: A secondary analysis of data from the program's evaluation. Paper presented at the American Political Science Association's annual meeting, San Francisco.

Hannaway, J., & Garner, W. (1980). *The private high school today.* Washington, DC: U.S. Department of Education.

Heckman, J. (1979). Sample selection bias as a specification error. *Econometrica, 47,* 153–161.

Henig, J. (1994). *Rethinking school choice: Limits of the market metaphor.* Princeton, NJ: Princeton University Press.

Hoffer, T., & Coleman, J. (1987). *Public and private high schools: The impact of communities.* New York: Basic Books.

Hoffer, T., Kilgore, S., & Coleman, J. (1982). *High school achievement: Public, Catholic and private schools compared.* New York: Basic Books.

Hoxby, C. (1996). Evidence on private school vouchers: Effects on school and students. In H. Ladd (Ed.), *Holding schools accountable* (pp. 177–208). Washington, DC: The Brookings Institution.

Huber, P. J. (1967). The behavior of maximum likelihood estimates under nonstandard conditions. *Proceedings of the Fifth Berkeley Symposium on Mathematical Statistics and Probability, 1,* 221–233.

Manski, C. (1992). Educational choice (vouchers) and social mobility. *Economics of Education Review,* 11 (December), 351–369.

Plank, S. et al. (1993). Effects of choice in education. In E. Rasell & R. Rothstein (Eds.), *School choice* (pp. 111–134). Washington, DC: Economic Policy Institute.

Rouse, C. (1997). Private school vouchers and student achievement: An evaluation of the Milwaukee Parental Choice Program. Unpublished manuscript, Princeton University, Princeton, NJ.

Smith, K., & Meier, K. (1995). *The case against school choice*. Armonk, NY: M. E. Sharpe.

Wahl, J. (1994). *Second-year report of the PAVE scholarship program*. Milwaukee, WI: Family Services of America.

Wells, A. S. (1993). *Time to choose: America at the crossroads of school choice policy*. New York: Hill and Wang.

White, H. (1980). A heteroskedasticity-consistent covariance matrix estimator and a direct test for heteroskedasticity. *Econometrica, 48*, 817–830.

Wisconsin Legislative Audit Bureau. (1995). *An evaluation of the Milwaukee Parental Choice Program*. Madison, WI: Author.

Witte, J. (1991). *First year report: Milwaukee Parental Choice Program*. Report prepared for the Wisconsin State Legislature, Department of Public Instruction, Madison, WI.

Witte, J. (1992). Private versus public school achievement: Should the findings affect the choice debate? *Economics of Education Review, 70* (fall), 371–394.

Witte, J. (1996). School choice and student performance. In H. Ladd (Ed.), *Holding schools accountable* (pp. 149–176). Washington, DC: The Brookings Institution.

Witte, J. (1997). The Milwaukee Parental Choice Program: Achievement test score results. Paper presented at the American Economic Association's annual meeting, New Orleans, LA.

Witte, J. (2000). *The market approach to education: An analysis of America's first voucher program*. Princeton, NJ: Princeton University Press.

Witte, J., & Rigdon, M. (1993). Education choice reforms: Will they change American schools? *Publius, 23*(Summer), 95–114.

Witte, J., & Thorn, C. (1995). *Who attends public and private schools in Wisconsin: With implications for the Milwaukee Choice Program*. Madison, WI: Robert LaFollette Institute of Public Affairs.

Witte, J., & Thorn, C. (1996). Who chooses? Vouchers and interdistrict choice programs in Milwaukee. *American Journal of Education, 104* (May), 186–217.

Witte, J., Rigdon, M., & Bailey, A. (1992). *Second year report: Milwaukee Parental Choice Program*. Report prepared for the Wisconsin State Legislature, Department of Public Instruction, Madison, WI.

Witte, J., Thorn, C., & Sterr, T. (1995). *Fifth year report: Milwaukee Parental Choice Program*. Report prepared for the Wisconsin State Legislature, Department of Public Instruction, Madison, WI.

Witte, J., Thorn, C., Pritchard, K., & Claibourn, M. (1994). *Fourth year report: Milwaukee Parental Choice Program*. Report prepared for the Wisconsin State Legislature, Department of Public Instruction, Madison, WI.

16

High Stakes in Chicago

Brian Jacob

As the first large urban school district to introduce a comprehensive accountability system, Chicago provides an exceptional case study of the effects of high-stakes testing—a reform strategy that will become omnipresent as the No Child Left Behind Act is implemented nationwide. One of the most serious criticisms of high-stakes testing is that it leads to "inflated" test scores that do not truly reflect students' knowledge or skills and therefore cannot be generalized to other tests. This article summarizes my research on whether the Chicago accountability system produced "real" gains in student achievement.

The first step in Chicago's accountability effort was to end the practice of "social promotion," whereby students were advanced to the next grade regardless of achievement level. Under the new policy, students in the 3rd, 6th, and 8th grades were required to meet minimum standards in reading and mathematics on the Iowa Test of Basic Skills (ITBS) in order to step up to the next grade. Students who didn't meet the standard were required to attend a six-week summer-school program, after which they took the exams again. Those who passed were able to move on to the next grade. Students who again failed to meet the standard were required to repeat the grade, with the exception of 15-year-olds who attended newly created "transition" centers. (Many students in special education and bilingual programs were exempt from these requirements.) In the fall of 1997, roughly 20 percent of Chicago's 3rd graders and 10 to 15 percent of 6th and 8th graders were held back.

Meanwhile, Chicago also instituted an "academic probation" program designed to hold teachers and schools accountable for student achievement. Schools in which fewer than 15 percent of students scored at or above national norms on the ITBS reading exam were placed on probation. If they did not exhibit sufficient improvement, these schools could be reconstituted, with teachers and school administrators dismissed or reassigned. In the 1996–97 school year, 71 elementary schools were placed on academic probation. While only recently has Chicago actually reconstituted several schools, as early as 1997 teachers and administrators in probationary schools reported being extremely worried about their job security, and staff in other schools reported a strong desire to avoid probation.

HIGH STAKES AND TEST SCORES

Scores on the ITBS increased substantially in Chicago in the second half of the 1990s. However, many factors besides the accountability policies may have influenced the achievement trends in Chicago. For instance, the population of students may have changed during the period in which high-stakes testing was implemented. An influx of recent immigrants during the mid- to late 1990s may depress the city's test scores, whereas they would be likely to rise with the return of middle-class students to the city. Similarly, policy changes at the state or national level, such as the efforts to reduce class sizes or mandate higher-quality teachers, if effective, would likely lead one to overestimate the impact of Chicago's policies.

The rich set of longitudinal, student-level data available for Chicago allowed me to overcome many of these concerns. I was able to adjust for observable changes in student composition, such as the district's racial and socioeconomic makeup and its students' prior achievement. Moreover, because achievement data were available back to 1990, six years prior to the introduction of the accountability policies, I was able to account for preexisting achievement trends within Chicago. Using this information, I looked for a sharp increase in achievement (a break in trend) following the introduction of high-stakes testing as evidence of a policy effect. Comparing achievement trends in Chicago with those in other urban districts in Illinois as well as in large midwestern cities outside Illinois enabled me to address the concern about actions at the state and federal level that might have influenced achievement.

The sample consisted of students who were in the 3rd, 6th, and 8th grades from 1993 to 2000. The new policy on social promotion caused a large number of low-performing students in these grades to be retained, substantially changing the student composition in these and subsequent grades beginning in the 1997–98 school year. For this reason I limited the sample to students who were in these three grades for the first time in their school career. Moreover, the results presented here are based on only those students who were tested and whose scores were included by the district for official reporting purposes. (Each year roughly 10 percent of students were not tested, and an additional 10 to 15 percent had scores that were not reported because of a special education or bilingual placement.) Analyses using a sample of all students who were tested yielded similar results. While special education placement rates appeared to increase following the introduction of the accountability policy in Chicago, this alone can explain only a small fraction of the observed achievement gains.

Using the observed achievement scores for successive cohorts of Chicago students from 1993 to 2000, predicted scores were obtained from a regression analysis that accounted for changes in student composition and prior

achievement levels as well as overall trends in achievement before the introduction of the accountability program. The results indicate that neither
observable changes in student composition nor preexisting achievement
trends in Chicago explain the substantial improvement in student performance since 1997. The trends predicted that achievement in math would
decrease or remain flat after 1996. In practice, however, achievement slipped
somewhat from 1993 to 1996, but increased sharply after 1996. By 2000,
math scores were roughly 0.3 standard deviations higher than predicted, an
improvement about one quarter the size of the difference in math performance between Chicago students in consecutive grades in 1995. A similar pattern was apparent in reading. Predicted and observed test scores were
relatively flat from 1993 to 1996. In 1997 the gap between observed and
predicted scores appeared to widen, and then grew substantially in 1998.
By 2000 students were scoring roughly 0.2 standard deviations higher than
predicted.

Still, it is possible that the achievement gains in Chicago simply reflected
improvements in student performance in the state or nation. The economy
was growing throughout the latter half of the 1990s, and there was a considerable emphasis on public education at the federal level. The achievement
of a nationwide sample of 4th and 8th grade students with the same racial
make-up as Chicago students, as measured by the National Assessment of
Educational Progress (NAEP), increased roughly 0.25 standard deviations in
math during the 1990s, though there was no gain in reading.

However, a comparison with other urban districts in Illinois and the
Midwest, such as Cincinnati, Gary, Indianapolis, Milwaukee, and St. Louis,
none of which created a similar accountability system during this period,
shows that Chicago's trend is unique. Trends in Chicago and the other cities
tracked one another remarkably well from 1993 to 1996, then began to
diverge in 1997. Math and reading achievement in the comparison districts
remained relatively constant from 1996 to 2000, while achievement levels in
Chicago rose sharply over this period—by roughly 0.3 standard deviations in
math and 0.2 standard deviations in reading.

Together, these results suggest that the accountability policy in Chicago
led to a substantial increase in math and reading achievement. It appears that
the effects were somewhat larger for math than for reading. This is consistent
with a number of studies that show larger effects in math than in reading,
presumably because reading achievement is more strongly influenced by
family and other factors besides schooling. The effects were also somewhat
larger for 8th grade students. This is consistent with the fact that 8th graders
faced the largest incentives: they could not move to high school with their
peers if they failed to meet the standards for promotion.

CHECKING ON INFLATION

The accountability policies that the Chicago school system put in place clearly
led to an increase in scores on the ITBS. Nevertheless, critics of high-stakes

testing wonder whether those increases reflect real gains in students' knowledge and skills—gains that ought to translate to students' performance in school and on other exams. When test scores are "inflated"—by, say, cheating or intense preparation that is geared to a specific exam—observed achievement gains are misleading because they do not reflect a more general mastery of the subject.

Researchers have found considerable evidence of test-score inflation throughout the country during the past two decades. In 1987, for example, John Jacob Cannell discovered what has become known as the "Lake Wobegon" effect—the fact that a disproportionate number of states and districts report being "above the national norm." More recently, researchers have demonstrated that Kentucky and Texas made substantially larger gains on state tests (the KIRIS and TAAS, respectively) than on the NAEP. This is one reason why the No Child Left Behind legislation requires states to consider NAEP scores along with scores from state exams.

An approach commonly used to investigate score inflation is to compare student performance trends across exams. The notion is that if the gains on the high-stakes exam are not accompanied by gains on other achievement exams, then the gains may not be generalizable.

In Chicago, elementary students have traditionally taken two exams. The district has administered the ITBS, one of several standardized, multiple-choice exams used by districts across the country, to students in 3rd to 8th grades for many years. Chicago's accountability sanctions were determined solely by student performance on the ITBS, making it the high-stakes exam. At the same time, Chicago elementary students took another standardized, multiple-choice exam administered by the state, known as the Illinois Goals Assessment Program (IGAP). Before 1996 the IGAP was arguably the higher-stakes exam, even though there were no direct consequences for students or schools tied to the IGAP, since results from it appeared annually in local newspapers. After 1996 the IGAP clearly became the low-stakes exam for students and teachers in Chicago in comparison with the ITBS.

In 1993, Chicago students scored between 0.4 and 0.8 standard deviations below students in other urban districts on the IGAP. During the mid-1990s, the achievement gap between Chicago and other districts appeared to narrow. However, this trend began, at least in 3rd and 6th grades, before the introduction of high-stakes testing in these grades, and there was no noticeable break in the trend in 1997, the first year of the accountability system. Achievement scores in the 8th grade, particularly in reading, showed some break beginning in 1996 (the accountability policy began for 8th graders in 1996).

What can be inferred from these trends? On the one hand, a simple comparison of student achievement at the beginning and end of the decade suggests that Chicago experienced roughly comparable improvement on the IGAP and the ITBS. This might lead to the conclusion that the achievement gains on both exams were largely generalizable. On the other hand, a comparison of how achievement in the late 1990s changed in relation to the preexisting trends on each exam suggests that the accountability policy had a large effect on ITBS scores but little if any effect on IGAP scores. This might lead to the conclusion that the ITBS gains in Chicago were driven largely by test-score inflation.

The data do not necessarily support either conclusion, however. One problem is that the ITBS and IGAP are different in both content and format. In mathematics, the ITBS places more emphasis on computation, while the IGAP appears to give greater weight to problem-solving skills. Indeed, the computation items on the IGAP are often asked in the context of a word problem. The general format of the reading comprehension sections on the two exams are similar—both ask students to read passages and then answer questions about the passage—the IGAP consists of fewer, but longer passages, whereas the ITBS contains a greater number of passages, each of which is shorter. Perhaps more important, the questions on the IGAP may have multiple correct responses in comparison with the ITBS, on which there is only one correct response. The fact that the two exams displayed different trends before the introduction of the accountability policy suggests that they measure somewhat different concepts.

The natural solution would be to adjust the ITBS and IGAP scores to account for such differences in content. For example, one might estimate what the IGAP scores would have been if both exams had the same distribution of question types. In practice, this exercise is probably only feasible in mathematics, where test items can be categorized with relative precision. Moreover, this requires detailed item-level information for both exams, which is not available for the IGAP.

A second difficulty in interpreting the differences in performance trends between the two exams involves student effort. Students undoubtedly began to increase test-day effort for the ITBS after 1996. It is unclear how, if at all, effort levels changed on the IGAP. One might imagine that effort increased somewhat given the new climate surrounding testing. Equally plausible, however, is the idea that effort has declined now that teachers and students view IGAP scores as largely irrelevant. If student effort on the ITBS increased at the same time that effort on the IGAP decreased, one would expect more rapid achievement growth on the ITBS even if the exams were identical or learning were completely generalizable.

In sum, given the differences in composition between the two exams along with possible changes in student effort over the time period, it is extremely difficult to determine what one should *expect* to see under the best of circumstances.

MEANINGFUL IMPROVEMENT

It is important not to exaggerate the importance of the fact that gains may not generalize to other exams. Even if an accountability program produces true, meaningful gains, we would not expect gains on one test to be completely reflected in data from other tests because of the inherent differences across exams. Even the most comprehensive achievement exam can cover only a fraction of the possible skills and topics within a particular domain. For this reason, different exams often lead to different inferences about student mastery, regardless of whether any type of accountability policy is in place.

Yet in discussing how to interpret test-score gains, even testing experts occasionally slip into language that seems to neglect the value of gains in particular areas. Harvard scholar Daniel Koretz notes, "When scores increase, students clearly have improved the mastery of the sample included in the test. This is of no interest, however, unless the improvement justifies the inference that students have attained greater mastery of the domain the test is intended to represent." Does this mean that if children improve their ability to add fractions, interpret line graphs, or identify the main idea of a written passage, this is of no interest?

Most people would agree that these improvements, while limited to specific skills or topics, are indeed important. This suggests an alternative criterion by which to judge changes in student performance—namely, that achievement gains on test items that measure particular skills or understandings may be *meaningful* even if the student's overall test score does not fully generalize to other exams. To be meaningful, achievement gains must result from greater student understanding, and they must be important in some educational sense.

Test-score gains that result from cheating on the part of students or teachers would of course not be considered meaningful. Similarly, most people would not view as meaningful increases in performance that result from an improvement in testing conditions. A less clear-cut case involves student effort. Various studies have shown that accountability policies lead students to take standardized exams more seriously, either by working harder during the school year or by simply concentrating harder during the actual exam (or both). While the former clearly represents meaningful gains, the latter may not. One could argue that teaching students to try hard in critical situations is a useful thing. But the observed improvements in student performance would represent greater effort rather than greater understanding.

A CLOSE LOOK AT THE QUESTIONS

One way to assess the meaningfulness of reported achievement gains is to see how changes in student performance varied across individual test questions. While item analysis is not a new technique, it may provide important insight in assessing the effects of testing policies. Consider test completion rates on the ITBS. Since there is no penalty for guessing on the ITBS (total score is determined solely by the number correct), the simplest way for a student to increase his or her expected score is to make sure that no items are left blank. Before the introduction of the accountability policy in Chicago, a surprisingly high proportion of students left one or more items of the ITBS exam blank. In 1994 only 58 and 77 percent of 8th grade students completed the entire math and reading exams, respectively.

Test-completion rates increased sharply under the high-stakes testing regime. For instance, the number of 8th graders who completed the entire math exam increased to nearly 63 percent in 1998, with the vast majority of students leaving only one or two items blank. The greatest impact was for low-achieving students, largely because the overwhelming majority of higher-achieving students had completed the exam before the onset of high-stakes testing.

Can guessing explain the observed achievement gains in Chicago? If the increased test scores were due solely to guessing, the percentage of questions answered would increase, but the percentage of questions answered *correctly* (as a percentage of all *answered* questions) would remain constant or perhaps even decline. In Chicago, the percentage of questions answered has increased, but the percentage answered correctly has also gone up, suggesting that the higher completion rates were not entirely due to guessing. A more detailed analysis suggests that guessing could explain only a small fraction of the overall achievement gains. Next consider student performance across skill areas. The ITBS math section measures students' understanding of five broad areas: number concepts, estimation, problem-solving, data interpretation, and computation. Questions in the reading section are broken into three broad categories: understanding factual information, evaluating written material (identifying the author's viewpoint, determining the main idea), and drawing inferences (inferring the feelings, motives, and traits of characters in a story, predicting likely outcomes).

The size of achievement gains following the introduction of the accountability policy differed across item areas. Students improved 7.1 percentage points on items involving number concepts and 6.8 percentage points on items involving computation. By contrast, students gained only 4.3 percentage points on problem-solving items and roughly 5.5 percentage points on data interpretation and estimation questions. Overall, these results suggest that math teachers may have focused on specific content areas in response to the accountability policy. Given the considerable weight placed on mathematical computation and number concepts in the ITBS, perhaps along with the perceived ease of teaching these skills, it would not be surprising if teachers chose to focus their energy in these areas. In reading, students made comparable improvement (roughly 5 percentage points) across question type, suggesting that test preparation may have played a larger role in math than in reading.

These aggregate results provide some insight, but the accountability policy affected students and schools differently based on previous achievement levels. In particular, observers have expressed concerns that the lowest-performing schools have responded to the policy by simply focusing on test preparation. If this were true, one would expect the patterns of test-score gains across items to differ for low- versus high-performing students and schools.

To explore this, I examined achievement changes by item type for low-, moderate-, and high-performing schools, as measured by the percentage of students scoring at or above national norms on the ITBS reading exam in 1995. Schools with fewer than 20 percent of students meeting norms were defined as low achieving; those with 20 to 30 percent meeting norms were moderate achieving; and those with at least 30 percent of students' meeting norms were high achieving (this created three groups of equal size). Two patterns stood out. In both reading and mathematics, low- and moderate-achieving schools made overall gains greater than those of high-achieving schools under the accountability policy. This is consistent with the incentives generated by the policy, which placed low-achieving schools on probation. Regardless of previous achievement level, however, all schools appeared to have improved more in computation and number concepts than in other math concepts. Interestingly, while low-achieving schools improved in areas such as problem-solving and data analysis, higher-achieving schools made little if any improvement in these areas. For reading, regardless of school performance level, students showed similar improvement on items measuring factual, inferential, and evaluative understandings.

CONCLUSIONS

Chicago's experience with accountability provides some lessons for other districts and states as they begin to implement the mandates of No Child Left Behind. The results of my analysis suggest that high-stakes testing substantially increases math and reading performance, with gains on the order of 0.20 to 0.30 standard deviations. Item-level analysis of test-score gains in Chicago during the 1990s reveals that math gains were disproportionately focused in certain areas, and therefore may not generalize to alternative performance measures, particularly those that tap other domains of knowledge. Nonetheless, this does not mean that the gains were not meaningful. They may well reflect an authentic increase in certain areas of knowledge and skills, underscoring the need for careful attention to the specific content of the exams used to hold schools and students accountable. Furthermore, it is important to note that the performance of Chicago's students on alternative assessments continued to increase in absolute terms, which may mean that there was no substantial tradeoff in skills learned. The broader lesson is that educators and policymakers must look beyond aggregate measures of student performance to assess the nature of observed performance trends, and they must carefully distinguish between concerns of generalizability and concerns of meaningfulness. Overall, these results suggest that high-stakes testing has the potential to improve student learning meaningfully, but attempts to generalize the results to other learning must be approached with caution.

Epilogue: The Uncertain Future of Urban Education

Jean Anyon is among the most thoughtful and astute observers of urban education in the United States today. In 1995 she published a searching examination of the issues facing educators who struggle with the day-to-day challenges of working in an inner-city school. She noted the frustrations these individuals faced, and the behavior they sometimes found themselves exhibiting in attempting to reach the children they were charged with educating. Most of them, she found, did not believe that educational reform would make much difference in the challenges they faced, or the possibilities of success for the children they taught. Anyon described the immense barriers that existed between the educators in this school and the children in their classes, a situation that occasionally resulted in abusive behavior on the part of both teachers and students.

The demands of teaching under these conditions were extraordinary, and even the most committed and talented individuals found it overwhelming as time passed. This does not mean that the schools in such areas do not occasionally achieve remarkable success, even against the great odds. Anyon pointed out that this was considered a "good school," and she also described the joy that these educators experienced in the achievements of their students. But fundamental change under these circumstances was improbable. As she put it, "sociocultural differences among participants in reform, an abusive school environment, and educator expectations of failed reform, occurring in a minority ghetto where the school population is racially and economically isolated constitute some of the powerful and devastating ways that concomitants of race and social class can intervene to determine what happens in inner-city schools." In other words, the problems of the racially segregated city, and the pervasive inequality in economic and social status that characterizes today's metropolitan society, make the prospects of meaningful change in urban schools quite uncertain.[1] One might add that this is likely to be true regardless of whether the schools are public or private, governed by central boards of education or local councils, or funded with state or federal dollars. In the end, the most compelling problems in urban education revolve around the children who attend (or drop out of) these schools and the adults who work in them. It is addressing these issues that reformers who propose to fix the city schools must consider.

Part of the problem, of course, is that the cities themselves had changed dramatically in a relatively short period of time, at least in historical terms. As noted in the introduction and several of the other chapters in this volume, the arrival of millions of African American and other minority families in the nation's largest metropolitan areas altered the dynamics of urban development in the latter half of the twentieth century. Deindustrialization, suburbanization, and racial segregation isolated these newcomers in declining inner-city neighborhoods, resulting in manifold difficulties. The concentration of poverty and related issues of nonemployment, crime, and changing family structures have been unprecedented in American history. Many of these problems existed in the past, of course, but not on the same scale nor to this degree. This means that the questions that urban educators serving the children from these areas must contend with are even more complex and exacting than those faced by previous generations of teachers, principals, and superintendents. This is a major part of the story behind the picture that Anyon has painted, the historical backdrop to the current "crisis" in urban education. The weight of history is quite heavy in the inner city neighborhoods of many large American cities these days.[2]

While it is tempting to dwell on the many problems of the cities, however, it would be wrong to conclude that these questions are the only side to the story. As Anyon has suggested, there also is the matter of the school themselves, and the educators who work in them. Here too the weight of history is significant indeed. As seen in earlier chapters, today's urban school regime developed during the nineteenth century, when the major challenges seemed to entail establishing systematic and consistent standards of performance, for students and educators alike. The dilemmas of the age were the haphazard teaching arrangements, inconsistent curricula and grading across the schools, and lack of uniform qualifications for teachers, administrators, and other school personnel. The response was the development of modern bureaucratic procedures for classifying and managing school employees, rules for teachers and students, and consistent curricula and performance standards for the schools. In the words of David Tyack, it was "the one best system," a method of school governance and administration that was spread from one city to another as a gospel of efficiency, order, and control.[3]

The resolution of one set of problems, however, too often leads to the rise of new ones. The reforms of the nineteenth and early twentieth century promised to deliver a consistent, reliable school experience, and provide a basic education to the greatest number of children at the most reasonable cost. In short, they resulted in what was a peculiarly industrial mode of school coordination and management, well suited to the demands of the rapidly growing cities of the industrial age. But the preoccupation with efficiency and standardization also may have carried the seeds of the system's demise. This is a lesson too often overlooked in the history of reform; today's answers to seemingly intractable dilemmas may eventually pose yet other problems unimaginable at the time. This has been all too clearly evident in the history of urban schooling. The large, bureaucratic school districts that existed in most major cities by the 1930s proved remarkably indifferent to the changing character of their communities during the postwar period. And this continues to be all too frequently evident even today. The nonresponsiveness and abuse that Anyon described on the part of teachers appears to have reflected this; in particular it represented a failure to recognize the specific social and cultural needs of their students. Blaming the students for their failure can be interpreted as symptomatic of the industrial mode of urban school organization. In the most egregious instances, it reflects a response of classification and assessment rather than education, labeling students instead of teaching them.[4]

As Anyon's other writings make quite clear, this was not a new situation.[5] Earlier chapters in this book have demonstrated that the response of school leaders to racial and ethnic inequity in educational resources, during the era of desegregation, too often was to deny that a problem even existed. Recalcitrant school boards fought bitterly against local campaigns to rectify long-standing inequities in resource allocation, and to fight discriminatory curricular and counseling policies in particular schools. They viewed their responsibility as defending the system, not changing it to address question of equality or social justice. If uniformity and impartiality were the watchwords of the system, after all, why should accommodations be made for a particular community? Why should a school district permit a particular school to adopt a curriculum for a single racial or ethnic group, especially one represented by students and their relatively uneducated parents? Such demands flew in the face of the professional ethos that governed the schools. While "the one best system" may have performed passably on the tasks of efficiently distributing resources and maintaining certain standards, it did not adapt well to change. Underlying relations of power and authority made it difficult to accommodate the demands of students and community groups during the 1960s and 1970s.[6] This created a crisis, one that in many respects has led to the current situation in urban educational reform.

This is not to say that educators in this period lacked imagination, nor that significant reforms were not undertaken. The many victories of the students and community members who protested inequality and injustice during these years did result in numerous changes. Curricula were modified to feature the history and culture of Blacks, Mexican Americans, and other minority groups, vocational education began to decline as fewer minority students were counseled to enter such programs, and tracking policies were challenged in a much wider number of districts. Magnet schools offered enriched academic programs of study to a relatively small number of students, and alternative schools provided innovative or experimental curricula to certain groups of students, usually at the secondary level. All of these developments represented important changes in the way urban schools were organized, and in the programs of instruction available to children in these communities. By and large, however, they did not address underlying issues related to the academic performance of their students. Dropout rates remained high (often in the 50 percent range), and adolescent crime and vandalism continued to be persistent problems. Despite the best of intentions, the reforms of the 1960s and 1970s did not produce enduring changes in the schools. Most importantly, they did not raise achievement, especially for the most needy students, and therein lay the problem. Only recently has educational reform in the United States taken up the improvement of scholarly performance as its primary (some would say exclusionary) concern. This has put the problems of urban schools into the limelight in a way that earlier questions of change had not.[7]

Today there is a new ethos of accountability in American public education, influenced in part by the example that Chicago provided in the mid-1990s. Schools across the country are expected to post the scores achieved by their students on tests of academic achievement linked to curriculum standards promulgated by the states. This has meant that students in the urban institutions often are compared, whether explicitly or implicitly, with their counterparts from wealthier suburban districts, children with advantages ranging from well-educated parents to generously funded schools. Such comparisons have made the deficiencies of the urban schools all too apparent, rendering it impossible to pretend that the performance of their students is nearly as high as those from other schools. While it may have been fine in the past to emphasize the diversity of urban schools, their multicultural curricula and innovative programs as points of strength, at the moment public attention has become focused on tests scores in specific domains of academic achievement, particularly reading and mathematics. The result has been the continued movement of middle-class families away from the most beleaguered urban districts, compounding the difficulties of the schools in these areas. The new accountability regime has also raised tensions within the city schools, in many instances leading educators to adjust the curriculum to emphasize test preparation at the expense of traditional subjects and to berate their students to perform better. As for the students, the growing emphasis upon their academic shortcomings can hardly be affirming in the long run.[8] Now it is all too evident that they are deficient, and as Jean Anyon poignantly points out, it is not uncommon for their teachers to tell them so.

Chicago is not the world, of course, but it may be an important bellwether. As suggested earlier, it was the low academic performance of the Chicago Public Schools that led Mayor Richard Daley to undertake the reforms that constituted the new accountability regime described in Brian Jacobs' chapter in this volume. The radical decentralization measures of the late 1980s, with parent-controlled local school councils determining curricular directions and budgetary decisions at individual schools, did not succeed in improving scholastic performance across the system. Despite Jacobs' positive assessment of the Chicago reforms, there are signs that Daley and other leaders are not altogether confident that this momentum can be sustained. As the experience of decentralization indicated, whatever the steps, a system as large as Chicago is very difficult to change. And potential pitfalls abound. In a recent election for control of the city's teachers union, reform-minded President Deborah Lynch narrowly lost a hotly contested campaign against a more traditionalist slate, which called for a return to conventional "bread and butter" unionism. This may be a signal that the district's teachers are growing weary of the constant drumbeat of reform and accountability, a regimen of continual improvement that places considerable stress on many of them, particularly those working in the most troubled schools.[9] If the teachers are growing restless, and disenchanted with reform, the prospects for the long-term success of "high stakes" school improvement are probably not very good. As Jean Anyon points out, the attitude and abilities of the teachers who work with urban children in classrooms on an everyday basis are among the most basic factors that ultimately will make any educational reform plan succeed or fail. And as Jeffrey Mirel demonstrated in his study of Detroit during the 1980s, teachers also have the power to stop reform dead in its tracks.

Given these developments, it probably should not be surprising that Mayor Daley recently announced a new reform initiative for the Chicago Public Schools. Labeled Renaissance 2010 it calls for converting some 100 schools into smaller institutions run under a variety of different arrangements, some of them as charter schools, others perhaps as private ventures, and yet others with unspecified external partners. Although it will be focused somewhat on the city's troubled public secondary institutions, it is intended to mark the start of an ongoing process of transformation, whereby the entire system is eventually changed into a universe of smaller, more responsive educational units. The announcement of this initiative, delivered with considerable fanfare, may have struck some observers as odd, especially given Chicago's long-standing commitment to a highly centralized accountability regime. But it also is a sign of the times. Other cities have undertaken similar reform measures, as they have tried to alter the traditional operating assumptions that have dominated the thinking of urban educators for decades on end. This has been evident in other big districts such as Philadelphia and New York, and even smaller ones like Baltimore and Kansas City have invited private school firms to run some of their schools. The underlying message is that things must change. The schools must be responsive to their constituents, and they must be flexible and agile in determining these needs and identifying strategies to meet them. Business as usual will no longer suffice. And traditional educational interest groups, such as teachers unions and similar organizations, will have to shift their priorities in order to remain relevant. This is the signal that Daley and other mayors and urban school leaders across the country are hoping to send. They are hoping to shake up the old system, and in this way create the possibility of greater improvement in their ailing city schools.[10]

It is an open question, however, whether even the most extreme changes to the operating principles of urban school systems will ultimately prove sufficient to address the underlying problems of urban education today. As Jean Anyon implied, in the end it is a matter of caring, responsive and highly competent adults working together to identify the educational needs of the children in their charge and determining ways to help them learn whatever they need to survive in tomorrow's world. The problem is convincing professionals with these characteristics to work in the urban schools, to remain in them, and to provide them with the resources, material and otherwise, that they will require for ultimate success. This will require money, certainly more of it than the cities are capable of supplying themselves. Proponents of educational choice, particularly voucher advocates, are fond of arguing that simply creating a competitive ethos among schools will improve their performance, and that the "market" will supply good schools to the inner city if sufficient demand can be generated by supplying families with resources (such as vouchers). The problem, however, is one of supply. As the Milwaukee experiment seems to have demonstrated, there do not seem to be great numbers of dedicated and talented educators waiting in the wings for an opportunity to open and run a highly effective urban school. Just as the private market does not supply inner-city neighborhoods with theaters, grocery stores, a variety of restaurants, and many other amenities, it is unlikely to provide an abundance of good schools. Instead, it seems that the most likely reform strategy would be to garner the resources necessary to recruit and retain the effective educators that observers like Anyon have argued are altogether too scarce in today's urban classrooms. This, of course, is not as easy as it sounds, but just getting a point such as this on the table in today's policy environment is a substantial accomplishment. Beyond that, however, a lot more work will be required.[11]

Even this sort of solution is not promising to the mind of Professor Anyon. Given the history of urban school reform, and the highly unlikely political possibility of wealthy and middle-class suburbanites subsidizing city schools with their tax dollars for an extended period of time, she believes that the only answer to the underlying problems of educational inequality is to eliminate the social and economic inequity that characterizes metropolitan life in the United States today. Since I cannot match her eloquence, nor offer a more sweeping and potent resolution to the problems of urban schooling, I will close with a quote from her article, the words she used herself to close.

> *Thus, I think the only solution to educational resignation and failure in the inner city is the ultimate elimination of poverty and racial degradation. The solution to educational failure in the ghetto is elimination of the ghetto. This prescription seems extremely difficult to implement. I acknowledge this, but urge you to view its assumed improbability differently. As James Baldwin suggests in The Fire Next Time, I know that what I am asking is impossible. But in our time, as in every time, the impossible is the least that one can demand—and one is, after all, emboldened by the spectacle of human history in general, and American Negro history in particular, for it testifies to nothing less than the perpetual achievement of the impossible . . . . If we do not now dare everything, the fulfillment of that prophecy, recreated from the Bible in song by a slave, is upon us: GOD GAVE NOAH THE RAINBOW SIGN, NO MORE WATER, THE FIRE NEXT TIME![12]*

NOTES

1. Jean Anyon, "Race, Social Class, and Educational Reform in an Inner-City School" *Teachers College Record* Fall 1995 97(1): 69–94.

2. For discussion of this historical legacy, see Michael B. Katz, ed., *The "Underclass" Debate: Views from History* (Princeton: Princeton University Press, 1993) Introduction and ch. 3.

3. David B. Tyack, *The One Best System: A History of American Urban Education* (Cambridge: Harvard University Press, 1974) Epilogue.

4. This is a long-standing critique of urban public education; see, for instance, Ray C. Rist, *The Urban School: A Factory for Failure: A Study of Education in American Society* (Cambridge, MA: M.I.T. Press, 1973) ch. 1. (This book has been reissued in recent years.) On the history of school reform, see David Tyack and Larry Cuban, *Tinkering Toward Utopia: A Century of Public School Reform* (Cambridge, MA: Harvard University Press, 1995) chs. 1 & 2.

5. Jean Anyon, *Ghetto Schooling: A Political Economy of Urban Educational Reform.* (New York: Teachers College Press, 1997) Part II.

6. The classic study of this is David Rogers, *110 Livingston Street: Politics and Bureaucracy in the New York City Schools* (New York: Random House, 1968). For a discussion of reform efforts, see Joseph P. Viteritti, "Managing 110 Livingston Street: Problems, Prospects, and Purpose" *Urban Education* April 1980 15(1): 103–114, and David Rogers and Norman H. Chung, *110 Livingston Street Revisited: Decentralization in Action* (New York: New York University Press, 1983).

7. For an assessment of curricular changes in urban secondary schools, see David L. Angus and Jeffrey E. Mirel, *The Failed Promise of the American High School, 1890–1995* (New York: Teachers College Press, 1999) ch. 5, and their article, "Equality, Curriculum, and the Decline of the Academic Ideal: Detroit, 1930–68" *History of Education Quarterly* Summer 1993 33(2): 177–207. Also see Jonathan Zimmerman, *Whose America?: Culture Wars in the Public Schools* (Cambridge: Harvard University Press, 2002) ch. 5, and Diane Ravitch, *The Troubled Crusade: American Education, 1945–1980* (New York: Basic Books, 1983) ch. 7.

8. For a critical view of the impact of standards and testing on an urban district, see Pauline Lipman, *High Stakes Education: Inequality, Globalization, and Urban School Reform* (New York: Routledge Falmer, 2004) chs. 3 & 4, and Linda M. McNeil, *Contradictions of Reform: Educational Costs of Standardized Testing* (New York: Routledge, 2000). For a more sanguine perspective regarding standards, see Diane Ravitch, *National Standards in American Education: A Citizen's Guide* (Washington, DC: Brookings Institution, 1995) chs. 4, 5, & 6. For insight into why Daley and other urban political leaders have become so interested in schools, see G. Donald Jud, "Public Schools and Urban Development" *Journal of the American Planning Association* 1985 51(1): 74–83.

9. Lipman, *High Stakes Education*, chs. 1 & 2, "Old Guard Takes Helm of Union in Chicago" *Education Week*, June 24, 2004.

10. For discussion of developments in Chicago and other cities, see "Chicago to Start Over with 100 Small Schools" *Education Week* July 14, 2004. This article also mentions reform initiatives in Philadelphia and New York, particularly the latter's "New Century High Schools" initiative, which also focuses on small schools. Also see the various essays on contemporary urban reform in Diane Ravitch and Joseph P. Viteritti, eds., *New Schools for a New Century: The Redesign of Urban Education* (New Haven: Yale University, 1997).

11. John F. Witte, *The Market Approach to Education: An Analysis of America's First Voucher Program* (Princeton: Princeton University Press, 2000) chs. 2 & 8.

12. Anyon, "Race, Social Class, and Educational Reform in an Inner-City School," 93–94.

INDEX

Academic achievement 343–5; and special classes (Atlanta) 119–21, 123–4, 126–30; and intelligence testing (Los Angeles) 163, 166–7; and race (Chicago) 224–6, 236–7; for Chicano students 259, 262, 266; late twentieth century 275–8; and vouchers 317–22; and "high stakes" accountability (Chicago) 333–40

Accountability 9, 69, 278, 333–5, 337–40, 344–5

Act for the Establishment and Support of Public Schools (Baltimore) 40–2, 45–8, 51

African Americans 6, 343; in Atlanta 122, 129; Los Angeles 176; Chicago 221, 225–30, 232; influence of in Houston 260; in Detroit 284, 287–300; and vouchers in Milwaukee 314, 328

Age-grading 58–60, 63–4, 66, 76, 80, 162–3

Anyon, Jean 341–7

Assimilation 3, 9

Atlanta 4, 70–1, 119–35

Attendance (truancy) officers 249–50

Backstage rules 214, 242–50, 252–3, 264

Baltimore 3, 14, 37–53, 214, 246–9, 251–2

Bennett, William 1, 232–3

Bilingual education 165, 171, 259, 269

Black education 8–9; ante-bellum Baltimore 52; St. Louis 58; Differentiated curricula 71; in Atlanta 119, 131–2; Los Angeles 138, 168–9, 172, 176; in post-war era 213–15; Chicago 224–6, 236; Detroit 284–7, 292–5; Milwaukee 315

Boston 2, 4, 39–40, 43–4, 80, 99–100, 103–8, 112

Brown Decision 213, 219

Budget problems 7

Bureaucracy 69–70, 342–3; in Portland 75–80, 82–4, 86–91, 94–5; and curricular differentiation (Atlanta) 126, 130; and special children 241–2; late twentieth century 276; Detroit 293

Businessmen 48, 69, 71, 121–2, 137–9, 144, 151–2, 183–95, 200, 202–4

Catholic Church 4, 13, 20

Certification 84

Charity schools 3, 13–14, 18, 23, 29–32, 38, 47, 102–5, 111

Charter schools 276

Chicago 1, 5, 7, 9, 137–8, 143–57, 210, 214, 219–39, 252, 278–9, 293, 298, 306, 333–40, 344–5

Chicago Teachers Federation (CTF) 138, 144–50

Chicanismo (Mexican-American youth movement) 260–5

Child labor 61–3, 181, 242

Civil Rights Movement 213, 215, 225–7, 260

Civil War 3–4, 17, 69, 97

Colonial schools 2, 18

Commercial education 126

Common schools 4, 17–18, 20–1, 31, 66, 76, 85–6, 122, 130, 241

Compulsory school attendance 121, 248

Corruption 5, 69, 84, 138, 145–9, 222–3, 228, 289–91, 326

Crime 7–8, 17, 40, 250–2, 285, 326, 342

Curriculum 4, 342–4; nineteenth century St. Louis 58, 63–5; Bureaucratic control 69–71, 75–6, 81–3, 86, 88–9; Kindergartens 98–100, 104–6, 108–9; Special classes (Atlanta) 126–7; Intelligence testing (Los Angeles) 162, 164–5; Detroit 180–1, 196–200, 210–11, 293–4, 301–2; Chicago 223; and student demands (Houston) 264

Daley, Richard J. 229–30
Daley, Richard M. 233–4, 278, 344–5
De facto segregation 213
Decentralization 276, 301, 344
Deindustrialization 7, 221–2, 275–6, 284
Denominational competition 45–6
Desegregation 7, 213, 228–33, 285
Detroit 5, 9, 139, 179–212, 214, 246–9, 276–8, 283–308, 345
Detroit Federation of Teachers 209, 277, 286–8, 292, 294–300
Dewey, John 79, 91, 95, 125, 222
Differentiation 71, 90, 109, 119–20, 125–6, 130, 133, 225, 234
Discipline 69, 77

Efficiency 90, 110, 162–3, 223, 242, 310, 342
Empowered schools (Detroit) 292–6, 298
Enrollment levels 5, 25; early St. Louis 57–64; in Kindergartens 81, 107; special classes (Atlanta) 123; Los Angeles 149; Detroit 180; Chicago 223, 226, 231; decline in Detroit 285; Milwaukee voucher schools 313–16
Ethnic diversity 3, 6–7, 17–18, 30, 222, 233
Evening schools 65

Federal government 201, 229, 232, 250, 260, 270, 310, 335, 341
Friedman, Milton 277
Froebel, Friederick 70, 98–9, 102, 109

Ghettos 6, 221, 346
Great Depression 5, 6, 138–9, 143, 152, 179, 181–212, 242, 250, 286

Haley, Margaret 138, 146–8, 150–2, 222
Hall, G. Stanley 99–100, 161
Harris, William Torrey 14, 64
High schools 4, 14–15, 343; nineteenth century St. Louis 57–9, 63–4; Portland 85–7; Massachusetts 107; Atlanta 125–6; Chicago 147, 149–50, 207, 224–5, 228, 243–53; Los Angeles 169, 172; Detroit 181, 188, 198, 285, 294, 302; Houston 264
HOPE Coalition (Detroit) 283, 289–300
Houston 7, 215, 257–73

Immigrants 3, 5, 6; Ante-bellum period 14; in New York 20–1, 32; and urban growth 70; and schools 80, 87; and Kindergartens 101–2, 106, 109, 111–12; home ownership (Chicago) 149; Mexican (Los Angeles) 160, 163–77; and "backstage rules" 214; industrialization (Chicago) 222; recent influx (Chicago) 334
Industrialization 3, 160, 179

Japanese-Americans 169–70, 177

Kansas City 345
Kindergartens 4, 57, 65, 70, 97–117, 119, 147, 188, 210

Latino (Hispanic) students 7, 214, 233–4, 315
Local school councils 278, 344
Los Angeles 5, 138–9, 159–77, 251–2, 265

Magnet schools 231, 293, 343
Mann, Horace 69, 76
Manual training 88, 125
Massachusetts 69–70, 97–117
Mexican-Americans 138, 160–9, 171–7, 215, 257–73, 343

Migration   6–7, 130, 213, 216, 220–2,
   225, 323–4
Milwaukee   9, 277–8, 309–29, 335
Monitorial schools   13, 50–1

Nation at Risk, A   275
National Assessment of Educational
   Progress (NAEP)   335
New England   14, 42–3, 45, 50–1,
   53, 64, 81
New York City   3, 13–14, 17–36, 124,
   162, 345
No Child Left Behind   278, 333
Normal schools   4, 57–9, 125
North   6, 14

Opposition to public schools
   37–8, 46
Outsiders (in schools)   250–1
Overcrowded schools   123, 226–8

Parochial (Catholic) schools   5, 63,
   222, 231, 276–7, 312
Philadelphia   14, 43, 214,
   252, 345
Population Growth   3, 5, 6, 342;
   New York   17; Baltimore   37–8;
   St. Louis   57; latter nineteenth
   century   69; Massachusetts   109;
   Atlanta   130; Los Angeles   160;
   Detroit   179; Chicago   220
Portland   4, 69–70, 75–95
Poverty   3, 8; ante-bellum New York
   17, 19, 21–2, 30; St. Louis   38–9,
   47; and kindergartens   100–6, 108;
   and intelligence tests (Los Angeles)
   171; Detroit during the depression
   181–2, 194; post-war Chicago   222;
   late twentieth century   275–6, 342,
   346; Detroit   284; Milwaukee
   311, 327
Private schools   3, 342; early New York
   22–3; Chicago   231; late twentieth
   century   276; Milwaukee   309–18,
   322–9
Progressive reform   4–5, 79,
   89–90, 95, 119, 125, 130, 160,
   172, 179–81, 186, 195–6, 199,
   214, 219, 222–4, 230, 242,
   283, 301

Psychological services (in schools)
   124, 161–9, 181, 195, 223,
   243, 249
Puerto Rican students   215

Reagan, Ronald   233, 275
Renaissance 2010 (Chicago)   345
Revolution, American   2–3, 18

St. Louis   3, 14, 37, 57–68, 77, 79,
   124, 335
School boards   343; proposed in
   Baltimore   41, 50; St. Louis   57;
   Portland   79, 84; and special classes
   (Atlanta)   120, 122, 124–6; political
   conflicts   138; Chicago   144,
   147–53, 227–8, 230, 232; Los
   Angeles   160, 162, 172; Detroit
   180–200, 285–93, 295–300, 306–7;
   Houston   258; Milwaukee   341
School choice   292–6, 300,
   310–29, 346
School reformers   4–5; in Baltimore
   37–51; latter nineteenth century
   69–70; Portland   75–7; and
   kindergartens   100–2; and special
   classes (Atlanta)   119–20, 131;
   Chicago   161, 233; Houston   265,
   269; late twentieth century   276–8;
   Detroit HOPE coalition   283–302
Schoolmasters   3, 13, 17, 21, 25–31
Segregation   6–7, 341; Los Angeles
   169–70; post-war era   213; Chicago
   229, 232–4, 236, 239; special
   students   241–6; Mexican students
   (Houston)   266; Detroit   284
Shaw, Mrs. Quincy Adams   102–6
Single parent families   8, 60, 275,
   315–16
Slums   70, 91, 100–2, 104, 108–9,
   112–13
Society of Associated Teachers of New
   York City   26–9
South   6, 14, 37, 54, 213, 225, 232
Special students   4, 70–1, 118–35,
   241–73, 312, 334
Standards (academic)   69, 166, 263–8,
   286, 302, 342
Suburbs   6–9, 214, 219–21, 230–1,
   233–4, 275

Sunday schools 38, 42
Superintendents (school) 4; St. Louis
  64; Portland 76–85, 87–91; Atlanta
  119–20, 122–5; Chicago 148, 219,
  223–33, 246; Los Angeles 162;
  Detroit 180, 188, 291–2, 297;
  Houston 267, 269
Suspensions (from school) 246–7

Taxes (for schools) 4, 346; early New
  York 27–31; Baltimore 40–2, 46,
  50; Portland 85; Massachusetts
  107–8; Chicago 138, 143–57,
  223; Detroit 179–82, 190–2,
  286–8
Teachers 5, 341–5; early New York
  22, 26, 29; Baltimore 50; and
  bureaucratic control 70–1; Portland
  75–6, 78–9, 82–4, 88–91; primary
  school 110; and special classes
  (Atlanta) 123–4, 126; and political
  conflict 137–9; Chicago 143–9,
  151–7; and intelligence testing
  (Los Angeles) 159–63, 166–73;
  Detroit during the depression
  181–92, 194–7, 199, 201, 207–8;
  post-war era 214–15; and backstage
  rules 243–8, 250; Detroit reform
  struggles 263–5, 269, 276–9,
  285–8, 293, 295–301; Milwaukee
  voucher reform 325–6; Chicago
  accountability 333, 339
Terman, Lewis 160–1

Testing 80–3, 93, 127, 138–9,
  159–76, 243, 285, 302, 318–20,
  323, 333–40, 344
Test item analysis 338–40
Test score inflation 336–7
Tracking 172, 244–5, 286

Unemployment 61, 181–2, 188, 194,
  221–2, 275, 284, 286, 342

Vocational education 129, 169,
  176, 188
Vouchers 9, 276–7, 309–29, 346

White-flight 6, 214, 231
Willis, Benjamin 214, 219, 223–30,
  232, 276
Washington, DC 7, 214, 244–9, 251
Women's education 15, 59–60, 62,
  66, 71, 294
Working (or lower) class 3, 14; early
  New York 23–5; Baltimore 38–9,
  42; St. Louis 58–62; late nineteenth
  century 70; and special classes
  129–30; Chicago 143, 149–50,
  153; Detroit 180; post-war era
  214; Chicago job losses 222;
  Detroit high schools 286; and
  vouchers (Milwaukee) 315
World War I 6, 69, 99, 105, 107, 244
World War II 6, 213, 241, 251

Young, Ella Flagg 148, 150, 222